Sam:

Can't understa... [barcode: D0788182] ...s find enjoyment reading such drivel, but I do hope you have a Merry Christmas!

Love,

Grand Dad

2011

The Yankees
Baseball Reader

The Yankees
Baseball Reader

A Collection of Writings
on the Game's Greatest Dynasty

Edited by Adam Brunner
and Josh Leventhal

MVP
BOOKS

First published in 2011 by MVP Books, an imprint of MBI Publishing Company and the Quayside Publishing Group, 400 First Avenue North, Suite 300, Minneapolis, MN 55401 USA

The information in this book is true and complete to the best of our knowledge. All recommendations are made without any guarantee on the part of the author or Publisher, who also disclaims any liability incurred in connection with the use of this data or specific details.

We recognize, further, that some words, model names, and designations mentioned herein are the property of the trademark holder. We use them for identification purposes only. This is not an official publication.

MVP Books titles are also available at discounts in bulk quantity for industrial or sales-promotional use. For details write to Special Sales Manager at Quayside Publishing Group, 400 First Avenue North, Suite 300, Minneapolis, MN 55401 USA.

To find out more about our books, visit us online at www.mvpbooks.com.

Library of Congress Cataloging-in-Publication Data

The Yankees baseball reader : a collection of writings on the game's greatest dynasty / edited by Adam Brunner and Josh Leventhal.
   p. cm.
ISBN 978-0-7603-4061-5 (hb w/ jkt)
1. New York Yankees (Baseball team)—Anecdotes. 2. Baseball stories, American.
I. Brunner, Adam. II. Leventhal, Josh, 1971-
GV875.N4Y23 2011
796.357'64097471—dc22
                    2010051507

Editor: Adam Brunner
Book designer: Chris Fayers
Cover designer: Rick Korab
Front Cover Photo by: Bruce Curtis
Printed in the United States of America
Credit Lines and Permissions appear at the end of the book

Contents

Introduction

by Josh Leventhal

Iconic. Storied. Legendary. Dominant. Evil. The words used to describe the New York Yankees have taken on an almost clichéd form as writers, players, fans, and other observers seek new ways to explain the team that has ruled the game of baseball like no other. The 27 World Series titles, 40 pennants, 20 Hall of Famers bearing the Yankee insignia on their Cooperstown plaque (and 19 more who spent some time with the club), and countless all-stars have been dissected, written about, and analyzed by so many followers of the game that hyperbole seems almost inevitable.

With such a rich collection of prose and poetry penned about this team, what better way to celebrate Yankee history, heroes, and moments than by bringing together the most classic, curious, and fascinating selections from more than a century of baseball literature. With all the journalists, historians, and authors who have covered the sport over its history, you can pretty much bet that if they've written about baseball, they've written about the Yankees. Accordingly, this collection includes writings by such influential early sportswriters as Grantland Rice, Ring Lardner, Damon Runyon, and Heywood Broun—all recipients of the esteemed J. G. Taylor Spink Award for "meritorious contributions to baseball writing"—as well as modern masters of the field, including Roger Angell, Thomas Boswell, Tom Verducci, Bill Madden, and others.

There are contributions from a wide spectrum of New York newspapers, past and present—Rice's *New York Daily Tribune*, Runyon's *New York American*, Broun's *New York World*, Madden's *New York Daily News*, Mike Vaccaro's *New York Post*, and multiple selections from the *New York Times* through the decades. But other cities' sports scribes get their say, too, including Lardner of the *Chicago Daily Tribune*, the incomparable Shirley Povich of the *Washington Post*, and Bob Hertzel from the Bergen County *Record*.

To be sure, leading national publications have contributed countless works of in-depth analysis on the "greatest team of all time." Excerpts from the classic *Baseball Magazine* illuminate moments and players from the first half of the 20th century, including profiles of less celebrated Yankee stars Wally Pipp, Tony Lazzeri, and Charlie Keller. Writers from the long-established *The Sporting News* similarly inform fans of the exploits of Waite Hoyt, Earle Combs, and Hank Bauer—Yankee greats who played in the shadows of Babe Ruth, Lou Gehrig, Joe DiMaggio, and Mickey Mantle, yet helped to bring the team unprecedented success. From more recent times, *Sports Illustrated* columnists William Leggett, E. M. Swift, Frank Lidz, Joe Posnanski, and Verducci put into context the accomplishments of the likes of Bobby Murcer, Don Mattingly, and the "Core Four" during the up-and-down-and-up-again days of the George Steinbrenner Era.

Through it all, it's the pinstripe-wearing players who have made this franchise the juggernaut that it has been at so many points during the last 110 years. While the finest biographers extol the virtues of baseball's great stars in shining prose—as Robert W. Creamer did for Ruth, Jonathan Eig for Gehrig, Richard Ben Cramer for DiMaggio, Jane Leavy for Mantle, and Marty Appel for Thurman Munson—the voices of the players themselves offer rare insight into the world of the Bronx Bombers.

Even before the team moved to the Bronx or wore uniforms with pinstripes, Highlander star and Hall of Famer Jack Chesbro described life as a pitcher during what would later be tagged the "dead-ball era." By the time the Yankees were a dynastic force, players large and small stepped forward to tell their tales. Whether it's Joe DiMaggio making sense of his unparalleled 56-game hitting streak in 1941 or Roger Maris reliving his record-breaking 61-homer season in '61; Yogi Berra describing playing in the bright lights of Yankee Stadium as a rookie or Jerry Coleman justifying being named World Series MVP on a star-studded squad; Whitey Ford and Elston Howard revealing the secrets of the game within the game; Graig Nettles and Dave Winfield portraying the functioning dysfunction of the Yankee family in the 1980s; or Jim Bouton and Sparky Lyle offering a peek behind the curtain at the madcap world of professional baseball players—there is no better way to understand the inner workings of this historic dynasty than from the men who made it happen.

The Yankees Baseball Reader is not simply a collection of writings about the New York Yankees, nor is it just a recounting of the franchise's signature moments and players. Ultimately, it is a history of an iconic/storied/legendary/dominant—and, yes to some, evil—team through the words of the men and women who played for, managed, or observed the greatest team of all time.

PART I

The Origins
of a Franchise
1903–1919

The New York Yankees hold such a deeply entrenched place in the American sports landscape that some might think they've been around as long as the game of baseball. In fact, the Yankees were not even part of the American League when the "junior circuit" was established in 1901. Opposition from the National League's New York Giants blocked efforts to place a competing team in the city, but AL president Ban Johnson kept fighting, knowing that his fledgling league needed a presence in the nation's largest metropolis.

After two years as the Baltimore Orioles, the league's last-place team in 1902 was relocated to Manhattan before the 1903 season. With home games played at Hilltop Park, the club was dubbed the Highlanders. Although it would be another decade before they became the Yankees, and nearly two decades before they won their first pennant, the seeds of a dynasty had been sown.

The articles included in this section explore the origins of the team, its early stars, and the advent of Yankee pinstripes. Wee Willie Keeler, already en route to the Hall of Fame for his credentials as a National Leaguer, makes an appearance, as does Happy Jack Chesbro, winner of an astounding 41 games in 1904 and the winningest pitcher in the team's first quarter century. Hal Chase, perhaps best known for being banished from baseball for gambling, and Carl Mays, whose biggest claim to fame was throwing a pitch that killed a batter in 1920, were among the top stars of the Yankees' early days.

Through the words of legendary writers like Grantland Rice and Ring Lardner as well as the players themselves, these pieces offer a revealing look at a forgotten era of Yankees baseball.

Wee Willie Keeler, 1906. *National Baseball Hall of Fame and Library, Cooperstown, NY*

The American League Makes Its Way to New York

"Home Nine Incorporated"
New York Times, March 15, 1903

Nothing came easily for Ban Johnson in his quest to bring an American League team to Manhattan. His plans were repeatedly thwarted by Tammany Hall politicians with connections to John McGraw and his New York Giants of the National League, but Johnson out-maneuvered them all in the end, securing a site in Washington Heights for his Highlanders ballclub.

The Greater New York Baseball Association was incorporated at Albany yesterday, with a capital of $100,000, to operate the American League baseball franchise in this city, to maintain athletic grounds and provide for the holding of athletic contests, including baseball, football, and general track events. The Directors are John R. Bushong, Samuel C. Worthen, and Jerome H. Buck of this city; Bernard T. Lynch of Brooklyn, and Henry T. Randall of East Orange, N.J.

Joseph Gordon, who is to be President of the new club, accompanied by some of the men closely identified with the organization, together with ex-Inspector of Police McAvoy, who has been awarded the contract for the leveling of the grounds and erection of grand stands and other equipments, visited the Washington Heights site yesterday. All day long the contractors' men were busily engaged carting engines, boilers, steam drills, and other paraphernalia to the grounds on which the work of blasting rock will begin to-morrow morning. There are some 5,000 cubic yards of rock to be removed and a great many trees to be cut down, but the contractor states that he will place a force of 500 men at work and they will labor night and day, until everything is completed, so that the opening game can be played there on April 30.

President Gordon did not seem in any way disconcerted over the rumors that other property holders in the Washington Heights district would oppose the opening of a ball park there. Reports to the effect that streets would be cut through the newly acquired property were not taken seriously by the representatives of the club, who believe that they will experience no trouble in this connection.

In order to facilitate the limited means of transportation to the grounds, arrangements are under way to have all the west side street car lines, including the Broadway line, run special cars to One Hundred and Sixty-fifth Street and Amsterdam Avenue every day during the playing season on which the new club has a game scheduled. The Third Avenue cars run direct to a point within 300 feet of the park.

Manager McGraw, accompanied by most of the New York National League's players, left here yesterday on their trip to Savannah via Washington, for their annual Spring practice. Several players, including Mathewson, Van Haltren, and Bresnahan, who are now traveling from other parts of the country, will join the team at Savannah tomorrow.

Wee Willie Keeler
Excels in the First Game

"New York Team Plays in Washington and Loses
to the Local Nine—Score, 3 to 1"
New York Times, April 22, 1903

*Wee Willie Keeler will forever be known for his sage advice to hitters:
"Keep your eye clear, and hit 'em where they ain't." He was already
a seasoned veteran with a Hall of Fame career when he joined the
Highlanders for their inaugural season. His experience was on display
in the team's first game, though it wasn't enough to catapult the
Highlanders to their first victory.*

The New York baseball team of the American League inaugurated the League season here to-day by meeting the Washington team. New York lost by 3 to 1 through inability to bat safely at opportune times. The game proved one of the most enjoyable ever witnessed by local cranks. It was closely contested at every point.

The game proved to be a pitchers' battle, and was won by Washington on the merits of a timely fusillade of safe hits in the fifth inning. New York was first to score, through a rare piece of base running by Willie Keeler. Keeler got his base on balls, and started for second, when Fultz singled to Delahanty. Delahanty immediately returned the ball to Coughlin, who jabbed at Keeler as the little wonder dropped to the ground and made an exceptionally long slide safely into third base, amid the applause of the multitude that occupied every available seat and completely surrounded the outfield.

Washington had three men passed to first on balls, with only one out in the first inning, when a quick double play by Chesbro, O'Connor, and Ganzel prevented any scoring. Delahanty was thrown out at third base in the fourth inning, while Carey reached second after singling. Demont's two bagger against the left field fence scored Carey. Three singles by Robinson, Selbach, and Delehanty, and an out gave Washington two more runs and the game in the fifth inning. Chesbro then settled down to perfect control of the ball and, except Coughlin's two-bagger, beginning at the sixth inning, the next twelve men went out in one, two, three order. Al Orth pitched in his best form for Washington and held the New Yorks practically at his mercy. The latter succeeded in securing as many as two hits in only one inning, which, however, proved unproductive. Hard luck robbed New York of at least one run in the seventh inning. Long was first to bat and reached third base, but was thrown out at the plate. O'Connor reached second base safely and was caught out between the bases, leaving Chesbro on first to be forced out at second on Davis's hit to Robinson. Long, Keeler, Williams, Fultz, Ganzel, and Conroy all played in their best style, but the masterly delivery of Orth baffled all of them except Fultz.

District Commissioner H. L. West and Senator Gorman participated in the formal opening of the game.

Happy Jack Explains His Famous Spitter

"Pitcher Chesbro Tells for the First Time of His Famous
'Spit Ball,' and Shows How It Is Thrown"
Boston Post, January 22, 1905

by Jack Chesbro and Frederic P. O'Connell

*Plenty has been written about the spitball, as Frederic P. O'Connell
suggests in this 1905 article, representing the first published
explanation of the puzzling pitch to come directly from the horse's
mouth. Here, Jack Chesbro, who won 128 games in his nearly seven
seasons with the Highlanders, dissects his famous pitch and also
touches on the fateful end to his 1904 season.*

GREATEST BOX ARTIST OF THE NATIONAL GAME IS SPENDING THE WINTER
AT HIS HOME AT CONWAY, MASS.—SAYS BOSTON WILL BE STRONG THIS
YEAR, BUT NEW YORK WILL WIN OUT

Jack Chesbro

The spit ball has come to stay, and in my opinion it will be the most effective
ball that can possibly be used.

I can make the spit ball drop two inches or a foot and a half.

It is an easy ball on the arm. I pitched 54 games last season, and my arm
never troubled me.

In the last 30 games of the season I pitched spit balls entirely. In those 30
games I didn't pitch over half a dozen balls that weren't spit balls.

I have not yet read any explanation of the spit ball that was any way
near correct.

You have never read of Gibson or Dineen telling how to throw spit balls.

Gibson of the Collins team had better control of the spit ball than any other pitcher I saw use it last season.

The spit ball is worked entirely by the thumb. The saliva one puts on the ball does not affect its course in any way.

The saliva is put on the ball for the sole purpose of making the fingers slip off the ball first.

Excepting the spit ball, every ball that goes from the pitcher leaves the fingers last. In throwing curves the fingers do the work.

By wetting the ball, it leaves the fingers first, and the thumb last, and the spit ball could be rightly called a thumb ball.

It is not necessary to thoroughly wet the ball. All you need to do is to moisten it so as to remove the friction from the part of the ball the fingers cover, and which slides off the fingers.

The ball is gripped the same as if you were throwing a curve.

Stricklett was the first pitcher I ever saw use it. I don't believe the ball was used before under other names as some people have claimed.

When I saw Stricklett throw it, I said to myself: "There is something, Mr. Chesbro, that you must learn." I studied Stricklett and soon discovered that the thumb did the work.

Clark Griffith didn't know last season how the ball was pitched. Few people know how Griffith throws his slow ball, and Griffith, in my opinion, has got the best slow ball in America.

I see Pop Anson claims he could hit the spit ball. Anson couldn't hit it in a thousand years, and I am ready to wager that Anson couldn't even catch it.

The spit ball is easy to control. It will not be a very hard ball for the catchers once the pitchers have mastered it.

It was only in the first part of the season that my catchers were bothered. Towards the end I signaled just how far the ball would drop and whether it would drop straight or to the outside.

The spit ball cannot be made to drop in towards a right-handed batsman. It drops straight or to the outside. Of course, to a left-handed batsman it will drop in towards him.

Sluggers of the Freeman type are apt to be bothered more by the spit ball than scientific place hitters like Keeler.

"Won't the batters run up to meet it?" [I] was asked, and [I] replied, "What if they do? They run up now to meet a curve. Any batter can hit a ball if he knows how it is coming."

It is up to the pitcher to try and see the batsman first, that is to try and find out if the batter is going to run up and to make his ball drop accordingly.

That last game in New York is still a dreadful nightmare.

Frederic P. O'Connell

No longer is the spit ball a mystery. Neither is the ball a supposition as many believe. Happy Jack Chesbro, the acknowledged king of the spit ball, the pitcher who won 41 games for the New York American team last season, the one man who Boston fans feared would deprive us of the pennant, and the same pitcher, who by a fatal wild throw allowed Criger to score from third with the run that gave Boston the pennant, tells for the first time of the spit ball, its effects, his discovery of it and its part in baseball's future.

Never before has Chesbro told, at least for publication, how he throws the spit ball. Manager Clark Griffith of the New York team tried in vain last season to discover Chesbro's method. Chesbro's fellow pitchers pleaded with him to let them "in," and from Napoleon Lajoie down, the American League batsmen could not connect with Chesbro's elusive delivery.

Chesbro's explanation of the spit ball will make many pitchers open their eyes in astonishment. It will make hundred of experts wonder, and it will make the ball players themselves gape. Since the pitch first came into vogue, column after column has been printed, explaining its virtues. Never, according to Chesbro, has a correct explanation of it been made, and the pitcher who won 41 games during last season, and who attributes the greater part of his success to his gift with the spit ball, should know whereof he speaks.

Spit Ball Is a Reality

It is useless to laugh at the spit ball. Years ago when the curved ball was first pitched many tried to laugh it down. The public as a rule likes to laugh at new discoveries. When the telegraph was first invented only a brave few took it seriously and the same was the case with the telephone.

The writer has seen the spit ball pitched by Chesbro, by Gibson and by Dineen. Lou Criger has gone on record regarding the spit ball; so has Lajoie, Wagner, Griffith, Collins, and all of baseball's leading players. It is, then, indeed foolish for many of the baseball fans to ridicule the spit ball.

The spit ball has come to stay. Every pitcher in the land is thinking these cold winter days of it. Chesbro next season expects even greater results. Chesbro's secret is now out and from coast to coast the pitchers will be able to begin the coming season with a definite knowledge of the ball that threatens in a way to revolutionize America's great sport.

Chesbro's explanation puts the ball in an entirely new light. It has been argued that the ball was made possible because of the saliva on it. It is only in a small way that the saliva has anything to do with the ball.

Could Be Called a Thumb Ball

Properly the ball could be called a thumb ball. Except with the spit ball every pitcher and everyone who ever threw a ball knows that baseball leaves the fingers last. The moistening of the ball makes it leave the fingers first and the thumb last, and from the thumb alone does Chesbro make the ball drop when it reaches the plate. As Chesbro says, he can make the ball drop two inches or he can make it drop 18 inches.

Chesbro was easily the best pitcher in either league last season. He pitched in 54 games and won 41. Another game he tied. Few pitchers in either league pitched over 30 games. Last season's schedule called for 154 games, so that Chesbro pitched over one-third of the games played by New York. Chesbro also won 14 straight games, this great winning streak being stopped by Norwood Gibson.

◆ ◆ ◆

Chesbro Didn't Tell All He Knows

Chesbro didn't tell all he knows about the spit ball. It was only after a long argument that Chesbro consented to tell about the part his thumb plays in pitching. He refused to tell how it is possible for him to make the ball drop two inches or 18 inches. The other pitchers must find out the secret themselves. Chesbro had no outside help, and no one can blame him for being secretive, for last year he baffled the batsmen by the use of the spit ball and would be indeed foolish to let his rival pitchers know the "something he now has on them."

Chesbro Loves the Sport

Chesbro loves baseball. He is in the sport for the glory there is in it. "I don't care about the money," said he. "I like to pitch and I like to win. I am well off. I have enough here to keep me for the rest of my life. I would rather have the credit of winning more games than any other pitcher than in being given the biggest salary. I have wanted to retire from baseball for the past three years, but when the spring comes around the baseball feeling gets into me, and the first thing I know I am off for the south.

"Baseball surely keeps one in the best of health. I have not had a sick day in ten years. How did I break in? Like all boys, I played baseball around North Adams. When but a youngster I discovered that I could pitch a little and played with several local teams. My pitching seemed to attract some attention, and in 1894 I was offered a job in the Middletown, N.Y., Insane Asylum. Part of the job was to pitch for the Middletown team. I had a good season and in '95 went to Springfield. In '96 I was with the Roanoke team, and in '97 went to Richmond, where I remained until July, 1899, when [I] joined the Pittsburgh Pirates."

Chesbro stayed with Pittsburgh until the spring of 1903, when with Tannehill and O'Connor he jumped the Pirates for the New York Americans.

That Great Game in New York

No game ever played in the history of baseball was more important than that memorable contest in New York on Oct. 12 last, between Boston and New York. A victory for Boston meant the pennant, while a victory for New York meant that Boston would have to win the second game in order to land the pennant.

Had New York won both games she would have captured the championship.

No man played a bigger part in that game than Chesbro. On Friday of the week before Chesbro beat Boston. On Saturday in Boston Chesbro was knocked out of the box. The test came on Monday and in the early part of the game Chesbro had smashed out a three-base hit. Leading Boston by two runs, New York's cause looked good.

Then came Williams' bad throw to the plate and the score was tied. The innings wore on and Criger was on third with Parent at the bat. Parent was down for two strikes and three balls, and Chesbro sized him up with deadly precision; but Chesbro realized the responsibility. In another second the whole aspect was changed, for Chesbro's ball had hit the grand stand and Criger ran home.

Chesbro Will Never Forget One Game

Chesbro will never forget that game, neither will the Boston rooters who were present, and reluctantly he told of that game, with the remark that he would never forget it.

"It is an old, old story," said Chesbro. "I have thought it over and over. I don't believe I will ever forget it. You were there when I made that wild pitch, and in all New York I don't believe there was a more sorrowful individual. I would have given my entire year's salary back could I but had the ball back. I wanted that game badly. It practically meant the pennant, for if we won the first we would have won the second. We had the game clinched at one time with a two-run lead.

"Boston was a lucky team without doubt, for in addition to my wild pitch Williams' low throw helped to give Boston her two runs that tied the game up.

"How did I make the wild pitch? How does any pitcher make one? I used a spit ball, but the spit ball had nothing to do with it. I simply put too much force into the throw. Then Dineen had been using the spit ball and had made the ball rather slippery. I am not blaming Dineen, however. I put too much force into the ball and that's all. It hit the grand stand, and it's a long story of what happened. We lost the pennant, but this year we will win it."

Chesbro Is a Modest Fellow

Chesbro was willing enough to talk baseball, but preferred to keep himself out of the discussion. In speaking of the spit ball Chesbro was obliged to bring himself in. What he said about the spit ball he meant. Chesbro, like all great players, is modest. He didn't want to tell about the ball until it was put up to him that he would be doing all young pitchers a big favor and that baseball would be the gainer.

Chesbro looks the part of a happy farmer. He is weighing 200 pounds, or 20 more than he does during the summer. In the middle of the next month he will come down to Harvard to teach the Crimson pitchers how to pitch. He may tell them something about the spit ball.

"Collins will have a great team this season," said Chesbro, as we drove to the station. "Burkett, in my mind, is a great player, although it will be a shame to see men as good as Selbach or Freeman sitting on the bench. Gibson had the spit ball down fine last year. Collins is a great general, and if New York doesn't win the flag this season, I look to see Boston capture it. Collins as a leader has few equals. His team never gives up, and I guess I faced them as often as any pitcher in the past two years, and I guess I know.

"Something I think should be done to increase the hitting. The spit ball is sure to work to the detriment of the batting game. I wouldn't mind having the foul strike abolished, provided the umpires would have the nerve to get after the men who foul balls on purpose. It is pretty tough to pitch to men who deliberately foul them off, and there are quite a few batters who can do the trick."

The visit came to an end almost too soon. It was a glorious day and behind Spit Ball the Berkshire hills never seemed more attractive. Chesbro is unselfish and he freely gave his views on the spit ball that will enable other pitchers to master it to be used against his own team.

Chesbro was the greatest pitcher in the game last year, and among the Berkshire hills, with his horses, dogs and cows, Chesbro is leading the Simple Life that will surely enable him to pitch winning ball the coming year.

Hal Chase Arrives in New York

From *The Black Prince of Baseball:
Hal Chase and the Mythology of Baseball*

by Donald Dewey and Nicholas Acocella

*Widely recognized as one of the finest fielders of his era, and perhaps
the first great star of the Yankees franchise, Hal Chase holds a
tenuous position in the game's history due to allegations of gambling
and game-fixing. In Chase's own words, "I'm the loser, just like all
gamblers are. I lived to make great plays. What did I gain? Nothing.
Everything was lost because I raised hell after hours."*

The biggest difference between the 1905 Highlanders and the team that came
together for spring training in Birmingham, Alabama, in March 1906 was
a Chase ready to jump from rookie celebrity to established star. And while
emerging as the club's best player, the first baseman also became a regular at a
lot more Manhattan spots than Hilltop Park.

Griffith knew Chase was a better hitter than his .249 average in 1905.
His initial solution had been to encourage the Californian to try batting left-
handed while playing with San Jose in fall of 1905, but whether because of
Chase's reluctance or inability, this went nowhere. In Birmingham, he turned
his budding star over to Keeler for instruction, but to Chase's embarrassment,
the outfielder he would always admire as the "best all-around" hitter he
had ever watched threw up his arms in defeat before the tutoring project.
Ironically, it was the teammate he would end up despising more than any
other, Kid Elberfeld, who introduced him to the shorter bat that would turn

around his offensive game. Moved from sixth or seventh to the cleanup spot in the batting order as the season progressed, he fulfilled all the potential that Griffith had glimpsed by batting .323 with 23 doubles, 10 triples, 76 runs batted and 28 stolen bases. In the style of the day, he gripped his bat down near the bottom, but loosely enough to allow him to move his hands up to adjust to the pitch and to movement on the field (Chase tested his bats by tasting the wood. A Highlander batboy attested to finding teethmarks in the wood.) He could be particularly dangerous during intentional walks—not only slapping at any careless pitch that got too close, but even running up out of the batter's box to stymie a deliberate walk (the ploy was still legitimate under baseball rules). But if there was one play that defined his hitting skills, it was the hit-and-run. As veteran American League manager Jimmy McAleer would tell *The Sporting News* in January 1909:

> Chase is in my opinion the best man in the league to hit with a runner. His ability in that line is as marked as his sensational fielding. He is in a class by himself in discovering whether the shortstop or second baseman is to cover second, can send the ball in either direction, and is without a peer in protecting the runner from a pitchout. Hal will hit or push his bat against the ball if it is possible for him to reach it, and if he gets it on the ground with the infield set for the play at second, the Californian will usually defeat it and get credit for a hit.

The redhead could also drive the ball. He reached double figures in doubles in every one of his 15 seasons (topping 20 nine times) and hit more than 10 triples six times. Moreover, according to his 1919 Giants teammate George Kelly, he could reach the fences whenever he wanted to switch off from his slap game:

> He never tried to hit the ball out of the park. But in batting practice, when a few dollars were known to change hands, the Prince always walked away with the money with the most home runs. He had more power when he wanted to than anyone on our club. I saw him hit a ball over the bullpen in left-center field in the Polo Grounds. It must have gone 440 feet.

As reflected by his triples count, Chase was, in spite of repeated ankle injuries, a speedy runner, especially early in his career. He accumulated 363 stolen bases, topped only by the Hall of Famers Frank Chance and George

Sisler among first basemen. By all accounts he was particularly adept at stealing third through the tactic of taking a long, wandering lead off second, drawing a throw from the catcher, and pushing himself into high gear as soon as he saw the ball in the air. It was the kind of running play, as dependent on deceitful smarts as leg speed, that didn't become popular again in the major leagues until the arrival of Jackie Robinson after World War II.

Chase wasn't afraid of physical contact, either, especially when he was the one initiating the impact. As the *New York Times* reported the next day, for instance, Washington third baseman Lave Cross took it too much for granted that a shot he hit into left-center field in a May 8 game against New York would go for a triple. "In circling first base," the paper recounted, "he ran into Chase, the latter's elbow striking Cross in the side of the head. The Washington third baseman fell to the ground senseless, but after a few minutes revived and was able to continue." Also during the 1906 season, Chase slid into home so hard in a contest against the White Sox that he knocked out catcher Billy Sullivan.

Chase's nimbleness on the diamond was of a piece with his general athleticism. There were few sports or games, indoors or outdoors, he didn't try at one time or another. Basketball, football, golf, bowling, boxing, wrestling, hunting—they were all good for bringing out his taste for physical and mental competition. Tales of his skill at pool and billiards were a constant from his youth in San Jose to his final years in Colusa and Williams. Did he truly play champion Willy Hoppe to a draw in a billiards match with $5,000 hanging on the outcome near the end of the 1910 season? His reputation with a cue was such that even contemporary skeptics were more prone to laughing at the alleged amount involved than at the rumored result of the game itself, and Hoppe was the first to admit losing another significant sum to him in a pool game in Arizona. And lest the morning hours go to waste, he was also an accomplished rider whose pre-game tune-ups for the Highlanders encompassed the bridle paths of Central Park. Commenting on this ritual in its January 25, 1913 edition, *Sporting Life* said: "He rides just as he plays ball—the personification of speed, with a bit of recklessness thrown in. Prince Hal . . . loves a good horse and is at home in the saddle. He is one of those fellows who do everything well."

◆ ◆ ◆

At Hilltop Park, meanwhile, the first baseman continued to spearhead New York's drive toward a pennant. By early September the Highlanders and White Sox seemed to have left the rest of the league behind with startling parallel streaks: While Chicago catapulted into first place with 19 consecutive victories, New York stayed in the race with 15 straight wins of its own. The streak included an astonishing sweep of five doubleheaders in a row between August 30 and September 4.

In the opener of the August 30 sweep of Washington, Slow Joe Doyle (named for the time he took between pitches) hurled his second straight shutout—the only two games he won all year. In the nightcap, Chase clouted three triples and a double to turn an 8-1 deficit in the sixth inning into a 9-8, 10-inning triumph. Then, on September 3, with 20,000 fans on hand to see New York taking on Philadelphia, Elberfeld showed why he was called the Tabasco Kid. Furious that an Athletics runner had been called safe at third on a close play, Elberfeld began chasing umpire Silk O'Loughlin around the field. To the astonishment of the shortstop, his own fans—bored with his regular eruptions and impatient to get on with the important game—started booing him. The mood turned so ugly that the police had to be dispatched to escort Elberfeld off the field. Philadelphia, however, drew the wrong moral from the incident: When some of its players began another lengthy argument in the second game, the fans had even less patience with them. Connie Mack finally called them off the field, and the contest was awarded to the Highlanders by forfeit.

While five straight doubleheaders might have exhausted most players, they weren't nearly enough baseball for Chase. On Sunday, September 2, the one off-day during the major league marathon, he did what he had been doing all season when he had been home—went off to Elizabeth, New Jersey, for a semi-pro doubleheader. He pitched the opening game for a team called the Invaders, then switched uniforms to return to first base for the opposing Amsterdams in the nightcap. At one juncture his casual moonlighting got him into trouble with the Newark Eastern League—the circuit claiming he was violating its territorial rights established with Organized Baseball. The infraction should have called for a fine, but he got off with a warning.

What gave the duel with Chicago added drama was the radical contrast in the makeup of the two clubs. While the Highlanders were a decidedly offensive club (finishing second in both batting and runs), the White Sox were the Hitless Wonders with a league-low .230 batting average. In the end, though, they prevailed. As near the end of the season as September 21, New York had a one-game lead, but then it won merely six of its last 14 games, allowing Chicago to streak past to the flag. The collapse served as the first opportunity for later-age historians to discern in retrospect suspicious play on the part of Chase. In fact, down the stretch of the season the first baseman went into a tailspin for a couple of weeks, losing his lead in the batting race and slipping down to the low .300s before righting himself again over the last handful of games: In another contest, his wild throw on a sacrifice cost New York a win. This has been sufficient for Bill James, to name one, to cite the dubious Lee Magee as a source for the contention that Chase's slump wasn't so natural (Magee was later involved with Chase in the throwing of games while both were with Cincinnati in 1918).

Chase himself told *Baseball Magazine* in 1917 that the main cause of his doldrums at the end of the year was an injury. But perhaps even more telling than that defense—or the hindsight pile-on that has characterized much of the writing about the Californian—was the perspective offered by Elberfeld in a 1942 interview with J. G. Taylor Spink of *The Sporting News*. Elberfeld, who never had any love for Chase even before the lapse of 36 years, blamed the first baseman for one thing—what he called "not having enough fight." But he was dumped into the same category as Keeler, whose crime was supposedly whistling in the outfield during the most tense moments of games, and every other player on the roster except himself, third baseman Wid Conroy, and second baseman Jimmy Williams. "We just didn't have many fighters on the club," the shortstop told Spink. "I mean players who fought for everything the way the old Orioles used to fight." Moreover, according to the Tabasco Kid, the team didn't catch many breaks toward the end of the year. "In all my experience in baseball I don't remember another week in which so many things went wrong on a club as happened to us when we were losing steadily," he said. "Grounders were taking bad hops, poor hitters were hitting balls they never hit before, we were misjudging flies, running into each other, until the club was almost off its head."

Farrell might not have won the pennant, but he had a few things to keep him warm during the winter. While the Highlanders finished three games between the White Sox, the equally second-place Giants wound up 20 games behind the all-time winning Cubs. In addition, the Highlander fans outnumbered the Polo Grounds faithful for the first time—434,709 to 402,850. This was particularly sweet after another contentious year between the two franchises. At various points in the season Farrell rebuffed a Giants invitation for a city series after the end of regular play (presumably in retaliation for earlier sneers from the Polo Grounds about taking the same field with "bush leaguers") and McGraw brushed off another Griffith proposal for a spring exhibition meeting. What appeared to rankle the Highlander owner more than anything, however, was the Giants' miserly contribution of $500 toward the relief of victims of the devastating April 18 earthquake in San Francisco.

By contrast, the Highlanders, with prominent area native Chase on the team, arranged a special Sunday exhibition with the Athletics and were able to turn over $10,000 to the emergency fund. Farrell himself led a parade of Tammany bigwigs to the game, each of them paying $100 a seat.

As Chase headed back to California for his own look at the results of the catastrophe, he had the satisfaction of knowing that, late-season slump or not, he was no longer regarded as a one-dimensional player. The sky still seemed to be the limit, and the baseball press was still looking up for him. A typical commentary was that which appeared in the June 9 edition of *Sporting Life*.

> We recall Griffith's remark in his long experience he had never had a player, veteran or cub, who was quicker to take advantage of the mistakes of opponents or who displayed better judgment than Chase. Well, the kid has 'come' and we beg to make the assertion that a more brilliant ball player never broke into base ball. As a first baseman Chase is in a class by himself. As a batter the big boy looms up stronger as the season progresses. No player bunts more artistically or successfully, and for headwork and agility Chase is an inspiration and before the season closes he will be regarded as the sensation of the base ball year. As a matter of fact, there are many who would not entertain a proposition to trade Chase for the great Napoleon Lajoie. . . . You can throw it back at us if the future does not prove Hal Chase the most valuable man in the game. Not that distant future either. If success does not turn that boy's head, with youth and natural brilliancy to aid him, he should shine as a leader in his profession for many years to come.

Stalling and Chasing

"From Griffith to Stallings to Chase—or Owner Frank
Farrell in search of someone who will give him
a ride for his money"
Chicago Daily Tribune, September 23, 1910

by Ring Lardner

*During the 1910 season, manager George Stallings accused Hal Chase
of "laying down" in a game at St. Louis. After an extended standoff
between the two, Stallings's accusations were dismissed, and the
manager was not asked back for the 1911 season. Chase, meanwhile,
was eventually blackballed from baseball for fixing games.*

I am tired of this stalling and chasing,
    And chasing and stalling again.
If I want to keep up with this ball game
    I must have a man who knows when
This outfit of mine's going badly,
    And can give it the brace that's required.
I want some one to slip me the wisdom
    I've had all the bunk till I'm tired.

I didn't know much about baseball,
    It never was part of my game,
I was raw when they gave me this franchise,
    But I've learned a whole lot just the same.
The principle's not unlike racing—
    When you notice your horse going wide
And losing good ground on the corners,
    Next time get a jock that can ride.

Even in Defeat, the Yankees Look "Natty" — The First Game in Pinstripes

"Yankees Lose with Victory in Sight"
New York Times, April 12, 1912

Harry Wolverton's term as manager began with a six-game losing streak, but that was not the most significant development of 1912. That season, the team made a simple change that would ultimately become synonymous with success: thin black vertical lines were added to the white uniforms. Yankee pinstripes were born, and to this day there is perhaps no more iconic uniform in the entire sporting world.

A ninth-inning batting rally by the Boston Red Sox furnished the only discordant note in an otherwise successful inaugural of the baseball season on the Hilltop yesterday afternoon, the Yankees losing their 1912 opener to the Beantown warriors by the score of 5 to 3. The rally arrived at a time when 12,000 fans were getting their throats in order to sing a few paeans of joy over the successful debut of Manager Harry Wolverton as a Yankee chieftain, a few more for the stellar mound work of "Slim" Ray Caldwell and some for the Yankee team. The storm of Boston bingles swept Caldwell from the scene, buried Wolverton and his Yankees in defeat, and drowned out all the bubbling enthusiasm.

All the usual first-day features attended the Yankees' opening. Flags of all nations decked the fence, vari-colored pennants floated to the chilling breeze above the stands, and both grand stand and bleachers were decorated with the Stars and Stripes. Prince's Military Band discoursed music of the popular brand before the game and between innings, and the usual official flavor was added to the occasion in the throwing out of the first ball. Supreme Court Justice Edward E. McCall did the honors in this particular and made a most creditable showing, although a trifle shy on both speed and control. Then there were presents for the new manager, and the usual welcoming cheers for all the old and new favorites.

The crowd did not come up to expectations. The conflict with the Giants-Superbas opening on the other side of the bridge had its effect on the attendance, and there was plenty of idle space on either end of the big stands. A lonesome rooter viewed the battle from the centre-field bleachers for four innings before he was joined by a companion. The twenty-five-cent section in the extreme right field corner was the only part of the stands which held a capacity crowd.

Splendid Welcome for Wolverton

Manager Harry Wolverton received many assurances of welcome from the crowd. He was recognized as soon as he emerged from the centre field clubhouse shortly after 2 o'clock, and the applause which started in the right field bleachers had traveled to the left field end of the stands before he reached the players' bench. Harry liked the demonstration, but his features did not betray the fact. When he took his first turn at the bat in the Yankees' preliminary practice, the noise burst forth again. But the real ovation was saved until the presentation of the floral horseshoe and the loving cup just before the game began. Across the floral piece was a silk ribbon marked "Success." This was the gift of local admirers. The loving cup, which was suitably engraved, was the gift of the Board of Trade of Oakland, Cal., where the new Yankee pilot spent the last two seasons as manager of the club representing that city in the Pacific Coast League.

The Boston team was the first to enter the field, coming from the clubhouse about 1:55 o'clock. The sight of anybody in baseball toggery was welcomed by the hungry fans, who had waited six long months for such a scene, and the 5,000 persons present at the time gave the visitors a hearty cheer. "Jake" Stahl, the new manager of the Red Sox, was picked out for special demonstration, and he had to doff his gray cap several times in acknowledgement. Five minutes later the Yankee squad burst forth from the clubhouse and there was a scene of general jubilation until all the athletes had reached the bench. The crowd looked in vain for several of the favorites, notably Manager Wolverton and Hal Chase. Chase did not arrive for fifteen minutes after the vanguard of the Hilltop army, and the reception to the peerless first sacker was second only to that accorded to Wolverton. Street and Wolter were other late arrivals, and the welcome-to-our-city noise was handed out in plenty to both athletes.

New Men With Yankees

The Yankees presented a natty appearance in their new uniforms of white with black pinstripes. George McConnell, the big hurler obtained from the Rochester Broncos at the close of last season, attracted considerable attention in the preliminary practice. The visitors were attired in the combination gray uniforms with red trimmings, the same as last year, the only difference being that "Red Sox" instead of "Boston" appears on the shirt.

Both managers sent out teams that differed slightly from the aggregations which closed the 1911 race. New York's only change was behind the bat where "Gabby" Street, the ex-Senator, did the honors. In every other position the line-up was the same as that which finished the last campaign. Boston, too, showed only one change and in this instance also a veteran was in charge, Jake Stahl being the player and first base the position. The only recruit who edged his way into the struggle was Simmons, the Rochester slugger, who was picked to unload a clean-up drive with two gone in the ninth inning. The best he could do was to pop a foul to Stahl.

Street's debut as a Yankee can hardly be termed a glittering success. He made two fancy throws to second base which turned back ambitious Speed Boys, one of his throws figuring as the second part of a double play. But he also made a throw to second which tore up the centre field, and on another attempted steal he helped out the Red Sox runner by dropping the ball. The worst was yet to come, and it was one of those performances which recall a certain celebrity named Barry. It happened in the fourth inning when Street dropped a third strike on Charley Wagner. The ex-Senator made a speedy pick-up and saw Duffy Lewis make a fake start from second to third base. He held the ball, debating with himself as to whether he should throw to first or second base and reached a decision about the same time that Wagner arrived at first base in safety.

Game Lacks Enthusiasm

The game itself was not of a nature to keep the several thousand fans keyed up to an enthusiastic pitch. There was a flying start by both teams which made the fans forget for the time about the chilling weather, and each team also favored with a rousing finish. During the interval the pitchers had the opposing batsmen so tightly in their grasp that there was little to enthuse about. In the third inning Harry Hooper brought the crowd to its feet with a sensational running catch of a drive to right field by Birdie Cree and in the eighth inning Cree made a spectacular stab of a long wallop by Tris Speaker. It was the only drive of the game good enough for more than one base, and Cree had to go back to the left field bulwarks to gather it in.

Joe Wood, always an enigma to the Yankees, had the hilltoppers well under control at all stages yesterday. A bit of wildness in the opening inning paved the way for New York's first run and an exhibition of outfield throwing by Nunamaker was responsible for the other tally, which the Yankees picked up in the first inning. The run scored in the ninth was a gift, coming because Charley Wagner chose to play for another base runner when the Red Sox held a three-run lead. Five scattered hits was the extent of the damage to Wood's speed and benders in the first eight innings, the only bunched hitting coming in the ninth inning, when Joe could afford to ease up a bit. The Yankees got only one runner beyond second base between the first and the ninth innings. Wood featured for both teams with the stick, getting a pair of sharp singles and losing another hit on a fancy catch by Harry Wolter. It was Joe's smashing single past Earl Gardner in the ninth inning which gave Boston the winning run and another count, which was not needed.

Caldwell's hit allowance up to the final inning was more scanty than that of Wood, but his control was bad and sharp fielding by his mates pulled him out of trouble on more than one occasion. He had the bad habit of passing the first batsman, and after twice escaping successfully under such conditions he repeated in the ninth inning and paved the way to his own defeat. In the final chapter he "blew up" completely, and the tail-end of the Red Sox batting order garnered four successive singles. Lewis got the first single of the quartet, after Street had dropped a high foul fly, but the new catcher had to bump against the box seats and reach into the crowd to get his hands on the ball so he can hardly be considered as an assisting party in the defeat which followed.

Red Sox Score First Run

The Red Sox started off auspiciously, Hooper getting a clean single to left field. After Yerkes had fanned, Hooper stole second and hustled along to third while Street's throw was mussing up the lawn in centre field. Stahl hit a long fly, which Cree grabbed close to the left field foul line, and Hooper registered.

Here come the Yankees. Wolter worked Wood for a pass and galloped along to second base when Bert Daniels drove a sizzler through the box and out to centre field. Chase sacrificed both runners along with a bunt to L. Gardner, and Wolter raced home, while Yerkes was throwing Cree out at first. Hartzell walked and stole. Nunamaker tried to get Daniels at third base and threw high, allowing Bert to score.

That ended the run getting until the ninth inning. The Red Sox had runners on their base in the second and fourth innings, but could not count. The Yankees saw third base in the third inning only, and a catch by Hooper prevented trouble. In the ninth after Stahl walked, L. Gardner sacrificed, and then followed singles by Lewis, Wagner, Nunamaker, and Wood, scoring four runs. Vaughn succeeded Caldwell after Wood's single, and quickly retired the side. For the Yankees Hartzell and Dolan opened with singles, Earl Gardner grounded out at first. Dolan was thrown out at third on Street's grounder to Wagner, and Simmons, batting for Vaughn, fouled out to Stahl.

The Giants Return
a Favor

"Giants to Share Polo Grounds with Yankees"
New York Daily Tribune, January 23, 1913

When the Yankees went looking for a new home in 1913, they found
willing landlords in the rival Giants, whom the Yanks had taken in two
years earlier after the Polo Grounds were ravaged by a fire. Although
they were planning to stay for only a single season, the American
Leaguers remained as tenants at the Polo Grounds until 1922.

FRANK FARRELL GLAD TO ACCEPT OFFER FOR HOMELESS TEAM—PLANS
ONLY TEMPORARY—CLUBHOUSE WILL BE BUILT FOR USE OF HILLTOP
BAND IN COOGAN'S HOLLOW.

The Giants and the Yankees will share the Polo Grounds this year, and American League Park, on the hilltop, will be closed forever to baseball. Frank J. Farrell is building a new home for his team near Van Cortlandt Park, but in the mean time he welcomed the opportunity to accept temporary shelter.

The offer of American League Park by Frank Farrell for the use of the Giants when the stands were destroyed by fire at the Polo Grounds in 1911 was always keenly appreciated by the late John T. Brush, and when it became apparent last fall that the new park of the Yankees would not be ready for occupancy this spring, while the old park would not be available, the then owner of the Giants immediately offered the use of the Polo Grounds to Mr. Farrell. The death of Mr. Brush temporarily held up proceedings, and many details which had to be attended to in the settling of the estate prevented the completion of the deal between the two clubs until yesterday, when Harry N. Hempstead, the new president, made the announcement.

If for any reason the diamond is needed on any particular day, the Yankees will be forced to vacate. The Giants reserve the right to rent the field for some of the college games that are played there annually, and in that case the Yankees will be compelled to postpone any games that are scheduled and lay them off in double headers.

While foundations are being laid for a clubhouse for the Yankees, it was announced that the present arrangement is not permanent. Neither Mr. Farrell nor Mr. Hempstead is in favor of both teams playing at the same park all the time, and while the relations between the two clubs are cordial yet it is felt that friendly rivalry should be maintained as far as possible. The visiting American League clubs will use the same dressing rooms as the visiting National League clubs.

Mr. Farrell was outspoken in his praise of the cordiality of the new owner of the Giants yesterday, and did not hesitate to say that the generosity of Mr. Hempstead was one of the finest things that had ever happened in the history of the game.

The following statement was issued by Mr. Hempstead yesterday from the office of the Giants:

John T. Brush, prior to his demise, learned that, by reason of a series of vexatious delays, it would be impossible for the new ground which is being built by Frank Farrell, at 225th Street, to be available for the use of his club at the beginning of the season of 1913. It later developed that the former grounds of the American League Club, at 168th Street, could not be had for another season under any circumstance.

Bearing in mind that the generous and timely offer which was made by Mr. Farrell, who extended the use of the American League Park to the Giants when the stands at the Polo Grounds were burned to ashes within an hour in April, 1911. Mr. Brush proffered to Mr. Farrell the use of the Polo Grounds for such dates in 1913 as would be needed by the owner of the New York American League club prior to the completion of his new park.

As the New York American League club finds itself homeless at the inauguration of the season of 1913, the New York National League club takes pleasure in offering to Mr. Farrell the privileges of the Polo Grounds during the season of 1913 only.

That the public may have a fair and intelligent understanding of this arrangement, the New York National League club desires specifically to state that this is in no sense a permanent agreement, but one which endeavors to apply the principles of the golden rule to baseball.

Except for the short stay of the Giants at the home of the Yankees in 1911, it is the first time in history of the game that clubs of the American and National leagues have made use of the same diamond for any length of time. It is a significant move in that it marks the end of all hostility between the two organizations in order that both may work together for the good of the game.

It was a bitter fight, especially in the early days, when the American League was first organized, but time has gradually taken the sting out of the rivalry until the relations between the two leagues have become cordial.

The Yankees expect to have their park ready for use by next season.

The American League's New Home Run King

"The Yankees' Chief Slugger: Walter Pipp, Who Robbed Frank Baker of His 'Home Run' Title" *Baseball Magazine*, January 1917

by J. J. Ward

In today's game, a season total of 12 home runs won't turn many heads. In 1916, that number was good enough to earn Wally Pipp the title of "home run king." Pipp was the first Yankee to earn such an honor, and he repeated as champ the following season with 9 homers. Pipp's main claim to fame, of course, is losing his first base job to Lou Gehrig in 1925.

He isn't the greatest first baseman in the American League. So long as Stuffy McInnes and George Sisler are at large perhaps he never will be. But he is a grand good player just the same, and the way he wallops that baseball has the pitchers sitting up and taking notice. Yes, Pipp is the American League's new Home Run King.

Walter Pipp is a concrete evidence of that good business principle which should rule in baseball affairs. Messrs. Huston and Ruppert bought the New York Yankees with the assurance of aid from other club owners. They believed this assurance, but like many other expressions of good will it proved rather vague and shadowy. There was one club owner, however, who made good in the promised co-operation to establish a strong American League club in the Great City. This club owner was Frank Navin, of Detroit, and his co-operation took the tangible form of a long lanky first baseman who had showed much inherent ability but hadn't quite arrived as yet.

Since that date when he joined the American League uplift movement on Manhattan, Pipp has arrived. Yes, indeed. He hasn't the grace of McInnes, nor the dazzling versatility of George Sisler. But he is a grand first baseman, and the tremendous force with which he wallops the ball stamps him as one of the battering ram sluggers of the old days.

Walter Pipp was born at Grand Rapids, Mich., in 1893. A kindly fortune endowed him with those valued assets of a first baseman—long legs and broad shoulders. Pipp measures six feet two inches overall as they say in shipbuilding circles, and pursuing the same plans and specifications his breadth of beam is great, but unknown. Very broad, in other words, are Pipp's shoulders, and when he swings that long heavy bat of his and gets his 180 pounds of rugged bone and muscle well behind the swing that little horsehide pellet usually describes a long, beautiful arc over the outfielders' heads. Pipp is a liberal patron of two baggers, three baggers and such, but his particular specialty is home runs.

The National League, owing to the limited size of some of its playing fields, far excels the rival circuit in number of four-ply wallops. For instance, Cactus Cravath startled the baseball world two years ago by piling up twenty-four home runs. But in accuracy it must be admitted that most of these runs were made in a park whose right field wall is the joke of the circuit. Not that Cactus isn't a direful slugger. He is. But Pipp's twelve home runs this season, while they look unimpressive compared with Cravath's grand record, are really a most substantial performance. For they were made under surroundings which were relatively unfavorable to circuit smashes.

Pipp started his baseball career in 1910 at Hastings, Mich., where he joined a semi-pro club, going later in the season to Grand Rapids of the Central League.

The next two years he spent at that great center of learning and refinement, Kalamazoo. From this town of the comic opera name Detroit rescued him in the fall of 1912. But the Tigers were well equipped with first base material, and farmed out Pipp to Providence and later to Scranton.

They recalled him in 1914, but only to send him to Rochester for further seasoning. And then as the Yankees changed hands they let the new owners secure Pipp at the waiver price, which was as near outright benevolence as a major league club owner ever gets.

With Rochester Pipp had hit well over .300. But amid more strenuous surroundings he slumped noticeably. However, he showed evidences of hitting with a punch when he did hit, and the long wallop is ever a prized possession of the first sacker.

This season Pipp has improved steadily, and now stands well up in the list of successful guardians of the initial corner. His great height and length of reach gave him a decided advantage over such men as McInnes, who in spite of their flawless fielding are handicapped by lack of inches. Anything that is aimed in the general direction of Pipp is pretty sure to find a safe landing place in his spacious glove.

But hitting, not fielding, is the chief delight of the lanky first baseman. He hasn't shown evidences of .300 form in the majors as yet, but he makes up for the infrequency of his wallops by their length. Take his home runs and other lusty drives and divide them into their component parts of single bases and his average would swell out of sight.

Frank Baker, long known as Home Run Baker, this season found a foeman worthy of his steel in young Pipp. The race between the two was carried merrily to a finish in October, and resulted in the complete triumph of the younger man. However, it is but due to Frank to admit that he was out of the game for a long time owing to injuries and might have continued in possession of the home run championship had he remained in good health.

But Pipp deserves all the credit in the world. He had other notable rivals besides Frank Baker. There were Joe Jackson and Sam Crawford and Ty Cobb and Tris Speaker, not to mention a dozen other redoubtable sluggers. Pipp mastered them all by a wide margin.

The great Speaker showed a proper respect for Pipp's prowess. "I usually play a short field," said he, "because I believe it is a decided advantage to do so. But of course in the case of such a batter as Pipp, it would be foolish to play in. You have to go away back for those sluggers."

Pipp believes that he is just beginning to find his batting eye. "I think I am better this year than I was last," he says, "and I ought to improve right along. If experience is worth anything, and they say it is, I don't think I have seen my best season yet. At least I hope not."

Pipp still resides in winter at Grand Rapids, the city of his birth, where he is known as a young man of exemplary habits and fine prospects. Like many other baseball players of the younger generation, Pipp is a college man, having attended Georgetown University. Whether or not he will make direct use of his education is unknown. But at present he is bringing whatever mathematical abilities he may possess to the problem of meeting a moving spherical object with the greatest possible force in a given direction. In other words, he is trying to sting the ball on the nose and sting it hard.

Before Reynolds, Larsen, Abbott, or Cone, There Was Mogridge— The First Yankee No-Hitter

"The Sport Light"
New York Daily Tribune, April 29, 1917

by Grantland Rice

*When New York hurler George Mogridge took the mound at Fenway
Park on April 24, 1917, he had one simple goal: beat the reigning
world champion Red Sox. At that point in history, seven Boston
pitchers had thrown no-hitters, while no Yankee had accomplished
the feat. In this piece, the incomparable Grantland Rice takes readers
into the mind of Mogridge as he recalls the first Yankee no-hitter.*

No-Hit Psychology

This is but a prelude to the psychology attached to pitching a no-hit game in
the major leagues.

We have always wondered how a pitcher felt as he was working his hitless
way along, once the fifth or sixth inning had been safely passed.

In order to get a line on this situation we decided to subpoena George
Mogridge, the New York southpaw, who a few days ago eased the Champion
Red Sox down without a solitary blow.

"In the early stages of the game," said George, "I only knew that I was cold and that I couldn't keep warmed up. So I spent all the spare time I had between innings trying to warm up and unravel the kinks.

"Now, there is a world of rivalry between the Red Sox and the Yankees, and my main idea, of course, was to win that ball game. When the seventh inning came they hadn't gotten a hit, but I hadn't realized it. They had scored in the last of the seventh, tying the game up. It was not until the first of the eighth I realized the fact that none of the enemy had tapped me for a safe drive. And I never realized it then until Bill Donovan came up and said: 'It would be a crime to lose this game, for they haven't even gotten a blow off you yet.'

At the Finish

"Even then, pitching the last of the eighth, I didn't feel nervous or excited or under any strain. It was not until the last of the ninth, with only three men to get, that I suddenly realized I'd like to have at least one no-hit game in my kit—and especially a no-hit affair against the World Champs. I still wasn't too nervous to speak, and it was not until two were out that I got my shock. I had only one man to get, and he tapped an easy one for an easy out. An error resulted, and, with such a fine chance gone, it occurred to me then that the next man up was about due. It generally happens that way. Leave an opening, and they nail you. Facing this last man was the first nervousness I felt. I knew the side should have been out, that he had no business up there, and that I ought to be on the way to the clubhouse with my no-hit game sewed up. But this time the upset didn't work out.

"If Donovan hadn't mentioned it in the eighth," remarked Mogridge, "I don't believe I would have known I had a no-hitter until after the game. If I had begun to figure on a no-hit game back in the fifth or sixth inning I doubt very much whether I would have landed one."

Carl Mays vs. Ban Johnson

"Carl Mays Twirls Yanks to Victory"
New York Times, August 8, 1919

Carl Mays may be the only professional baseball player ever suspended for going fishing. In the middle of the 1919 season, Mays, then a member of the Red Sox, decided he'd had enough and left the team. Boston dealt Mays to the Yankees, but American League president Ban Johnson suspended him for "conduct detrimental to the general welfare of the game." Mays fought the suspension and went on to become the ace of the Yankee staff.

BROWNS HELPLESS BEFORE BOXMAN WHOSE SUSPENSION WAS RAISED BY COURT ORDER.—FANS 9 MEN, GIVES 6 HITS—HUGGINS'S MEN DROP OPENING GAME, 6 TO 3, THEN HIT HARD AND WIN SECOND, 8 TO 2.

Carl Mays, completely surrounded by the protection of a blanket injunction from the Supreme Court, broke through Ban Johnson's suspension yesterday and pitched the second game of a double-header at the Polo Grounds against the St. Louis Browns. And what's more, Carl won his game, the score being 8 to 2. In the preliminary skirmish of the afternoon, the Browns got a little uppish and beat the Yanks 6 to 3. Some 16,000 people were anxious to see how the injunction would work and all hands seemed well pleased when it operated as advertised.

The injection of the legal arm of the commonwealth on the base ball diamond aroused much curiosity. Some of the fans thought when Mays appeared that the hurry-up wagon would roll out on the field with a squad of bluecoats and give Mays a ride down to the Tombs. Nothing of the kind happened. The injunction said that Ban Johnson, his umpires, Manager

Jimmy Burke of the Browns, and all of the aforesaid Johnson's agents, henchmen, et cetera, must keep their well-known hands off Carl Mays and they did. The injunction ran true to form and so did Mays. He fanned nine of the Browns, held them to six hits and had his submarine shoots playing tricks with the St. Looey bats.

The only inhabitants of the park who seemed worried were the umpires, Hildebrand and Moriarty. When the coloratura soprano who does the announcing told the people that Mays would pitch, the umpires called a convention between themselves at the home plate and had a long chest-to-chest talk. They argued the case pro and con and decided that there were two sides to it. According to their boss, Ban Johnson, Mays was under suspension, while, according to the Supreme Court of the State of New York, Mays could play ball and cut up around the ball field just as he blamed pleased. The umpires had to use their noodles in deciding just what to do.

Ban Runs Second

They concluded to string along with the Supreme Court and the game went on. They kept a close watch on Mays throughout the game. They examined the horsehide ball every time Carl rubbed it and did the old Hawkshaw examination of the cover several times to see if Mays was using beeswax, resin, emery, or any of those things. Hildebrand discovered something on one of the balls and put it in his back pocket to be submitted to Boss Ban as evidence.

Mays got the greatest reception a ball player has received in Harlem in many a day. When he fanned the three St. Louis players—Austin, Bronkie, and Jacobson—in the first inning, the crowd stood up and cheered his journey back to the bench. Then men got up in all parts of the grand stand, threw up their hats, and led cheer after cheer for Carl. "Three cheers for Mays," they cried, and the chorus of hurrahs was taken up by the fans in all parts of the spacious stands.

Allan Sothoron was pitted against Mays, and although the Yanks hit him freely they were unable to squeeze many runs across until they fairly bombarded him in the seventh. New York broke into the run business in the third when Home Run Baker hit the ball into the right field grand stand. St. Louis tied it up in the fourth when Baby Doll Jacobson punched another home run into the left field bleachers. The Yanks sneaked ahead in their half of the same inning when Bodie singled to centre and went down on Hannah's sacrifice. Mays got an infield hit to first and Fewster hoisted a fly to Jacobson. The Baby Doll in left muffed the ball and Bodie scored.

The Big Seventh Inning

It was a see-saw session and the Browns tied it again in the fifth. Sothoron singled and was forced by Austin. After Bronkie fanned, Austin stole second. Jacobson was hit by a pitched ball and Sisler crashed a single to centre, scoring Austin, Sisler going to second on Bodie's fumble.

The Yanks scampered off with the game in the seventh. After Pipp skied to Smith, Pratt singled and stole second. Bodie got a pass and Hannah hoisted one to Smith. Mays singled to centre, scoring Pratt, and Carl took second on Williams' error, Bodie going to third. Fewster was hit by a pitched ball, filling the bases.

Samuel Vick from Tennessee then made everybody happy by banging a home run into the left field bleachers, accomplishing a feat which is the ambition of every ball player—to hit a homer with the bases jammed.

Austin walked in the opening inning of the first game and Bronkie sacrificed. Jacobson pasted a single to right, scoring Austin. Sisler forced Jacobson at second and Williams died at first. The Yanks got the run back in the same inning. Fewster singled to centre and Peck [Roger Peckinpaugh] skied to Jacobson. Baker's single to left sent Fewster to third. On a squeeze play Lewis bunted to Shocker, who made the play at the plate, Fewster scoring.

Huggins and O'Connor Exiled

Manager Huggins and Coach Pat O'Connor kicked so hard at this decision that Hildebrand put them out of the picture.

St. Louis went to the front in the second. Earl Smith singled to left and Gerber was safe on Baker's fumble. After Severeid popped to Baker, Shocker forced Gerber at second, Pratt to Peck, but Pipp muffed Peck's high toss when he tried for a double play and Smith scored.

Peck was injured when Severeid slid into a second in the fifth and in the next inning he retired, Fewster going to short while Vick went to right field.

The Browns landed on Quinn hard in the sixth. Williams singled to right and Smith did likewise. Gerber's single to centre scored Williams. Severeid was walked purposely, filling the bases. This was a poor move, for Shocker rapped a single to Vick and Smith and Gerber scored.

Bronkie singled to centre in the seventh and went to second on Jacobson's line drive over Fewster's head. Sisler contributed a sacrifice, and when Williams rolled to Fewster he threw Bronkie out at the plate. Jacobson and Williams reeled off a double steal, Jacobson scoring.

Yanks Make a Rally

The Yanks made a dying gasp rally in the eighth. After Lewis fouled to Austin, Pipp bounded a double off Bronkie's shins and went to third on Williams's wild toss in returning the ball. Pratt singled to centre, scoring Pipp, Bodie singled to left, sending Pratt to third. At this critical moment Muddy Ruel fanned. Even worse than that was Al Wickland, who, pinch hitting for Quinn, hoisted a measly fly to Williams.

Sam Vick caused a little excitement in the ninth. With one gone Samuel tripled to centre and scored while Baker was being tossed out at first.

PART II

Ruth, Gehrig, and the Birth of a Dynasty

1920–1935

The acquisition of George Herman "Babe" Ruth from the Boston Red Sox in January 1920 (for the grand sum of $100,000) wasn't just the turning point in the fortunes of two baseball franchises, it was a pivotal moment in the history of the sport. Although the Babe first began his assault on the record books as a member of the Red Sox—belting a then-unheard-of 29 homers in 1919 while making the transition from dominant pitcher to awe-inspiring slugger—it was not until he arrived in New York that baseball's dead-ball era was brought to a decisive end.

The statistics and accomplishments of the legendary Ruth are well known to students of the game, but the writings of venerable baseball scribes Frank Graham, Heywood Broun, and Robert W. Creamer contextualize those accomplishments with exquisite prose.

Of course, the Yankee dynasty of the 1920s and early 1930s was not built solely on the shoulders of Ruth. His main partner in domination, Lou Gehrig, was a legend in his own right, establishing records of strength and stamina, often in the shadow of his larger-than-life teammate. Gehrig's story is both inspiring and, ultimately, tragic.

Those who played beneath the double shadow of Ruth and Gehrig, yet made essential contributions to an unforgettable dynasty, also get their due. "Schoolboy" Waite Hoyt, Earle "The Kentucky Colonel" Combs, and "Poosh 'Em Up" Tony Lazzeri each spent at least 10 seasons while helping to build one of the greatest teams ever assembled.

Babe Ruth and Lou Gehrig, 1927. *National Baseball Hall of Fame and Library, Cooperstown, NY*

The Early Days of the Babe Ruth Era

From *New York Yankees: An Informal History*

by Frank Graham

There has been no more significant transaction in the history of baseball than the sale of Babe Ruth from the Red Sox to the Yankees in 1920. At the time of the deal, Boston had won five World Series titles, more than any team in baseball, while the Yankees hadn't even won an American League pennant. The fortunes of the two teams were about to change dramatically.

Never before had the transfer of one ball player created such a stir. Ruth not only had smashed existing home run records in 1919 but plainly was at the very beginning of a career as a hitter that would revolutionize baseball. There were other great hitters in the game—Cobb, Speaker, Jackson, Sisler, Hornsby. But in one year the Babe had swept past all of them. If the fans in Boston were in despair at losing him, those in New York were overjoyed at the prospect of seeing him in seventy-seven games a year at the Polo Grounds.

Innocent bystanders hit by this deal were the Giants. Up to this time they had kept the edge in the patronage fight, but they had no one (who had?) to match Ruth, and it was certain the Yankees soon would be the top team in the town. Nor did the Giants have to wait until the season opened to realize what, from their standpoint, the Babe meant in a Yankee uniform. Sensible of his drawing power in the provinces, as far back as November they had arranged a spring tour with the Red Sox and had planned to bill the Babe like a circus all through the South. Now it was spring, and they were touring with the Red Sox—but a few days ahead of them the Yankees were cleaning up with Ruth.

Bob Meusel had been added to the roster, coming up from Vernon in the Coast League to play third base or the outfield, Ward or Baker also being available for use at third. Freddy Hoffmann had joined Hannah and Ruel back of the bat, and "Two Gun" Rip Collins from Texas was retained as a pitcher.

But, at home or abroad, Ruth was the one. As early as May he was pulling crowds through the Polo Grounds turnstiles that far outnumbered any the Yankees had seen. And he was giving them something to rave about as he hammered the ball into the stands, or on one occasion, over the stand. He played right field at the Polo Grounds, left field in most of the other parks. He said he didn't like to play the sunfield, and Huggins had no mind to press the point. After all, the big guy was in a spot where he could have things his way.

Ruppert [Team owner Colonel Jacob Ruppert] went to the games more often now. Huston was there practically every day. Cap—he never could get used to being called Colonel, so nobody ever called him that any more—was the greatest Ruth fan in a town rapidly going wild over the Babe. The presence of Ruth almost—but not quite—made Cap forget the presence of Huggins. There was no chance Cap would ever warm up to Hug, but the sight of the Babe walking up to the plate and slugging the ball out of sight made him forget who was running the team on the field. It made virtually everybody else forget, too, including most of the baseball writers. The only time Hug got his name in the paper was when the Yankees lost. When they won the headlines went to Ruth—or Pipp or Shawkey, or someone else.

On May 7 Harry Sparrow died [Business Manager for the Yankees]. His health had not been good since his almost fatal heart attack three years before, but he had been as smiling, as willing, and hard-working as ever. On the evening of May 7 he left the ball park after the game in apparent good health, but that night, at his home, his heart just stopped.

Ruth went swinging from town to town—on and off the field. Technically, he was Ping Bodie's roommate, but the only time Ping ever saw him was on a train or in the ball park.

"Who are you rooming with, Ping?" one of the other players asked him one day.

"With a suitcase," Ping said.

The crack went around the league. It was Ping's major contribution to the history of baseball.

One day Joe Judge, first baseman of the Senators, met the Babe coming out of the Willard in Washington.

"Your ball club stop here?" he asked.

"No," the Babe said. "They're over at the—the what's-it, down the street."

He gestured vaguely.

"But I'm staying here," he said.

Judge shook his head. "It must be nice to be rich," he said. "How much do they soak you, Babe?"

"A hundred bucks a day for a suite."

"A hundred bucks a day!"

"Well," the Babe growled, "a fellow's got to entertain, don't he?"

He tied his home-run record against Bill Burwell of the Browns at the Polo Grounds on July 15. On July 19, also at the Polo Grounds, he broke it by hitting two off Dick Kerr of the White Sox. By this time everybody on the club was swinging with him. Meusel, Bodie, Pipp, Peckinpaugh. The craze for home runs spread—and fattened on a lively ball introduced surreptitiously into the American League. (The National League got it the next year.) Somebody apparently had figured that if one Babe Ruth was so popular, ten Ruths would be ten times as popular and, accordingly, hopped up the ball. Home-run totals mounted, of course. But there was only one Ruth, and nobody could keep within a million miles of him.

With the Babe showing the way, the Yankees moved into a three-cornered fight for the pennant with the Indians and the White Sox. Later it was believed that the Sox, who admitted having chucked the 1919 World Series, had chucked this pennant race, too, winning or losing games according to the bets they made. But the Yankees and Indians were on the level, at any rate, and were hammering away at each other in midseason when tragedy struck. In a game at the Polo Grounds on August 16, Mays, pitching for the Yankees, hit Ray Chapman, Cleveland shortstop, in the head. Chapman was carried unconscious from the field and removed to a hospital where, early the following morning, he died.

In the wide-spread grief over Chapman's death there was an undertone of anger. There was no evidence or reason to believe that Mays had intended to hit Chapman, but the bean ball or duster was very much in use at that time, and some of the players either intimated or charged outright that, while Mays had not meant to injure the batsman, he had sought to drive him back from the plate. Cobb was quoted by a press association as saying that he believed the pitcher had thrown at the hitter. Appearing in New York a day or two later, he was booed from the time he left the clubhouse in center field until he reached the dugout. Then he said he had been misquoted.

The Yankees hotly defended Mays, although few of them liked him personally—Huggins, who had no use for him, being one of his most loyal supporters. Mays, for his part, said the ball had sailed. Public opinion was on his side, naturally, and the bitterness engendered by the tragedy subsided as Chapman was buried in Cleveland on August 20. Two days later Mays returned to the box, beating Chicago.

The White Sox scandal broke late in September. It looked as though the honest survivors of the blast still might win the pennant, but the Indians got the nod in a photo finish, winding up two games in front of Chicago and three games in front of the Yanks.

There was, however, rejoicing in New York. Although the Yanks had finished third, they had won ninety-five games. Ruth had hit .376, fourth in the league behind Sisler, Speaker, and Jackson, and had made the astonishing, almost unbelievable total of fifty-four home runs. Because of him a new type of fan was appearing at the Polo Grounds. This was the fan who didn't know where first base was but had heard of Babe Ruth and wanted to see him hit a home run. When the Babe hit one, the fan went back the next day to see him hit another. Pretty soon he was a regular, and knew not only where first base was but second base as well.

1921—The Yankees' First World Series

"Manhattan Fandom Finally Realizes Dream of 18 Years
By Triumph of Its Two Clubs"
New York Daily Tribune, October 2, 1921

by Grantland Rice

*After struggling through nearly 20 lean seasons, the Yankees finally
arrived on the World Series stage in 1921, where they were to face
off with the rival New York Giants in a best-of-nine series for the
championship. The final results were not what they'd hoped for, but
the Yankees would get their chance to topple the Giants two years
later with their first championship.*

RICE SAYS THIS SHOULD BE FEATURE WORLD'S SERIES OF HISTORY,
FROM VIEWPOINT OF STAGE SETTINGS, ALL-STAR CASTS AND ROOTING
OF DIVIDED METROPOLIS

For the second time in world's series history one massed collection of civic
taxpayers will enjoy the rare privilege of witnessing a championship clash
without journeying from their own firesides or leaving the fragrant odor of
home cooking far behind.

For it's the Giants and Yankees at last!

After all these years the golden dream of the Manhattan fan has at last
come true. The Big Town with its waiting millions shares its post-season glory
with no other city, and whatever happens New York becomes the world's series
capital of the only universe that matters very much as we glide to press.

Fifteen years ago Chicago emerged from the lists with two pennant winning teams, and while Cubs and White Sox battled, the city was in the grip of civil war. Now, fifteen years later, it is Giants and Yankees.

The Giants under McGraw have come into their seventh pennant, but the Yankees, after twenty barren years, have at least crossed the Red Sea of failure upon the big bat of "Babe" Ruth. They are debutants in the land of glory, newcomers into the championship joust. They were forced to fight their way into the throne room through a line of gallant defenders in the Cleveland club, but when the final test came the mighty mace of "Babe" Ruth hammered out a gap wide enough to clear the way.

Prove Gameness in the Stretch

Almost outclassed until the stretch was reached, the Giants proved their greatness and their gameness by catching and crushing the Pirates just as they were sailing into port. They broke through only after one of the greatest uphill fights in baseball lore, cutting away a lead of seven and one-half games in less than a fortnight.

Each club was called upon to prove its fitness by stopping its leading rival, and now, out of the double scrimmage, the two New York winners stand face to face upon the same home field where the greatest crowds that ever saw a post-season championship are waiting for the opening rush.

The fanatical multitude, now practicing quick starts in the direction of the Polo Grounds, will not only see the two Big Town clubs decide the matter of baseball's supremacy, but they will also see the greatest slugger of all time in action against a new set of pitchers, swinging his fifty-four-ounce bludgeon against an enemy from another league.

It will be the first time that Ruth has had the chance to display his wares in world's series conflict since he came to home run greatness. It will be the first time in a world's series party that he has worn his crown, for in 1916 and 1918 he was merely a left-hander taking his turn in the box.

Many Stars on Contending Teams

Considering all these possibilities for drama, no wonder Manhattan Island is now in the convulsive throes of a baseball fit. No wonder the clamor of the multitude and the polite chit-chat of the day are all turned upon the approaching carnival which has gripped the fancy of the world's largest city.

Ruth will not be the only card. Both clubs will send platoons of star talent to the field, with two evenly matched machines contesting the issue. There will be the two slugging Meusels, adjusting their heavy artillery fire from opposite sides of the line. There will be Bancroft and Peckinpaugh in a bristling duel at short that should be one of the features of the year. There will be the brilliant Frisch and the hard-hitting Ward, with the outfield play of Young and Burns.

Backed up by confident supporters, the two clubs will put on top speed to control the destiny of the home town, and it can be written down now that each contest will be fought out bitterly to the final blow.

Civil war is always more nerve-wracking than any other brand. When neighbors fall out the trouble is usually increased twofold. And now, after struggling for New York patronage through a rivalry of twenty years, one can understand the feeling of both fans and players as the big day closes in wherein John J. McGraw and Miller Huggins will make their first pitching selections and leave the rest to fate.

Must Spike "Big Gun" of Yanks

McGraw's main attempt will be to select pitchers who have a better chance of spiking the Big Gun, "Babe" Ruth. For this reason he will use Art Nehf at every open chance and the star left-hander is now his leading hope.

Considering all the intimate details, if the possibilities of drama work out as they should, this should be the feature world's series of the game from the viewpoint of stage settings, all-star casts and the fanatical uproar of a divided metropolis.

A vast horde of fans has watched the two machines in the long dash that began last April, and now that both have crossed the finish line in front of their respective fields, the same vast horde is waiting to pour like a tidal wave upon the battlefield to see the clash of champions in the final test.

In Defense of Miller Huggins

"Sport Editorial: Huggins"
New York American, October 3, 1921

by Damon Runyon

*Though Miller Huggins had led his team to the pennant in 1921,
accomplishing what no Yankee manager before him had been able to,
he was met with harsh criticism when his ballclub failed to seal the
deal in the World Series. Here, the legendary Damon Runyon takes
a moment to extol the virtues of Huggins, reminding fans of the
depths from which the club had risen.*

Miller Huggins has brought the American League's first pennant to Manhattan Island.

The feat speaks for itself.

The crafty (Clark) Griffith (the first Yankee manager, from 1903 to 1908), with a hand-picked club, failed to do it. (George) Stallings (Yankee manager, '09, and '10), the "Miracle Man" of 1914 (as manager of the World Series–winning Boston Braves); (Frank Chance) the "Peerless Leader" of the old Cubs; (Hal) Chase, the ball-playing sensation of his time; (Kid) Elberfeld, (Harry) Wolverton, ("Wild" Bill) Donovan, all fell ingloriously by the wayside in pursuit of the same enterprise.

It has remained for the little flat-footed lawyer-ballplayer from Cincinnati to finally fulfill that hope deferred for 19 long years to the Yankee fans of this town.

We repeat, the feat speaks for itself.

Huggins has won against tradition, against opposition and criticism such as few managers have ever encountered.

Assembling his ball club piece by piece, plodding along with astounding patience, the small leader of the Yanks has scored one of the greatest triumphs in baseball history, after one of the bitterest fights.

We have heard carping critics that Huggins ought to win because he is backed by two liberal millionaire sportsmen, (Jacob) Ruppert and (Til) Huston, willing to gratify his lightest whim in the way of baseball purchase. The same thing has been said of John J. McGraw with the rich Charley Stoneham behind the Giants.

This is the veriest nonsense.

The Fleischmann millions backed the Cincinnati club for years, and the Reds invariably finished in the ruck. The millions of Wrigley and Armour are behind the Chicago National Leaguers, and where is the club in the race?

The not inconsiderable fortune of (Charles) Comiskey is the financial bolster of the White Sox; the wealthy Shibes are interested in the Philadelphia Athletics; and every other club in both leagues has plenty of backing.

You can buy the various parts of the finest automobile in the world, but what good are they unless you have a man who can properly assemble them? If you purchased all the greatest ballplayers in the two big leagues, they couldn't win a pennant without able direction.

Huggins has done well.

He is entitled to all the credit and the glory that goes with the leadership of a pennant-winning ball club.

He is entitled to an apology from those who have belittled his efforts.

Waite Hoyt's Dreams
Come True

"Dream As School Boy Comes True for Hoyt"
The Sporting News October 13, 1921

*Waite Hoyt's is a feel-good story, giving hope to little-leaguers
everywhere that they too might fulfill the dream of starring in the
World Series for the local nine. The Brooklyn-born pitcher quickly
became a Yankee hero after coming over from the Red Sox in 1921,
helping the team to three titles in ten seasons. When Hoyt retired in
1938, he had more World Series wins than any pitcher in history.*

YOUNGSTER FROM BROOKLYN HAD VISION AS LAD OF DAY HE WOULD
BE PITCHER IN WORLD'S SERIES

Young America, romance is not dead. No, indeed. Things can happen, even
to a boy. Father and mother and big brother may laugh at your day dreams of
one day marching home as a conquering hero at the head of your troops, or of
marching down Commercial Street as master of a circus parade.

They may smile at all your air castles, for grown folks are that way. They
don't understand. They don't understand that things can happen, even to a boy.

They may grin at your pet dream of one day being the hero pitcher of a
World's Series game, with cheering thousands crying your name and bands
blaring, and men and women fighting to shake your hands.

They may tell you that such things do not happen outside storybooks,
and that even if they do happen they do not happen to a boy, but you tell 'em
they don't know what they are talking about.

Hoyt's Dream Comes True

You tell 'em the story as you read it of "Schoolboy" Waite Hoyt, a Brooklyn lad, who lived this very thing at the Polo Grounds and whose boy-dream came true in the materialistic form of pitching the Yankees to a 3-0 shut-out against the mighty New York Giants in his first start in a World's Series, then, when everything seemed going against his team, came back in another game and turned the tide that had set in against the Yankees.

Now for the earlier chapters of the school boy's dream that came true at the Polo Grounds this October.

Waite was born in Brooklyn and when he was 15 years old he attended Erasmus High School, at Flatbush and Church avenues. This is a pretty good high school. All the boys and girls of Brooklyn's best families go there, and its baseball and football teams are famous in the scholastic world.

Waite pitched for the baseball team and he pitched so well that he made a name for himself around the schools. Between ball games and lessons he stood in front of a drugstore near a bank with other boys and watched the girls or carved his initials in the trees of Prospect Park.

He Dreamed of the Day

Meantime he dreamed of one day being a big league pitcher. That was his idea of complete glory. Especially a pitcher for the New York Giants, although he lived in Brooklyn. The Giants were his boyhood idea of everything in baseball.

Waite's father was a member of the Lamb's Club and so was John J. McGraw, manager of the Giants—then. You emphasize the then.

Pa Hoyt knew McGraw, and told him of his son, and one day he took Waite to the Polo Grounds to let McGraw see him pitch.

The great McGraw must have been impressed, because although Waite then was only 15 years old he was signed to a big league contract, the youngest player ever so signed.

In time Waite went to the minors for seasoning.

Jack Dunn, manager of the Baltimore team, took him into the Baltimore team of the International League through a deal with Rochester.

Eventually Frazee, of the Boston Red Sox, bought Waite from Dunn. He pitched great ball for the Red Sox for a time, and then his arm seemed to weaken and the Boston owners thought he was through.

Huggins, manager of the Yanks, always liked his style and took him in a deal that involved a number of players, and Waite, now 22 years old, finally found himself in the uniform, not of his old dreams, but of New York, pitching his team to victory in a World's Series.

The Ruth Is Mighty and Shall Prevail

"Ruth Comes into His Own with Two Homers, Clinching
Second for Yanks, 4 to 2"
New York World, October 12, 1923

by Heywood Broun

*After losing two straight World Series to the Giants, and failing to
win even a single Series game in 1922, Babe Ruth took matters into
his own hands in 1923, slugging the Yanks to victory in Game 2 with
two homers and three RBI. The classic first line of Heywood Broun's
account of the game says it all: "The Ruth is mighty and shall prevail."*

The Ruth is mighty and shall prevail. He did yesterday. Babe made two home
runs and the Yankees won from the Giants at the Polo Grounds by a score of 4
to 2. This evens up the World's Series, with one game for each contender.

It was the first game the Yankees won from the Giants since Oct. 10, 1921,
and it ended a string of eight successive victories for the latter, with one tie
thrown in.

Victory came to the American League champions through a change in
tactics. Miller Huggins could hardly fail to have observed Wednesday that
terrible things were almost certain to happen to his men if they paused any
place along the line from first to home.

In order to prevent blunders in base running he wisely decided to
eliminate it. The batter who hits a ball into the stands cannot possibly be
caught napping off any base.

The Yankees prevented Kelly, Frisch and the rest from performing tricks
in black magic by consistently hammering the ball out of the park or into
sections of the stand where only amateurs were seated.

Though simplicity itself, the system worked like a charm. Three of the Yankees' four runs were the product of homers, and this was enough for a winning total. Erin Ward was Ruth's assistant. Irish Meusel of the Giants also made a home run, but yesterday's show belonged to Ruth.

For the first time since coming to New York, Babe achieved his full brilliance in a World's Series game. Before this he has varied between pretty good and simply awful, but yesterday he was magnificent.

Just before the game John McGraw remarked:

"Why shouldn't we pitch to Ruth? I've said before, and I'll say it again, we pitch to better hitters than Ruth in the National League."

Ere the sun had set on McGraw's rash and presumptuous words, the Babe had flashed across the sky fiery portents which should have been sufficient to strike terror and conviction into the hearts of all infidels. But John McGraw clung to his heresy with a courage worthy of better cause.

In the fourth inning Ruth drove the ball completely out of the premises. McQuillan was pitching at the time, and the count was two balls and one strike. The strike was a fast ball shoulder high, at which Ruth had lunged with almost comic ferocity and ineptitude.

Snyder peeked at the bench to get a signal from McGraw. Catching for the Giants must be a terrific strain on the neck muscles, for apparently it is etiquette to take the signals from the bench manager furtively. The catcher is supposed to pretend he is merely glancing around to see if the girl in the red hat is anywhere in the grand stand, although all the time his eyes are intent on McGraw.

Of course the nature of the code is secret, but this time McGraw scratched his nose, to indicate: "Try another of those shoulder high fast ones on the Big Bam and let's see if we can't make him break his back again."

But Babe didn't break his back, for he had something solid to check his terrific swing. The ball started climbing from the moment it left the plate. It was a pop fly with a brand new gland and, though it flew high, it also flew far.

When last seen the ball was crossing the roof of the stand in deep right field at an attitude of 315 feet. We wonder whether new baseballs conversing together in the original package ever remark: "Join Ruth and see the world."

In the fifth Ruth was up again and by this time McQuillan had left the park utterly and Jack Bentley was pitching. The count crept up to two strikes and two balls. Snyder sneaked a look at the little logician in the dugout. McGraw blinked twice, pulled up trousers and thrust the forefinger of his right hand into his left eye. Snyder knew that he meant, "Try Bozo on a slow curve around his knees and don't forget to throw to first if you happen to drop the third strike."

Snyder called for the delivery as directed and Ruth topped a line drive over the wall of the lower stand right field. With that drive the Babe tied a record. Benny Kauff and Duffy Lewis are the only other players who ever made two home runs in a single World's Series game.

But was McGraw convinced and did he rush out of the dugout and kneel before Ruth with a cry of "Maestro," as the Babe crossed the plate? He did not. He nibbled at not a single word he has ever uttered in disparagement of the prowess of the Yankee slugger. In the ninth Ruth came to bat with two outs and a runner on second base. By every consideration of prudent tactics an intentional pass seemed indicated.

Snyder jerked his head around and observed that McGraw was blowing his nose. The Giant catcher was puzzled, for that was a signal he had never learned. By a process of pure reasoning he attempted to figure out just what it was that his chief was trying to convey to him.

"Maybe he means if we pitch to Ruth we'll blow the game," thought Snyder, but he looked toward the bench again just to make sure.

Now McGraw intended no signal at all when he blew his nose. That was not tactics, but only a head cold. On the second glance, Snyder observed that the little Napoleon gritted his teeth. Then he proceeded to spell out with the first three fingers of his right hand: "The Old Guard dies, but never surrenders." That was a signal Snyder recognized, although it never had passed between him and his manager before.

McGraw was saying: "Pitch to the big bum if he hammers every ball in the park into the North River."

And so, at Snyder's request, Bentley did pitch to Ruth and the Babe drove the ball deep into right centre; so deep that Casey Stengel could feel the hot breath of the bleacherites on his back as the ball came down and he caught it. If that drive had been just a shade to the right, it would have been a third home run for Ruth. As it was, the Babe had a great day, with two home runs, a terrific long fly and two bases on balls.

Neither pass was intentional. For that McGraw should receive due credit. His fame deserves to be recorded along with the man who said, "Lay on, MacDuff," "Sink me the ship, Master Gunner, split her in twain," and "I'll fight it out on this line if it takes all summer." For John McGraw also went down eyes front and his thumb on his nose.

Some of the sportsmanship of the afternoon was not so admirable. In the sixth inning Pep Young prevented a Yankee double play by diving at the legs of Ward, who was just about to throw to first after a force-out. Tack Hardwick never took out an opposing back more neatly. Half the spectators booed Young and the other half applauded him.

It did not seem to us that there was any very good reason for booing Young, since the tradition of professional baseball always has been agreeably free of chivalry. The rule is, "Do anything you can get away with."

But Young never should have been permitted to get away with that interference. The runner on first ought to have been declared out. In coming down to second Young had complete rights to the baseline and the bag, but those rights should not have permitted him the privilege of diving all the way across the bag to tackle Ward around the ankles.

It was a most palpably incompetent decision by Hart, the National League umpire on second base. Fortunately the blunder had no effect on the game, since the next Giant batter hit into a double play in which the Giant rushline was unable to reach Ward in time to do anything about it.

Ruth crushed to earth shall rise again. Herb Pennock, the assistant hero of the afternoon, did the same thing. In the fourth inning, Jack Bentley topped the slim Yankee left-hander into a crumpled heap by hitting him in the back with a fast ball. Pennock went down with a groan which could be heard even in the $1 seats. All the players gathered around him as he writhed, and what with sympathy and some judicious massage, he was up again within three or four minutes and his pitching efficiency seemed to be in nowise impaired. It was, of course, wholly an accident, as the kidney punch is barred in baseball.

Entirely aside from his injury, Pennock looked none too stalwart. He is a meagre athlete who winds up with great deliberation, as if fearful about what the opposing batter will do with the ball. And it was mostly slow curves that he fed to the Giants, but they did nothing much in crucial moments. Every now and then Pennock switched to a fast one, and the change of pace had McGraw's men baffled throughout.

Just once Pennock was in grave danger. It looked as if his three-run lead might be swept away in the sixth inning. Groh, Frisch and Young, the three Giants to face him at that point, all singled solidly. It seemed the part of wisdom to remove Pennock immediately after Young's single had scored Groh. Here Huggins was shrewd. He guessed wisely and stuck to Pennock.

Irish Meusel forced Young, and it would have been a double play but for Young's interference with Ward's throw. Cunningham, who followed, did hit into a double play, Scott to Ward to Pipp. The Giants' rally thus was limited to one run.

Their other score came in the second inning, when Irish Meusel drove a home run into the upper tier of the left field stands. It was a long wallop and served to tie the score at that stage of the game, as Erin Ward had made a home run for the Yankees in the first half of the inning. Ward's homer was less lusty, but went in the same general direction.

In the fourth the Yankees broke the tie. Ruth began it with his over-the-fence smash, and another run came across on a single by Pipp, Schang's hit to right—which Young fumbled long enough to let Pipp reach third—and Scott's clean line hit to centre. This is said to be Scott's last year as a regular and he seems intent on making a good exit, for, in addition to fielding spryly, he made two singles.

The defensive star of the afternoon was Joe Dugan, third baseman of the Yankees. He specialized on bunts. McQuillan caught him flatfooted with an unexpected tap, in the third inning, and Dugan made a marvelous throw on the dead run in time to get his man at first.

Again he made a great play against Kelly, first batter up in the last half of the ninth. Kelly just nicked the ball with a vicious swing and the result was a treacherous spinning grounder that rolled only half way down to third. Dugan had to run and throw in conjunction this time, too, but he got his man.

For the Giants, Frisch, Young and Meusel batted hard and Jack Bentley pitched well after relieving McQuillan in the fourth. He was hit fairly hard and he was a trifle wild, but the only run scored against him was Ruth's homer in the fifth.

As for the local color, the only bit we saw was around the neck of a spectator in a large white hat. The big handkerchief, which was spread completely over the gentleman's chest, was green and yellow, with purple spots. The rooter said his name was Tom Mix, but offered no other explanation.

Champions at Last

"Yanks Win Title; 6-4 Victory Ends $1,063,815 Series"
New York Times, October 16, 1923

*With 27 World Series titles under their belt at the time of this book's
printing, it's worth taking a look back at the Series that started it all
for the New York Yankees. In 1923, on the shoulders of Joe Dugan
and Babe Ruth, the Yankees finally crossed the Rubicon, arriving on
the other side as champions of the baseball world.*

The Yankees are the champions. In the greatest game of the greatest world's
series they beat the Giants yesterday at the Polo Grounds, 6 to 4, winning in
the eighth inning when Arthur Nehf collapsed and Bob Meusel drove a single
to centre field with the bases full.

Dreams came true in the eighth inning. The Yankees reached the journey's
end, and a world's championship flag will fly in the Yankee Stadium next year.
Dreams also went up in a puff of smoke, for when Meusel made that hit and
the Giants went crashing down, the life-long hope of John J. McGraw for three
world's championships went down with them.

This dramatic eighth inning finish was a fitting climax for the great three-
year battle that had been waged by the two New York teams. Twice McGraw's
baseball machine had emerged the winners and only as late as last Friday it
seemed invincible. Then the Yankees with their backs to the wall staged one
of the most remarkable fights in the history of the sport and swept everything
before them for three consecutive victories and the championship. Twice the
Giants had taken the lead and twice the Yankees had overhauled them before
Miller Huggins's team, with a determination that would not be denied, swept
on to a complete triumph and its first world's championship.

Great as was this series in the tenseness of the games played and in the
varying fortunes of the combatants, it was probably most remarkable of all
for the great interest it stirred in fandom. Large new grounds, just completed,
and built with an eye to the future, proved inadequate to accommodate the

thousands who rushed the gates to be spectators at this gigantic struggle. Scores of thousands were turned away, but 301,430 did get in to witness the six games played, for which they paid the sum of $1,063,815, both figures eclipsing all former records for baseball.

The Better Team Won

The better team won, and, moreover, it was a game team. When the eighth inning opened, the Yankees apparently were soundly thrashed. Nehf, the last hope of the old guard, had allowed only two hits in seven frames and only one run, a homer by Babe Ruth in the first inning. With two more chances, the Yanks were three runs behind, and, although they had fought bravely in this series, hardly a person in the big crowd paid them the tribute of believing that they would come through this crisis.

Nehf had been too powerful for them. With terrific speed and a side-breaking curve, with gameness and grim determination back of every pitch, the stocky left-hander had made the Yankee sluggers look like schoolboys. Two hits in the first two innings, and then a row of blanks. From the third to the eighth, the Yanks went hitless, and in five innings they went out in one-two-three order.

Nor was the start of the eighth any better. Aaron Ward lifted a feeble fly which George Kelly caught, making the eighteenth batter who had faced Nehf without hitting.

The goal was almost in sight for Nehf, but on the very next pitch fate tripped him up. The ball was high and at Schang's ear. Trying to escape it, Schang's bat hit the ball a glancing blow and drove it over third base for a single. Everett Scott followed up this "break" of the game by smashing a single sharply past Kelly. Schang dashed for third and made it, and then Miller Huggins rushed Freddy Hofmann to the plate to bat for Herb Pennock, the Yankee pitcher.

Nehf, his face literally as white as a sheet, was in the tightest hole of his life. After the contest the Yankee players accused him of lack of gameness, but it is a question if the stoutest heart in the world wouldn't have quailed and the steadfast hand trembled in this situation. On what he did in the next few minutes rested all the Giants' hopes for keeping their championship. Nehf, while probably nervous and fearful, was not a coward.

Something snapped inside him. Something gave way, and with it went every vestige of the superb control that had marked his pitching up to that time. In the twinkling of an eye he went down, conquered by something, perhaps by Yankee gameness, or by physical weakness after only a two days rest—or by the enormity of the burden that had been put on his shoulders.

While 34,172 looked on, he gave Hoffman four straight balls and filled the bases. He gave Joe Bush, batting for Witt, four more balls, and forced Schang over with a run that made the score 4 to 2. Then Nehf went out, with his head down, his shoulders bent, the most tragic figure that had appeared in this world's series.

Bill Ryan came in to salvage what he could from the wreckage. Even to hold the Yankees to one more run would have been enough, for the Giants could have won in that case. Ryan gave them that one run by also throwing four balls without a strike to Dugan, and after Scott had been forced over the plate Babe Ruth came up to face his greatest opportunity of the series. The 34,172 rose in their seats and pleaded for a home run, a triple, even a single—and then the Babe struck out!

It didn't check the Yankees, but it did make Ruth again the big failure of the series. With all his home runs and his fielding and his batting that had made McGraw's pitchers pass him, Ruth failed pitifully in the biggest crisis of all. Of all the Yankee players he figured slightest in the final victory that brought the title.

Now Ryan seemed almost out of the woods. He curved a strike over on Bob Meusel that made the Giant partisans howl with joy. But the next ball Meusel hit squarely. It went slightly to the right of Ryan on the bound, and it seemed that the pitcher might have tried to break it down, as McGraw himself pointed out after the game. Instead, he turned away from the hit and let it roll out to centre field. There Cunningham stopped it and threw desperately to the only base open to him—third base—whither Dugan was flying like the wind. The ball was straight at Groh, but it hopped badly as Heinie jumped for it and went rolling to the edge of the stand.

Hinkey Haines, running for Hoffmann, scored from third. Johnson, running for Bush, scampered in from second. Dugan did his own running and came all the way from first to the plate, while Meusel slid safely into third. Three runs on one hit, five for the inning, and the world's series was nearly over.

That eighth-inning rally put the stamp of gameness on the Yankee team. For the last time will some critic raise his voice to observe that the Yankees are a great team, but lack the courage to come from behind? Besides winning the championship, the Yankees removed with a single stroke the only blot that still marred their escutcheon in the minds of many, and Colonel Jacob Ruppert, in a little speech he made after the battle, seemed as delighted by the Yankees' gameness as by the fact that they had finally won a world's title.

◆ ◆ ◆

The Giants had finally been beaten. In three years of championship play they had never before met their match. With uncanny, almost superhuman, ability they had risen to meet every crisis fairly, and they could make the boast of every champion that they had never felt defeat. This series put before them their hardest test: could they break all baseball tradition and win three world's titles in a row? They could not, and so yesterday a great team finally went down.

At the same time another great team came up. Perhaps the Yanks next year will make it four pennants in as many years and equal the record of the old Chicago White Stockings made before the birth of the National League. Certainly the Hugmen are the most powerful team in baseball. With pitching, with batting, with team spirit and with Ruth, the Yanks stand out as real champions.

The best team won the greatest of all world's series. Except in fielding, smartness and finish of team play, the Giants were outplayed, for they were outbatted and outpitched by a smashing margin. In the two games that they did win, the champions were extended to the last limit of strength. In a measure, the terrific strain that the McGraw men were under even in victory led to their undoing, for their pitchers cracked in the last three games and even their superb defense showed signs of wear and tear.

This fact is the best of tributes to the power that the Yanks can apply when they are aroused. As water wears away a stone, only faster did the Yanks wear down the Giants, forcing them, step by step, to the wall until yesterday's breakdown became inevitable.

For the first time in three years the Yanks showed their real form, and this may be attributed not so much to Ruth as to the finer spirit and the deeper determination behind their every move. If the 1923 series did nothing else, it showed the value of discipline.

In attendance and receipts, of course, the series will not be equaled in many years, perhaps never—unless the same two teams should come together again and a way could be found to squeeze more people into a given space than were squeezed recently. If the promised enlargement of Colonel Ruppert's park is made, new records may be seen.

But, leaving aside the financial aspect, the series will rank high among its fellows. The first game, for one thing, was the greatest series game ever played in the opinion of John McGraw and hundreds of others who have seen baseball come and go. Nehf's third-game pitching, along with Jones's, was almost unequaled. Great crowds, but also great sensations and many thrills and bitter fighting, made the games stand out.

The hero? Joe Dugan, who was of greatest all-around value to his team; Ward was close behind him, and also Meusel, Witt, Ruth and Pipp. If by hero is meant the best player, Frisch was the man on the Giants. But if the hero is the obscure chap who was last in the experts' calculation, then Casey Stengel and Everett Scott win laurel wreaths. They deserve equal rank with the Rohes, the Rawlings and the Hendricksons of world's series baseball.

In the Shadow of the Babe

"Fate Unkind to Young Star of Yankees"
The Sporting News, February 4, 1926

by Billy Evans

Although he often played second (or even third) fiddle to Babe Ruth, Earle Combs had a key role in the Yankees' mighty "Murderer's Row" lineup. A well-rounded player, Combs was loved by his manager both for his contributions on the field and his demeanor off of it. The Hall of Fame centerfielder had a lifetime batting average of .325 in 12 seasons, all with the Yankees.

The greatest outfielder that has broken into the American League since Cobb and Speaker made their big league debut. That is Miller Huggins' opinion of Earle Combs. The mite manager of the Yankees is wise in the ways of baseball. He spilled big praise in behalf of Combs, but it was deserved.

Despite the admitted greatness of Combs, it is doubtful if any star of equal magnitude has ever been less press-agented. Two huge obstacles have stood in the way of Combs getting the publicity his play deserved.

The commanding figure of Babe Ruth proved the greatest handicap. It was a tough break for a young star to join the Yanks with Ruth cutting high jinks with his home run swing. Combs found himself in that very position.

The year that Combs came to the Yankees, Babe was going big. The rest of the personnel of the New York outfield was such that even so great a youngster as the "Kentucky Colonel," as Combs is known to his teammates, was unable to break into the line-up.

Then fate paved the way for the big opportunity that he had so long awaited. A Yankee batting slump was the cause. Sent into the New York line-up in a series against Detroit, he went over big. He made it evident by his brilliant play that it was going to be a tough job to get him out of the line-up.

Cleveland was next on the schedule after Detroit. Almost before he had a chance to show his real worth to the fans of that city, Combs suffered a broken leg in sliding into the home plate.

Fate could have scarcely been more unkind. First the greatness of Babe Ruth had kept him under the cover of the bench, just as a substitute. Then, after weeks of patient waiting, a broken leg put him out of the running for the rest of the season, perhaps forever. But Earle Combs is not the run-of-the-mine player; he is made of sterner stuff. Very fast on his feet, it was freely predicted that Combs was through, that the accident would rob him of much of his speed and most of his confidence.

When the Yankees reported at St. Petersburg, Fla., Combs was the big question mark, but he didn't remain that way very long. Almost instantly he became the exclamation point with the New York sport writers. He soon showed that he was as fast as ever. It didn't take much longer to demonstrate that he had the same sublime confidence in his ability to make good.

Earle Combs is just about ready to blossom out as one of the real stars of the American League. He is a great hitter despite the fact that his style is rather unorthodox and many of his base hits savor of the fluke.

Combs has a peculiar crouch at the plate and chops at the ball rather than swings. Many of his hits drop just out of the reach of either the infield or outfield and rival players often refer to him as a "lucky stiff" but Earle just smiles.

If Combs has a single fault it is a rather weak arm. But tell me what outfielders are throwing runners out at the plate? He will also become a better base runner.

The Babe Ruth
of the Rockies

"'Poosh-'Em-Out' Tony Lazzeri and His Colorful Record"
Baseball Magazine, April 1927

by F. C. Lane

*Tony Lazerri was nicknamed "Poosh 'Em Up," a bad translation
of an Italian phrase meaning "hit it out," as his Italian fans used to
cheer him on wildly from the stands. One of six players from the 1927
Yankees enshrined in the Hall of Fame, Lazzeri drove in at least 100
runs in 7 of 12 seasons in New York, including 114 as a rookie in 1926.*

LAZZERI IS A BORN BALL PLAYER. NOT ONLY CAN HE STING THE BALL
WITH TRUE HOME RUN FERVOR BUT HE IS A FINISHED PERFORMER
AT VARIOUS INFIELD POSITIONS.

A prime favorite among the younger players of the Big League diamond
is Tony Lazzeri. Baseball, the game of many nationalities, has attracted
comparatively few from sunny Italy; Germans and Irishmen have fairly
swarmed in the baseball records, but the Italians who have risen to stardom
have been relatively rare. Tony is an exception.

A year ago fabulous tales floated eastward from the mountains of a
slugging Wop in Salt Lake City who could hammer the ball a mile. He was sort
of Babe Ruth of the Rockies, a bludgeon-wielding terror to opposing pitchers,
a potential strong man of the ash. Hence, more than one Major League
magnate picked up his ears in response to such rumors. The ears of Colonel
Ruppert, however, millionaire magnate of the New York Yankees, were a little
more keenly in tune with the situation, or perhaps his bank balance was a
trifle larger. At any rate, he extended the right hand of friendship, with a fifty

thousand dollar check neatly folded in the palm, toward the Salt Lake City owner and the latter, with a sigh of resignation, grabbed the check.

Tony came to New York with the best wishes of the multitude. He got a slightly fishy eye from the assembled scribes. The gentlemen of the press recalled that other phenoms had made a great noise in Salt Lake City, only to fade away to a scarce audible whisper in the Big Leagues. There seemed something in the bracing climate of the Mormon metropolis upon which batting averages throve amazingly. The park there wasn't too big, the air was light, resistance to a catapulting baseball was at a minimum. Why not home runs? No wonder the gentlemen of the press were dubious.

But Tony shouldered his sturdy bat and proceeded to show them. Now standing in his well darned sox, Tony weighs just 157 pounds. He is 5 feet 11 inches tall, but he's built on the Bob Fitzsimmons plan, stringy and wiry. His wrists are not over large, his hands do not appear unduly muscular. His shoulders are lost in the shadow of Babe Ruth's ponderous torso. But Lazzeri, in a straight-away, swinging fashion, can hit the ball with a solid smash that would do credit to Babe himself.

I asked Tony the secret of his ability to hit so hard. "I don't know," he said. "I could always hit hard." Ty Cobb came ambling by at the moment and Tony addressed him. "Why can I hit hard?" he said. Ty looked at him with his half friendly, half sarcastic smile and said, "It comes from eating spaghetti and drinking wop wine."

Herb Pennock offered another more plausible explanation. "It's because he worked in a boiler factory for years and developed a lot of wiry strength." Tony, however, was non-committal. The subject was beyond his ken. Hitting hard was a gift. He could hit hard much easier than he could explain how or why.

Tony is not only a hard hitter, but he is, in the shrewd analysis of leading batters, a good hitter. That is, he generally hits to right field or right center, though he is a right handed batter and this is because he hits from habit, little late, sizing up the ball and taking his fun only at the last instant.

Tony's batting average, as revealed by the records, entirely fails to do him justice. He hit for .275, which is good enough, but it wasn't the quantity of Tony's hits so much as the quality which counted. Among other impressive features of his batting were 28 two baggers, 14 triples, and 18 home runs. Tony came to the Yankees as a direful slugger and he lived up to this reputation.

But Tony was not simply a slugger who specialized in fence crashing clout. He was a finished fielder and that finish came from the underlying fact that he was a born ball player. "Tony is a great natural player," said Miller Huggins with conviction. "Make no mistake about that. This is his first year in the Majors, but he's a finished player now and his hitting is no flash in the pan. He should improve."

In his Minor League days Tony played every infield position. He is as good a shortstop as he is a second baseman. In fact, he is good anywhere in the infield. He has a natural fielding knack and an excellent throwing arm. Colonel Ruppert has long since put down that initial cost of fifty thousand dollars among his wiser investments.

Tony suffers somewhat from the slugger's liability to frequent strike-outs. During the season he whiffed the air no fewer than 96 times. No doubt his most historic fanning bee was in the final game of the World's Series when he faced Alexander with the bases filled and opportunity vocal in the throats of forty thousand frenzied rooters. That opportunity faded from gilt to grey, however, when Alec, cool as ice, put over a third strike. It was a disappointment for Tony but no one blamed him. Alexander has fanned much more experienced batters than Lazzeri. It was Alexander's banner day in the sunset of his career. Tony has many more days to which he can look forward.

"It is easier to hit at Salt Lake City," admitted Tony, "than at New York. But I do believe the right field fence at Salt Lake was much closer than it is at the Stadium. The pitching is different and you can drive the ball further with less strength behind it because the air is light."

When Tony goes to bat, the crowd indulges in good-natured encouragement. "Poosh 'em out," they yell in chorus. They are thinking, evidently, of that fellow countryman of Tony's, Ping Bodie, who was a colorful asset to the American League years ago. Bodie was a good natured, clownish type of player who could hit but do little else. There could be no greater contrast between this volatile, rather excited Italian, and the sober minded, quiet Lazzeri. There isn't a more serious, studious player in baseball than Tony Lazzeri. More power to his wallops.

Lou Gehrig:
Built to Conquer

From *Luckiest Man: The Life and Death of Lou Gehrig*

by Jonathan Eig

*Never have two teammates been in a more remarkable offensive
competition than the one between Babe Ruth and Lou Gehrig in
1927. Though Ruth's record total of 60 home runs received the lion's
share of media attention, Gehrig (whose 47 homers were second-most
in the league) edged out the mighty Ruth with 175 RBI and a .373
batting average against the Babe's measly totals of 164 and .356.*

As the Yankees jumped to an early lead in the American League pennant
race, the team began to enjoy the rhythms of a baseball season, on and off
the field. With ball games beginning at three in the afternoon and ending
before dark, there were long nights of leisure, particularly when the team was
on the road, away from wives and families. On train trips, they would climb
aboard carrying boxes of barbecued ribs and bottles of booze. As darkness
fell, gnawed rib bones and empty bottles would fly from the train's windows,
and the men would sing "The Beer Barrel Polka."

The Yankee roster included a former schoolteacher, several farmers, a
seaman, a logger, a would-be priest, and a barkeep. They were diverse in their
occupations yet fairly homogenous in their working-class backgrounds. They
were anything but spoiled celebrities. Only Ruth enjoyed nationwide celebrity,
although Tony Lazzeri was fast becoming a big star in Italian communities
across the country. Six players from the club would eventually gain election
to the Hall of Fame—Ruth, Gehrig, Lazzeri, Combs, Pennock and Hoyt. But
there were more mortals than deities on the squad.

Among pitchers, Hoyt was the ace. Pennock, with a wicked curve and fine control, was the staff's best lefty. Dutch Ruether was considered too old and too inebriated by most other teams, but Huggins liked him and Ruether consistently rewarded his manager's confidence. Shocker, a silent, brooding man who threw a baffling assortment of slow curves, rounded out the rotation, winning game after game even as he scuffed along in nearly constant pain. George Pipgras, after knocking around the minor leagues for three years, became a starter in the middle of the season and finished with a 10-3 record. Wilcy Moore, an Oklahoma dirt farmer, was a rookie with a beguiling sinker who often worked out of the bullpen.

It wasn't just the pitching that proved better than anyone expected in 1927. Gehrig was playing better-than-average defense at first base and hitting the ball with more power than ever. Lazzeri, a slashing hitter, played a nearly flawless second base. Koenig still made too many errors at shortstop, but he had nice range and a strong arm and Huggins believed he would cut down the errors with time. Third baseman Joe Dugan was nearing the end of his career and no longer hitting for either power or average. But the Yankees had enough pop in the lineup that they could live without his bat. His experience helped steady the infield. The only weakness in the lineup was a catcher. Joe Collins, Benny Bengough, and Johnny Grabowski were all fine on defense but fairly useless at the plate. As the season stretched on, none of them would ever get hot enough to solidify his place as the starter. Collins would get the greatest share of the playing time, but he never hit well enough (.275, 7 HRs, 36 RBIs) to prove he deserved it.

The outfield was superb. Bob Meusel, a Yankee since 1920, was one of the league's most graceful athletes. He drank heavily and enjoyed chasing women with Ruth, but while the Babe pursued these activities with a childish joy and an endless fascination with all that the world had to offer him, Meusel behaved churlishly, as if he were owed something. A scowl seemed his natural expression, a grunt his favorite means of communication. He loped around the outfield, turning easy catches into hard ones and hard catches into hits, his pinstripes perpetually unstained. He seemed not to care for his fans, his teammates, or his coaches. But when he felt like playing ball, he was one of the best in the league, his arm a cannon, his swing simply gorgeous. Fortunately for the Yankees in 1927, Meusel felt like playing most of the time.

In center field, the Yanks had Earle Combs, a smooth fielder, a swift sprinter, and perhaps the finest leadoff hitter the game had ever seen. Born to a big family from the mountains of Kentucky, Combs could never understand the lazy work habits of men like Meusel. Combs knew he was lucky to be making money at baseball. Huggins gave him a job—get on base and wait for Ruth and Gehrig to drive you in—and Combs performed it brilliantly. He hit for high average—that season he would bat .356—drew a lot of walks, and ran the bases with a perfect balance of caution and zeal. Along with Gehrig, Combs was one of the manager's favorites. "If you had nine Combses on your ball club, you could go to bed every night and sleep like a baby," the manager once said.

Ruth, of course, was the right fielder. He not only led the Yankees in the pennant race, he led them in fun. He hit, fielded, joked, drank, strutted, and cackled. And no matter how selfishly he behaved at times, teammates couldn't help adoring him. In 1927, Ruth made a running gag out of Wilcy Moore's horrendous hitting. He bet the pitcher fifteen dollars at twenty-to-one odds that Moore would get no more than three hits all year. Moore's season-long pursuit of those three hits became a terrific source of entertainment for the Yankees. On August 26 in Detroit, Moore topped a feeble ground ball that rolled to a stop in the grass for hit number three. After the game, he bragged: "This is just an easy park to hit in." When he won the bet, Moore used Ruth's $300 payoff to buy two mules for his farm back in Oklahoma. He said he named one ass Babe and the other Ruth.

Even without the Babe, the Yankees might have been good enough to win it all in 1927. Of course, trying to imagine the '27 Yankees without Ruth is like trying to imagine the American Revolution without George Washington. Today, the '27 Yankees are the standard against which all great teams are judged. Other clubs have won more games. As batters have gotten bigger and stronger, other players have hit more home runs than Ruth and Gehrig. Yet no club has ever displayed anything near their sparkle or swagger. No team has been so exalted. No team has ever been such a gas.

"When we got to the ballpark," Pipgras told a writer once, "we knew we were going to win. That's all there was to it. We weren't cocky. I wouldn't call it confidence, either. We just *knew*. Like when you go to sleep you know the sun is going to come up in the morning."

It didn't take long for the Yankees to leave behind the competition. Philadelphia started slowly and never recovered. The White Sox, led by pitcher Ted Lyons, got off to a strong start, and for a short time it appeared they might give the Yankees a run for the pennant. The Sox came to New York on June 7 for a four-game series trailing the Yankees by only a game and a half in the standings. Ruth and Gehrig (referred to by the *New York Post* as the Babe's "little boy friend") hit back-to-back homers in the first game, a 4-1 Yankee win. In the next game—a 12-11 Yankee win—Lazzeri became the first Yankee to hit three home runs in a regular-season contest. By the time the Yankees won the third game on a three-run homer in the seventh inning by the little-known Ray Morehart (filling in at second for Lazzeri), the pennant race was effectively over. Lyons salvaged the final game of the series for the Sox, but by then the Yankees had made their point.

The team's nickname, "Murderers' Row," dated to 1921, when every member of the starting lineup had hit at least four home runs, but it was never more apt than in 1927. The White Sox as a team would hit thirty-six home runs in 1927. The Athletics, the second most powerful team in the league after the Yankees, would hit fifty-six. The Yankees would finish with 158. The team won so many games with dramatic, late-inning blasts that writers began to refer to the phenomenon as "five o'clock lightning." The nicknames piled up as fast as the wins.

◆ ◆ ◆

On June 22, the Babe smashed two home runs in the opening game of a doubleheader against the Red Sox, putting him slightly ahead of his 1921 pace, with twenty-four for the season. With each homer, Ruth would put another small notch in the barrel of his bat. The day after Ruth's two homers, Gehrig hit three in one game for the first time in his career; that gave him twenty-one for the season. He didn't notch his bat, or engage in any other form of braggadocio, so Ruth did it for him: "There's only one man who will ever have a chance of breaking my record," the Babe said in one interview, "and that's Lou Gehrig. He's a great kid." And Gehrig returned the compliment. "There will never be another guy like the Babe," he said. "I get more kick out of seeing him hit one more than I do from hitting one myself."

A great contest was shaping up. By July 1, Ruth and Gehrig were tied with twenty-five homers each. When Ruth hit a homer, Gehrig would wait at home plate to greet him before taking his turn at bat. If Ruth happened to be on base when Gehrig belted one, the Babe would wait to greet Lou and the two men would laugh their way back to the dugout as the fans stood and cheered and waved their straw hats. They cheered for the two sluggers, reported the *New York World*, "and other happenings meant nothing."

As Gehrig began to gain fame, Ruth's ambitious business manager, Christy Walsh, spotted an opportunity for his client. Ruth was in no danger of being eclipsed by Gehrig as a celebrity. The Kid didn't have the personality for it. But he was handsome and wholesome, clean-shaven and polite—attributes that played nicely in contrast to Ruth's boorish image. Walsh thought he could sell the sluggers as a pair—Babe and Buster, the legend and the kid, the rascal and the choirboy. He encouraged photographers to shoot the men side by side and pushed writers to play up the theme of a friendly competition. He invited Ruth and Gehrig on fishing trips to create the impression that the men socialized together. "Every day brings this chronicler a dozen queries regarding the social state of affairs existing between the Babe and the Buster," a *Times* writer dutifully told readers. "The answer is that they're pals."

In truth, there was no great friendship. Not yet, anyway. For one thing, Ruth and Gehrig were sharply divided on the subject of Huggins. Gehrig, naturally inclined to obey authority, saw in Huggins yet another father figure, a man of iron will and great determination, a mentor. Ruth saw a worthless little squirt. If not for Walsh's prompting, it seems unlikely that a Ruth-Gehrig relationship beyond the playing field, locker room, and Pullman car would have developed. Ruth's social calendar was such that he did not spend a lot of time nurturing new friendships.

As summer heated up, the Yankees kept winning. Combs seemed to be on base every inning. Lazzeri was driving in almost as many runs as Gehrig or Ruth; Meusel was playing with surprising tenacity. The pitching staff, to almost everyone's surprise, had emerged as the league's best. By July, the Yankees—"the frolicking, rollicking, walloping Yankees," as Richards Vidmer of *The Times* wrote—were running away with the pennant. Rumors circulated that Huggins was spotted wearing a smile.

Bigger crowds than ever greeted the Yankees when they traveled. And while these throngs had once been satisfied when Ruth stepped outside the train to wave and utter a few words, now they wanted something new: Gehrig, the wunderkind. Ruth had to cajole his young teammate to come outside. Sometimes the crowds gathered long after midnight, when Ruth and Gehrig thought their train would pass unnoticed. Still, the men would rarely disappoint. They would put down their cards or get up from their narrow berths to put on some clothes and smile and shake hands. Even when roused from his sleep, Ruth was energized by an audience. Gehrig, no matter the hour, never seemed to enjoy the attention. He would stand with his hands in his pockets, glancing nervously at Ruth, as if waiting to be told what to do. Then, looking like the child who wished not to be called on by his teacher, he would mumble a few words into his chest.

On days off the Yankees often scheduled exhibition games in minor-league cities like St. Paul, Dayton, Buffalo, and Indianapolis. Requests came even from big-league cities like Cincinnati and Pittsburgh, where the Yankees rarely played because there were no American League teams. As a result, players seldom had a day off. And Ruth and Gehrig could scarcely ask to sit out the exhibitions. Customers didn't pay to see Bengough and Gazella take their swings. Still,

Ruth did manage to rest his legs a bit during some of these exhibition games by switching from the outfield to first base. That meant Gehrig had to stumble around in right field, but he was younger and not one to gripe.

In 1927, audiences at Yankee Stadium were so large that the team had to hire a second announcer—a big-voiced man with megaphone—to stand on the field and shout the names of the pitchers and batters. As a result of the overflow audiences, increasing numbers of radio stations began broadcasting games. At first, owners of major-league teams protested, concerned that fans would no longer pay to come to the park if they could hear baseball at home for free. But their fears quickly dissipated. Radio, it turned out, was the best advertising the game had ever had, carrying the sport to countless people who otherwise might never have fallen under its spell.

Nineteen twenty-seven was a critical year in the development of baseball. Seven years after the "Black Sox" scandal, fans finally began to embrace the game again. The emergence of Lou Gehrig—this sweet, dimpled child with seemingly superhuman strength—played a big part in the revival. Suddenly, baseball had more than a big star—it had a big star and a dramatic narrative. It had a home-run race, referred to by writers as "The Great Home Run Derby." It had a notorious character and a squeaky-clean one battling for supremacy, a sinner and a saint.

Homers were flying so fast that fans began bringing baseball gloves to games, hoping to grab souvenirs. Die-hards complained that the integrity of the sport had been dealt a blow by all these "circuit blasts," that fans no longer appreciated the subtlety of the sport, that they went away disappointed even by terrific games if these famous sluggers failed to hit at least one ball out of the park. Similar cries are heard today. But then, as now, the majority of fans were thrilled by the display of power and lusted for more. America's love of the home run said something about the nation's expectations in 1927, about the population's delight in muscle and spectacle. Across the country, highways were sprouting from cornfields. Industrial output was soaring. Stock prices were rising and rising. Once, thrift had been a virtue. Now Americans wanted more, more, more. More toasters, irons, and vacuum cleaners. More refrigerators. More radios. More cars. More airplanes. More home runs.

By mid-summer some newspapers were predicting that Gehrig would not only win the home-run derby but go on to shatter all the Babe's records. His youth and superior conditioning, they said, would carry him long after Ruth tired. The pressure of these expectations must have been enormous, but Gehrig handled it well. He never tried to convert his celebrity status into a more prominent position in the team's social order. He never tried to cash in on endorsements. He never made demands of management. When each game ended, he sat on a stool in front of his locker and dressed as quickly as he could, while Ruth held court before the media a few feet away.

All his life, Gehrig wrestled with his ego. He was built to conquer, yet programmed for failure. He had a subtle and active mind, yet he lived and worked in an environment in which the expression of deep thoughts often incited teasing. Now, in only his third year with the Yankees, things were going better than he could have hoped. Babe Ruth, his hero, had become his friend. He was batting fourth and starting at first base for a winning team. He had the complete trust of his manager and the respect of the fans. Still, Gehrig did not so much set aside his self-doubt as manage it. He learned once again that he could always count on his body, that his brawny legs, wide chest, and enormous shoulders could be trained to do almost anything. The young man who once wanted to be an engineer now treated baseball as a mechanical affair. See the ball; hit the ball. He developed a smooth, simple swing—one much more compact than Ruth's—until he became almost frighteningly consistent. It was inside the straight white lines of the batter's box that he seemed most comfortable.

Most of the force generated in the swing of a bat comes from the thighs and torso, and Gehrig was built hugely around the middle. He lowered his center of gravity when he swung so that his left knee almost scraped the ground. He didn't need to flail. Ruth, with his wild, up-from-the-heels swing, hit soaring rockets that disappeared high in the air and then fell to earth, often in the bleachers. Gehrig swung from the shoulder, as if wielding an ax. His home runs seemed to zip just over the second baseman's head and continue rising until they banged off a seat in the right-field bleachers. His shots almost seemed to whistle.

"I have as much respect for a home run as anybody," Gehrig told *Baseball Magazine* in the summer of 1927, "but I like straightaway hitting. I believe it's the proper way to hit. If a fellow has met the ball just right, on the nose, he's done what he set out to do. A lot of home runs are lucky. I've seen more than one ball carried into the stands by the wind. But there's nothing lucky about a solid smash, straight out over the diamond. It means only one thing—that the batter has connected just right."

◆ ◆ ◆

On August 8, the Yankees left New York for their longest road trip of the year. They would travel to Philadelphia, Washington, D.C., Chicago, Cleveland, Detroit, and St. Louis. Then, after just one game back home in New York on

August 31, they would take off again for Philadelphia and Boston. For more than a month they lived in hotels and railroad cars. Sometimes a player would forget where he was. Even more difficult was remembering where he had been. The pretty blonde waitress in the tight, white uniform—was that Cleveland or Detroit? Everything blurred but the baseball.

Ruth seemed to have every advantage in the home-run competition as it entered its final stage. First, he adored the attention. But more important, in a practical sense, he had the good fortune of batting before Gehrig in the team's lineup. "I'd rather see Ruth than Gehrig in a tight place," said Dan Howley, manager of the St, Louis Browns. "Sometimes you can figure what the Babe is going to do, but you can never tell about Gehrig. He is likely to hit any kind of ball to any field."

Gehrig enjoyed his success, but he never seemed to believe that he could be Babe Ruth's equal, much less his superior. "The only real home run hitter that has ever lived," he said in reference to Ruth. "I'm fortunate to be even close to him."

On September 3, in the first inning of another game at Shibe Park in Philadelphia, Ruth hit a towering shot into the right-center field stands for his forty-fourth homer, taking a lead of three on Gehrig. But on the next pitch, Gehrig smacked one over the rooftops of the neighboring cottages. One inning later, Gehrig hit another, bringing his total to forty-three.

The men were neck-and-neck heading into the final turn. On September 5 in Boston, more than 70,000 fans showed up outside Fenway Park, hoping to get in to see the Yankees. Almost half of them were turned away. When the seats in the stadium filled, fans began sitting atop the outfield fence and along the foul lines in the outfield, which inspired the umpires to declare that any fair ball that rolled into the foul territory and hit a fan would be declared a double. Those fans not lucky enough to get in watched from beneath the grandstand or from rooftops in the surrounding neighborhood.

In the third inning of the first game, Gehrig saw a pitch from Charlie Ruffing that he liked. He swung and hit it squarely. The ball carried into the right-field bleachers for a long home run. The Boston crowd, usually hostile toward the Yankees, screamed in delight. Gehrig and Ruth were tied at forty-four with twenty-three games to go. For either man to break the Babe's record of fifty-nine, he would have to hit homers at a terrific pace—more than one for every two games. And yet the question gripping fans wasn't whether the record would be broken, but who would break it.

"The most astonishing thing that has ever happened in organized baseball is the home run race between George Herman Ruth and Henry Louis Gehrig," wrote Paul Gallico. "Gehrig, of course, cannot approach Ruth as a showman and an eccentric, but there is still time for that. Lou is only a kid. Wait until he develops a little more and runs up against the temptations that beset a popular hero. Ruth without temptations might be a pretty ordinary fellow. Part of his charm lies in the manner with which he succumbs to every temptation that comes his way. That doesn't mean Henry Louis must take up sin to become a box office attraction. Rather one waits to see his reactions to life, which same reactions make a man interesting or not. Right now he seems devoted to fishing, devouring pickled eels, and hitting home runs, of which three things the last alone is of interest to the baseball public. For this reason it is a little more difficult to write about Henry Louis than George Herman. Ruth is either planning to cut loose, is cutting loose, or is repenting the last time he cut loose. He is a news story on legs going about looking for a place to happen. He has not lived a model life, while Henry Louis has, and if Ruth wins the home run race it will come as a great blow to the pure."

It wouldn't be the first time, or the last, that the Babe had dealt purity a blow. On September 6, Ruth hit three home runs in a doubleheader. He had the lead again. Then, the next day, he hit two more—numbers 48 and 49.

Gehrig entered the game on September 7 batting .389, with 45 home runs and 161 runs batted in (he was driving in an astonishing 1.2 runs per game). Ruth had the slight edge in home runs, but Gehrig was putting together the most productive season the game had ever seen. He could have stopped on that date, nearly a month early, and still have had one of the greatest seasons any baseball player had ever enjoyed. If he had continued at the same pace, he would have finished with 52 home runs and 186 runs batted in to go along with his .389 average. No one, not even Ruth, had ever hit for such a high average and so much power.

His slump began not long after the Yankees returned from their long road trip. It was not uncommon for young men to get worn down over the course of 154 games, what with the cramped and stuffy train cars, the strange beds, the frequent doubleheaders, the numerous exhibition games, and the inescapable heat. Was Gehrig tired? Did his nerves get the best of him? It's possible. But Fred Lieb said Gehrig struggled because he was worried about his mother, who had developed a goiter (an inflammation of the thyroid) and needed surgery. "I'm so worried about Mom that I can't see straight," Gehrig said.

Over the last twenty-two games of the season, he hit only .275, with two home runs, two triples, and five doubles. He committed four errors and drove in only fourteen runs.

On September 29, with three games remaining in the regular season, Ruth hit two more home runs—numbers 58 and 59—to tie his record. The next afternoon, in the eighth inning of a game against the Washington Senators, he sent one arcing into the right-field bleachers for his sixtieth. The Babe waddled around the bases, waving his cap to the delirious crowd. Gehrig greeted his teammate with an energetic handshake and a pat on the back.

The final game of the year was meaningless. Only 20,000 turned out at Yankee Stadium. Gehrig could have sat it out and rested for the start of the World Series. But he knew he had played every game that season, same as the year before, and he was proud of it. Perhaps, too, he was hoping a few more swings would help him break out of his slump in time for the World Series. So he trotted out to first base again. Even Ruth declined to take the day off. The two men had been having fun. Their home-run challenge had never become burdensome. They had never griped about the media attention or the unrealistic expectations of the fact that some pitchers threw them few good pitches to hit. On the last day of the regular season, Gehrig hit his forty-seventh home run. The fans cheered, but without enthusiasm. Franklin Pierce Adams, a columnist for the *Herald Tribune*, wrote that Gehrig would be remembered as "the guy who hit all those home runs the year Ruth broke the record."

It was just Gehrig's luck to have his accomplishments overshadowed. Even with his slump. He set a major-league record with 175 runs batted in for the season and he hit .373. Ruth drove in 164 runs and hit .356. Gehrig won the most valuable player award, referred to at the time as the League Award, but even that honor came with an asterisk: Ruth was ineligible because he had already won it once.

Most of the talk around baseball revolved around what Ruth would do for an encore. Would he hit sixty-five in 1928? Why not seventy? If the stock market could keep going up, up, up, why couldn't Ruth? The Babe had this to say: "Will I ever break this again? I don't know and I don't care. But if I don't, I know who will. Wait 'til that bozo over there"—he pointed across the locker room to Gehrig—"gets waded into them again and they may forget that a guy named Ruth ever lived."

The Greatest Team in the History of Baseball

From *The Wonder Team: The True Story of the Incomparable 1927 New York Yankees*

by Leo Trachtenberg

Of all the dominant teams in the history of this game, no star-studded lineup measures up to the bar set by the 1927 Yankees. Leo Trachtenberg simply and eloquently sums up this squad, describing them as a once-in-a-lifetime collection of "supremely gifted, irresistibly confident athletes who dominated baseball like some colossus casting a shadow beyond its time."

It was 1927. Calvin Coolidge was president, Prohibition was the law of the land, Lindbergh had just flown to Paris, and the movies were still silent. But none of this mattered to me, a nine-year-old sitting with his father in Yankee Stadium watching my first major league baseball game. I don't remember who the Yankees played that radiant summer afternoon before a crowd of tumultuous fans, a day when the grass on the field seemed greener than it ever would again. Nor do I recall who pitched for either team, or who won the game. What I do remember is a barrel-chested, skinny-legged man in a pinstriped uniform who stepped up to the plate in the first inning.

"That's Babe Ruth," my father said. "Watch. He could hit a home run."

I don't recall the count or if I had my fingers crossed, but the prodigious swing of Babe's bat, the sharp crack as it met the ball, and the roar of the immense crowd remain etched in my memory. High into the air soared the ball, a white dot ascending with extravagant and splendid velocity towards the right field bleachers where it dropped into a forest of outstretched hands.

I watched excitedly as the Babe circled the bases, touched home, and tipped his hat to the adoring fans. At that moment I became, then and forever after, a fan of baseball, the New York Yankees, and George Herman "Babe" Ruth.

"Does he always hit home runs?" I asked my father. "No, not always," he said laughing, "but plenty of times. More than anybody."

I was to see the Babe hit other home runs, and I've been lucky enough during 60-plus years as a Yankee fan to see the likes of Joe DiMaggio, Mickey Mantle, Reggie Jackson, Yogi Berra and other pinstriped sluggers whack the ball into the stands. But none compared to the homer Babe hit that afternoon in 1927—for me.

A few months later, on October 8, Yankee second baseman "Poosh 'em up" Tony Lazzeri stood at that same Stadium home plate. It was the fourth game of the 1927 World Series (the Yankees had taken the first three games from the Pittsburgh Pirates), the bottom of the ninth with the score 3-3 and two out.

On third was Yankee center fielder Earle Combs. Pirates hurler John "Big Serb" Miljus got the signal and loosed an errant pitch towards home. The ball flew past the desperate grasp of Pirate catcher Johnny Gooch's outstretched mitt. 60,000 fans erupted when Combs scuttled in from third, touched home, and a legend was born.

The ball club that won the 4-3 game that October day, completing a four game sweep of the world series, was the 1927 Yankees, judged by many as the greatest of all teams in the long and splendid history of professional baseball. In the 60-some years since those "Murderers' Row" Yanks shattered the opposition with prodigal skills and awesome power they have become the recognized model of singular baseball achievement. A few excellent teams preceded them, others followed, but none were quite their equal.

Scarcely had the series tumult died away when James R. Harrison, a sportswriter not easily given to overstatement, wrote in the *New York Times* of October 9, 1927, "They must not be far wrong who assert that these Yankees are the greatest team in the more than fifty years of baseball history."

H. I. Phillips, writing in the *New York Sun* of October 10,1927, with no trace of Harrison's small equivocation, stated, "Their original ideal that they (the Pirates) might win a game from what is beyond the greatest team of all time was definitely and finally snuffed out when . . . pitcher Miljus threw a ball at an invisible catcher." The Yankees, he wrote waggishly, "are the first team in history to have magicians, miracle men, jinns, a Beowulf and a couple of Thors on it." Then, in a moment of insight and divination he added, "It is a team out of folklore and mythology."

Phillips was on to something. For the remarkable ball club that had swaggered through baseball and taken the measure of the best in both leagues has in fact become part of our American folk lore tradition. And though years have passed, and admirable ball clubs have come and gone, the sovereign reputation of the 1927 Yankees remains undiminished. Indeed, in the recent years of profound changes in our national pastime—expanded leagues, night ball, the designated hitter, pool table playing surfaces, indoor stadiums, a ball so juiced up that the homers are commonplace instead of feats of special accomplishment—that reputation has taken on added luster with each passing season.

In the May 1951 issue of *Sport Magazine*, Paul Gallico, who began his prominent writing career as a sports reporter and columnist, called the '27 Yanks "the greatest all-around baseball team ever to trot up the dugout steps onto the diamond—and unquestionably the greatest collection of assassins of pitchers."

The same magazine, in an October 1962 article by Josh Greenfeld, quotes Wilbert Robinson, a charter member of that famous gang of diamond depredators, the Baltimore "Old Orioles." Said Robinson, "This Yankee team would have murdered the old Orioles. We never saw the day we could make runs like Huggins' mob."

And though you'd think that by 1963 some other ball club would be jostling the '27 Yanks in the contest for all-time supremacy, that year 84 out of 100 sports editors voted the 1927 Yankees number 1. Reporting these results in the *Sporting News* of June 8, 1963, veteran sports writer Dan Daniel stated: "They'll never be matched." Today, with the twentieth century waning, Daniel's prediction stands unchallenged.

Of course, other great ball clubs have come on the scene since the departure of the 1927 Yankees, notably Connie Mack's 1929–31 Philadelphia A's, Joe McCarthy's 1936 Yankees, and Sparky Anderson's "Big Red Machine" Cincinnati Reds of the 1970s. You can crunch their numbers in approved Quanto-History style, examine their virtues, and acclaim their eminence; but significantly, hardly ever do we hear them selected as the "greatest" in the history of the game. That accolade, at least until now, has been reserved for the 1927 Yankees, a golden team for a golden time.

Who were the 1927 Yankees, the team of "Five O'Clock Lightning" and Babe's epochal 60 homers? What sort of men were those supremely gifted, irresistibly confident athletes who dominated baseball like some colossus casting a shadow beyond its time? Who brought them together for that glorious season? And what exactly did they accomplish in the climactic year of the 1920s, that time between the great wars when the unemployment rate was 3.2 percent, taxes were low, optimism high, we were sure of ourselves as a nation and a people, and sports thrived in its first Golden Age? Looking back at that time of cheerful expectations and high confidence, it's a small wonder that historian Paul Johnson, in his book, *Modern Times*, dubbed the 1920s "The Last Arcadia."

Six of the 1927 club are in the Hall of Fame in Cooperstown, New York: Babe Ruth, Lou Gehrig, Tony Lazzeri, Earle Combs, Waite Hoyt, Herb Pennock. So are Miller Huggins, their great manager, and Ed Barrow, the business manager who wheeled and dealed to bring superb players to New York.

The most famous, of course, was their right fielder, the lusty, roistering child/man George Herman "Babe" Ruth, a player gifted beyond the reasonable, a force of nature responding to the crowd as no other ballplayer before or since.

Patrolling center field was Earle Combs, the Bible-reading "Kentucky Colonel" from the Cumberland, swift, graceful, the best leadoff man ever. Bob Meusel, with his icy stare and surly disposition, the picture swing and rifle arm, was the left fielder.

The Yankee infield was equally gifted. Playing first base was the strapping, even-tempered "Iron Man," Lou Gehrig, a true baseball immortal who with Ruth comprised the most devastating one-two punch the game has ever known. "Poosh 'em up," Tony Lazzeri, a take-charge fielder and slashing hitter, the first of a long line of brilliant Italian-American Yankees, covered second. Mark Koenig, the man sportswriters once said would never make it in the majors, played short and found immortality on the great team. "Jumping Joe" Dugan, nearing the end of his playing days, yet still peerless at the hot corner, picked 'em at third. Joe Collins, Benny Bengough, and Johnny Grabowski, all sterling catchers, shared the assignments behind home plate.

The pitching staff was top rank, a manager's dream. The ace righty was the free-spirited "Schoolboy," Waite Hoyt. Herb Pennock, the wily, brainy Quaker countryman with a wicked curve and fine control, was their dominant lefty hurler. Rookie Wilcy Moore was there, the Oklahoma dirt farmer with steady nerves and a bewildering sinker. So was that most courageous of pitchers, Urban Shocker, winning eighteen while slowly dying of heart disease. Rounding out the staff was George Pipgras, finally coming into his own after discouraging years on the bench, and Dutch Ruether, ending his major league career as a winning hurler. On the strong Yank bench were sterling backups— Mike Gazella, Cedric Durst, Ben Paschal, Ray Morehart—men lost in time whom few recall, who never had the slightest chance of winning a plaque in

Cooperstown yet found themselves, through the benign touch of fate, a piece with true greatness.

Not least, there was Miller Huggins (manager), Edward Grant Barrow (business manager), Colonel Jacob Ruppert (owner): three men who came together to form a management alliance that was made in some baseball heaven. Who, in the apogee year of a beguiling decade—before the Great Depression, Hitler, World War II, and the nagging anxieties of the nuclear age—saw their '27 Yankees triumph with an exuberance that mirrored the time.

The word "great" is defined in my Webster's as "remarkable in magnitude, degree, or effectiveness," a definition that surely fits the 1927 New York Yankees. For they were a remarkable ball club in every way by which superior achievement is judged in baseball. Brought together and attaining a kind of radiant perfection in that one magnificent year, their accomplishments will continue to resonate as long as the game is played.

One of the dwindling number who saw those '27 Yankees play, I have carried with me the luminous memory of the ball club that came into my life that summer afternoon. Now, in remembrance of joyous days in the company of Babe, Lou, and their memorable teammates, I invite you to join me in playing baseball with the 1927 New York Yankees.

The Babe Calls His Shot

From *Babe: The Legend Comes to Life*

by Robert W. Creamer

*Babe Ruth's called shot—re-enacted by kids and adults alike on
sandlots everywhere. Who among us hasn't calmly pointed a bat
toward the far reaches of a ball field, indicating exactly where we plan
to hit the next pitch? Whether Ruth was truly calling his shot with
his gesture during the 1932 World Series, nobody seems to know for
certain—but it sure is fun to believe.*

Almost 50,000 people were jammed into every part of Wrigley Field, and
most of them were yelling at Ruth. Wherever a ball was lofted his way in
pregame practice, a lemon or two would come flying out of the bleachers.
Each time, Babe picked up the lemons and threw them back. He was in a good
mood. There was a strong wind blowing toward right field, and during batting
practice he and Gehrig put on an awesome show, far more spectacular than
the one in Pittsburgh a few years earlier. Babe hit nine balls into the stands,
Gehrig seven. Ruth yelled at the Cubs, "I'd play for half my salary if I could
hit in this dump all the time." Gomez, the non-hitting pitcher, said, "With that
wind, I could hit a home run today."

The jockeying between the two teams, or, to be more accurate, between
Ruth and the Cubs, became more intense as the game began. Charlie Root was
the starting pitcher for Chicago, but Bush and Grimes and Malone were on the
top step of the Cub dugout, leading the verbal barrage on Ruth. Andy Lotshaw,
the Cubs' trainer, yelled, "If I had you, I'd hitch you to a wagon, you potbelly,"
Ruth said afterwards, "I didn't mind no ballplayers yelling at me, but the
trainer cutting in—that made me sore." As he waited to bat in the first inning,
according to Richards Vidmer in the *New York Herald Tribune*, "He paused to
jest with the raging Cubs, pointed to the right field bleachers and grinned."

The game started badly for the Cubs. Koenig had hurt his wrist in New York and was out the rest of the Series. His replacement, Billy Jurges, fielded the first ball hit by the Yankees—a grounder by Earle Combs—and threw it all the way into the stands behind first base. Joe Sewell walked, and Ruth came to bat with men on first and second and no one out. Root threw a pitch outside for ball one, another one inside for ball two. Then he threw a fastball on the outside corner and Ruth, swinging at the ball for the first time in a game in Wrigley Field, hit a three-run homer into the right field bleachers to put the Yankees ahead 3-0, before an out had been made.

Gehrig hit a homer in the third with the bases empty (and Ruth hit a fly to the right center field fence), but the Cubs rallied and in the fourth inning tied the game 4-4. The tying run was scored by Jurges, who reached second base with a double when Ruth, to the great delight of the crowd, looked foolish missing a try at a shoestring catch.

And so it was 4-4 in a rowdy game as the Yankees came to bat in the fifth. Another lemon bounced toward Ruth as he waited in the on-deck circle while Sewell went out. Boos and hoots rose to a crescendo as he stepped into the batter's box. The Cubs were on the top of the dugout steps, Bush cupping his hands around his mouth as he taunted Ruth. Babe grinned, then stepped in to face Root. The pitcher threw. It was called a strike. The crowd cheered, and the Cubs razzed Ruth louder than ever. Still grinning, holding his bat loosely in his left hand, he looked over at the Cubs and raised one finger of his right hand. Root pitched again, in close, for ball one. He pitched again, this time outside, and it was ball two. The crowd stirred in disappointment, and the razzing from the Cubs let up slightly. Again Root pitched, and it was called strike two. The crowd roared, and the Cubs yammered with renewed vigor. Bush was so excited he ran a step or two onto the grass in front of the dugout, yelling at Ruth. Grimes was shouting something. Ruth waved the exultant Cubs back toward their dugout and held up two fingers. Gabby Hartnett, the Chicago catcher, heard him say, "It only takes one to hit it." Root said something from the mound, and Ruth said something back. Gehrig, who was in the on-deck circle, said, "Babe was jawing with Root and what he said was, 'I'm going to knock the next pitch right down your goddamned throat.'"

Root threw again, a changeup curve, low and away. Ruth swung and hit a tremendous line-drive home run deep into the bleachers in center field. Johnny Moore, the center fielder, ran back and stood there looking up as it went far over his head into the stands. It was the longest home run that had ever been hit in Wrigley Field. Ruth ran down the first base line laughing. "You lucky bum," he said to himself. "You lucky, lucky bum." He said something to

Charlie Grimm, the Cubs' player-manager first baseman. He said something to second baseman Billy Herman. He shook his clasped hands over his head like a victorious fighter, and as he rounded third base, still laughing, he yelled, "Squeeze the eagle club!" to the now silent Chicago dugout. In a box near home plate Franklin D. Roosevelt, who was running for President against Herbert Hoover, put his head back and laughed, and after the Babe crossed home plate Roosevelt's eyes followed him all the way into the dugout, where he was mauled and pounded by his gleeful Yankee teammates.

Gehrig stepped to the plate, Root threw one pitch and Gehrig hit a home run. Two pitches, two home runs; the Yankees led, 6-4, all their runs coming on homers by Ruth and Gehrig. Root was taken out of the game, and it ended with the Yankees winning, 7-5.

The New York clubhouse roared with noise afterwards. Ruth yelled, "Did Mr. Ruth chase those guys back into the dugout? Mr. Ruth sure did!"

The next day Bush was Chicago's starting pitcher. When Ruth came to bat in the first inning, Bush hit him on the arm with a blistering fastball. Babe pretended to flick something off his arm as he trotted down to first base. "Hey, Lop Ears," he yelled to Bush, "was that your fastball? I thought it was a gnat." To Gehrig, he called, "Don't look for nothing, Lou. He ain't got it." And Bush didn't. He faced five men in the inning, got one out and was lifted from the game. Lazzeri hit two homers, Combs one, Gehrig batted in three runs, and the Yankees won, 13-6. Ruth had only one single in five at bats and in the clubhouse afterwards put hot towels on his arm, which was flaming red and badly swollen where Bush's gnat had bitten it. Doc Painter, the trainer, said that if the Series had gone another game, Ruth could not possibly have played in it. But despite the pain, Ruth was gloriously happy. He even went over to McCarthy and shook his hand. "What a victory!" he said. "My hat is off to you, Mac." A few days later, back in New York, he said, "That's the first time I ever got the players and the fans going at the same time. I never had so much fun in all my life."

Now. What about the legend? What about the story, often affirmed, often denied, that Babe pointed to a spot in center field and then hit the ball precisely to that spot? It is an argument over nothing, and the fact that Ruth did not point to center field before his home run does not diminish in the least what he did. He did challenge the Cubs before 50,000 people, did indicate he was going to hit a home run and did hit a home run. What more could you ask?

The legend grew, obviously, because people gild lilies and because sometimes we remember vividly seeing things we did not see. Most of the contemporary accounts of the game talked about Ruth calling his shot, but only one that I could find said specifically that he pointed at the fence. That, written by Joe Williams, sports editor of the Scripps-Howard newspapers, appeared in late editions of afternoon newspapers on Saturday, October 1, the day of the game. The headline over Williams' story in the *New York World-Telegram* said, "RUTH CALLS SHOT AS HE PUTS HOMER NO. 2 IN SIDE POCKET," and part of his account said, "In the fifth, with the Cubs riding him unmercifully from the bench, Ruth pointed to center and punched a screaming liner to a spot where no ball had ever been hit before." That is the only place in the story where specific reference is made to pointing to center field. Elsewhere in his copy Williams wrote, "The first strike was called, and the razzing from the Cub bench increased. Ruth laughed and held up one finger. Two balls were pitched and Babe jeered the Cub bench, the fans and Root, grinning broadly all the time. Another strike was called and Bush ran part way out of the dugout to tell the Babe that he was just a tramp. Ruth hit the next pitch farther than any other ball was hit in this park."

Westbrook Pegler, who wrote a column but not a running account of the game, said, "Bush pushed back his big ears, funneled his hands at his mouth and yelled raspingly at the great man to upset him. The Babe laughed derisively and gestured at him—wait, mugg, I'm going to hit one out of the yard. Root threw a strike past him and he held up a finger to Bush whose ears flapped excitedly as he renewed his insults. Another strike passed him and Bush crawled almost out of the hole to extend his remarks. The Babe held up two fingers this time. Root wasted two balls and Babe put up two fingers on his other hand. Then with a warning gesture of his hand to Bush, he sent the signal for the customers to see. Now, it said, this is the one, look. And that one went riding on the longest home run ever hit in the park. . . . Many a hitter may make two home runs, possibly three, in World Series play in years to come, but not the way Ruth hit these two. Nor will you ever see an artist call his shot before hitting one of the longest drives ever made on the ground in a World Series game, laughing at and mocking the enemy, two strikes gone."

The story by Williams was the only one I found of those written on the day of the game that interpreted Ruth's gestures as pointing towards center, but two days later Paul Gallico of the *New York Daily News*, a rococo and flamboyant writer, wrote, "He painted like a duelist to the spot where he expected to send his rapier home." A day after that Bill Corum of the Hearst newspapers wrote that Ruth "pointed out where he was going to hit the next one, and hit it there," but in his game account the day it happened Corum neglected to mention the fact.

Tom Meany, who worked for Williams and sat next to him at the game on Saturday, wrote a story the following Tuesday that said, "Babe's interviewer then interrupted to point out the hold in which Babe put himself Saturday when he pointed out the spot in which he intended hitting his homer and asked the great man if he realized how ridiculous he would have appeared if he had struck out. 'I never thought of that,' said Babe." But it is not clear in Meany's story if the phrase about pointing was in the question put to Ruth or was merely incorporated in the copy as a clarifying description.

Williams was a positive, opinionated observer, and a vigorous journalist. Taking an opposite tack some months later, he suggested to Gehrig that Root let Babe hit the ball ("Like hell he did," said Gehrig). Meany was a fine reporter, a gifted writer and a superior raconteur of baseball anecdotes. I believe that Williams' strong personality and the wide circulation given his original story in Scripps-Howard newspapers as well as Meany's repeated accounts of that colorful World Series are what got the legend started and kept it going. That the pointing version was often questioned is shown in Meany's biography of Ruth, published in 1947. In it Meany wrote, "It was then the big fellow made what many believe to be the *beau geste* of his entire career. He pointed in the direction of dead centerfield. Some say it was merely a gesture toward Root, others that he was just letting the Cub bench know that he still had the big one left. Ruth himself has changed his version a couple of times. . . . Whatever the intent of the gesture, the result was, as they say in Hollywood, slightly colossal."

Ruth told John Carmichael, a highly respected Chicago sportswriter, "I didn't exactly point to any spot. All I wanted to do was give that thing a ride out of the park, anywhere. I used to pop off a lot about hitting homers, but mostly among the Yankees. Combs and Lazzeri and Fletcher used to yell, 'Come on, Babe, hit one.' So I'd come back and say, 'Okay, you bums. I'll hit one!' Sometimes I did. Sometimes I didn't. Hell, it was fun."

His autobiography, published in 1947, not only says he did it but adds the embroidery that he began to think about it the night before the game, after he and Claire were spat on when they entered their hotel. It says he was angry and hurt because of the taunts of the Chicago players and fans. It says that before the first pitch he pointed to center field and that when Root threw the ball, Babe held up a finger and yelled, "Strike one," before the umpire could call the pitch. And held up two fingers and yelled, "Strike two," after the second pitch. And before the third pitch, he stepped out of the box and pointed to the bleachers again. And then hit the third pitch for the home run. This version is the one that was substantially followed by Hollywood in the movie of Ruth's life that starred William Bendix, and as bad as the movie was it gave the legend a permanence of concrete.

Both autobiography and movie infuriated Charlie Root, who turned the film company down flat when they asked him to portray himself. "Not if you're going to have him pointing," he said. He refused to have anything to do with it, and he went to his grave denying that Ruth had pointed to center field. "If he had I would have knocked him on his ass with the next pitch," he always insisted. Yet Root's memory was hazy on detail. In the mid 1950s he said, "George Magerkurth, the plate umpire, said in a magazine story that Ruth did point to center field. But to show how far wrong Magerkurth was, he had the count three and two when it was really two strikes and no balls. To me, the count was significant. Why should Ruth point to show where he was going to hit a ball when, with two strikes and no balls, he knew he wasn't apt to get a pitch he could hit at all?" But both Magerkurth and Root were wrong. The count was neither three balls and two strikes nor two strikes and no balls. It was two strikes and two balls. And Magerkurth umpired at first base that day, not behind the plate.

Such fuzziness of detail is evident in several contemporary accounts of the game. Pegler, quoted above, said the count went strike, strike, ball, ball, whereas it was strike, ball, ball, strike. Corum said the count was three and two, and so did the play-by-play account in the *New York Times*. Meany's biography and Ruth's autobiography both say, as Root did, that it was two strikes and no balls. Any lawyer will concede that honest witnesses see the same things differently.

Here are what some witnesses said about it.

Charlie Root: "Ruth did not point at the fence before he swung. If he had made a gesture like that, well, anybody who knows me knows that Ruth would have ended up on his ass. The legend didn't get started until later. I fed him a changeup curve. It wasn't a foot off the ground and it was three or four inches outside, certainly not a good pitch to hit. But that was the one he smacked. He told me the next day that if I'd have thrown him a fastball he would have struck out. 'I was guessing with you,' he said."

Gabby Hartnett, the Chicago catcher: "Babe came up in the fifth and took two called strikes. After each one the Cub bench gave him the business, stuff like he was choking and he was washed up. Babe waved his hand across the plate toward our bench on the third base side. One finger was up. At the same time he said softly, and I think only the umpire and I heard him, 'It only takes one to hit it.' Root came in with a fast one and it went into the center field seats. Babe didn't say a word when he passed me after the home run. If he had pointed out at the bleachers, I'd be the first to say so."

Doc Painter, the Yankee trainer: "Before taking his stance he swept his left arm full length and pointed to the center field fence. When he got back to the bench, Herb Pennock said, 'Suppose you missed? You would have looked like an awful bum.' Ruth was taking a drink from the water cooler, and he lifted his head and laughed. 'I never thought of that,' he said."

Joe McCarthy, the Yankee manager: "I'm not going to say he didn't do it. Maybe I didn't see it. Maybe I was looking the other way. Anyway, I'm not going to say he didn't do it."

Jimmy Isaminger, Philadelphia sportswriter: "He made a satiric gesture to the Cub bench and followed it with a resounding belt that had so much force behind it that it landed in the bleachers in dead center."

The *San Francisco Examiner*, October 2, 1932: "He called his shot theatrically, with derisive gestures towards the Cubs' dugout."

The Reach Guide, covering the 1932 season: "Ruth hit the ball over the center field fence, a tremendous drive, after indicating in pantomime to his hostile admirers what he proposed to do, and did."

Warren Brown, Chicago sportswriter: "The Babe indicated he had one strike, the big one, left. The vituperative Cub bench knew what he meant. Harnett heard Ruth growl that this was what he meant. Ruth, for a long while, had no other version, nor was any other sought from him."

Ford Frick, who was not at the game, tried to pin Ruth down on the subject when the two were talking about the Series some time later.

"Did you really point to the bleachers?" Frick asked.

Ruth, always honest, shrugged. "It's in the papers, isn't it?" he said.

"Yeah," Frick said. "It's in the papers. But did you really point to the stands?"

"Why don't you read the papers? It's all right there in the papers."

Which, Frick said, means he never said he did and he never said he didn't.

The Mahatma Comes to the Stadium

"Gandhi at the Bat"
The New Yorker, June 20, 1983

by Chet Williamson

If you've ever wondered what it would be like to see Gandhi step up to the plate at the House that Ruth Built, look no further. In this fictional account, novelist and short-story writer Chet Williamson sends Gandhi, "a little brown man in a loincloth and wire-rimmed specs," to the plate to face Hall of Famer Lefty Grove.

History books and available newspaper files hold no record of the visit to America in 1933 made by Mohandas K. Gandhi. For reasons of a sensitive political nature that have not yet come to light, all contemporary accounts of the visit were suppressed at the request of President Roosevelt. Although Gandhi repeatedly appeared in public during his three-month stay, the cloak of journalistic silence was seamless, and all that remains of the great man's celebrated tour is this long-secreted glimpse of one of the Mahatma's unexpected nonpolitical appearances, written by an anonymous press-box denizen of the day.

Yankee Stadium is used to roaring crowds. But never did a crowd roar louder than on yesterday afternoon, when a little brown man in a loincloth and wire-rimmed specs put some wood on a Lefty Grove fastball and completely bamboozled Connie Mack's A's.

It all started when Mayor John J. O'Brien invited M. K. ("Mahatma") Gandhi to see the Yanks play Philadelphia up at "The House that Ruth Built." Gandhi, whose ballplaying experience was limited to a few wallops with a cricket bat, jumped at the chance, and 12 noon saw the Mayor's party in the

Yankee locker room, where the Mahatma met the Bronx Bombers. A zippy exchange occurred when the Mayor introduced the Lord of the Loincloth to the Bambino. "Mr. Gandhi," Hizoner said, "I want you to meet Babe Ruth, the Sultan of Swat."

Gandhi's eyes sparkled behind his Moxie-bottle lenses, and he chuckled. "Swat," quoth he, "is a sultanate of which I am not aware. Is it by any chance near Maharashtra?"

"Say," laughed the Babe, laying a meaty hand on the frail brown shoulder, "you're all right, kiddo. I'll hit one out of the park for you today."

"No hitting, please," the Mahatma quipped.

In the Mayor's front-row private box, the little Indian turned down the offer of a hot dog and requested a box of Cracker Jack instead. The prize inside was a tin whistle, which he blew gleefully whenever the Bambino waddled up to bat.

The grinning guru enjoyed the game immensely—far more than the A's, who were down 3-1 by the fifth. Ruth, as promised, did smash a homer in the seventh, to Gandhi's delight. "Hey, Gunga Din!" Ruth cried jovially on his way to the Yankee dugout. "Know why my battin' reminds folks of India? 'Cause I can really Bangalore!"

"That is a very good one, Mr. Ruth!" cried the economy-size Asian.

By the top of the ninth, the Yanks had scored two more runs. After Mickey Cochrane whiffed on a Red Ruffing fastball, Gandhi remarked how difficult it must be to hit such a swiftly thrown missile and said, "I should like to try it very much."

"Are you serious?" Mayor O'Brien asked.

"If it would not be too much trouble. Perhaps after the exhibition is over," his visitor suggested.

There was no time to lose. O'Brien, displaying a panache that would have done credit to his predecessor, Jimmy Walker, leaped up and shouted to the umpire, who called a time-out. Managers McCarthy and Mack were beckoned to the Mayor's side, along with Bill Dinneen, the home-plate umpire, and soon all of Yankee Stadium heard an unprecedented announcement:

"Ladies and gentleman, regardless of the score, the Yankees will come to bat to finish the ninth inning."

The excited crowd soon learned that the reason for such a breach of tradition was a little brown pinch-hitter shorter than his bat. When the pinstriped Bronx Bombers returned to their dugout after the last Philadelphia batter had been retired in the ninth, the Nabob of Nonviolence received a hasty batting lesson from Babe Ruth under the stands.

Lazzeri led off the bottom of the stanza, hitting a short chop to Bishop, who rifled to Foxx for the out. Then, after Crosetti fouled out to Cochrane, the stadium became hushed as the announcer intoned, "Pinch-hitting for Ruffing, Mohandas K. Gandhi."

The crowd erupted as the white-robed holy man, a fungo bat propped jauntily on his shoulder, strode to the plate, where he remarked to the crouching Mickey Cochrane, "It is a very big field, and a very small ball."

"C'mon, Moe!" Ruth called loudly to the dead-game bantam batter. "Show 'em the old pepper!"

"I will try, Mr. Baby!" Gandhi called back, and went into a batting stance unique in the annals of the great game—his sheet-draped posterior facing the catcher, and his bat held high over his head, as if to clobber the ball into submission. While Joe McCarthy called time, the Babe trotted out and politely corrected the little Indian's position in the box.

The time-out over, Grove threw a screaming fastball right over the plate. The bat stayed on Gandhi's shoulder. "Oh, my," he said as he turned and observed the ball firmly ensconced in Cochrane's glove. "That *was* speedy."

PART III

Joltin' Joe and
Baseball's Golden Age
1936–1948

The departure of Babe Ruth in 1934 and the premature end to Lou Gehrig's career in 1939 did not send the Yankee franchise into a tailspin. Quite the contrary. The arrival of Joe DiMaggio launched a new era of dominance, one that was extended by the emergence of Phil Rizzuto and Yogi Berra, among others. Winners of four straight titles to close out the 1930s, and four more in the 1940s, the Yanks boasted a supporting cast flush with all-stars. The exploits of two of those stars, Red Ruffing and Charlie Keller, are presented here in contemporary accounts from the renowned publication *Baseball Magazine*.

Tales of the rookie campaigns of Rizzuto and Berra explore what it was like for young players—an Italian American from Brooklyn and an Italian American from the heartland in St. Louis—to enter a locker room filled with World Series heroes and the ghosts of all-time greats. Both more than amply lived up to the expectations that came with wearing Yankee pinstripes.

Bill Dickey, the Cooperstown-bound catcher who preceded Berra, straddled the Ruth/Gehrig and DiMaggio eras as a member of seven world champion teams between 1932 and 1943. He masterfully caught pitchers Lefty Gomez, Herb Pennock, and Red Ruffing while asserting his place as one of the game's best hitting backstops.

But Yankee history from 1936 to 1951 was dominated by the man known as Joltin' Joe. An excerpt from the landmark biography by Richard Ben Cramer and DiMaggio's own reflections of his historic hitting streak of 1941 can only begin to touch on the greatness of the Yankee Clipper.

Joe DiMaggio, 1941. *Bob Wands/AP Images*

One for Stardom's Book

From *Joe DiMaggio: The Hero's Life*

by Richard Ben Cramer

There was no shortage of heroics in the great career of Joe DiMaggio, even in his rookie season. DiMaggio's performance against the Giants in the 1936 World Series was one for the ages, convincing Giants first baseman and manager Bill Terry that Joltin' Joe had single-handedly been the difference in the Yankees' World Series victory.

Two weeks after the All-Star Game, DiMaggio almost screwed up in a mortal way. He was back on track at the plate, playing right field steadily—his embarrassment in Boston was fading into memory—when, in a game against the Tigers, DiMaggio raced into right center, chasing a high drive off the bat of Goose Goslin.

The center fielder that day was Myril Hoag, who also took off after Goslin's liner. DiMaggio and Hoag collided at full speed—head-to-head—and both dropped to the ground like they'd been shot. Goslin scored an inside-the-park home run; after several minutes, DiMaggio and Hoag finally rose, and both men played out the inning. But Hoag was still woozy on the bench and sat out the rest of the game. Clearly, DiMaggio had caused the foul-up: The center fielder has the right of way on any ball he can get to. But no one said anything. The Yankees won the game. And Hoag was still in the lineup the following day.

Two days later, Hoag was found unconscious in his hotel room. At Harper Hospital in Detroit, doctors suspected his collision with DiMaggio had caused a blood clot in Hoag's brain. The Yankees had to move on. Their train was rolling toward Cleveland as surgeons drilled three holes to relieve the pressure in Hoag's skull, and then waited . . . there was nothing more they could do. Brain surgery was an infant science in 1936. Hoag might die, or might live on with brain damage—no one could predict. The Yankees learned by long-distance telephone that Hoag had survived the operation. In time he would recover fully, and play for another eight years in the bigs.

The collision with Hoag could have made Joe one of those sad specters of baseball history—like Carl Mays, who could never live down his fatal beaning of Ray Chapman in 1920. But as it turned out, Joe was unscathed. Instead of a specter, he became a center fielder. McCarthy said he had that spot in mind from the start.

"Finally, I decided he was ready so I moved him into center field," McCarthy told Maury Allen, in *Where Have You Gone, Joe DiMaggio?* " . . . He never would have become the great outfielder he was if I hadn't moved him. He needed that room to roam in Yankee Stadium. That's the toughest center field in baseball and only the real great ones can play out there.

" . . . Once he got out there he stayed out there. He did everything so easily. That's why they never appreciated him as much as they should. You never saw him make a great catch. You never saw him fall down or go diving for a ball. He didn't have to. He just knew where the ball was hit and he went and got it. That's what you're supposed to do. The idea is to catch the ball. The idea isn't to make exciting catches."

Last-ditch drama wasn't McCarthy's style. With the rookie DiMaggio in center field, the Yankees clinched the pennant on September 9, the earliest date in the history of major league baseball. And they finished nineteen and a half games ahead of the second-place Tigers. After that season, the baseball writers awarded Lou Gehrig (.354, 49 HRs, 152 RBIs) the title of American League MVP. In those exacting days, no rookie would be considered for that prize. But the difference in Yanks' performance—in every account that autumn—was credited to Joe. There was no Rookie of the Year ballot (that wasn't invented till 1940), but in '36, they wouldn't have needed a vote. The only question was whether Joe D. (.323, 29 HRs, 125 RBIs) was the best rookie *in history*. . . . But that debate wouldn't begin in earnest until the Yanks met the Giants for the title of titles—World Champs—in the subway Series of 1936.

In New York, the Giants still bore the mantle of class they'd earned through the long reign (1902–1932) of John J. McGraw. Now they held sway in the National League under their player-manager (and future Hall of Famer), first baseman Bill Terry. In the outfield, they were led by another all-time great, the National League home run leader, Mel Ott. And on the mound, they had the stopper of the age (and National League MVP), "King" Carl Hubbell.

It was a measure of the excitement that Young Joe's Yanks had stirred that they were favored eight-to-five by the bookies. But in Game One, the

Yanks were mesmerized by Hubbell's screwball—they were beaten soundly, 6-1—and the Giants' outfield didn't have to make a putout all day.

That would be the last time the Yanks could be put to sleep. They came back in Game Two with eighteen runs and won in a laugher. Game Three was squeaky-tight, a 2-1 Yankee win. And the next day, the Yanks got revenge on Hubbell, when Gehrig won the game with a two-run homer.

The Giants were down three games to one—but they wouldn't fold. In Game Five, they eked out a 5-4 win in the tenth inning, to send the Series back to their home park, the Polo Grounds. In Game Six, the Yanks jumped out to a commanding three-run lead, but the Giants chipped away, chipped away—single runs in the fifth, the seventh, and the eighth. By the ninth inning, the Yanks were clinging to a one-run lead, and facing the possibility that they'd let the Giants back into the Series—then everything would rest on Game Seven, in the Polo Grounds—perhaps with the hypnotist, Hubbell, on the mound again . . .

But it never got that far. In the ninth inning of Game Six, DiMaggio led off with a line single into left field. Gehrig singled and DiMaggio raced around to third. The next hitter, Dickey, bounced a sharp one-hopper to first baseman Bill Terry, who made the right play—he grabbed the ball and looked across the diamond, to freeze DiMaggio on third base. . . . But DiMaggio wasn't on third. He'd broken for home as the ball left the bat. Now he stopped in no-man's land, while the crowd (and the Giants) screamed for Terry to gun him down.

Terry fired the ball to third—but DiMaggio broke again for home. Third baseman Eddie Mayo whipped the ball past Joe to the plate, and the catcher, Harry Danning, blocked the baseline, crouched for collision.

But DiMaggio didn't run into Danning. Joe didn't even slide. Instead, he launched himself into the air—head first, over the tag, completely over Danning . . . and in the air, Joe twisted his body, still falling . . . till he landed back of Danning, in the dirt, with his hand on the Polo Grounds plate.

And that was the end of the Giants. Danning was so flustered he juggled the ball while two remaining Yankee runners each took a base. Then the rest of the Giants came unglued . . . and the Yanks poured seven runs across (the last on Joe's second hit of the inning). The final tally was 13-5. The Yankees were the World Champions—and a new era of their dynasty was launched.

Joe had hit .346 for the Series. In the aftermath, the Giants' manager, Terry, could only pay homage: "I've always heard that one player could make the difference between a losing team and a winner, and I never believed it. Now I know, it's true."

Withal, those words from Terry were not the highest accolade for Joe in that Series. The topper came after the second game, also in the vast oval Polo

Grounds—in fact, at the farthest reach of that oval. It was near the end of the Yankee blowout—18-4, the scoreboard read—and as the Giants took their last at bats, many of the 43,543 fans were on their way to the exits. That's when the public address announcer asked all present to stay at their seats, until one special fan, Franklin D. Roosevelt, could get to his open limousine and ride off the field through the center field gates.

It was just moments thereafter that the Giants' slugger, Hank Leiber, swung at a fastball from the weary Lefty Gomez and launched it like a mortar shell toward the fence in center field.

DiMaggio was off before the crack of the bat could be heard in the stands. He turned his back and raced for the deepest curve of the horseshoe. He was 475 feet from the plate when he made the impossible catch—over his shoulder, still running flat out . . . in fact, he just kept running, through the notch in the fence, up the steep stairs that led to the players' clubhouse, in deepest center field. Then, he remembered—*Roosevelt!*

Near the top of the stairs, Joe stopped, turned and stood with the ball in his glove, while the car came toward him. There he was—the nation's savior—in the back seat, with his hat cocked up, his trademark grin around the cigarette holder. Joe, without thinking, stiffened to attention as the car rounded the center field gravel track, with all eyes upon it—save for Roosevelt's eyes. He looked to the stands, then to the stairway, until he found Joe . . . and then FDR lifted a hand in a jaunty wave from the brim of his hat. And from the crowd there was a final, rippling cheer, as the Dago boy from Fisherman's Wharf was saluted by the President of the United States.

King Kong Keller Joins an Elite Outfield

"The Maryland Mauler"
Baseball Magazine, June 1941

by Arthur O. W. Anderson

Though he wasn't a fan of the "King Kong" nickname, Charlie Keller earned it with his brute strength. Batting between Hall of Famers Joe DiMaggio and Bill Dickey in the lineup, Keller had a remarkable 1941 season, belting 33 home runs and 122 RBI—both career bests. Keller is also remembered for big performances in the biggest games, driving in 18 runs in 19 World Series contests.

Charlie Keller came up to the majors under a double handicap. He was a rookie on an apparently set team that had ridden roughshod over the American League for three successive seasons and had romped through the World Series with consummate ease. The club was rated by many experts as one of the greatest ever assembled. An outsider seemed to have little chance of breaking into the line-up regularly on this combination of stars. Even to be retained as a substitute amounted to victory.

In addition Keller arrived at his first Yankee camp with a reputation. He was a great ballplayer who couldn't miss even with the world champions. The ballyhoo drums rumbled and roared. He was featured in newspapers and magazines. This extravagant, premature publicity was a millstone about his neck. Such propaganda had ruined many a bright prospect before him, if not ruined, at least delayed his progress.

Keller, however, wasn't to be denied. With a grim determination to succeed that isn't surpassed by any athlete in any sport, and matched by only a few, he went to work. He soon made the predictions of the scouts look as good as he made the opposing pitchers look bad. He broke into the outfield combination of Selkirk, Henrich and DiMaggio and belonged. Belonged? Next to DiMaggio who led the American League in hitting in 1939, Keller had the highest batting average on the Yankee ball club, .334.

Freshman stars in World Series are frequently subject to the jitters and play far below the form that enabled them to get into the classic. Not so with Charlie Keller. He was hotter than a six alarm fire and copped the highest batting honors among the regulars with the flourishing average of .438. He fashioned this on seven hits in 16 times at bat, and five of those bingles were devastating extra base wallops, three homers, a triple and a double. His batting helped materially to set down the Reds of Cincy in four straight games.

The Yankee windup of that 1939 World Series was one of the most extraordinary ever staged. It would tax the ingenuity of a Hollywood playwright to produce one more weird or fantastic. You may recall it, big Ernie Lombardi, the Reds catcher, sitting at the plate in a daze, the ball a few feet from him, as New York scored their final winning run. Keller was the man directly responsible for this Cincinnati humiliation. He was on first when DiMaggio shot a single to Ival Goodman in right field who erred on the play, enabling Charlie to try for home. Ball and man arrived at the pay-off station about the same time and down went Lombardi, bowled over by the flying outfielder.

Keller can't recall hitting the bulky catcher and to this day doesn't believe he did despite the overwhelming evidence to the contrary. His mind was centered solely on scoring and the impact didn't register. On that much discussed play he was running as fast as he could possibly go and felt that he would make better time going into the plate standing up than by sliding.

The standout rookie of 1939 made such a profound impression all over the circuit that it was the consensus of opinion that he wouldn't be bothered by any sophomore jinx. He was too good a natural hitter. Keller himself doesn't figure that any one year can be any harder than any other. He doesn't see how it could be if a fellow is serious and keeps his ambition.

Keller had just as much desire for superiority in 1940 as in 1939, he's that kind of a player, he was just as earnest in his endeavors, but his batting average dropped almost fifty percentage points to .286. Had the opposing pitchers suddenly discovered some tell-tale weakness in his makeup? A further check on his record wouldn't tend to make on believe so. He batted in ten more runs in 1940 than in his initial year and hit just that many more homers. That may be a partial answer to his slump in average. A great straight away hitter, he may have been trying too frequently to pull that ball into the stands for the round trip. Even Babe Ruth could have stepped up his average had he not being pointing so often for round trippers.

This angle is speculation. There is another. Keller was in poor health a good part of the season and finally had to have his tonsils yanked to get some of the poison out of his system. The day he left his bed after the operation he appeared in a ball game. Weak and wan, he returned to action too soon, which didn't help. Charlie is a worrisome fellow about his hits. Failure to get them with fair consistency makes him press. Watch him sometime at the plate. If he should be batting .390, he won't relax.

Keller is one of the few major league ballplayers to hail from Maryland, one of the thirteen original states of the U.S.A. He was born September 12, 1916, at Middletown and spent the early years of his life on a 125-acre farm. Though relatively short—he's five feet ten inches—he's powerfully built with long arms and the large and sinewy hands of the Village Blacksmith. He weighs 190 pounds and there isn't an ounce of superfluous fat on his frame. Hard work on the farm developed him into the fine physical specimen that he is. Charlie's been behind the plow and he has milked his twenty-five cows a day.

He wasn't one to neglect school either and before hitting the majors took a Bachelor of Science degree at the University of Maryland. He was a standout, from his freshman year on, at basketball and baseball. He had attended a very small high school that didn't have a football team so he lost out in that sport in his first year at college. In fact he didn't go out for the team as he had an appendectomy the summer before he entered Maryland U.

His natural athletic ability led him out on the gridiron in his sophomore year, however. He played in most of the games, but because of his inexperience he didn't know how to protect himself too well and was banged up plenty. With a baseball career in the offing Keller wisely decided to give up the grid frolic before sustaining some injury that might put him out of the running for keeps.

Charlie played summer ball at Kinston, North Carolina, and it was there that the major league scouts caught up with him. A half dozen, from as many clubs, were soon elbowing each other trying to get him to sign on the dotted line. Keller was cagey. He sat tight and let the scouts fight it out.

White tie Gene McCann and the Yankee ivory hunter got on the job, and after sizing up the situation he sent a hurry call to New York for assistance. Trouble shooter Paul Krichell was hurriedly summoned to the Barrow office and ordered to pack his bag and join the party at Kinston. Keller must not escape.

The two New York scouts teamed perfectly. While one kept a weather eye on Charlie to see that he didn't sign with some other club, the other went to his home and talked to his father, sold him on the advantages of a young fellow like Charlie starting in the Yankees organization. The traveler then visited the coach at the University of Maryland and won his support.

Working together it wasn't long before Keller capitulated. It had been his wish all along to sign with a club where he would have a chance to play regularly and one that would be in the running.

Charlie was started off with the Newark Bears of the International League in 1937. It was a team that dominated the loop and ranked among the greatest minor league outfits of all time. It won the pennant by more than twenty-five games and went on to snatch the Little World Series from Columbus of the American Association after losing the first three games of the set.

Freshman Keller was a success from the start and won the batting championship of the circuit by a comfortable margin with a percentage of .353. Playing in 113 games he gathered 180 hits among which were interspersed 34 doubles, 14 triples and 13 home runs. He scored 120 runs and batted in 88 teammates.

The comeback of the Newark club to win the Junior World Series of 1937 after trailing by three games gave Keller as big a thrill as he was later to experience helping to knock off the Reds at Cincinnati. And well it might, for he led all the regular players in the series by clouting a sensational .478 and he ranked second in total bases.

Oscar Vitt was Keller's first manager in pro ball. Shortly after the season was ended Ol' Oz was appointed pilot of the Cleveland Indians, succeeding Steve O'Neill. The Newark post for 1938 was given to Johnny Neun who faced a difficult assignment in following a 25 1/2 game winner that had been shorn of ten of its stars. But Neun had Keller to build his club around, and the Maryland strong boy set such a fine example that the Newark club again ran away with the pennant.

His 1938 record literally demands close examination. His batting average was .363, which was tops among those who played in a hundred or more games. Charlie was head man in scoring runs, notching his spikes in the plate 149 times. He was the leader in drawing bases on balls with 108, and he made the most hits, 211. He batted in 129 runs which needs no apology in any league. After that hitting display there was no question of his immediate promotion to the parent club.

Keller, while good in the field, isn't the best grass patrolman who ever caged a far-flung fly, but we have never seen him loaf on a ball or give up in disgust when one slipped through his legs.

"The play that may seem hardest at one time," he says, "may not be the next. Perhaps the most trying chance an outfielder has is one of those either you do or don't plays. By that I mean rushing in to pick up a grounder and then throwing out the runner who is carrying that important tally in a close ball game. One can't afford to fumble momentarily, and he has to get the ball away fast and accurate. Sometimes those balls do not bound true and their erratic course may not be discernible from the press coop and the outfielder is unjustly charged with an error."

On batting, Charlie offers this expression, "All pitchers are hard to hit, but when you are hitting, you will hit them all and when you are not, you won't hit any of them."

Keller has collected handsomely for the time he has been in baseball and he isn't one to squander his money foolishly. Greatly devoted to his family—he was like a lost sheep without them in training camp this past spring—he expects to save enough before he hangs up his glove to give them security for the rest of their lives. That is the spirit that maintains his determination to succeed. And a fine spirit it is to have.

Exit Crosetti,
Enter the Scooter

From *The Scooter: The Phil Rizzuto Story*

by Gene Schoor

*One of the game's classic small-ball players, Phil Rizzuto was a perfect
fit for the middle of the Yankees' infield. With a slew of feared sluggers
filling out the rest of the Bombers' lineup, Rizzuto's speed and nifty
glove work added a new dimension to an already formidable team.
During his 13-season tenure, New York won an astounding
10 pennants and 7 world championships.*

For almost a month, Phil sat on the bench, his eyes wide, studying the game, soaking up all the wisdom he could from one of the greatest managers in the history of baseball. When Frank Crosetti was spiked and taken out of the game, the Scooter was ready.

"Get in there, kid," said McCarthy, and this time Scooter went in to play for a long, long time.

Joe DiMaggio, Bill Dickey, Charlie Keller, Tommy Henrich, and Joe Gordon were hammering the ball, driving opposing pitchers out of the box with regularity. The club was hitting at a .300 clip. The Yanks were at the top of the league and running away from the pack. The New York club had regained its confidence and was headed once more for the pennant and a World Series.

With that kind of atmosphere in the clubhouse and on the diamond, the pressure on the rookie Rizzuto was off. He played up to his potential in the field and, with Joe Gordon at second, the Yanks had an outstanding combination up the middle. They were so good that even the players on the opposing teams would stop to watch the brilliant duo go through their routines in the pregame workout.

That month on the bench, with Joe McCarthy at his side, had worked wonders for the Scooter. Even McCarthy was surprised by the change in the play of his rookie, the sharpness, the keenness, the enthusiasm—and it was his enthusiasm that was infectious. If the club hadn't paid much attention to the rookie down at spring training and into the first weeks of the '41 season, they were all well aware of him now, and they couldn't help but loving him both for his enthusiasm and his obvious boyish naiveté. He invited kidding and all those tricks they played on him, though not when Joe McCarthy was skipper—Joe was too serious a man for that kind of tomfoolery.

The fans grew to love the Scooter quickly, too, and he proved to be the sensation they had expected. No, he wasn't a slugger like Joe DiMaggio, but he had other attributes. In his first season with the Yankees, both in the field and at bat, he was outstanding. He was the team's second best hitter, next to DiMaggio, compiling a .307 average in 133 games, with twenty doubles, nine triples, and three home runs. He scored sixty-five times, batted in forty-six runs, and stole fourteen bases. Phil was good enough in his first season as a Yankee to win accolades as the Yankees' number one rookie of the year.

And, on the verge of playing in the World Series, nobody was more excited than Phil. A World Series, and in his first year! It was a dream come true.

The Yankees were World Series veterans. They had won sixteen games and lost only three in the four World Series from 1936 through 1939. It was a relatively calm bunch of ballplayers who approached the world championship games. Not so their opponents, the Brooklyn Dodgers. The Dodgers, led by the fiery Leo (Lippy) Durocher, the man who was fond of saying, "Nice guys finish last," were to play in the World Series for the first time in twenty-one years.

Durocher, who had played shortstop for the Gas House Gang of St. Louis, had molded his club in the image of the rough-and-tough, give-no-quarter Cardinals of 1934. They were a fist-fighting, beanballing, cursing and spitting crew, and no one, not even umpires, were safe from the rowdiest brand of ball the majors had ever witnessed. No skipper was thrown out of more games in the history of the diamond than ringleader Lippy, and Hugh Casey, the ace relief pitcher for the Dodgers, was once accused, not without reason, of trying to bean an umpire. Dodger spikes came high into second base every time there was a throw to that sack, especially when there was a possibility of breaking up a double play. The Scooter and Joe Gordon were not going to have an easy time of it.

The Yankees, of course, were ready to retaliate. They were just as tough as Durocher's gang, and they weren't going to be intimidated by the Dodgers' roughhouse tactics.

Every game of the Series proved to be a close one. The closer the game, the more intense the play and the greater the mayhem. As was expected, the greatest mayhem occurred around the midway sack.

The Dodgers started it by plowing into Gordon and Rizzuto, their base runners, spikes high, trying to cut down the shortstop and second baseman. The Yankees responded in kind, smashing into Pee Wee Reese and Billy Herman, then Pete Coscarart, who had come in to replace an injured Herman. Mickey Owen, the Dodger catcher, went ten feet out of the baseline to slide into the Scooter in a futile effort to break up a double play. Pee Wee Reese took a beating from hard-sliding, barreling Tommy Henrich, Charlie Keller, and Joe Gordon. It was a hard-nosed baseball and every player was a target.

Then there was the beanball. There isn't a pitcher who doesn't throw a fast, inside ball, "the duster," to loosen up a hitter at the plate. The beanball, headed for a man's head, is something else. Too many players have had their heads cracked and their careers ended by a beanball. But Leo Durocher's pitchers were famous for it, especially their ace right-hander, Whitlow Wyatt. Wyatt threw a few too many close ones at Joe DiMaggio during the Series, and the usually quiet and mild-mannered DiMaggio came near to punching the pitcher out of the game. Wyatt and DiMaggio, both big men, squared off at the pitching mound. They glared at each other and said a few choice words. But, fortunately, the affair was broken up by teammates who rushed in to separate the two players. It was a rough, tough Series. It was also a well-played Series.

The two teams split the first two games, at Yankee Stadium, by the same scores, 3-2. Marius Russo, from the Scooter's old school, Richmond Hill High, won the third game, at Ebbets Field, 2-1, pitching against the Dodgers' knuckleballer Fat Fred Fitzsimmons, Hugh Casey, and the two other relievers. In the fourth game, the Dodgers had a 4-3 lead going into the ninth inning and looked sure to tie the Series at 2 and 2.

Hugh Casey was pitching, and he retired the first two Yankee batters without any problem. One more out and Durocher's men would have their win. The Dodger fans were wild, anticipating a victory. They grew wilder and the noise in Ebbets Field was deafening as Casey, dealing to Tommy Henrich, ran the count to 3-2.

One more strike and it was all over, and Hugh Casey got that strike, as Tommy, fooled by a wide-breaking curve ball, took his cut and missed. But . . . sudden silence descended over the stands at Ebbets Field as the sure-handed Mickey Owen couldn't hold on to the ball, and there he was chasing the white pellet to the backstop as Tommy Henrich scooted down to first base.

Pandemonium. The special police fighting to keep the fans in their seats and off the field. Cops pushing back Leo Durocher, who had run out onto the field, yelling at Owen to get the ball.

When things quieted down again, there was Joe DiMaggio standing at the plate and Hugh Casey so mad that all he could throw was the fastball, and Joltin' Joe immediately lined the pitch to left for a clean single, sending Tommy to third. Then up came Charlie Keller with a double off the right field screen to score Tommy and Joe that put the Yanks ahead, 5-4.

Why Durocher didn't call time-out so that Casey could settle down, or pull Casey from the game entirely, is still a matter of conjecture. He was probably just as upset as his pitcher at this point. In any case, Casey stayed on the mound and the Yanks went on to win that fourth game of the Series, 7-4. Ernie Bonham pitched the final game of the championship, defeating a dispirited Dodger club, 3-1. Once more, the New York Yankees were champions of the baseball world.

It wasn't the best of World Series for the Scooter. He had gotten only two hits, for a .111 average. However, he had made eighteen assists and twelve putouts at short and compiled a .968 fielding average. He would have better Series in the years to come, though.

All things considered, he could look back on his first year in the major leagues with considerable satisfaction. He was a Yankee. He had proved himself worthy of the pinstripe uniform. He was, in everyone's opinion, one of the leading rookies in the game.

But the year wasn't quite over. There was the firemen's banquet in Newark, and there was Cora. Especially, there was Cora.

Thank You, Mickey Owen

"Casey in the Box"
New York Times, 1941

by Meyer Berger

*Adopting the format Ernest Thayer made famous with his legendary
baseball poem "Casey at the Bat," Meyer Berger tells the story of
Game 4 of the 1941 World Series, which the Dodgers led by a score of
4–3 going into the 9th inning.*

The prospects seemed all rosy for the Dodger nine that day,
Four to three the score stood, with one man left to play.
And so when Sturm died and Rolfe the Red went out,
In the tall weeds of Canarsie you could hear the Dodgers' shout.

A measly few got up to go as screaming rent the air. The rest
Were held deep-rooted by Fear's gnaw eternal at the human breast.
They thought with Henrich, Hugh Casey had a cinch.
They could depend on Casey when things stood in the pinch.

There was ease in Casey's manner as he stood there in the box.
There was pride in Casey's bearing, from his cap down to his sox.
And when, responding to the cheers, he took up his trousers' sag.
No stranger in the crowd could doubt, he had them in the bag.

Sixty thousand eyes were on him when Casey toed the dirt.
Thirty thousand tongues applauded as he rubbed his Dodger shirt.
Then while the writhing Henrich stood swaying at the hip.
Contempt gleamed high in Casey's eye. A sneer curled Casey's lip.

And now the leather-covered sphere came hurtling through the air,
And Henrich stood awaiting it, with pale and frightened stare.
Close by the trembling Henrich the ball unheeded sped.
"He don't like my style," said Casey. "Strike one!" the umpire said.

From the benches black with people there went up a muffled roar,
Like the thunder of dark storm waves on the Coney Island shore.
"Get him! Get him, Casey!" shouted someone in the stand.
Hugh Casey smiled with confidence. Hugh Casey raised his hand.

With a smile of kindly charity Great Casey's visage shone.
He stifled the Faithful's screaming. He bade the game go on.
He caught Mickey Owen's signal. Once more the spheroid flew.
But Henrich still ignored it. The umpire bawled, "Strike two!"

"Yay!" screamed the maddened thousands, and the echo answered, "YAY!"
But another smile from Casey. He held them under sway.
They saw his strong jaws tighten. They saw his muscles strain,
And they knew that Hughie Casey would get his man again.

Pale as the lily Henrich's lips; his teeth were clenched in hate.
He pounded with cruel violence his bat upon the plate.
And now Great Casey held the ball, and now he let it go,
And Brooklyn was shattered by the whiff of Henrich's blow.

But Mickey Owen missed this strike. The ball rolled far behind.
And Henrich speeded to first base, like Clipper on the wind.
Upon the stricken multitude grim melancholy perched.
Dark disbelief bowed Hughie's head. It seemed as if he lurched.

DiMaggio got a single. Keller sent one to the wall.
Two runs came pounding o'er the dish and oh, this wasn't all.
For Dickey walked and Gordon a resounding double smashed.
And Dodger fans were sickened. And Dodger hopes were bashed.

Oh somewhere North of Harlem the sun is shining bright.
Bands are playing in the Bronx and up there hearts are light.
In Hunt's Point men are laughing, on the Concourse children shout.
But there is no joy in Flatbush. Fate had knocked their Casey out.

The Greatest Streak

From *Lucky to Be a Yankee*

by Joe DiMaggio

It remains one of the most elusive records in baseball—over the course of two months, Joe DiMaggio took the field in 56 straight games and came away with at least one hit every time. No other player in major league history has accomplished a hitting streak of even 50 games; since DiMaggio's achievement, nobody has gotten closer than Pete Rose's 44 games in 1978.

"Where do you get your power?" was asked of me at least once by every writer in camp. I'd just shrug and laugh it off but the persistency with which it cropped up started me thinking. I talked it over with Lefty Gomez.

"Forget about the answer as long as you have the power," advised Gomez. "The time to worry is when they ask you where you *lost* your power."

This is one of the first questions New York sports writers asked me after they had seen me take my first workout in St. Petersburg. It was something I had never thought about and I found it difficult to give an answer to it.

I have a very short swing, which undoubtedly was the reason for the question in the first place. It's deceptive in that it doesn't seem possible that a ball can be hit for distance with such a short swing. I hit a ball with a natural snap of the wrists and a long follow-through. Lefty O'Doul coached me for hours on the Coast to follow the ball from the time it left the pitcher's hand until it was right on top of me. That's where the short swing is useful. You can take your cut at the last possible split second.

O'Doul told me, too, that the word had been passed on to him that one of the great old-time-hitters, Wildfire Frank Schulte of the Cubs, claimed he got his longest base hits "right out of the catcher's glove." I was told my hitting style resembled his, although, of course, I had never seen him play.

Outside of O'Doul's coaching on following the ball, the only other advice on style I ever received all followed the one pattern—be natural, be comfortable. Joe Cronin and others whom I asked for pointers told me not to alter my style. I never have.

It is obvious, however, that to a hitter of my type, timing is all important and I've been pretty lucky in rarely getting off the beam in my timing. I have had a few slumps in my career and I had one of my worst in 1940, the year I beat out Luke Appling of the White Sox for the batting championship by .352 to .348. In August of that season, I couldn't buy a base hit and my average dropped steadily. It was my wife, Dorothy, of all people, who gave me a clue to the reason for my slump.

One night at dinner, and I always ate heartily, base hits or no base hits, Dorothy spoke up.

"Joe," she said timidly, because she felt she was approaching forbidden territory, "I noticed something at the ball park today."

I asked her what she noticed, assuming it was going to be something new one of the other player's wives was wearing.

"I noticed what's wrong with your hitting," answered Dorothy. "The number on your shirt is in a different position. You're not swinging the way you used to."

It sounds silly, but it was the answer. Dorothy sat in the same seat every day and looked at me from the same angle. The figure "5" on the back of my uniform was in a different position when I completed my swing, so therefore, reasoned Dorothy, I was swinging differently. I had developed a hitch in my swing, probably under the pressure of being shut out a few times. Next day I altered my stance a little, eased up and got three for four. From there on, everything was lovely.

I made it pretty clear, I think, early in this book that you have to be lucky to hang on to a consecutive hitting streak. I was lucky on the Coast when I went through 61 games without being blanked and I was lucky in 1941 when I established a major league record for hitting in 56 straight games. As a matter of fact, and just so you won't think I'm being overly modest, I think I was unlucky in the game in which my streak was stopped. I hit the ball harder in that game than I did in some of the games in which I had made hits and kept the string intact.

I won't admit that it was anything more than a coincidence that the streak started on the pay day, May 15, against Ed Smith, the stocky little left hander of the White Sox. I made only one hit in four times up in this game in the Stadium but that's how hitting streaks start.

The hardest part of a hitting streak is building it to the point where it is a streak worthy of being noticed. And once it is attracting attention, then you find the pressure on you. Nobody, including myself, paid any attention to my hitting streak, or its humble beginning, until it had passed 20.

The pressure was tightest, from Game No. 40, when I approached the records of Willie Keeler and George Sisler, to Game No. 53, when I had safely passed them, the Yankees were off on a streak of their own, a winning streak of 14 straight, which just about eliminated all competition from the pennant race, including the Tigers who had stopped us by winning the pennant the year before.

Manager McCarthy was a great help to me in keeping my streak going. He never gave me the "take" sign once. In other words, I was free to swing at any ball I chose. And Joe often gave me the "hit" sign when it was three balls and no strikes, or three balls and one strike. Most managers—McCarthy among them—don't encourage their hitters to pick on the "cripple," the 3-and-0 and the 3-and-1 pitch, but Joe, to prolong my string, was giving me a free rein up at the dish.

Even with this help from McCarthy, and the help my teammates gave me in never talking about my streak while it was under way, lest they put what ball players called a "whammy" on it, the pressure cropped out in spots.

I found that out when I needed a couple of games more to equal Sisler's record of 41 straight. For the first time in my life I looked back at an umpire, something Tommy Connolly, chief of staff of American League umpires, once had congratulated me upon never doing. I'm glad Tommy wasn't at the ballpark that day.

It was called a strike (naturally) that caused me to turn around and look back at the umpire but before I could say anything, he blurted out, "Honest to Gawd, Joe, it was right down the middle."

The idea of an umpire being apologetic for his decision appealed to me and helped ease the strain.

I've always tried never to get excited, because I found relaxation is the best way to keep hitting but the effect of a batting streak is cumulative. The tension started mounting on June 20 in the clubhouse at the Stadium after I had made four hits against Bobo Newsom and Archie McKain of the Tigers. I learned then that I had passed Rogers Hornsby's National League mark of 33 straight games.

It was in a double header at Washington on June 29 that I tried and broke Sisler's record. I doubled off Dutch Leonard in the sixth inning of the opener to make it 41 straight and in the second game I got my only other hit of the day, a single off Arnie Anderson to break Sisler's record, which had lasted since 1922. The Yankee bench really made a demonstration over the hit against Anderson, particularly because I was using a new bat in this game, using it for the first time. A souvenir-hunting fan had swiped the bat I had used in the previous 41 games. He later returned it to me.

In a double header against the Red Sox on July 1, I got two hits off Mike Ryba in the first game to come within one of Keeler's record. And in the first inning of the second game, I tied Keeler's mark of 44 games, a 43-year record, with a single off Jack Wilson in the first inning. Here, again, I was lucky, as it was not only the only hit I got in the game but the game was called at the end of five innings because of rain.

The next day was my shot at a new major league record and I knew it wasn't going to be a cinch when Heber Newsome went out to warm up for the Red Sox, for he was no "cousin" of mine. Lefty Gomez was our pitcher and I figured that was a good sign because I usually hit well when Lefty was pitching for us and most of the time managed to get hold of one for a home run.

In the first inning, I really lit into a pitch. I thought it was going right out of the Yankee Stadium but Stan Spence went back and made a great catch. The next time up it was my own brother, Dom, who got on his bike and took out after a long drive to make the catch. I felt a little down at the moment, because I had hit Newsome hard twice and that's about as often as I figured to hit him under the law of averages. And when Dom came up with the ball, I thought that while it might have been a great tribute to the integrity of baseball it was kind of rubbing it in to be robbed of a record by your own brother, especially when he was coming over to my house for dinner that same night!

In the fifth inning, my old Gomez good luck charm worked. I tagged Newsome for a home run and the record was in—44 straight games. I got quite a hand from the fans and quite a reception from our bench, particularly from Gomez who couldn't resist the opportunity to sneak in a wise crack.

"You not only broke Keeler's record, Joe," said Lefty, "but you used Keeler's formula to do it—hitting 'em where they ain't. And, incidentally, hitting them into the seats is one way of making sure your own family won't cheat you out of a record."

I wasn't exactly Dead-pan Joe from there on. I really played the rest of the game in a trance. I remember once on the bench, apropos of nothing at all, asking Gomez when he and his wife, June, were going to go on another picnic to Bear Mountain with Dorothy and me. I don't know what prompted me to ask that, unless maybe I was trying to be nonchalant and make out that I wasn't impressed with my record.

With the record behind me, there wasn't as much pressure and I kept going through the 56 games until I was cooled off on the night of July 17, out in Cleveland's Municipal Stadium before a mob of 67,468.

Al Smith started for the Indians and he was one pitcher I hadn't faced in the streak, even though we had played Cleveland two series earlier during the string. Still, Al was left-handed, so the percentage, if any, figured to be with me. In the first, I rifled one down the third baseline but Ken Keltner made a dandy play on the ball. Smith walked me in the fourth and in the seventh Keltner made another good stop.

We scored twice in the eighth and I got another shot, this time against Jim Bagby who had relived Smith. I hit the ball cleanly but Lou Boudreau came up with it, even though it took a bad hop, and turned it into a double play. That was the end of the streak. It ended in a night game and I've never had much of an average under lights but I couldn't complain about that night, because I had connected solidly in each of my three turns at the plate, particularly the two balls I hit at Keltner. In fact most of the stories about the end of the streak said that I was "stopped by Smith, Bagby and Keltner."

I had no regrets when it was over. During the streak I had gone to bat 223 times, made 91 hits for an average of .408, scored an even 56 runs, drove in 55 more, hit 15 homers, 4 triples and 16 doubles. I had walked 21 times, struck out seven times and had been hit by a pitcher twice. And during the lifetime of the streak, which endured just over two months, the Yankees had just about wrapped up the pennant.

Immediately after the streak was over, I went off on another tear, this time for 16 straight, so that if I had been able to get one of those shots by Keltner that night in Cleveland, I would have had a consecutive game record of 73. Of course, the "ifs" don't count, for "if" I had missed anywhere along the line, I wouldn't have had 56 straight.

A Duo Not to Be Denied

"The Best Battery the Bronx Ever Had"
Baseball Magazine, March 1946

by Ed Rumill

*Few relationships in professional sports are as essential as that
between a pitcher and a catcher, and few batteries were as effective as
pitcher Red Ruffing and catcher Bill Dickey. Ruffing, who had been
a career loser in Boston before coming to New York in 1930, became
a new man with Dickey as his backstop, winning 65 percent of his
decisions as a Yankee.*

Glancing mentally backward through the below-par war years in the major
leagues, there are a few things which stand out. For instance, there was the
weighty remark of Marse Joe McCarthy one hot mid-July afternoon as he sat
in the visiting dugout at Fenway Park and watched his odd collection of New
York Yankees move through the motions of pre-game batting practice.

"In the clubhouse a few minutes ago I heard a couple of baseball writers
talking about famous batteries," commented the manager of the Gotham
American Leaguers. "And there have been some great ones, as you know.
Fellows like Christy Mathewson and Roger Bresnahan of the Giants, and Big
Ed Walsh and Billy Sullivan of the old White Sox. But did anybody ever take
the time to check back over the records of Ruffing and Dickey?"

McCarthy chewed a little more violently on his gum for a moment, then
added: "I'll bet you a hatful of silver dollars that Ruffing and Dickey had the
best winning percentage of any battery in the history of the game, if there is
any way you can tell. Especially when the chips were down. They weren't very
often beaten in clutch games."

Only two or three ballplayers overheard the Yankee skipper and nobody seemed to pay particular attention among those who did. But a while later your correspondent did as Joe suggested. We checked back through the figure-jammed pages of *The Little Red Book* and of *Who's Who In Baseball,* and they emphasize rather emphatically that the team of Red Ruffing and Bill Dickey was one of the greatest of all time.

To go back to the beginning, the battery of Ruffing and Dickey first tackled the hitters of the American League in 1930. It was on May 6, 1930, that the Boston Red Sox, their book in red ink, traded pitcher Ruffing to the New York club for outfielder Cedric Durst and approximately $50,000 in cold cash. Dickey, the lanky, slow-footed Louisiana boy, had joined the Yankees two years earlier and in 1929, under little Miller Huggins, had settled in the number one backstopping berth in the stadium that borders on the bank of the Harlem River.

A losing pitcher with Boston for more than half a dozen years, Ruffing began immediately to climb in the victory column under the magic touch of the talented young Dickey. Together they out-guessed and out-smarted Yankee rivals, improving year by year, until they became blueprinted as the toughest battery in the American League. It was Ruffing and slim Lefty Gomez, with the aid of Dickey, who played the key battery roles as almost unbeatable Yankee clubs rolled over badly outclassed rivals in the regular season and World's Series play through the 1930s and early '40s.

The Yankees were a third-place outfit when big Red arrived on the scene in 1930. The following year, after Joe McCarthy had succeeded one-year Bob Shawkey, the team climbed up a notch to the runner-up spot in the race. And by 1932, with Ruffing winning eighteen games and losing only seven, the Yanks had won the pennant, McCarthy's first in the Will Harridge circuit.

From then on, until the war unpredictably scrambled the majors, the Yanks were the most dominating ball club in the dusty annals of the game. They won four straight pennants and world championships from 1936 through 1939, finishing off the string with eleven straight World's Series victories over the Giants, Cubs and Reds, and the battery of Ruffing and Dickey was McCarthy's pride and joy. It was this pair that Joe turned to when he needed that big game—when the pressure was on. And they rarely failed him.

In those triumphant years of 1936, '37, '38 and '39, the team of Ruffing and Dickey tacked up the fine total of eighty-two victories and thirty-three defeats, for a flattering .707 winning percentage. As a bonus to the Yankee management, they won four World's Series engagements and lost a mere one.

It was hardly their fault that the mighty Yankee machine finally ran out of gas and stalled to a sudden and unexpected halt in 1940, when everybody was expecting it to further steamroll the American League.

From the time that big Red donned a New York uniform in distant 1930 until he discarded it at the close of the 1942 campaign to go into the Army, he piled up 219 triumphs for a winning percentage of .640.

The brilliance of this winning figure is emphasized when it is compared with those of other mound greats, most of whom are but dim memories to the modern fan.

Herb Pennock's winning percentage in the American League was .598. Rube Waddell's was just .587. In the .600 class were Walter Johnson at an even .600, Cy Young at .619, Carl Hubbell at .622, Chief Bender at .623 and Eddie Plank at .630. Grover Alexander, at .642, obviously beat Ruffing's Yankee pace by just two points. But as this was written, Red was still in there firing, with an opportunity to enlarge upon his grand record.

And while the name of Bill Dickey is not often mentioned when the top-heavy victories of Ruffing are recalled in the dugout, or in print, the hard-hitting catcher was in there every day, nursing big Red through the tough innings and, in the bargain, helping to wreck the dreams of opposing hurlers when it came his turn to walk to the plate and swing a bat.

It was in the World's Series competition that the battery of Ruffing and Dickey most often made the headlines. Ten times "Ruff" stepped to the rubber as the starting Yankee pitcher in the big classic, a figure which ties Waite Hoyt and the all-time Series record. On seven occasions Ruffing was the winning pitcher, a standard which he holds undisputed.

The Ruffing-Dickey team defeated Guy Bush of the Chicago Cubs in the World's Series opener of 1932. Carl Hubbell, screwball ace of the New York Giants, beat the Yankee stars in the 1936 classic inaugural, but Red and Bill bounced back to edge Cliff Melton of the Giants in the second game of the 1937 classic. In '38 the big right-hander of McCarthy's staff beat Bill Lee of the Cubs twice, by 3-1 in the opener and by 8-3 in the final and clincher.

In 1939 Ruffing took a curtain-raising thriller from Paul Derringer of the Cincinnati Reds, 2-1, for one of the toughest decisions Paul ever lost, and in 1941 Ruffing beat Curtis Davis of the rowdy and cocky Brooklyn Dodgers in the October opener. In the memorable 1942 Series, as the surprising St. Louis Cardinals crushed the uninspired Yankees in a battle of five games, "Ruff" beat Mort Cooper in the inaugural, but bowed to rookie Johnny Beazley in the fifth and deciding contest for the Redbirds.

That was a somewhat bitter pill for Charley The Red to take, for he must have known that he would soon be in the Army and perhaps at the end of his active career in the major leagues. But it only slightly dimmed the grand record which he and Dickey had previously carved on the walls of the Yankee dugout.

There are those who are inclined to soft pedal the team work of Dickey and Ruffing, because of the all-around strength of the ball clubs with which they have labored. Some folks suggest that your Aunt Hattie could have pitched and won for those great, well-balanced Yankee outfits of the pre-war past. But critics who followed the Yanks around the circuit in those days will tell you, and with gestures, that one of the chief reasons for this monopolizing power was the battery of Ruffing and Dickey. They would have been a winning combination, even in the second division.

But, of course, no ball club with Ruffing taking a turn on the rubber every fourth or fifth day and Dickey receiving and hitting would have lingered for long in the lower regions of the standing. Not only did this pair have the mound finesse and savvy of a championship battery, but they produced a bit of power themselves.

Through the aforementioned four-year period between 1936 and '40, as the Yanks were at their peak, Dickey drove in a total of 460 runs, or an average of 115 per season. During his entire sixteen springs, summers and falls in the American League prior to entering the Navy in March, 1944, he batted across 1,199 New York teammates.

As a hitting pitcher, Ruffing had few equals through his lush years beside the Harlem River. He could hit the ball and hit it hard. McCarthy many times waved him off the bench, on days he was not pitching, to pinch bat in crucial spots. Red usually hit over the charmed .300 level. Unlike the average hurler, he could consistently murder a curve ball. When he was on the rubber, not even the number nine slot in the batting order represented a breathing space for the opposing moundsman. In fact, Red was a better sticker than a few of the other Yankee regulars.

McCarthy, too, must rate the battery of Gomez and Dickey high in his hall of memories. Lefty was a standout pitcher when he was on top and a rough customer particularly when the world championship or Yankee honor were at stake. As a matter of fact, while the slender Californian needed relief assistance in a couple of his World's Series appearances, never once in October did the National League succeed in beating him.

Gomez defeated Lon Warneke of the Cubs in the 1932 classic, added both Hal Schumacher and Freddy Fitzsimmons of the Giants in 1936, took Hubbell and Melton of the same club in the fall of 1937 and polished off a fine money career by defeating Dizzy Dean and the Cubs in the memorable second game of the 1938 Series at Wrigley Field, the day Old Diz put on his great exhibition of slow-ball pitching. That made it six victories and no setbacks for Gomez, a World's Series record for kid mound aces of the future to shoot at.

The team of Gomez and Dickey also functioned with brilliance in All-Star Games. Four times the American League handed Lefty the warmup ball in the mid-summer classic and only once did he fail them. He was the winning pitcher in the Julys of 1933, '35 and '37, and was charged with his lone defeat in 1938.

However, despite this challenge of Gomez, Ruffing—over the long haul—stands out as the number one battery-mate of the great Dickey, and it is the team of Red and Bill which hangs the highest in the Yankee offices now occupied by Larry MacPhail and his two associates, Topping and Webb.

Who might crowd Ruffing and Dickey in the all-time book of batteries?

The Philadelphia crowd will point to Lefty Grove and Mickey Cochrane, and for good reason. They were hot during the last years that Connie Mack's Athletics were up there on top of the heap. Cochrane can give Dickey a battle in the all-time catching department, and for his overpowering of the hitters of his era, Grove stood head and shoulders above the rank and file. But Joe McCarthy would take his boys, Ruffing and Dickey, and Joe has been around for some time.

Old-timers hold out for such renown combinations as Alexander and Killefer, Johnson and Ainsmith, and the two that McCarthy mentioned—Mathewson and Bresnahan and Walsh and Sullivan—in the long history of batteries, which goes back to A. G. Spalding and Deacon White in the days of handlebar mustaches. The Johnny-come-latelies in the vicinity of Detroit may stump for Hal Newhouser and Paul Richards, the top-ranking wartime battery.

But from Spalding and White to Newhouser and Richards, any pitching and catching team you care to mention would have to step to hold its own against the Ruffing and Dickey of 1936, '37, '38 and '39.

Yogi Arrives
on the Scene

From *Ten Rings: My Championship Seasons*

by Yogi Berra with Dave Kaplan

*As the Bill Dickey era came to an end in the Bronx, the Yankees were
fortunate to have a young prospect waiting to take his place. Donning
Dickey's number 8, Yogi Berra was a legend in the making. As the title
of his book suggests, Berra won a remarkable 10 World Series titles
with the Yankees, and he holds several Series hitting records.*

Less than two weeks after Opening Day I felt more emotion in a ballpark than
I ever experienced. It was Babe Ruth Day. He'd just been diagnosed with throat
cancer, and it was obvious he only had a short time to live. I'd never met him
before but was too nervous to say hello. It was sad seeing him shrunken and
weak, wearing that camel's-hair polo coat and cap that matched, his voice just
a rasp. But I'll never forget his speech. He thanked baseball for everything,
saying it was the best game. At the time he was involved with American Legion
baseball, which is the first organized ball I played, and am still indebted to.
When Babe finished talking, he started walking, a little unsteady, toward
the dugout. Some of us were wondering if we should give him a hand, but
somebody said, "Leave him alone. He knows where the dugout is." I did meet
Babe later in the season at Sportman's Park, part of his farewell tour. We posed
for a picture, in which you can see I was still nervous and in awe. Less than a
year after, the Babe was gone.

That rookie season with the Yankees was full of ups and downs. We had
lots of injuries, but someone always stepped in to do the job. Our pitching was
great. Reynolds went 19-8 and Shea was right behind at 14-5, and Page was
tremendous in relief, going 14-8 with seventeen saves. We picked up Bobo

Newsom, who was forty years old, and he went 7-5. We weren't the classic Yankee slugging team, nobody had a hundred RBIs and only DiMaggio had more than twenty homers.

But there was a lot of leadership with DiMag and Henrich. They were the old pros and kind of drilled into you that if you were on the Yankees, you were entering a tradition. That tradition meant going all out, pulling for one another, or you wouldn't win.

DiMag was usually quiet and always hustled, and expected everyone to do the same. Once I was unhappy after I popped up and sort of moped out to right field after the inning. Joe trotted over to me and said, "Always run out to your position, kid. It doesn't look good when you walk. The other team may have gotten you down, but don't let 'em know it."

It wasn't all smooth and easy in the clubhouse. Most of the guys were fed up with MacPhail, who was always meddling and fining players for the littlest things. He even fined DiMag for refusing to pose for a newsreel film. Before one game at the Stadium in May we actually took a vote to strike. But DiMag, mad as he was, convinced everyone that it would do more harm than good. Then MacPhail began to back off, and by the end of June we were really clicking. We went on a nineteen-game winning streak, including a double-header sweep against the Browns when I made an unassisted double play on a squeeze play in the ninth inning to save a 2-1 win. That made me feel pretty good because I wasn't exactly a rousing success behind the plate.

I didn't do too bad in the outfield, though there were times I looked that way. Especially the day DiMaggio finally came back after recovering from his heel operation. I bowled him over in center while chasing a fly ball and felt terrible. I felt much better when DiMag excused me and told the writers they should lay off since I was only trying to help him out, which I was because I figured he was favoring his foot. When DiMag called, I thought he meant to take the play. From then on, DiMag told me, if I heard his voice, better keep away. If he heard mine, I'd better catch it.

Maybe my worst night was in July in St. Louis, when some friends and neighbors from The Hill arranged to have Yogi Berra Night in Sportsman's Park. It was bad enough I had a strep infection, worse was having to talk in front of a crowd, which included my family. I'd never made a speech before. I asked my pal Bobby Brown to help me, and he said the best thing was to keep it short. He wrote it out and helped me memorize it: "I'm a lucky guy and happy to be with the Yankees. I want to thank everyone for making this night possible." But when the time came, after I was presented with a nice pile of gifts, including a Nash sedan, I got kind of nervous and said, "I want to thank everyone for making this night *necessary*."

Eventually that year I caught as often as Robinson. It was hard to tell who was the first-string catcher. The main thing is, Bucky wanted me in the lineup. More important, we plowed ahead to the pennant, winning by twelve games over Detroit. I didn't do bad for a rookie, hitting .280 with eleven homers and fifty-four RBIs in eighty-three games. But my catching was still not getting any better, especially throwing.

Late in the season I was so concerned, I asked some advice from Birdie Tebbetts, who was catching for the Red Sox. He told me not to worry about guys stealing on me, because they didn't steal on me, they stole on the pitcher. He told me when I saw the runners going, to just let the ball go and I'd do okay. He said he's seen catchers with worse arms. I took that as a compliment, I think.

Brooklyn won the National League pennant, and the city was all charged up about the World Series. Reporters asked how I was going to handle all the Dodgers, especially Jackie Robinson, on the bases. I wasn't trying to brag, but I said Jackie had never stolen on me with Montreal. As it turned out, the Dodgers stole everything on me but my chest protector. That didn't settle my nerves any. Honestly, I think I almost was too scared to do any good. Talk about a contrast. I think me and Spec Shea were the first rookie battery to start a World Series. Spec was all calm before the game, telling the writers it was just another ball game when you still have to get twenty-seven outs. Me? DiMaggio told me later that he could see my knees shaking from center field—and could even hear them rattling. But the Series was an amazing experience—Game 1 at the Stadium drew a record crowd of over seventy-three thousand—and it was the first Series ever televised.

The games were intense, exciting, though not the crispest. I was one of the worst culprits. Even though we won the first two games, the Dodgers stole five bases on me. "Worst World Series catching I ever saw," said Connie Mack. That was real nice, coming from a former catcher who broke into baseball around 1900. I was benched the next game but hit the first pinch home run in the Series history, off Ralph Branca. We lost the game but still led the Series, 2-1.

Bucky wanted my bat in there so he could also play Johnny Lindell in the outfield. So I was batting third again and catching Game 4, which is the one nobody forgets. Bill Bevens was pitching and was wild, but had great stuff. He had a no-hitter with two out in the ninth. He was up to 137 pitches and would've made it if I'd thrown out Al Gionfriddo trying to steal second. He got a good jump, and my throw was a little high, though Phil Rizzuto thought we had him. Then Bucky went against the book and walked Pete Reiser intentionally, putting on the winning run.

He got second-guessed to death, but I agreed with his decision. Cookie Lavagetto was thirty-five and on his last legs and the scouting report said you could get him with fastballs. But he hit an outside fastball to right for a double, and Eddie Miksis (running for Reiser) slid across with the winning run. Bevens was in tears when he walked off the mound. I felt just as bad. He should've made history but ended up with a defeat. Nobody knew at the time, but he would also end up with a dead arm.

I sat out Game 5 and got two hits in Game 6, although we lost when Gionfriddo made that great catch on DiMag. I was in right field for Game 7 in Yankee Stadium. All our pitchers were exhausted, but Joe Page did a hell of a job relieving Bevens, who had relieved Shea. And I was also relieved for defensive purposes in the late innings. The big thing is, we won, 5-2. The world championship was ours.

All I can say is, playing and winning my first World Series was a thrilling experience. It kind of felt like a dream. Even though I played lousy—my catching was terrible, and I got only three hits in nineteen at-bats—I wasn't feeling lousy. Our clubhouse was a madhouse; everyone was whooping and spraying champagne. I found Bucky, thanked him for his faith in me, and asked if he expected me back the next year. He told me yes, and he said they planned to make me the full-time catcher.

Amid all the craziness, MacPhail charged into the room waving a bottle of beer and announced that he was retiring. None of us believed him. He was flushed and teary-faced, and we all thought he was simply drunk. That night we had a big victory party at the Biltmore Hotel, and MacPhail was still carrying on, yelling at people, and even punched our road secretary, John McDonald. But he was serious about retiring, because he did. George Weiss, the farm director, would be taking over as GM, and he was as different from MacPhail as could be. It was a wild end to an unforgettable year.

Within a week or so the World Series check came from the commissioner's office. I'd made $5,000 for the whole season, because that was the minimum. Now I'd gotten a new $5,830 check for a winning Series share . . . not bad for a week's work. I came home to The Hill and showed the check to Mom and Pop, and they took a long look at it before I brought it to the bank. I think they realized then that baseball was not a bum's game.

PART IV

The Greatest Dynasty of All Time

1949–1964

Between 1921 and 1948, the Yankees claimed 15 American League pennants—meaning that, in a 28-year period, the Bronx Bombers won more AL flags than any other team in league history except one (the Philadelphia/Oakland A's, winners of exactly 15 in their 110 years). Even more amazingly, that wasn't the pinnacle of Yankee domination. Over the 16 subsequent seasons (1949–1964), New York won all but two league pennants while winning nine World Series.

That thrilling era of Yankee baseball began with one of the most memorable seasons in the game's annals, a season that is captured in an equally memorable piece of sports writing: David Halberstam's *Summer of '49*. From there, the journey through greatness leads to unique characters like Billy Martin and Jerry Coleman, sage and witty baseball men Casey Stengel and Yogi Berra, and all-time greats such as Mickey Mantle, Roger Maris, and Whitey Ford.

As with any great team, success did not come exclusively from Hall of Famers. Indeed, numerous role players and clutch performers were integral to the Yankee dynasty. Hank Bauer gets his due from longtime baseball writer Dan Daniel, himself enshrined in Cooperstown. Allie Reynolds, Vic Raschi, and Eddie Lopat had five 20-win seasons and 10 all-star selections among them—but no Cooperstown plaques—so we allow Sol Gittleman to impart the contributions of the "Big Three." And while Don Larsen never played in the midsummer classic or won more than 11 games in a single season, his incomparable performance in Game 5 of the 1956 World Series inspired a stirring tribute by celebrated *Washington Post* columnist Shirley Povich.

Yogi Berra and Don Larsen, 1956. *Diamond Images/Getty Images*

The Yanks, the Sox, and the Summer of 1949

From *Summer of '49*

by David Halberstam

It's Joe DiMaggio vs. Ted Williams, the Yankees vs. the Red Sox—no wonder Summer of '49 *is a baseball classic. Required reading for every fan of America's pastime, Halberstam's book guides readers through the entire season, including the remarkable pennant race that came down to the wire—the dramatic end of which is recounted in this piece.*

Charlie Silvera, the backup catcher, lived on Gerard Avenue, about a block from the Stadium. To his amazement, the noise from the crowd started late Saturday afternoon and grew through the evening as fans gathered in the parking lot and formed a line waiting for bleacher seats. Throughout the night, as game time approached, the noise grew steadily louder. Curt Gowdy was equally impressed by the noise of the crowd. He thought of it as a war of fans—the Yankee fans cheering wildly, then their noise answered by deafening volleys from the many Red Sox fans who had driven down from New England. Gowdy's job was to help Mel Allen, for this was Mel's game. Gowdy was impressed at how calm Allen was, as if he had been broadcasting games like this all his life. "We've been so full of tension all year long, that honest-to-goodness today I'm just forgetting about everything," Allen told his audience at the beginning of the game. "Whatever happens, happens. Something's gotta happen today. That's just the way it's going to be. The Yankees have done an out-of-this-world job this year, and the Red Sox have just been magnificent."

Vic Raschi heard none if it. He thought only about the Red Sox. Keep Dominic DiMaggio off the bases. That was important because Pesky was a much better hitter when Dominic was on base. Pitch carefully to Williams and walk him if necessary. Williams could kill a right-handed fastball pitcher in the Stadium. No curveballs to Junior Stephens, who murdered Raschi's curve. Nothing but high fastballs slightly outside. Let Stevie do battle with Death Valley in left center. To Bobby Doerr, as good a hitter as they had, with no real weakness, just pitch carefully and around the edges.

Raschi saw Joe DiMaggio in the locker room. DiMaggio looked gray and wan and was moving poorly. Raschi knew he was sick and exhausted. He wondered if DiMaggio was really well enough to play that day. Probably not, he decided, but nobody on this team was going to tell Joe DiMaggio that he should not be playing.

At last Raschi went out to the mound, and started to pitch. Within minutes he was pleased. Everything was working that day; he had speed, placement, and his little curve. This was not the day to go out and find that one of his pitches was missing, or that he could not put the ball where he wanted. And he was pleased to be pitching against Ellis Kinder. Kinder was tough too, a man who, in the phrase that Raschi liked to apply to himself and his friend Allie Reynolds, liked to make hitters smell the leather. Kinder would almost surely pitch well and make the game close. Raschi wanted that; he wanted a close game where the pressure was on the pitcher.

Dom DiMaggio and Pesky went out quickly. After he got a man out, Raschi would always observe a certain ritual: He would straighten his cap, pull his sweat shirt down toward his wrist, and fix the mound. Then he would plant his right foot on the rubber. All the while the infielders would throw the ball around. Then Raschi was ready to receive the ball from the third baseman, either Bobby Brown or Billy Johnson. He wanted the ball thrown right at his glove so that he wouldn't have to move. Sometimes when the Yankees had a big lead, Johnson or Brown would throw the ball slightly behind him, forcing him to leave the rubber. He hated it. There would be none of that today. With two out, Ted Williams came to the plate. Raschi kept everything close to the plate, but he also walked Williams on four pitches. Then he got Junior Stephens out.

Rizzuto was the lead-off man in the bottom of the first. By then he had come to share the Yankees' admiration for Kinder, who had so completely mastered them that season. Four victories. If there was one advantage Rizzuto had over his teammates when it came to hitting against Kinder, it was that he was not a power hitter. Instead he went with the ball. With a pitcher as smart as Kinder, Rizzuto never tried to guess. The pitch came in, somewhat on the inside, and Rizzuto swung. It was a slider, not a fastball, he realized immediately, because a fastball that much inside would have broken his bat. Because it was slightly off-speed, Rizzuto got out ahead of it. He slapped it down the line, past Pesky at third base, and he knew immediately it was extra bases. The ball hugged the left-field line and went into the corner, and as Rizzuto raced for a second, he watched Ted Williams go into the corner. Williams played back slightly, waiting for the ball to come back to him the way it would at Fenway. Rizzuto knew the fence better, and he raced for third. The ball stayed along the contours of the park, more like a hockey puck than a baseball, and went past Williams. Rizzuto had an easy triple. He watched with relief as McCarthy played the infield back.

Henrich was up now, the perfect batter for this situation. Kinder pitched and Henrich choked up on the bat. With the softest swing imaginable, he hit a grounder toward Bobby Doerr. Classic Henrich, Rizzuto thought, giving himself up and getting the run. No ego in the way. The Yankees had a one-run lead.

Inning after inning passed. The lead held up. Raschi was on top of his game, and the Yankees could do nothing with Kinder. If anything, he was even more in control than Raschi. His placement was almost perfect. When he missed the corner with a pitch, it was because he wanted to miss the corner. He was varying his speed nicely. And he showed no signs of getting tired.

In the eighth, the first batter was Tebbetts, and he went out; then it was Kinder's turn up. Kinder badly wanted to bat; he was sure he was as good a hitter as anyone on the bench, but McCarthy played the percentages. He sent up Tom Wright, a player just called up from the minors, to bat for Kinder. On the Yankee bench the players had been watching McCarthy closely. When he made his signal, there was among the Yankee players a collective sigh of relief and gratitude. Kinder was out and the Red Sox had a notoriously weak bullpen. On the Red Sox bench, Matt Batts, the catcher, who liked McCarthy more than most of the bench players (McCarthy had given him his chance at the majors), thought, God, don't do it; that's a mistake. We're down only one run, they can't touch Ellis, and we are weak, I mean *weak* in the bullpen. Kinder was furious. Wright walked, but Dominic DiMaggio grounded to Rizzuto, who turned it into a double play. The inning was over and Kinder, to the relief of the Yankees, was out of the game.

The first two Yankee batters in the eighth, Henrich and Berra, were both left-handed, so McCarthy again played the percentages and went to Parnell, his pitcher from yesterday. Sitting by himself in his attic in South Hadley, eleven-year-old Bart Giamatti heard Jim Britt say that Parnell was coming in to relieve Kinder. Giamatti was young, but he knew that Parnell had pitched too often in recent weeks, and that he had pitched the day before and must be exhausted. He had an immediate sense that this was a gallant but futile gesture. Giamatti was filled with sadness. Something in Jim Britt's voice over the radio made it clear that he was equally pessimistic.

Giamatti was right to be pessimistic. Parnell's was to be a short appearance. He was tired, and he had lost his edge. Henrich had hit him hard in the past ("My nemesis," Parnell later called him), and now was eager to bat against someone other than Ellis Kinder. Lefty or no, he saw the ball better with Parnell than with Kinder. This time Parnell threw him a fastball. Henrich hit it about ten rows back into the right-field seats and the Yankees got their cushion, 2-0. Then Berra singled and McCarthy called to the bullpen for Tex Hughson. Hughson turned to Joe Dobson and said, "Well, Joe, they've finally gone to the bottom of the barrel." It was odd, Hughson thought, that McCarthy had shown nothing but contempt for him all season, and now at this most important moment he had decided to use him.

DiMaggio hit into a double play, and there were two outs and no one was on. But Lindell singled and Hank Bauer was sent in as a pinch runner. Then Billy Johnson singled, and when Williams juggled the ball, Bauer went to third. Then Hughson deliberately walked Mapes to get to the rookie, Jerry Coleman.

Coleman had thought in the early part of the season that he liked to hit against Kinder, and then gradually as the season progressed he decided he was wrong. Kinder had seemed to improve as a pitcher in every outing. You just never got a good pitch. There was the change, the sudden fastball, and then, of course, the last-second slider. Like his teammates, he had been relieved when McCarthy had played by the book and pulled Kinder for a pinch hitter. Now in the eighth, he was up with the bases loaded. The Yankees were ahead, but even so Coleman did not want to look foolish at this moment. This season might be nearly over, he might have done everything the Yankees wanted of him and more, but he had never felt more on trial.

Hughson was absolutely sure he could handle the rookie. Tex could still throw hard, and the ball came in letter-high and inside. Hughson was delighted. He had placed it almost perfectly, an impossible pitch for a hitter to do anything with, he thought, and he was right; Coleman did very little with it. He hit it right on the trademark of the bat and sliced the ball, a pop-up, just past second base; Coleman was disgusted with himself.

In right field Al Zarilla was not playing Coleman particularly deep. Bases loaded, he thought, two out, short right-field runs. Coleman was not a power hitter. For Zarilla, the ability to come in on a pop fly or a soft liner was more important than going back on a ball, particularly with two out. Zarilla watched Hughson's pitch and he thought, That is a lovely pitch. Then he saw the ball leave the bat and he knew at once that it was trouble—too far back for Bobby Doerr, the ball spinning away toward the line, a dying swan if there ever was one. It had to be Zarilla's ball. He charged it, and kept charging, but the ball kept slicing away from him. At the last second Zarilla was sure he had a play. He dove for it, his fingers and glove outstretched. He was diving at the expense of his body, for he was not positioned to break a fall. He missed it by perhaps two inches. By the time the ball came down, Zarilla realized later, it was almost on the foul line.

When Coleman saw that it was too deep for Doerr and that Zarilla was desperately charging, he knew the ball was going to drop. He turned past second and raced for third. He was out at third, but three runs had scored. The lead was 5-0. When he came back into the dugout, everyone patted Coleman on the back as if he were an old veteran and an RBI leader. But he thought of it as a cheap hit, and was more than a little ashamed of himself. A three-run double in the box score, he thought, and a cheap pop-up on the field.

He was ashamed of it for a long time afterward. Then three years later he ran into Joe McCarthy at a banquet. He started to mumble something about it being a bloop hit, but McCarthy interrupted him. "You swung at it, didn't you?" he asked, and Coleman nodded. Coleman understood McCarthy's meaning immediately—you didn't strike out and they didn't put anything past you. So don't apologize, you did your job.

The Red Sox gave it one more shot. In the top of the ninth, they rallied for three runs. Pesky fouled out, and then Williams walked. Stephens singled to center. Then Bobby Doerr hit a long drive to center field. It was a well-hit ball, but the kind that Joe DiMaggio normally handled readily. This time, his legs cramping up, it went over his head and Doerr had a triple. DiMaggio signaled for time and took himself out of the game. His long regular season was over. Two runs were in. Zarilla flied out to Mapes. Two outs. But Goodman singled through center, and Doerr scored. The score was 5-3.

The next batter was Birdie Tebbetts. Since they had fattened their lead, the Yankee bench jockies had been needling the needler mercilessly: "Hey, Birdie, get the kid [Quinn] to lend you some of his money for your World Series share." "Hey, Birdie, we'll send you over a bottle of our champagne." Tommy Henrich was playing first, and he walked over to Raschi to give him a small pep talk, to remind him that he needed only one more out. "Give me the goddamn ball and get the hell out of here!" Raschi snarled. Henrich turned, and grinned to himself. We've got it, it's a lock, he thought, there is no way Birdie Tebbetts is going to get a hit off this man right now. Tebbetts popped up in foul territory. Coleman started calling for it, but Henrich yelled him off. "It's my ball," he shouted, and he thought to himself, It's the one I've been looking for all year. The regular season was over.

That Cocky Kid from the Coast

From *Damn Yankee: The Billy Martin Story*

by Maury Allen

*Over the course of his tumultuous Yankee career, the New York
media used plenty of colorful adjectives to describe Billy Martin,
and they hit the nail on the head from day one with "cocky"
and "effervescent." Martin made an immediate impact, coming to
bat twice in a long eighth inning rally in his debut game and
driving in runs on both occasions.*

On April 18, 1950, Martin awoke early, sipped at a cup of coffee for breakfast, read the morning *Globe*, saw his name was not in Casey Stengel's starting lineup, growled at a waitress, and took a cab with Rizzuto out to Fenway Park. There would be a full house, 31,822 people, to see the hated Yankees beat the Red Sox. Cleveland had beaten Boston in a 1948 playoff when manager Lou Boudreau had hit two home runs. The Yankees had beaten the Red Sox, 5-4, on the final Saturday and 5-3 on the final Sunday of the 1949 season to win the flag. Now there was a new season and the ever-hopeful Red Sox fans were looking to Ted Williams, Dom DiMaggio, Mel Parnell, and Johnny Pesky to lead their team to a pennant.

It was one of the strangest opening day games in baseball history. Lefthander Mel Parnell of the Red Sox coasted to a 9-0 lead in Fenway. The fans were screaming their heads off. The Red Sox were humiliating the hated opposition. It wouldn't make up for the debacle of 1949 but it was a good start to a new season. In the sixth inning, Stengel, still fighting to get into the game, sent Dick Wakefield, one of baseball's first big bonus players from the University of Michigan, up to pinch-hit for second baseman Jerry Coleman.

"Get a glove, kid, and get ready," Stengel ordered Martin.

"I think he put me in there to get me away from him," says Martin, with a smile. "I had been up and down all afternoon on that bench. I was disappointed I didn't start. I agitated Casey to put me in. When he did, we started winning. I had something to do with it."

So, on the 175th anniversary of Paul Revere's ride from Lexington to Concord, on a day Senator Joseph McCarthy of Wisconsin submitted the names of two witnesses in his red-baiting case against historian Owen Lattimore, on the afternoon the first jet liner from Toronto landed at New York's Idlewild Airport, and on the day Russian planes shot down an American aircraft over the Baltic Sea, Billy Martin played in his first major league game.

The Yankees got four runs in the sixth. In the eighth inning Martin cracked a 1-1 pitch from Parnell off the left field wall in his first big league turn at bat. The Yankees continued to score and Martin batted again in the eighth with bases loaded. He hit a line single to left field for two runs. In two times at bat in the same inning Martin made two hits in his first two major-league appearances, a record that has stood for twenty-nine years and may stand forever.

The lead story on the *New York Times* sports page the next day was about the surprising Yankee comeback. Under the main headline was a subhead reading, "3 hits for Joe DiMaggio, Henrich smashes two triples, Martin, Berra, Mize excel." Sportswriter John Drebinger wrote, "The 1950 edition of Joe McCarthy's Red Sox opened the season with a grand flourish today but the Yankees almost closed it on the spot with an explosion that all but leveled Bunker Hill."

After describing the Red Sox' 9-0 lead and the Yankee's four-run rally in the sixth, Drebinger turned to the incredible nine-run eighth inning that won the game. "Rookie Billy Martin came up with two hits in that devastating round," Drebinger wrote. He described how Yogi Berra opened the inning with a single, Billy Johnson walked, Johnny Lindell flied out, "but Martin, the effervescent rookie from the coast, doubled off the left-field wall. It was the first time he had ever seen the wall and he liked it."

Drebinger ended his description of the scoring by saying, "Martin, up for the second time in the inning, singled runs 8 and 9 across."

Columnist Arthur Daley, also on hand for the Boston opener, wrote of the big inning, "Up to the plate stepped Billy Martin, a cocky 21-year-old from the coast, for his major league debut at bat. Billy was so awed and terrified that he spilled a double off the left-field wall."

"Yeah, I did so good," says Billy, "I didn't play again for a month."

The MVP of the 1950 World Series

From *An American Journey: My Life on the Field, in the Air, and on the Air*

by Jerry Coleman

The 1950 World Series wasn't exactly a high-scoring affair—the Yankees scored 11 runs in their four-game sweep of the Phillies—so it's fitting that the Babe Ruth Award for the series' most valuable player went to defensive star Jerry Coleman. His 3 RBI were tops for the series, and the second baseman's solid defensive play bolstered the infield in the Yanks' second straight World Series victory.

The 1950 season was probably my best year with the Yankees, though nothing would beat that thrill of edging out the Red Sox and winning a pennant for the first time. I played all but one game that year and hit .287, my highest average ever. I hit six home runs and drove in 69 runs. Those weren't exactly DiMaggio numbers, but I would never match those totals again. And Rizzuto and I were teaming once more for smooth middle-infield play.

But halfway through the season came the news that stunned an America only recently emerged from World War II. Just like Pearl Harbor Day, it was a Sunday morning (Saturday night in Washington). On June 25 thousands of North Korean troops crossed the 38th parallel, dividing two Koreas, and began a rout of our South Korean allies.

The Yankees split a Sunday doubleheader with the Tigers in Detroit, but I doubt that anyone was paying much attention beyond the ballpark. President Truman rushed back to Washington from a trip to his hometown of Independence, Missouri, and pledged to push back the Communists. Fighting under a United Nations resolution, America would be at war again, not even five full years after VJ-Day.

The nation's armed forces had been cut severely since the end of World War II, and the Marines were no exception. In fact, the Corps was fortunate to have fended off a proposal that the air force absorb its aviation units. But the Marines quickly went into action. Two weeks after the North Koreans invaded the south, the 1st Provisional Marine Brigade, consisting of 6,500 ground troops and aviation personnel, was activated at Camp Pendleton, California. It sailed for Korea from San Diego in mid-July.

Marines began coming ashore on August 2 to protect the southern port of Pusan, the South Korean capital of Seoul having already fallen. The next day Marine pilots flying gull-winged Corsair fighters raided North Korean installations, taking off from the escort carrier *Sicily*. They were soon joined by Corsairs flying off the escort carrier *Baedong Strait*.

On September 15 the 1st Marine Division led the first major counterattack by United Nations forces with a surprise amphibious assault at the North Korean-occupied port of Inchon. Two weeks later the Marines had wrested Seoul from Communist control.

What did all this mean to me personally? When the Korean War broke out, the Marines realized, "Wow, we don't have any pilots." At least not enough. I was on the reserve list. When officers got out of the service after World War II, they were put on an inactive status, so they didn't really get out. That's what happened to me. The draft was on, but you can't draft a pilot—and it takes a year and a half to train one. I had no thought of being called up. This was Korea, a little peninsula. It was a "police action," it was "over there." It was 10,000 miles away. The war in Korea wasn't something I gave much thought to, so far as my personal situation went.

I had enough to be excited about, what with the prospect of another pennant victory and, before that, my first appearance at an All-Star Game, in Chicago's Comiskey Park. Bobby Doerr of the Red Sox started at second base, but I came in for him. I had one chance and booted it, and I got up twice and struck out. (It was a worse day for Ted Williams, who hit the wall making a catch in the first inning and learned later he had broken his elbow.)

But I was there, and it turned out to be one of the more exciting All-Star Games and the first one to go into extra innings. The St. Louis Cardinals' second baseman, Red Schoendienst, won it for the National League, 4-3, with a home run in the fourteenth inning.

Back then there were none of the trappings you have today, like the home-run derby and all those parties. When he owned the Padres, Ray Kroc was the guy who started all that hype. He opened the San Diego ballpark for the workout the day before they had the All-Star Game there in 1978, and 30,000 people came. Dave Winfield threw a cookie-and-doughnuts party for 10,000 youngsters at a hotel hall in San Diego. A half-dozen players from both teams joined him in talking to the kids. Baseball realized it had something more than the game itself. Back in 1950 I took an overnight train from New York to Chicago, played the game, and that night I took another train home. That was it. Nobody paid any attention otherwise—the All-Star Game was it.

After all those years where the game was simply an exhibition—a chance to see baseball's best—now they've tagged on this thing where the league that wins the All-Star Game gains the home-field advantage for its pennant-winner in the World Series. I don't agree with that. The home-field edge should alternate between leagues the way it had been. Home field is a big deal. It's insignificant as to which team wins the All-Star Game. Nobody cares. But it is a showpiece for baseball, and there should be a penalty for any player who opts out for reasons other than injury. It's important to bring your best out there. You want to see the superstars compete.

In that 1950 season the Yankees still had great pitching with Raschi, Reynolds, Lopat, and Byrne, but we got even stronger when we brought up a left-hander from our Kansas City farm club—Whitey Ford. He went 9-0, then finally lost a game while pitching in relief. He was facing the Athletics' Sam Chapman, a right-handed batting outfielder with good power and, incidentally, a former All-American football player at California. Chapman hit one over the left-field wall in the ninth inning at Philadelphia's Shibe Park for a game-winning two-run homer. But Ford was just brilliant that year.

We beat out the Detroit Tigers by three games for the pennant, and this time we faced the Philadelphia Phillies in the World Series—the team known as the Whiz Kids because they had so many young players. They had good pitching with Jim Konstanty, Robin Roberts, and Curt Simmons, and a lineup including Richie Ashburn and Del Ennis in the outfield.

It was a low-scoring Series, but I got some timely hits. In Game 1 at Shibe Park, my fly ball in the fourth inning drove in Bobby Brown, who had doubled, for a 1-0 win over Konstanty. The next day I scored a run and then DiMaggio gave us a 2-1 victory with a tenth-inning home run.

When the Series arrived at Yankee Stadium, I came to the plate in the ninth inning with the game tied, 2-2, two men on and two out. I already had two of the Yankees' six hits that day and I scored the second run.

In his "Views of Sport" column in the *New York Herald Tribune* the next day, Red Smith described the scene:

Now he was up again but most of the 64,505 witnesses weren't looking. Most of them were watching Russ Meyer, a somewhat flamboyant Philadelphia pitcher who bears watching because he does interesting things, like getting his nose bitten in saloons.

"He never loses his swagger," a Philadelphia newspaperman was saying of Meyer. "He lost nine games in a row this summer and he never lost that strut."

"He may lose it in a second," a guy said.

In a second, Coleman had his third hit.

It was a long fly to left center which the Philadelphia outfielders chased hopelessly for a little while and then gave up. Coleman ran to first base and Gene Woodling ran home with the winning run, and Meyer dropped like an old, ungartered sock.

Across the infield, Coleman was trotting toward the Yankee bench, and Bill Dickey, who had been coaching at first, trotted behind him whacking him where he sits. The Yankees were one game away from their 13th world championship.

I was self-effacing after the game in describing the hit for the sportswriters.

The Associated Press quoted me as saying, "I thought the team was going to win, but I didn't think I'd be that instrumental in the victory."

The Associated Press's Ted Smits wrote, "Yes, that's the way he talks, smiling all the time and looking more as if he belonged on a college team than on the Yankees."

As for my single, I described it this way: "Actually, I think it was a ball that should have been caught. Richie Ashburn was playing me in right-center and it looked as if Jack Mayo in left field was too close to the foul line. The ball went right between them."

Stengel wasn't all that exuberant, considering that we had won three times and were on the brink of a sweep. Casey dwelled on the fact we had played three low-scoring games. As he put it, "Their pitches are awful good or else we're in a terrible slump."

Whitey Ford was pitching in Game 4 at the Stadium. He had a 5-0 shutout with two down in the ninth, but Woodling dropped a fly ball to left. It was sunny and bright in left field and hard to pick up the ball. Stengel wanted Ford to get a shutout, but Woodling's muff brought in two runs. Stengel took Ford out, bringing Allie Reynolds in. This is where Woodling and Stengel ended up as mortal enemies forever. Stengel ran on top of the dugout steps and waved back, back to Woodling, thinking he was playing too shallow. It showed Gene up very badly, and Gene never forgave Stengel for that. Both of them are probably arguing about it in heaven someplace. We won the game anyway, 5-2, for a sweep and our second straight World Series championship.

I was given the Babe Ruth plaque as the Most Valuable Player of the World Series. We scored only 11 runs, but I had knocked in three of them, twice producing the game-winner.

Hank Bauer and the '51 Yankees

"Bauer Proves Double Hero in Series Clincher"
The Sporting News, October 17, 1951

by Dan Daniel

*Hank Bauer joined the Yankees as a 25-year-old rookie in
September 1948, and he went on to be a part of nine pennant
winners and three all-star teams in his 11 full seasons in New York.
Although the outfielder collected only three hits in the 1951 series,
his bases-loaded triple in the clinching sixth game made him the
hero of the hour.*

HIS BASE-CLEARING TRIPLE AND GAME-ENDING CATCH STAND OUT
IN FINALE—DRAMATIC CLIMAX MAKES UP FOR PART-TIME ROLE
IN '51—STENGEL HIGH ON EX-MARINE'S LONG-DISTANCE POWER—
FAST ON THE BASES AND IN FIELD, DESPITE HIS SIZE

NEW YORK, NY—To Hank Bauer went the distinction of being a double hero in the sixth and final game of the World's Series.

The outfielder's triple with the bases loaded not only won the game for the Yankees in the sixth inning, but his amazing catch of Pinch-Hitter Sal Yvars' drive to end the battle saved the victory for the Bombers, 4 to 3, with the tying tally on second base.

Yvars, usually a left field hitter, apparently tried to drive the ball into right and almost succeeded in putting Relief Pitcher Bob Kuzava in very hot water. Bauer's diving catch clinched the Yankees' fourteenth world's championship in 18 series, their fifth consecutive title and their fourth in a row over the Giants.

Bauer's base-clearing triple was hit off a three-two pitch and, but for the contrary wind, would have gone into the left field stands and duplicated the grand-slam homer which Rookie Gil McDougald had achieved the day before.

Bauer was one of many Yankee heroes. But he had one advantage over the others. He shone last.

Phil Rizzuto's spectacular play day after day, his 39 chances accepted, for a six-game Series high, his participation in nine of the Bombers' record ten double plays, his topping Yankee regulars with a mark of .320, all combined to make him the writer's choice as the hero of the Series.

Ed Lopat's two brilliant victories, in which he gave the Giants two walks, ten hits and one earned run, made the lefthander formidable competition for The Scooter.

Then there was McDougald and his four-run homer, unprecedented for a rookie.

Only a Part-Timer

And finally, the ex-Marine, Hank Bauer. He had not had too happy a season. Being shunted in and out of the lineup did not appeal to Hank, because it made him a part-time player, and that type does not land in the higher salary brackets.

The Series climax, however, made up for Bauer's pennant-season disappointments.

Hank's triumphs in the finale now stand out in a most interesting Yankee career which has yet to see him at his best.

Back in June, 1950, when the Yankees were trying to close a deal with the White Sox for Pitcher Bill Wight, General Manager Frank Lane of the Chicago club kept insisting that Bauer be included in the swap.

"Man, you are asking us to turn over to you one of the coming ball players of the major leagues, the successor to Joe DiMaggio," Casey Stengel protested.

Stengel is highly enamored of Bauer as a ball player, as a batter of extra-base proclivities, as a hustler, and an all-around, determined, young man.

There are quite a few fast movers on the New York club. And Hank is among them. He can run and he knows how to use that spectacular asset.

Looks Like Fighter

Hank looks like an athlete. He looks the fighter. That dented nose and other mementos bespeak a lively youth around East St. Louis, where he was born on July 31, 1922. He is a six-footer and weighs about 190.

Hank has the distinction of having had perhaps the longest term of service in our military set-up of anybody in Organized Ball.

He was with the Marines for more than four years. He was in the Pacific Theater for 34 months, on Okinawa, Guam, Guadalcanal and Japan. He has two Purple Hearts, two Bronze Stars. He came out a platoon sergeant.

Bauer reported to the Yankees from their Kansas City farm on September 3, 1948. On the eve of his flight to the Stadium, he received an award as the most popular Kansas City player.

Hank had appeared in 132 contests with K.C. and had batted .305.

George Weiss was not keen for rushing Hank into the Yankee situation before the spring of 1949. He felt that Bauer was not quite ready, despite his impressive record in the Triple-A company. But Bucky Harris was desperate, and he wanted all the help he possibly could summon from the Yankee farm system.

Weiss' assay of Bauer's 1948 potentialities was supported by what happened.

Bauer displayed some damning weaknesses, as a righthanded batter against righthanded pitching. He was especially weak against sidearm hurling and was prone to go fishing for the high outside curve. Hank got into 19 games before the close of that season, for a lackluster .180.

When the spring training season of 1949 rolled around, with Casey Stengel in the place of Harris, it was taken for granted by most of the writers covering the St. Petersburg camp that Hank would be sent back to Kansas City.

However, neither Bauer nor Stengel would have any part of that plan.

It took just two days for Casey to become sold 100 per cent on the big outfielder.

"There is a man who by 1952 will be ranked with the standouts of the big leagues," exuberated Casey.

"I know, he still is a little green at the plate, and he has something to learn in the field. But he has the physical equipment and tremendous confidence. I am going to stick with this lad."

Under the encouraging aegis of Stengel, Bauer got into 103 games in 1949, for a .272 rating. He hit ten homers, and achieved some interesting feats in the field. Not the least important of his possessions was a great arm.

In 1950, playing 113 games, Bauer hit .320, with 13 homers and 70 RBIs. During the past season, he batted .296, with nine homers and 53 RBIs.

On October 22, 1949, Hank married Charlene Bernadine Friede, whom he had met when she was on the office staff of the Kansas City club.

Bauer is the personal discovery of Danny Menendez, once business manager of the Joplin (Western Association) club in the Yankee chain, then with Kansas City and last season with Hollywood. Menendez spotted Bauer after Hank had returned from service in 1945, and in 1946, the outfielder signed with Quincy, Ill., the Bombers' Three-I League subsidiary.

"I played ball in school in East St. Louis for St. Elizabeth's, to begin with," Bauer said. "I was at St. Elizabeth's until 1936, and then went to Clark Junior High. In 1937, I shifted to Central Catholic High and was graduated in 1940, also played American Legion ball.

"Quite a few local scouts were after me, and in 1941, I signed with Oshkosh. I got into 108 games. And hardly busted down the fences of the Wisconsin State League. I hit .262.

Hand Fling at Pitching

"They thought I had a pretty good arm, and got the notion that I might do better as a pitcher than an outfielder or infielder," Hank continued. "I worked in 11 games, pitching 34 innings, with a 2-1 record and 30 strikeouts. I was not keen for the conversion.

"In 1942, I joined the Marines, and, as you know, did not get back to baseball until 1946.

"I did not play ball in service. In the places where we were located, there was little time for games, believe me."

Bauer hit .323 for Quincy and gained promotion to Kansas City in 1947. His rating for that year was .313.

In 1948, he batted .305, with 23 homers and 100 runs accounted for—and then came the summons to Yankee Stadium.

Hank is of Austro-Hungarian extraction. He has an off-season trade—that of steamfitter. However, it appears certain that from now on, Hank's baseball salary will make it possible for him to sell his wrenches and other paraphernalia, and take off during the winter months.

In the winter, the Yankee front office mailed a questionnaire to each of the Bombers. One of the questions read like this: "What ball player, past or present, do you most admire?"

Bauer's answer was: "Joe DiMaggio. Because he is a good hustler, with great team spirit. He has all-around greatness and is always willing to help the others improve their play."

As the 1951 season, with its capping classic, unfolded itself, Bauer appeared to be getting a decision over his own big batting handicap, weakness against sidearm pitching.

Once the tenacious Hank goes after anything, he shows the determination of the service branch with which he saw four years of fighting—the Marines.

The View from the Dugout

From *Casey at the Bat*

by Casey Stengel and Harry T. Paxton

*Every hero eventually wears out, grows old, or falls victim to injury.
In this piece, the great Casey Stengel describes the challenges of
replacing a retired superstar like Joe DiMaggio while keeping a team
of veterans focused on the 1952 pennant race. One of the great feats of
the Yankee organization has been its ability to adapt and discover the
"next great Yankee"—again and again.*

Everybody knows we had a lot of playing talent during the years I was managing the Yankees, but a lot of people don't realize how fast the talent kept wearing out. By the time of the 1952 World Series, we had only two of the regulars that had started my first World Series for me in 1949—Berra and Rizzuto. The others were all traded or retired or in the military service.

One of our biggest problems in 1952 was to replace DiMaggio in center field. We didn't think we could move Mantle over there from right field because he was handicapped in covering ground with his knee that he'd hurt in the 1951 World Series. And it also turned out that he'd had osteomyelitis in one leg, which is a very serious thing.

That kept him out of the draft. He was examined three times in different cities and turned down. This bothered him, because people would yell from the stands and ask him why he wasn't in the Army. On the field he could run fast and everything.

But for three or four years Mantle couldn't turn and cut quick because of that knee. He could only run in a straight line. On the bases he'd have to swing wide around first instead of cutting sharp toward second. And in the outfield he was very troubled on balls hit over his head. Later on he found a way where he could circle back better and overtake the baseball at times.

Another possibility for center field was Jackie Jensen. We had gotten him and Billy Martin from Oakland in 1950. But we decided that Jensen's best position was right field, where we already had Mantle. So in May of 1952 we gave up Jensen to get Irv Noren, a center fielder with the Washington club.

Noren had been sensational playing against us, but after we got him, he misjudged the first ball that was hit to him in center field. And we found out that he also had had knee trouble. So it ended up that Mantle became the center-fielder after all, while Noren was used mostly in left field. Next to Woodling, he did the best defensive work for me there—he was a very good thrower.

Well, we were in another hot pennant fight with Cleveland that season, and there was one point in September when it looked like we weren't going to win our fourth straight. We got in a slump, and in Philadelphia we lost a game I never expected to lose. In the clubhouse afterward I kept myself from handing out any comments, as when you're burned up, it's generally better to talk to your ballplayers the next day.

And the men commenced to get cans of beer in the clubhouse, and instead of walking over and dropping them in the trash can when they finished, they'd let them fly. It wasn't a very large trash can, and they'd miss, and the empty cans of beer would bounce around and go ting-a-ling, ting-a-ling. There were so many ting-a-lings that it began to get my goat. It looked to me like they were kidding around too much and not taking this slump seriously. And I could see it was getting on one of the pitcher's nerves, too.

But I got out of there without saying anything. Then in the dining car to Washington they started this game called Twenty Questions. The game got going good, and they were laughing and joking, and it wasn't so funny to me. I jumped up and asked for their attention. I asked if they realized that hardly a one of them had earned his salary that day. I told them it wasn't any laughing matter, and they didn't know what their salary would be for the following year or where they'd be playing, as it looked like this season was going to be a failure. I gave them as good a jacking up as I could, and it may have helped to keep them bearing down hard the rest of the year.

We won the pennant by two games over Cleveland, and in the 1952 World Series we played Brooklyn. We got down to the seventh inning of the seventh game with a 4-2 lead, and then they filled the bases with two out and Jackie Robinson at bat.

Bob Kuzava came in to pitch for us. You weren't supposed to be able to pitch to left-handers against those Brooklyn right-handed hitters, especially in Ebbets Field, but Kuzava made Robinson pop this high infield fly. It went so high it looked like it would go over the Washington Monument if you were in Washington. And while it was up in the air, each player looked at the others and said, "I don't want it, you take it." It was like that ball was a bomb that nobody wanted to handle.

At second base we had Billy Martin, who had taken over the position when Jerry Coleman was called back into the military service on account of the Korean War. This pop fly wasn't Martin's ball, but he started running for it. He ran right up near home plate and made a diving grab of the ball four inches from his knees. If that ball hadn't been caught, all the men on the bases would have scored, because everybody was running, and Robinson would have gotten around maybe to third.

In 1953 Martin was a World Series hero against Brooklyn again with twelve hits in twenty-four times at bat. Later on, of course, he got traded away in 1957. This was after some sort of fight broke out at the Copacabana night club when some of our players and their wives had a party there to celebrate Martin's birthday. If I ever go into the restaurant business, I think I'll invite some ballplayers and their wives to come there at night, because the Copacabana got the most publicity out of that I ever saw.

I don't know anything about the fight. I didn't see it. But the bad part was that we had a game the next day. Originally it was to be an off day, but then we had to make up a game that had been rained out. Martin's group had made their plans for that night in advance, and they went ahead with the party anyway. They didn't come and ask me if they could. If I'd said yes, it would have been all right. But when you don't get permission from the manager, then you're going at your own risk.

The owners and Mr. Weiss didn't like that at all, and didn't think the manager was handling his players right. Some fines were made. I don't know the exact amount, because it was done by the office. And about a month afterward Billy Martin was traded to Kansas City.

Now here's the situation with Martin. He was a young man that came out of a neighborhood, which we have in every city, which they did try to watch. He'd had a stepfather. Martin was a small man. He thought he could whip anybody. And when anybody tells you Martin can't fight, that's a big joke. Martin can fight good.

He gave me a lot of spirit and everything else. Sometimes you have to have a noisy man on the team. You can have too many quiet players, and you need a man to jack them up. Martin could yell and yell at the other side, and he was a game player. And Martin is a skilled player. He knows all the plays, knows what's coming up, and he can catch the signs.

There was one thing that no doubt got him in a little bad with our ball club. He could not see the ideas of some men that were up in the front office. He was a man that was better for the players or better for the manager—if you could handle him. I could handle Billy Martin.

Did I approve of trading him? Well, the office had been after me three or four times to get rid of him. But I gave in only when they arranged to get me a left-handed hitter, Harry Simpson, who I thought would help us in Yankee Stadium. And we had Bobby Richardson coming along to play second base for us. As it worked out, Simpson didn't help us much. Anyway, I will have to say that there were very rare occasions on that ball club that they could slip around and get rid of a player if I didn't approve of the deal.

The Big Three

From *Reynolds, Raschi, and Lopat: New York's Big Three and the Great Yankee Dynasty of 1949–1953*

by Sol Gittleman

On a team that won five consecutive world championships and featured such iconic figures as DiMaggio, Berra, Rizzuto, and Mantle, the names Reynolds, Raschi, and Lopat tend to get overshadowed. But righthanders Vic Raschi and Allie Reynolds and southpaw Eddie Lopat provided a formidable mound trio, earning wins in 15 of the 20 Yankee victories in the five World Series from 1949 to 1953.

"Our pitchers were getting old—Reynolds was thirty-eight, Lopat thirty-five and Raschi thirty-four. But, everybody seemed to help everybody else at just the right time." —Yogi Berra

This time, the journalists were not taking any chances. Having gotten it wrong four years running, they were not going to be fooled again: all ten reporters covering the Yankee spring training camp picked the Yankees to win the American League pennant. Ironically, they chose to ignore what they saw. Eddie Lopat did not throw a ball in a Grapefruit League game; Reynolds and Raschi were shelled together regularly, and there was a clear diminution of Vic's velocity. He could not push off his damaged knee and shrunken leg. Berra was injured or ill much of the time. But, no one cared, because Mickey Mantle was hitting gigantic home runs over everything in Florida. No ballpark could contain him. That, plus the return of Whitey Ford from his two-year military service to the Yankee rotation, focused the press's attention on him, and not on the aging core of Stengel's pitching staff. Often in the newspapers they were still referred to as "the Big Three," and after so many years of consistent excellence, Reynolds, Raschi and Lopat arrived at a taken-for-granted immortality that suggested to the New York City working press that they would go on forever. The journalists did not notice that forever was coming to an end.

Ironically, they got it right this time. In 1953, the Yankees exploded out of the starting gate and held first place in the American League for 158 of the season's 167 days, from May 11 to the end. On May 28, they cemented their grip on first place by beginning an eighteen-game winning streak—the final fourteen on the road—that destroyed the rest of the contenders, namely Cleveland and Chicago. They took on the Indians during this road trip and in four games swept Wynn, Feller, Lemon and Garcia, the great Cleveland rotation. These four games represented a microcosm of the entire season. A Cleveland sweep would have reduced the Yankee lead to 2 1/2 games. Instead, the Yankees left Cleveland's Municipal Stadium and 74,708 shocked fans after a Sunday doubleheader on June 14 with the Indians 10 1/2 games behind. The winning Yankee pitchers were Ford, Lopat, Sain and Raschi; Reynolds saved two games for Ford and Sain, pitching five innings of shutout relief. As Louis Effrat reported in the *New York Times*, Stengel "called for Reynolds, and that was that." Allie, now the Yankee stopper as well as a starter, had not lost in relief since August 22, 1951. Ford and Lopat, after their victories against Cleveland, were a combined 14-0, each with seven victories and no defeats. Allie had seven saves so far in the season in seven opportunities and had not been scored on in his last eleven relief appearances. By the end of June, he was being used exclusively out of the bullpen. Casey had spoken with Topping and Webb. He wanted it made clear that if Reynolds went to the bullpen, he would still get a salary appropriate for a successful starting pitcher. The owners agreed.

Only Vic was showing signs of severe wear. This complete game 3-0 shutout of Cleveland brought his record to 4-3, far from the level of the previous Yankee years. Still, he was on the mound for every turn, doggedly pitching for his friends, his coach and his team. As long as his arm allowed, he would not quit, even as his body failed him. This shutout revealed a different pitcher. He gave up three hits, but struck out only two. He was throwing to spots, increasingly using his slider and curve, changing speeds and location. Allie, during the years rooming with Lopat and endless conversations about pitching, had learned Lopat's craft: the art of pitching, the cunning that even a power pitcher could use. He didn't have to bear down on every pitch. Instead, he used the whole field, and took advantage of the hitter's false enthusiasm and misguided belief that he could hit a lesser pitch thrown in the perfect place. Reynolds had learned guile from Lopat. Vic was a profoundly focused man, deeply wedded to what he considered the ethics of his pitching philosophy: give it all you have on every pitch. Stengel used to marvel at Raschi's single-minded intensity, throwing as hard as he could for as long as he could, never letting up. In his autobiography, Casey wrote: "Raschi was the greatest pitcher I ever had to be sure to win. And he would never give in any time that he pitched, even when his stuff was ordinary. . . . He wasn't a graceful pitcher—he just put so much on it."

Now the vaunted Raschi fastball was a weapon of the past. Only the concentration and ferocity of competition was still driving him. The heart that beat, the one that Stengel, Turner and his two comrades knew so well, was as true as ever. Turner, whom Vic trusted as an older brother, spoke quietly to him. Eddie and Allie would sit with Vic, then walk to the mound and try things out. It was time to use other weapons, they told him; he learned well.

After this explosion, the Yankees teased the opposition by losing nine straight, including three to the Indians in Yankee Stadium, but by then the gap never closed sufficiently to give Stengel any worries. On June 28, the second-place Cleveland Indians were 39-26, a respectable .600 pace. But, they were seven games behind New York, who, with an incredible 46-19 record, had a .708 won-lost percentage. The White Sox went on a tear, winning seven straight—and made up only one-half game. On July 5, they were in second place, ahead of the Indians, at 44-29. The Yankees had "slumped" to .694 with a 50-22 record. For the rest of the season, the Yankees coasted. But, there was still high drama, and much of it involved Allie.

On the night of July 7, the Yankees bus was heading for the train station in Philadelphia after a game with the A's. As the speeding bus came within sight of the station, the Yankees players started out of their seats to get ready to disembark. The driver took a wrong turn into a taxi lane and slammed into a low bridge overhead pass at considerable speed. The players were thrown in every direction. The bus driver went through the window and lay unconscious. Reynolds smashed into the seat railing behind him, wrenching his back. Of all the injuries suffered in this accident, Allie's would prove to be the most serious. It virtually ended his career.

For the rest of the season, Reynolds was not the same pitcher. He had his usual velocity for three or four innings, then back spasms would come along, and he would lose location. He could not control his fastball. The trainer would freeze up his back with a spray during games, just so he could keep going. Reynolds was basically finished as a starter for the rest of the season.

The other career-threatening event involved the fragile young Mantle, who already had damaged his knee in the first game of the 1951 World Series. Now, in an early August game against the White Sox, cutting sharply in the outfield, he came down hard on the same right knee, and it buckled under him.

Mantle had torn more ligaments and damaged the cartilage. Mickey would miss almost thirty games in the 1953 season, and he had to play with what at the time was a bulky and awkward knee brace that hampered his running. Yet Mantle was not a quitter, and it was this characteristic that later endeared him to his teammates and made life-long cheerleaders and genuinely loyal friends out of older veterans like Woodling and Bauer, friends who were willing to look the other way when Mickey showed up hung over before a game. They would see him bandage his legs with yards of tape, put on a brace, play with extraordinary pain, and never complain. He never lacked courage. But, Mickey was no natural leader and refused to play that role; nor did his other buddy with the potential star status, Whitey Ford.

George Weiss just could not believe it. What made this team so much better than the previous four, when the Yankees barely won the American League pennants by 1, 3, 5 and 2 games? His friend Casey *must* be a genius. He always knew that Stengel had one of the best baseball brains in the business. It was Stengel who told Weiss in mid-season: get me a backup shortstop, someone who could play defense for four or five innings, in case I have to hit for the little Dago. Rizzuto was going on thirty-six, an advanced age for a premier shortstop, especially one with a weak arm to start with. Stengel had a strong corps of pinch hitters and was increasingly inclined to use them early. On June 12, New York purchased the contract of a slick-fielding, weak-hitting shortstop from the ever-accommodating St. Louis Browns. Willie Miranda was exactly what Casey was looking for, and as soon as Miranda arrived, Rizzuto was vulnerable to be lifted, if the situation warranted it, even before his first at-bat. Rizzuto, never an admirer of Casey, resented being hit for early in the game and was embarrassed. But, when he saw Reynolds heading down to the bullpen every day, he understood what sacrifices had to be made to win.

The tight-jawed Weiss kept watching all season from his seat in Yankee Stadium. No matter what happens, he thought, there will be changes. Individuals are not performing and they will still want to get paid. No. There will be changes.

As the season moved to its end, Yogi Berra could praise himself for his best year of generalship. He had gotten the most out of his aging veterans, who looked with great satisfaction on the product of their attention. Berra was now, with Roy Campanella, the premier catcher in the major leagues. Yogi was more durable, less injury-prone than Campy. He was agile behind the plate, a lethal clutch hitter, and recognized by everyone as one of the most valuable players in baseball. He became a three-time MVP, and during the great Yankee run from 1949 to 1953, was always in the top five voting. In this season, he also proved to be a subtle and intuitive master of his position. He could sense how much Vic, Allie or Eddie had left once the game got underway. Berra had lived inside their minds, at first hesitantly, for five years. He had attained a level of comfort and understanding that gave them complete confidence in his judgment. It could only have happened if the three pitchers had permitted it; and indeed, they did. They invited Berra into their thoughts, allowed him to study how they pitched, their strategies, their cunning and authority. He grew to understand the fear that Reynolds could engender in a hitting when one of his 100 mile-per-hour fastballs shook the spikes loose from the batter's box. When the batter stepped back in, he was a changed, often frightened man. Berra, who brought his own affable and warm personality to his position, loved to keep up a friendly chatter behind the plate. "Boy, am I glad I don't have to hit against the Chief today," he would say, even to the lordly Ted Williams, who would turn around and yell, "Yogi, shut the fuck up!" But Berra just kept chattering.

By the 1953 season, it was as if there was only one mind involved, regardless of who was pitching. The rapport between Berra and his pitchers was complete. Befitting their relationship and experience, Ford deferred to Berra in the calling of the game. Whitey admitted it with his usual matter-of-fact candor: Yogi knew the hitters, knew the situation. Whatever Yogi called for, Whitey would throw.

The great challenge for Yogi this year was to understand what limitations their bodies now put on his three older mentors. After the bus accident, Allie's arsenal of weapons was significantly diminished; he lost his consistency, even when he maintained his velocity. He and Vic both pitched in pain. This year, Yogi no longer taunted his fellow Italian-American, whom he would playfully insult just to get his attention and to add a little more steam to his fastball. For Vic, it had been critical to have the extra yard, because Yogi knew that, unlike Allie, he really would not throw at a hitter. If a batter started crowding in on Raschi, looking for a fastball over the plate, Berra would mutter, loud enough to be heard, "Jeez, don't get hit by one of this Dago's fastballs. It could kill you!" But, this year, it was different. Vic could not reach back for the little extra; it wasn't there. When Raschi's record was a miserable 3-3 in June, Yogi sat first with Turner, then with Vic to talk strategy. He became part of the friendly conspiracy that encircled their wounded and vulnerable comrade. "We can change speeds better, move the ball around, get them to hit balls out of the strike zone. Eddie's been living that way all his life!" Vic now trusted Berra as much as he trusted Eddie, Allie, Jim or even his wife Sally; this was the special relationship of a pitcher to a catcher whom had learned to trust with one another's life, like a marriage.

At this stage of his career, with time drawing short, Vic listened and became a different pitcher. He turned the season around, finishing the year with a respectable 13-6 record, a winning percentage of .684, yielding only 150 hits in the 181 innings pitched, the fewest he had thrown since becoming the most reliable starter in post-war Yankee history. His statistics reveal the extent of the metamorphosis that he willed for himself and that his teammates and coach urged on him. He completely remade himself as a pitcher. For the first time in five years, Vic was not in the top ten strikeouts, innings pitched, and games started or completed. He took the ball as a starter twenty-six times, and was still holding it at the end in only seven games. No longer the power pitcher that he had been for his entire career, Raschi's control improved. He had the second best record of hits and walks allowed per game, surpassed only by teammate Eddie Lopat. He had four shutouts, his highest total for a season over this five-year stretch. His record was a tribute to his character and to Berra's intelligence.

As a catcher, Berra always had a special relationship with Eddie Lopat. By 1951, the synergy had been completed: Yogi could anticipate Eddie's pitches so well, had gotten inside his head so completely, that they stopped having signals between them. For Berra, there was no danger that a ferocious fastball would smash into his facemask; it was like playing catch with a pal. He always had time to react to Eddie's variety of pitches and arm directions. It proved to be for Lopat, Berra, and the Yankees an unbelievable year. Mostly starting once a week because of what was now chronic tendinitis, Eddie produced a spectacular 16-4 record. He only completed nine games, and Berra was a master of the moment for both Vic and Eddie. They both now were perfectly willing to tell their catcher if they were tiring. What a change from the first year, when they were prepared to murder their catcher if he gave any signal to Stengel or Turner! Lopat threw fewer innings than Raschi, 178, but he had a league-leading ERA of a miserly 2.43. He had the best won-lost percentage in baseball at a gaudy .800, led the majors in fewest walks per nine innings of pitching, and for good measure threw three shutouts, as usual dominating the Cleveland Indians.

Whitey Ford was the only Yankee pitcher who had thirty starts. Yet, he, too, did not take the ball into the clubhouse at game's end very often: he completed only eleven. He threw a staff-high 207 innings, a far cry from previous years when the Big Three each would have more than 200 innings. His 18-6 record placed the twenty-four-year-old Ford now at the top of the pitching chain. He had an ERA exactly at 3.00. But, he did not kid himself. He knew who made this all possible: the Chief in the bullpen.

There may not have been a comparable year for any pitcher in recent baseball history similar to the one that Allie Reynolds had in 1953. He appeared in forty-one games—the most on the Yankee staff—won thirteen (13-7, 3.41 ERA, .650 won-lost percentage), started fifteen, completed five, and had a shutout. He relieved in twenty-six, won seven, saved thirteen more (third in the league), and finished twenty-three. Vic, Eddie, and Whitey knew who made it happen for them that year: it was Allie coming in from the bullpen, even after the terrible injury in July. No matter how deep the spasms or how much pain he felt, he somehow would reach back and find the old flame for two or three innings. Yogi was the timekeeper for the starters, and he kept Vic, Eddie, and Whitey going for as long as they could go, pacing and resting them inning by inning. Johnny Sain, a lower case version of Reynolds who could also start and relieve, had been a big help in sparing Allie, but in the big games, Stengel would turn to his Chief. He couldn't break old habits. Reynolds pitched only 145 innings, struck out just eighty-six batters, but in his manager's mind, when he saw his Indian put a leg over the bullpen railing, he knew in his heart that batters still grew faint.

In a two-game series against Cleveland on September 13 and 14 in Yankee Stadium, Stengel ended the misery for the Indians. Two days earlier he had begun preparing for the World Series by bringing Allie Reynolds back into the starting rotation. Allie, who had not thrown a complete game since June 30, went ten innings against Detroit, gave them seven hits, struck out five, and walked one. It was only the fourth time he had gone the distance. Although losing 3-2, everyone was satisfied. Allie had controlled the back spasms and was ready for October. His offerings would be needed to stop the powerful right-handed bats in the lineup of the mighty Brooklyn Dodgers, who had clinched the pennant in record time on September 11.

The Yankees needed a win in the first game of the series to clinch the tie. With Reynolds not available, Casey went to his other valiant big-game winner. Vic Raschi was not the same force he had been, but Stengel often found his hunches validated in his heart. Vic did not let him down. In front of 48,492 cheering Sunday fans, Raschi clinched the fifth pennant for Casey, beating Cleveland's Mike Garcia, 6-3, with yet another cagey six-hitter for his thirteenth win of the season. He walked three and struck out three: again, not the overpowering Vic Raschi, but a winner nonetheless.

Next day, Casey wanted to give the new big kid on the block a chance to pitch the game that made history, the fifth consecutive pennant clincher, and handed the ball to Whitey Ford. Ford got shelled in the third inning and left the game trailing 5-0. But, this was a team destined to make history, and they wanted to do it against the closest competition. The Yankee bats exploded against Cleveland ace Early Wynn, and Casey had his fifth in a row with an 8-5 comeback victory. Johnny Sain got the win in relief. Cleveland left New York City trailing by 13 games. There were nearly three weeks left in the season with little to do. The Yankees coasted to an 8½-game final lead, finishing with a 99-52 record, the best of their five straight pennant-winning seasons. Casey had surpassed his mentor, John McGraw, and the earlier Yankee legend, Joe McCarthy. The Yankees had made baseball history.

Mickey's Triple Crown

From *The Last Boy: Mickey Mantle and the End of America's Childhood*

by Jane Leavy

Though we need no further reminders that Mickey Mantle was a once-in-a-lifetime talent, they are hidden everywhere in the details of his illustrious career. Even his 1956 triple crown, remarkably impressive by definition, stands out amongst the handful of others achieved in the history of the game—his 52 home runs have never been matched by another triple crown winner.

On opening day in the nation's capital, Mantle relocated two Camilo Pascual fastballs beyond the center field fence in Griffith Stadium—past the flagpole, over the thirty-one-foot wall and into the boughs of the beloved backyard tree that caused the ballpark to be built around it. The first of the two gargantuan left-handed efforts sailed over the tree and landed on the roof of a house beyond the 408-foot sign and bounced across Fifth Street. The second disturbed birds nesting in the bower. Most papers said it was an oak left over from virgin forest; others called it a maple. Pascual called it "Mickey's tree."

Pedro Ramos, his voluble countryman and teammate—generously characterized by Mantle as "one fucking bright Cuban"—waved a white towel at Pascual as Mantle rounded the bases again. "He hit one *into* the tree and the next one went *over* the tree," Ramos said, the force of the two 500-footers having conflated his recollections. "They are still looking for those balls. That tree *remembers* Mickey."

"*Tree*-mendous," Casey Stengel declared. "They tell me that the only other feller which hit that tree was Ruth. He shook some kids outta the tree when the ball landed. But the tree's gotten bigger in twenty-five years, and so I guess have the kids The Babe shook outta it."

In the sixth spring of his major league career, Mantle had arrived at the tipping point. The 1955 season had been a good one. He led the American League in triples (11), home runs (37), walks (113), runs (129), slugging (.611), and on-base percentage (.433). That May he had the only three-home-run game of his career, hitting two left-handed, one right-handed. But on September 16, he pulled his right hamstring trying to beat out a bunt and made only two more regular-season appearances, both as a pinch-hitter. He was limited to ten at-bats in the World Series, remembered in Brooklyn for sweet redemption and in the Bronx for Mantle's absence from the lineup. When the Yankees gathered in St. Petersburg the next spring, sports columnist Dan Daniel posed the question everyone in baseball had been mulling all winter: "Which way will his career turn?"

The exhibition season offered tantalizing clues and cautionary omens. Mantle's hamstring was still weak, and he quickly reinjured it. But he struck out only once (not until the twelfth game) and hit six home runs, two of which found their way into Tampa Bay beyond Al Lang Field. A third prompted Stan Musial to say, "No home run has ever cleared my head by so much as long as I can remember."

The new Mantle announced himself in the first game of the regular season. "Mickey attained maturity on opening day," Jerry Coleman said. "It was—boom! boom!—and he had two home runs without even trying."

Mantle said he had quit trying to hit homers. "I'm beginning to learn that easy does it," he told *Times* columnist Arthur Daley.

Within a month, this new, laid-back slugger had churned up a tide of dread in opposing pitchers.

May 5 vs. Kansas City: 3 for 4, 3 RBI, 2 home runs, one of which threatened to leave Yankee Stadium.

May 18 at Chicago: 4 for 4. 2 RBI, 2 home runs (one left-handed, one right-handed), a double, and a walk. His ninth-inning home run tied the game, which the Yankees won in the tenth inning.

May 24 at Detroit: 5 for 5, 1 home run, 1 RBI.

Five days later, little Billy Crystal of Long Beach, Long Island, attended his first game at Yankee Stadium. At age eight, he was young enough to believe that Miller Huggins, Babe Ruth, and Lou Gehrig were buried beneath their monuments in center field.

Rain dampened the uniforms of the Marine color guard as the flag was raised in center field before the first game of the Memorial Day doubleheader. The soggy forecast also diminished the expected holiday crowd. There were not quite 30,000 fans in the ballpark when the players assembled along the baselines for a moment of silence. A mist shrouded the copper filigree of the Stadium's frieze and hovered over the bullpens where the starting pitchers, Pedro Ramos and Johnny Kucks, were trying to get warm. A bugler played taps.

Jack Crystal owned the Commodore Record Shop in Times Square, *the* jazz emporium in New York. Louis Armstrong had given him his tickets. A priest was seated in the row before them along the third base line. So when Mantle came to the plate in the fifth inning and Ramos came in with a waist-high fastball on a 2-2 pitch, Billy didn't see the sweet left-handed swing or the collision between ash and cowhide. Nor could he see the trajectory that carried the ball where no other had gone before. "The priest stood up and blocked my view of the ball hitting the façade," he said. "Though I do remember standing up on my chair, 'cause everybody else just went 'Aaaaaaaaah.' It was just huge. It just went up and up and up, and it just settled down at the last second. And the priest actually said, 'Holy fucking shit!'"

In the Yankee bullpen, Tommy Byrne gazed at the heavens. "You just keep lookin' and you keep wonderin', 'Well, how far is the damn thing goin' to go?'"

As Mantle rounded third base, Pascual stood on the dugout steps, waving a white towel at his compatriot on the mound. "Look what he did to you! He rocket up in right field!"

Between games, team officials consulted the archives and the blueprints and determined that the rocket had traveled 370 feet, hitting the façade 118 feet above field level, 18 inches from oblivion. Ramos thought the ball had left New York. Indeed, it ended up in Eddie Robinson's Baltimore restaurant, a gift from The Mick to the Yankee first baseman.

Much to Pascual's regret, Mantle declined Stengel's offer to rest his aching hamstring and take the rest of the afternoon off. In the fifth inning of the second game, he hit his third home run of the year off Pascual, the 141st of his career. It was a modest effort that landed only halfway up the right field bleachers. At the end of the day he was leading the majors in six offensive categories: runs (45), hits (65), total bases (135), home runs (20), RBI (50), and batting average (.425). He had struck out only twenty-one times. Even the usually imperturbable Harold Rosenthal of the *Herald Tribune* was moved to excess: The "Merry Mortician" was burying the rest of the league.

By the time the Detroit Tigers arrived two days later, the façade home run had been memorialized in front-page photographs adorned with soaring arrows. Outfielder Harvey Kuenn eyed the distance and demanded corroboration from a young sportscaster named Howard Cosell who had witnessed the clout. "Did he really hit it up there? *Really?* His strength isn't human."

Whitey Herzog, the future Hall of Fame manager who played left field for the Senators that day had been traded to Washington on Easter Sunday. Summoned to the manager's office after church services, Herzog learned his fate. "You're pretty good but you're not as good as the guy I got," Stengel said.

"Shit, I know that," Herzog replied.

How good was Casey's guy?

"Nobody could play baseball better than Mickey Mantle played it in 1956," Herzog said. For once he wasn't sabotaged by physiology. He was batting .371 with 29 home runs—ahead of Babe Ruth's 1927 pace—against the Red Sox on the Fourth of July. The Yankees held their collective breath after he charged a ball hit his way in the eleventh inning of the first game of a doubleheader. He thought he could prevent the winning run from scoring. Then he felt a familiar twinge in his right knee. "Sprained ligament on the outer aspect," said team physician Sidney Gaynor. Mantle missed the next four games.

The pain went "all around the leg" but it did not derail him for long. He won the Triple Crown, leading the American League in home runs (52), RBIs (130), and batting average (.353). He was the *Sporting News* Major League Player of the Year and the Associated Press Male Athlete of the Year. He received the Hickok Belt, awarded to the top professional athlete of the year, as well as the first-ever Babe Ruth Sultan of Swat crown as the major leagues' top slugger.

The First Perfect Yankee

"Larsen Pitches 1st Perfect Game in Series History"
Washington Post, October 9, 1956

by Shirley Povich

Of all the once-seemingly-unbreakable records—Ruth's home run total, Gehrig's "Iron Man" streak, DiMaggio's hitting streak—Don Larsen's perfect game in the 1956 World Series is perhaps most untouchable. There has been one other no-hitter in the history of postseason play (Roy Halladay in the 2010 divisional series), but Larsen's work of perfection on the grand stage of the World Series was cut from a different cloth.

NEW YORK, OCT. 8—The million-to-one shot came in. Hell froze over. A month of Sundays hit the calendar. Don Larsen today pitched a no-hit, no-run, no-man-reach-first game in a World Series.

On the mound at Yankee Stadium, the same guy who was knocked out in two innings by the Dodgers on Friday came up today with one for the record books, posting it there in solo grandeur as the only Perfect Game in World Series history.

With it, the Yankee right-hander shattered the Dodgers, 2-0, and beat Sal Maglie, while taking 64,519 suspense-limp fans into his act.

First there was mild speculation, then there was hope, then breaths were held in slackened jaws in the late innings as the big mob wondered if the big Yankee right-hander could bring off for them the most fabulous of all World Series games.

Yanks Grab 3–2 Series Lead

He did it, and the Yanks took the Series lead three games to two, to leave the Dodgers as thunderstruck as Larsen himself appeared to be at the finish of his feat.

Larsen whizzed a third strike past pinch hitter Dale Mitchell in the ninth. That was all. It was over. Automatically, the massive 226-pounder from San Diego started walking from the mound toward the dugout, as pitchers are supposed to do at the finish.

But this time there was woodenness in his steps and his stride was that of a man in a daze. The spell was broken for Larsen when Yogi Berra ran onto the infield to embrace him.

It was not Larsen jumping for joy. It was the more demonstrative Berra. His battery mate leaped full tilt at the big guy. In self-defense, Larsen caught Berra in mid-air as one would catch a frolicking child, and that's how they made their way toward the Yankee bench, Larsen carrying Berra.

There wasn't a Brooklyn partisan left among the 64,519, it seemed, at the finish. Loyalties to the Dodgers evaporated in sheer enthrallment at the show big Larsen was giving them, for this was a day when the fans could boast that they were there.

So at the finish, Larsen had brought it off, and erected for himself a special throne in baseball's Hall of Fame, with the first Perfect Game pitched in major-league baseball since Charlie Robertson of the White Sox against Detroit 34 years ago.

Maglie Just Watches

But this was one more special. This one was in a World Series. Three times, pitchers had almost come through with no-hitters, and there were three one-hitters in the World Series books, but never a no-man-reach-base classic.

The tragic victim of it all, sitting on the Dodger bench, was sad Sal Maglie, himself a five-hit pitcher today in his bid for a second Series victory over the Yankees. He was out of the game, technically, but he was staying to see it out and it must have been in disbelief that he saw himself beaten by another guy's World Series no-hitter.

Mickey Mantle hit a home run today in the fourth inning and that was all the impetus the Yankees needed, but no game-winning home run ever wound up with such emphatic second billing as Mantle's this afternoon.

It was an exciting wallop but in the fourth inning only, because after that Larsen was the story today, and the dumbfounded Dodgers could wonder how this same guy who couldn't last out two innings in the second game could master them so thoroughly today.

He did it with a tremendous assortment of pitches that seemed to have five forward speeds, including a slow one that ought to have been equipped with back-up lights.

Larsen had them in hand all day. He used only 97 pitches, not an abnormally low number because 11 pitches an inning is about normal for a good day's work. But he was the boss from the outset. Only against Pee Wee Reese in the first inning did he lapse to a three-ball count, and then he struck Reese out. No other Dodger was ever favored with more than two called balls by Umpire Babe Pinelli.

Behind him, his Yankee teammates made three spectacular fielding plays to put Larsen in the Hall of Fame. There was one in the second inning that calls for special description. In the fifth, Mickey Mantle ranged far back into left center to haul in Gil Hodges' long drive with a backhand shoetop grab that was a beaut. In the eighth, the same Hodges made another bid to break it up, but Third Baseman Andy Carey speared his line drive.

Little did Larsen, the Yankees, the Dodgers or anybody among the 64,519 in the stands suspect that when Jackie Robinson was robbed of a line-drive hit in the second inning, the stage was being set for a Perfect Game.

McDougald Saves It

Robinson murdered the ball so hard that Third Baseman Andy Carey barely had time to fling his glove upward in a desperate attempt to get the ball. He could only deflect it. But, luckily, shortstop Gil McDougald was backing up, and able to grab the ball on one bounce. By a half-step, McDougald got Robinson at first base, and Larsen tonight can be grateful that it was not the younger, fleeter Robinson of a few years back but a heavy-legged, 40-year-old Jackie.

As the game wore on, Larsen lost the edge that gave him five strikeouts in the first four innings, and added only two in the last five. He had opened up by slipping called third strikes past both Gilliam and Reese in the first inning.

Came the sixth, and he got Furillo and Campanella on pops, fanned Maglie. Gilliam, Reese and Snider were easy in the seventh. Robinson tapped out, Hodges lined out and Amoros flied out in the eighth. And now it was the ninth, and the big Scandinavian-American was going for the works with a calm that was exclusive with him.

Furrilo gave him a bit of a battle, fouled off four pitches, then flied mildly to Bauer. He got two quick strikes on Campanella, got him on a slow roller to Martin.

Now it was the left-handed Dale Mitchell, pinch hitting for Maglie.

Ball one came in high. Larsen got a called strike.

On the next pitch, Mitchell swung for strike two.

Then the last pitch of the game, Mitchell started to swing, but didn't go through with it.

But it made no difference because Umpire Pinelli was calling it Strike Number Three, and baseball history was being made.

Maglie's Brilliance Forgotten

Maglie himself was a magnificent figure out there all day, pitching hitless balls and leaving the Yankees a perplexed gang, until suddenly with two out in the fourth, Mickey Mantle, with two called strikes against him, lashed the next pitch on a line into the right-field seats to give the Yanks a 1-0 lead.

There was doubt about that Mantle homer because the ball was curving and would it stay fair? It did. In their own half of the inning, the Dodgers had no such luck. Duke Snider's drive into the same seats had curved foul by a few feet. The disgusted Snider eventually took a third strike.

The Dodgers were a luckless gang and Larsen a fortunate fellow in the fifth. Like Mantle, Sandy Amoros lined one into the seats in right, and that one was a near thing for the Yankees. By what seemed only inches, it curved foul, the umpires ruled.

Going into the sixth, Maglie was pitching a one-hitter—Mantle's homer— and being outpitched. The old guy lost some of his stuff in the sixth, though, and the Yankees came up with their other run.

Extra Run Unnecessary

Carey led off with a single to center, and Larsen sacrificed him to second on a daring third-strike bunt. Hank Bauer got the run in with a single to left. There might have been a close play at the plate had Amoros come up with the ball cleanly, but he didn't and Carey scored unmolested.

Now there were Yanks still on first and third with only one out, but they could get no more. Hodges made a scintillating pickup of Mantle's smash, stepped on first and threw to home for a double play on Bauer, who was trying to score. Bauer was trapped in a rundown and caught despite a low throw by Campanella that caused Robinson to fall into the dirt.

But the Yankees weren't needing any more runs for Larsen today. They didn't even need their second one, because they were getting a pitching job for the books this memorable day in baseball.

Meet Me at the Copa

from *When You Come to a Fork in the Road, Take It!*

by Yogi Berra

Though Casey Stengel was a bit vague in his recollection of the infamous Copacabana incident and the aftermath that led to the trade of Billy Martin (see pages 152–155), Yogi Berra offers a firsthand account of the evening's events. As only Yogi could put it, "Nobody did nothin' to nobody."

Nobody Did Nothin' to Nobody

When you're part of a team, you stand up for your teammates. Your loyalty is to them. You protect them through good and bad, because they'd do the same for you. The Yankee teams I played on were real close-knit guys always pulling for each other, always looking out for one another—on the field and off. Everybody got along, everybody fit in.

When Elston Howard joined us in 1955, he was the first black man on the Yankees, but we always made sure Ellie felt part of us. There was segregation in the South, and Ellie was forced to stay in separate hotels in Florida in those days. George Weiss, our general manager, got some heat for taking so long to get a black player, but we players always made Ellie feel like he belonged. We always tried to make things as pleasant for him as we could. Phil Rizzuto was like a father to him, always talking to him. I used to go with Ellie shopping for clothes and to the movies, and he always played in our card games. If a bunch of us went out, we asked Ellie to come along.

As I said, we were a team. We ate together. We socialized and played cards together. Sometimes we went out with our wives together. Unfortunately, that's what happened on May 16, 1957, when we took Billy Martin out to celebrate his birthday—his twenty-ninth. Billy was a bachelor, but Whitey Ford, Mickey Mantle, Hank Bauer, and I brought our wives, since we didn't have a game the next afternoon. I also brought Johnny Kucks, who was one of our young pitchers, to join us. Carmen thought going out would help relax me since I wasn't hitting too well at the time. She suggested we all see the singer Johnny Ray at the Waldorf and then go to the Copacabana, which was a real popular club on West 51st Street, to see Sammy Davis.

Well, a drunk customer began heckling Sammy Davis, and Bauer told the guy to shut up. Then one of the guy's friends challenged Hank to a fight. We all got up but were separated from the drunk's friends by the restaurant staff. The drunk went into the men's room, and minutes later when Hank went in, the drunk was knocked out on the floor with a broken nose. It looked like Hank had slugged him, but in actuality it was one of the Copacabana bouncers. We all left through the kitchen, hoping nobody would see us or we'd be in big trouble. But Hank got a call from a crime reporter at 4:30 in the morning because the drunk was at the police station swearing out a warrant for his arrest. The next day all hell broke loose. "Bauer in Brawl in Copa" was the headline on page one, and George Weiss was furious. He was sure Billy Martin had started the whole thing and called all of us into his office to get the real story, but nobody admitted to hitting the guy. Then he called me aside, I think knowing I was always honest and would tell what really happened. That's when I said, "Nobody did nothin' to nobody." Still, Weiss was convinced we were all covering up to protect Martin, and he was real angry we'd gone out on the town. The owner, Dan Topping, thought we had hurt the Yankee image and immediately fined us all $1,000, which was a lot of money in those days.

But in a way, the Copacabana incident brought us even closer together. We were all angry about the fines, which came before the hearing and made it look like we were all guilty. And Weiss was still angry at us for being at the Copa. I think he thought we had no business going out with our wives, and that made us angry, too. We were in third place when the Copacabana thing happened. I won't say it rallied us, but we did go on to win the pennant. As it turned out, the case was dropped for lack of evidence, but Billy still got the blame—he was traded to Kansas City soon after.

The Major Takes the Reins

From *Season of Glory: The Amazing Saga of the 1961 New York Yankees*

by Ralph Houk and Robert W. Creamer

When both Ralph Houk and Mickey Mantle speak up to say that 1961 was the best season they ever experienced, you just might want to listen. Interspersed with commentary from baseball historian and renowned Babe Ruth biographer, Robert W. Creamer, these passages from the "Major" himself help explain why 1961 was such a magical time to be a Yankee.

After watching Mantle leave the game in his bloodstained uniform, Ford said, "The bandages were so thick I couldn't believe the blood could come through." But Mantle only said, "It looked worse than it was. It was bleeding, but it didn't really hurt that bad." Maybe so, but those Yankees who ducked back into the clubhouse to watch the trainer apply fresh dressings to the wound winced when they saw the gaping, bleeding hole in Mantle's buttock. "It was as deep as a golf ball," Blanchard said, "with blood oozing out of it." [Mantle had an abscess in his hip.] Yet Mantle had batted twice, had hit the ball hard twice, and had run hard to first base twice. In the outfield in the second inning, he had run toward right to back up Maris on a long fly ball.

After Mantle left the game, Maris scored on a double play and the Yankees took a 1-0 lead. They scored another run in the fifth, two in the sixth, and three in the seventh when Lopez, playing for Mantle, drove in two and scored a third, to win 7-0.

◆ ◆ ◆

The Yankees were now ahead three games to one in the Series, and the Reds looked thoroughly beaten. But Houk was worried. Mantle was out for the Series. So was Ford. Berra had been hurt in the seventh inning of the fourth game when he slid face-first into a tag at third base, cutting his eye, wrenching his neck, and injuring his shoulder, and he couldn't play. Stafford had a stiff wrist. Cerv had torn cartilage in his knee a week before the season ended and missed the entire Series. Terry, who was due to start the fifth game, had been hit hard by the Reds in his earlier start. If the Reds beat Terry with Jay (who had already defeated the Yankees), the Series would go back to New York, where, if Stafford was unable to start, Coates would have to go against Purkey, who had pitched so well against the Yankees in the third game. Without Mantle and Berra, the Yankee attack was not as strong against righthanders, and Jay and Purkey were good right-handers. If Jay and Purkey both won, the Series would be tied at three games apiece, with Ford no longer available to pitch the showdown seventh game.

Ralph Houk:

> I was worried, and I wasn't making believe. We had a 3-1 lead in the Series but we were running pretty thin, and it's been proved recently that you don't always win with a 3-1 lead in games. I'd seen us come back from a 3-1 deficit in 1958 to beat the Braves. Maybe everybody else thought we had it locked up, but I didn't. I thought we could lose and then lose again, and we'd come down to a seventh game and I wouldn't have Ford. I was worried. I was plenty worried. I wanted to win that fifth game bad.
>
> The thing was, I didn't know who I'd have playing in the sixth and seventh games if we had to play two more. Ford was out. I'd been expecting to have Whitey ready if it ever went to a seventh game, and now I didn't have him. He could hardly walk with that toe. Mantle was out for the Series, and Yogi was through, with his neck and his shoulder and his eye where that ball hit him in the face. He could hardly see. He couldn't have played anymore. We didn't have Cerv. And Stafford had that stiff wrist.
>
> I'm telling you, people didn't realize it but we were in pretty bad shape. No Ford, no Mantle, no Yogi, and we were down to the point where I was looking around for starters. The night before that fifth game I just lay there in bed thinking about it. I didn't sleep all night. Really, I don't think I slept at all, and usually I can always sleep a little bit. I kept seeing Mickey coming off the field with the blood

coming out of his pants, and that kind of upset the whole thing. To win a World Series without Mantle was pretty hard. And not having Yogi and Ford—hell, I was worried. That fifth game was a very, very big ball game. If we didn't win it, we could blow the whole Series. I wanted to win that fifth game bad.

He didn't stay worried long. Richardson opened the game with a single. After Kubek and Maris flied out, Blanchard hit a two-run homer. Howard followed with a double, and Skowron hit a long single to score Howard. At this point Jay, the Cincinnati starter, had faced six men and had given up two singles, a double, a home run, and two long fly balls. Hutchinson took him out and brought in 21-year-old Jim Maloney, later a sensational pitcher for Cincinnati, but then an uncertain youngster. Lopez, playing left field for Berra, hit a triple off Maloney, and Boyer hit a double to give the Yankees a 5-0 lead, and in the second inning Maris doubled Kubek home with another run.

But then Terry gave up three hits himself in the first two innings and in the bottom of the third came unraveled as the Reds scored three times to force their way back into the game. Robinson's huge home run over the fence in deep right center in the third was the sixth hit off Terry, and that was enough for Houk. Out went Terry and in came Daley, who had pitched only a third of an inning thus far in the Series. Daley got out of the inning, but the Yankees' big lead had been cut in half.

Almost automatically, they responded in their next time at bat. Kubek singled, Blanchard doubled, Howard walked, Skowron drove in two runs with a single, and Lopez, making up for his disappointing season, followed his earlier triple with a three-run homer over the center-field fence. The Yankees led 11-3.

Post hit a two-run homer off Daley an inning later, but again the Yankees reacted. Lopez got his third straight hit—a squeeze bunt with the bases loaded—and Daley hit a sacrifice fly. Hutchinson, trudging wearily back and forth to the mound, used eight pitchers in the game trying to quench the flood of Yankee power. Daley pitched six and two-thirds innings and gave up only one more hit after Post's home run. The Yankees won the game 13-5, and Houk, the rookie manager, had won the World Series.

"Gosh, I'm happy," Blanchard said after the game.

His manager, the old company commander, smiled and said, "Our thin gray line did pretty well out there today."

◆ ◆ ◆

After a joyful train ride back to New York, with a steak and champagne celebration on board, the Yankees had a formal victory party at the Savoy Hilton, where Houk's managerial career had begun a year earlier. In keeping with the dignity the Yankees were so proud of in those days, the party was quiet. Not all the players were there. Mantle, feeling poorly, had gone straight home from Cincinnati, and so had Maris, Kubek, and Blanchard.

Maris, back home in Kansas City with his family, said, "I'm a little tired of baseball. I'm ready to tie up for a while."

Mantle said, later, "I don't like to pick teams, because I played on some good ones—the first team I played on, in 1951, won five straight World Series—but my favorite was the '61 Yankees. Kubek, Richardson, Boyer, Skowron—that was the best infield I ever saw. And Roger—when people think of Roger they think of home runs, but he was a great all-around player. Never threw to the wrong base, always went from first to third on a base hit, broke up double plays. And he was a great outfielder.

"We had a great team that year. John Blanchard, a hell of a pinch-hitter. Whitey Ford, won 25 games. That was a great ball team. That was a fun year."

Two days after the Series ended—the 365th day of the year that began with Mazeroski's home run—Houk signed a new two-year contract for $50,000 a year, a 30-percent raise. "For the first time in all my years in baseball I have security," he said. "I also have a hell of a chance of winning the pennant again."

He did, in 1962 and 1963. Then he moved up to the front office for a few years before returning to the dugout to manage the Yankees from 1966 through 1973, the Tigers from 1974 through 1978, and the Red Sox from 1981 through 1984.

He put in 20 seasons as a big league manager, but none ever meant as much to him as the first one, when the Yankees won it all in 1961.

Ralph Houk:

That was the greatest year I ever had in baseball. My biggest *day* was when the Yankees kept me in 1947, which I didn't expect, and next biggest was being named manager in 1960. But for a season, it was winning the pennant and the World Series in my first year. I mean, you can't hardly top that. I certainly never made enough hits to top it. And then I got the new two-year contract at $50,000. People don't realize how much money that was then, or anyway how much it was for me.

It was a just a great year, a great year. Usually during a season, no matter what club you manage or how well you do, you have a few problems off the field with some of the players, trouble they get into during the season. Except for the Duren thing in spring training, we never had any of that all year.

It was a pleasure managing that team. They played so *good*. They played so good all season.

It kind of gives you a chill when you think back. You'd like to see it all again. God, what great years those guys had. What a season that was!

61 in '61

From *Roger Maris at Bat*

by Roger Maris and Jim Ogle

Adding to the excitement and mystique of the '61 season was Roger Maris' pursuit of Babe Ruth's storied record of 60 home runs, set in the legendary 1927 season. Jimmie Foxx and Hank Greenberg had each come within two blasts of the Babe in the 1930s, but it was fitting that the man to break the record did it in Yankee pinstripes. Maris's record would stand even longer than Ruth's had.

When I got to the park for the last game, there was one thing I was certain of—this was the end. There were no more games, there could be no more excitement about the home runs. Whatever happened today would close the book. That, in itself, was a relief. I knew that this would be do or die, sink or swim, but whatever happened there was nothing I could do, so I wasn't going to worry about it.

Once again there was that air of excitement hanging over the park. Everyone looked strangely at me. I was thinking that I knew now how the monkeys in the zoo must feel. But, at least, it would all end after today. I knew that I had hit sixty. I was happy, and no matter what happened on this final day I could tell myself that I had given it my best shot.

I knew that I would have only four, perhaps five, chances to try for the sixty-first. If I didn't get it, then I just didn't. I never had a feeling that perhaps if I did hit it, people would feel that I had topped an idol by beating Ruth. Babe had his record for 154 games, but perhaps I could get one for 162 games.

Tracy Stallard, a young right-hander, was the Boston pitcher. I knew that I wasn't going to take any walks. I was just hoping that perhaps he would be pitching trying to get me out, not to walk me. No one was going to walk me that day, I was going down swinging.

The pressure in this game, despite all it meant to me personally, was not as severe as in the 154th game. Nothing will ever equal the way I felt that day. This one, of course, was the second toughest game. I was determined to do the same as I had in the 154th . . . give it my best, go down swinging with everything I had. If I hit one, then it would be the greatest thing that ever happened to an individual. If I didn't, no one could say I didn't try.

There was a man on second when I came up in the first. I hit a long drive to left field. I found myself wishing I had pulled it. If I had and if it had gone that far to right field, it would have been in the seats. At least Stallard was trying to work on me. He threw me a fast ball low on the outside corner. It so happened that I went with the pitch and didn't try to pull it.

It was 0-0 as I came up with two out in the fourth. Each time I came up there would be a stirring in the right-field stands, but otherwise it was so quiet that I almost felt the Stadium was empty. There were no cameramen on the field. They aren't allowed on the field at the Stadium. Once again it was between Stallard and me. Every eye in the Stadium was on us. Would he pitch to me again?

There was a lot of pressure on the pitcher too. He knew what was happening. His first pitch was a ball; the crowd booed. Then the second pitch was also a ball; the boos grew louder. I knew everyone was pulling for me and I dug in a little deeper. Perhaps the booing had made Stallard mad. He's a proud young man and was only doing his job.

He wound up and delivered the 2-0 pitch. It was a good fast ball, but maybe he had got it too good. I was ready and I connected. As soon as I hit it, I knew it was number sixty-one. . . . It was the only time that the number of the homer ever flashed into my mind as I hit it. Then I heard the tremendous roar from the crowd. I could see them all standing, then my mind went blank again.

I couldn't even think as I went around the bases. I couldn't tell you what crossed my mind; I don't think anything did. I was in a daze. I was all fogged out from a very, very hectic season and an extremely difficult month. It is difficult to explain how I felt or what I thought of.

I began to come to as I got to the dugout. All my teammates were there to greet me, pound my back, and congratulate me. I saw the fans standing, giving me a wonderful ovation. I didn't know what to do. I stood up on the dugout steps and waved my hat. I was afraid I was being corny and tried to get back into the dugout, but my teammates held me up on the steps and wouldn't let me get down. It began to feel as if they would never let me down.

Even as I was standing up on the steps, something inside was telling me that now I had hit more home runs than anyone in history had ever hit in a single season. I felt very proud, but also humble. I knew I hadn't done it alone. I knew I had been helped along the way. I felt that I was a very fortunate man.

After the next half inning, I was taken under the stands to meet Sal Durante, the young man who had caught the ball. He seemed like a nice kid. He even tried to give me the ball right then, but I told him there was a reward for it and that he had better keep it so he could get his money. He gave the ball to a Yankee official for safe keeping, then stayed around until after the game. He has since got the reward and married the girl he was with that day. I wish them both good fortune.

I went to bat twice more in that game. I felt looser than I had in weeks. I felt as carefree as when I used to play on the sand lots. I just didn't care what happened at that point. I had done something no one else had ever done. I couldn't believe it. Sometimes I still find it hard to believe.

I would have been happy to leave the game after I hit the homer, but never would have. I felt I owed it to the fans to stay in all the way. I was still in a daze when the game ended, 1-0. Oddly enough it was the first 1-0 game I had ever won with a home run. Then I found that the run had also given me the RBI title again by one. That made me even happier. As I have said, I am proud of that RBI title.

Maybe I was ready to crack up at this point. I found myself thinking about the game and the score, then got the silly idea that it was lucky that I had hit the homer or we would have had to play extra innings. Certainly I was in no mood to be playing extra innings that day.

I was as happy as it is possible for anyone to be. I didn't care about it being in 162 games. It was the biggest home run of my life. What is the use of saying anything else? It was the greatest thrill that I have ever had or hope to have.

I was very happy for many reasons, but I was happiest because now it was all over. The pressure, the excitement, the anxiety were gone. There can be no more talk of homerun records. It is all in the book, and the book is closed.

I was tremendously happy to go past Ruth's record even if my season ran a little longer. I would have liked to have broken it in 154 games, but perhaps it is just as well that I didn't. At the time I still couldn't explain that feeling, but I believe I can now.

I believe that it is probably best that his record goes right on and that I have mine in 162 games. There is just something about Ruth and his record of sixty that seems to set it apart from other records. Mr. Ruth still has his record for 154 games, and I have mine for 162. Nothing has been ruined or shattered. He still has his record, and now I have mine. I am completely satisfied with it that way.

The wonderful ovation the fans had given me had convinced me that they were accepting me as the new record holder with no strings attached. Definitely, I didn't feel that they were accepting me as the home-run king. That still belongs to Babe Ruth.

Yankee Fans,
Make This One Last

"Yanks Beat Giants, 1-0; Win World Series"
New York Times, October 17, 1962

by John Drebinger

When the Yankees took on the former cross-town rival Giants, now in San Francisco, in the 1962 World Series, the result was one of the greatest series contests between two storied franchises. After alternating wins through the first six games, the Yanks pulled out a 1-0 nail-biter in the clincher. Little did fans and players know that this classic would be the last Yankee championship for 15 years.

TERRY YIELDS ONLY 4 HITS AS BOMBERS TAKE 20TH TITLE

SAN FRANCISCO, OCT. 16—Baseball's longest season ended today with the New York Yankees still the world champions.

Manager Ralph Houk's Bombers, behind the four-hit pitching of their ace right-hander, Ralph Terry, turned back the Giants, 1 to 0, in the seventh and deciding game of the 1962 World Series.

That gave the Yanks the Series, four games to three, and brought to their Stadium in the Bronx their 20th world championship.

Only seven times since 1921 have the Yanks been defeated in a World Series. But they came mighty close to losing another one today.

For in the last of the ninth, as a crowd of 43,948 looked on, the issue hung for a split second on the last play of the game.

With runners on second and third and two out, huge Willie McCovey blasted a line drive that appeared headed for right field. Had it reached its destination, two runs would have scored and folks would be dancing in the streets of San Francisco tonight.

But the ball landed squarely in the glove of the Yankee second baseman, Bobby Richardson. With that, Manager Alvin Dark's spunky Giants, who had performed spectacular feats through the long campaign, breathed their last.

Although the Yankees' tally, scored off Jack Sanford in the fifth inning, was achieved in prosaic fashion, this struggle, fought by both sides against a spanking 35-mile-an-hour wind that blew in from dead center, was perhaps the tensest and most dramatic of the Series. For Terry and Sanford this was their third meeting. Sanford had won the first one, Terry the second. This was the rubber match that was to decide everything.

And though the home folks at the time refused to believe it, it was settled in the fifth inning when Sanford, suffering a brief letdown, saw the Yanks fill the bases with nobody out on singles by Bill Skowron and Cletis Boyer and a walk to Terry.

A routine double-play that Tony Kubek plowed into drove in Skowron with the run that was to settle the issue.

Sanford Gets Single

Desperately bucking the head winds, the Giants' vaunted sluggers strove to overcome that puny tally. But in six innings a lone single, by their pitcher, Sanford, no less, was all the headway they could make against the blazing fast ball and tantalizing let-up pitches of the long and lean Yankee right-hander.

In the seventh came the Giants' second hit and this one could have wreaked havoc. For it was a tremendous triple that McCovey sent roaring into the wind. But the bases were empty, thanks to a sparkling catch in left field by young Tom Tresh. That catch made it two out and Terry fanned Orlando Cepeda for the third one.

More thrills followed in the eighth. The Yanks filled the bases and routed Sanford with nobody out, only to be halted scoreless by Billy O'Dell.

Then came the dramatics in the ninth. Matty Alou, in the role of pinch-hitter, caught the Yankee inner defense flat-footed with a beautifully executed drag bunt to the right of the mound for a hit—the third off Terry.

An expectant roar went up from the crowd, but it turned to groans as Felipe Alou and Chuck Hiller struck out. However, Terry still had to dispose of Willie Mays.

Mays Smacks Double

Willie the Wonder, whose bat had kept the Giants alive time after time during the thrill-packed days of the National League pennant race, came through again. It was his drive that Tresh had caught in left field in the seventh. But this time Willie smashed a double down the right-field line.

Only swift work by Roger Maris in the right-hand corner of the field prevented Matty Alou from scoring the tying run. However, the Giants were still breathing. They had the potential tying and winning runs on third and second, and at the plate was the 6-foot-4 inch McCovey.

Out of the Yankee dugout came Houk for a conference on the mound. Down in the Yankee bullpen Bill Stafford, winner of the third game, and Bud Daley were warming up furiously.

But the one-time Army major decided that he would sink or swim with the fellow still on the hill. McCovey took a swing and hit a tremendous drive that curved foul down the right-field line.

He swung again, and for an instant it looked like the payoff for San Francisco. But Richardson froze to the ball as it landed in his glove with a thud and in the next instant the jubilant Yanks were smothering and pounding Terry on the back.

Terry Is Two-Time Winner

The 26-year-old Oklahoman had gone into this Series with three defeats against no victories in post-season play. To this he added a fourth setback when Sanford beat him in the second game. But now, with his superb four-hitter, he was bowing out of this Series a two-time winner.

Minutes after the game, it was announced that the smiling Westerner had made off with the eighth annual *Sport Magazine* Corvette Award as the outstanding player of the 1962 Series.

For the transplanted New York Giants, who in their fifth season here had given San Francisco its first National League pennant, this was their 10th Series defeat against five victories.

However, there was no denying they had waged a spectacular fight. With only seven games remaining in the regular championship season, they were trailing the Los Angeles Dodgers by four games. But in an amazing finish, the Dodgers managed to blow their lead until the two wound up in a tie on the final day. That necessitated a playoff, which the Giants won, two games to one.

But today the Yankees, determined to give Houk his second world championship in his two years as successor to the illustrious Casey Stengel, proved a little too much for them.

The weather, still out to atone for the grand mess it had made of things by causing four postponements—one in New York and three here—turned on another sunny day. The breeze was considerably stiffer than it was yesterday, but that helped remove virtually all traces of the rain that had drenched the playing field over the weekend.

In fact, the field looked like something fresh out of a barber shop. For the overnight winds had sufficiently dried the grass to permit a much needed mowing of the outfield.

Winds Present Problem

There were no preliminaries beyond the singing of the National Anthem and both sides wasted no time getting down to the business at hand. Almost from the start, this was a matter of bucking the wind.

Veering from its customary left-field to right-field course, the wind blew straight in from dead center. As the wind increased from 25 to 35 miles an hour, right-handed as well as left-handed batters found themselves at a distinct disadvantage.

Even more trying was the wind on the fielders, who cut all sorts of fancy capers as they followed the gyrations of twisting fly balls. Once Mickey Mantle, drifting over from center for a comparatively easy pop fly, wound up plucking the ball out of Roger Maris' waiting hands in right field.

The Yanks finally solved the vexing problem. Skowron, up first in the fifth, smacked one close to the ground between short and third and into left for a single. Boyer followed with a low line-drive single to left center that swept Skowron to third.

This seemed to unsettle Sanford. Up to here the Giant right-hander, though not so near-perfect as Terry, had kept the Yanks well in hand. He had walked Richardson in the first inning and again in the third after Kubek had singled for the Bombers' first hit. But the rest he handled with comparative ease.

But here Sanford's control momentarily deserted him at a most inopportune time. With the count three balls and two strikes, he walked Terry, filling the bases with nobody out.

The Giant board of strategy elected to play it safe. Instead of moving in with the idea of cutting off the run at the plate, even at the risk of having a single poked through the drawn-in infield, they dropped back for the double play by way of second.

Kubek Grounds to Short

In this the Yankee batter, Kubek, obliged. He grounded the ball to the shortstop, Jose Pagan. But while Tony and Terry were being rubbed out, Skowron lumbered over the plate.

Richardson then fouled out, but the Yankees were one in front. As the struggle moved along, that tally loomed larger and larger.

The wind, which occasionally bothered Sanford, seemed made to order for Terry. For five innings the tall Oklahoman allowed no Giant to get on base. In fact, he still had a perfect game with two out in the sixth when his mound adversary, Sanford, ended that dream with a single to center.

But nothing came of this modest threat. It wasn't until two were out in the seventh that the Giants made their first substantial move. The second out was a spectacular running catch by Tom Tresh in the extreme left handed corner of the playing field of a vicious low drive by Mays.

Had that fallen in for a hit, the score minutes later would at least have been tied. For McCovey followed with a powerful smash into the teeth of the gale. It cleared Mantle's head to the left of center and went for a triple.

But the Giants still couldn't send that all-important tally across. For Terry here put everything he had on the ball and fanned Orlando Cepeda for the second time and that ended the inning.

In the eighth the Yanks threatened to widen the gap as they again filled the bases with nobody out. That finished Sanford, but the left-handed O'Dell turned in a brilliant relief job that kept the Bombers from scoring.

The inning opened with Pagan throwing wide to first for an error on Richardson's grounder. Tresh got an infield hit, and Mantle, hitless in thirteen official times at bat, slammed a single to right. It was only the third hit of the series for The Switcher, who'll never look back on this one with pride. In the sixth he had drawn a pass only to get picked off first base.

However, his hit here, though too sharp to drive in Richardson, filled the bases and there still was nobody out. But O'Dell came on with five pitches and stopped the Bombers in their tracks.

Whitey Tells All

From *Whitey and Mickey*

by Whitey Ford with Joseph Durso

Though he was once thought of as simply a nice addition to New York's renowned "big three" rotation (Reynolds, Raschi, and Lopat), it didn't take long for Whitey Ford to rise to the top. He was a pitcher who did whatever it took to win, and as his strength and health declined with age, he got creative with the ball. In this piece, Whitey lets us in on a few secrets.

Okay, so much for the mud and the cuts and the spitters. They were child's play compared to the main event: the *Ring*. I always figured that he'd be a secret forever, but since I'm laying it all on the line, I might as well go all the way.

The ring. I had this friend who was a jeweler, and I had him make up a ring for me. This was late in my career, and I was really using my street-smart overtime. I told him exactly what I wanted—a half-inch-by-quarter-inch piece of a rasp, all nice and scratchy like a file. Then we got this stainless steel ring and he welded it onto the hunk of rasp.

I'd wear the ring on my right hand like a wedding ring and, since I'm left-handed, that was my glove hand. So, during games, I'd just stand behind the mound like any other pitcher rubbing up a new ball and I'd take the glove off and rub up the ball. That rasp would do some job on it, too. Whenever I needed a ground ball, I'd cut it good. It was as though I had my own tool bench out there with me.

To hide it, I even got a skin-colored Band-Aid and wrapped it around the ring to match my finger. Camouflage and all.

I also worked out some signs with Elston to warn him which way the ball was going to break. I'd flap my glove, meaning that I was going to try something, the way pitchers flap their glove when they're recycling the catcher's signals or adding numbers to them. You know, like a quarterback calling an automatic at the line of scrimmage. But in my case, the flap told the catcher to keep his eyes open because I had something going. Then I'd brush my glove down or across my body to give him an extra clue what to expect.

I've got to admit it worked like a charm. Nobody got on to it, and I didn't go around talking about it in the dugout or anything like that—guys get traded to other teams, and I didn't want *that* to get around. Then one day we were playing Cleveland in Yankee Stadium and my ring and I pitched together for the last time. They caught me using it. They didn't realize exactly what was going on, but it was a close call, too close to keep tempting fate with.

I had just struck out a guy and Elston rolled the ball back to the mound because it was the third out in the inning. Then the Indians' pitcher, Mudcat Grant, came out to pitch and he picked up the ball. Right away he showed it to the umpire, who for some reason didn't say anything.

For a minute, I thought maybe I was getting a reprieve. But it didn't last. Alvin Dark, who was the Indians' manager, started saving foul balls that were hit into their dugout, and finally he showed them to the umpire, Hank Soar. And Soar came over to me and said, "How are you cutting the ball?"

Then he spotted my ring and got to the point. "What's that?" he asked me. And—Joannie forgive me—I said, "My wedding ring."

Well, all hell didn't break loose, as I thought it would. But they were on to me, so I slipped the old rasp-ring into my pants and got rid of it after the inning was over. I couldn't afford to be caught with the evidence on me.

After a game in those days, I used to give the ring to our trainer, Joe Soares, and he'd wrap it up in some gauze and hide it in the bottom of one of his trunks with the pills and bandages and medical supplies. The year after I quit pitching, I was going to show the ring to Steve Hamilton, one of our pitchers, who was also a professor down in Kentucky in the off-season. So I went to Joe and said, "Where's the ring?" He said, "I threw it out the day after you retired. I wasn't going to get caught with that thing in my medical case."

Imagine that. After all those delicate moves on the mound, Joe Soares chickened out. I guess I should've been happy that I'd never been caught, either. But I was sort of teed off.

"Hell," I said, kind of irritated, "it cost me a hundred bucks to have it made."

PART V

The Fall and Rise of the Bronx Bombers

1965–1981

If you followed professional baseball anytime between the inauguration of President Warren G. Harding in 1921 and the election of Lyndon Baines Johnson in 1964, you might have assumed that the Yankees were simply preordained to win. But, if you came of age as a baseball fan in the mid-1960s (and had no awareness of the sport's history), you may not have viewed the Yankees any differently than you did, say, the Cleveland Indians or even the Washington Senators. After winning five consecutive pennants from 1960 to 1964—but "only" two World Series titles—the Yanks began a precipitous slide into the second division, including their first last place finish since 1912.

Not that the rosters of this era were devoid of talent. Catcher Elston Howard continued his mastery of handling pitchers, even as those pitchers won fewer and fewer games for New York. Thurman Munson assumed the mantle of great backstops in the following decade, tearing up the league as a rookie in 1970. Munson's life would ultimately come to a tragic end in the decade's final year—those bookend moments are captured here by renowned writers Marty Appel and Thomas Boswell.

By the late 1970s, the Bombers were back on top of the standings and the front pages, led by the combustible combination of owner George Steinbrenner, manager Billy Martin, and star player Reggie Jackson.

In addition to marking the resurgence of a once and future dynasty, this period in Yankee history featured two landmark and highly entertaining "tell-all" books by the players who were there: Jim Bouton's *Ball Four* and Sparky Lyle's *Bronx Zoo*.

Thurman Munson, Chris Chambliss, and Reggie Jackson, 1977. *NY Daily News/Getty Images*

How to Care for Your Very Own Pitcher

From *Catching*

by Elston Howard

Meet Elston Howard, catcher for the New York Yankees and part-time psychologist. The supposed mental fragility of major league pitchers is an intriguing phenomenon that Howard succinctly sums up: pitchers are human. This pieces offers readers a glimpse into the relationship between a catcher and his pitching staff, as told by a Yankee great who caught the likes of Whitey Ford, Jim Bouton, and Mel Stottlemyre.

Psychology

No matter what anyone may say to the contrary, pitchers are human. They all have human weaknesses and peculiarities, and every one is different. A catcher, to be successful in organized baseball, has to be a little bit of a psychologist. He has to know what sort of treatment a pitcher will respond to and what each man's weaknesses are. For it is up to the catcher to keep the pitcher from blowing his cool in an emergency or from going to pieces after a few bad breaks. Nearly every pitcher, like nearly every ballplayer, responds well to encouragement and praise. And you are the man who has to supply it. Above all, you must never blow your own stack under pressure, or let your own courage droop. If you ever lose your courage and aggressiveness, not only the pitcher but the whole team will go downhill.

You have to know exactly what to offer every pitcher in the way of a target and what to do when his good pitch does not seem to be coming into the strike zone. If the man is wild, it is your job to settle him down. If he gets angry, you have to cool him off. If he loses heart, you have got to build him up again. And if he gets careless, you may have to needle him awake.

The Hard Throwers

One of the wildest pitchers I ever handled, and the hardest thrower, was Ryne Duren, onetime relief pitcher with the Yankees, who could throw a baseball through a bale of hay, pretty near. Before Ralph Houk got hold of Ryne in Denver, Duren could walk ten in a row. He was so wild it wasn't safe to stand anywhere near the plate, for his fast ball would knock a horse over. About all Ryne had besides his fast ball was a little slider. But that's all he needed, for most batters never saw anything but a blur when he let his fast ball go. In Denver, Ryne learned control so that he could pitch in the big leagues. But he was always right on the edge of wildness, and you had to offer him that great big target—legs spread, body half erect, glove centered against the body-protector, so you became a sort of giant bull's-eye for him to aim at.

Another hard thrower in his day, who also had a tendency to go wild, was Bob Turley. When he was unsteady, he became wild high and was likely to let a ball fly right over your head to the backstop. I always gave him a good low target, down on one knee, with the glove right on the ground.

Jim Coates was another wild man. He was very likely to lose his control after a man got a hit. He did not believe *any* man had a right to get a hit off him, and his neck would get red as soon as anybody belted a ball into fair territory. And Jim could throw exceptionally hard, too. He once actually broke his own forearm through snapping off his curve so hard. The treatment for Jim was to talk to him a lot. I believe I spent more time talking to Jim than to any other pitcher I ever knew. I would just urge him to slow down, to cool off, and to keep that good pitch coming. I would tell him the hit was lucky, that the pitch had been good, and that the next guy was probably going to pop one up.

That sort of talk is good for any pitcher. Even the best of them have to be reminded that they really can get the batters out and that their best pitch is still working. Sometimes you don't need to do much more than carry the ball a short way out toward the mound to give the pitcher a chance to settle down. For most wild men have a tendency to work too fast.

A pitcher who works fast is too often just what the batter hopes for. The longer the batter has to wait between pitches, the more likely the tension is to build in some hitters, and so you should never let your pitcher speed up too much.

Talking to the Pitcher

Many people will ask what the catcher says to the pitcher when he walks out to talk to him. Well, he doesn't say anything too profound. It's usually just a reminder of what they decided to throw to this man when they were talking over the line-up before the game. Or, if the last man has got a solid hit, it may just be to tell the pitcher that he threw a good pitch, that he should not let the hit get him down, that the man at bat can be got out on a good pitch. Or if the pitcher has been getting wild high, the catcher may tell him he is going to provide a low target and he should forget the batter and concentrate on the target.

Sometimes you go out to remind the pitcher that there is a fast man on first and that the man at bat is a good hit-and-run man so there is no need to keep the runner close. Or tell him to forget about what has gone before. "Just hold them now, and we'll get those runs back. Come into the strike zone with something on the ball. Don't let up! This next guy is our problem now."

Every now and then you do run up against a pitcher who has to be needled a little to make him work hard, who has to be reminded to hustle his tail over to first on a ball hit to his left, and who has to be told over and over again that the situation is serious. But there aren't many of those, and even some of those have to be handled with kid gloves and a little flattery. I think pitchers in general are more likely to get discouraged than they are to get lazy.

The hard ones to deal with are the ones who keep shaking you off. You never want your pitcher to throw a pitch he does not want to pitch, so it is sometimes necessary to go out and explain your call—that this man is looking for the curve, that he has edged a little closer to the plate, or that the pitcher's good pitch has lost some of its hum and he should use it as a waste pitch for awhile, until it comes back.

The Strikeout Pitch

As I said before, it is extremely important that you know what your pitcher can throw, and how his pitches act. Some pitchers have difficulty getting the breaking ball into the strike zone consistently, and you must have that in mind as you work with that type. Some pitchers throw a fast ball that has a slight break on it, like a slider. Then there are the guys who can put all their pitches where they want to—on the days when they are good. Whitey Ford, my favorite pitcher, is one of these. As I have said earlier, on three-and-two I can ask Whitey for anything. But fellows like that, luckily for the hitters, do not show up too often. There are plenty of good pitchers who just can't be trusted to put the curve ball or slider into the strike zone on three-and-two. Then you have to stick with your fast ball for the strikeout pitch.

But actually there is no better strikeout pitch in my book than a letter-high fast ball. When Al Downing is right, he can really get you out on that pitch and I like to depend on it. But Downing has a fine slider too, so we can often fool the batter who likes the fast ball, or if his fast ball is coming in too high we can keep mixing in those good sliders until Al gets so he can keep the fast ball low again.

I think the best slider I ever caught was thrown by Mel Stottlemyre. He can keep it low, too, and it is so good the batter just cannot lay off. It is ideal for giving you that nice ground ball that provides the double plays.

You have to catalogue all these things about your pitchers, just as you keep book on the batters, for you don't want to be guilty of asking a pitcher to throw something he can't control. And you can't count on the pitcher to know what pitch is working best. There are some guys who want to throw the fast ball regardless, or who want to get tricky when the fast ball is needed.

The Next Great
Yankee Captain

From *Munson: Life and Death of a Yankee Captain*

by Marty Appel

*The best Yankee teams featured elite catchers—Bill Dickey won
8 championships, Yogi Berra won 10, and Elston Howard won 4.
But Thurman Munson was more than just the next in line. He was
the heart and soul of the franchise as it returned to greatness in the
1970s, and the first Yankee captain since Lou Gehrig.*

The 1970 Yankees had only two players remaining from their last World Series
in 1964—Mel Stottlemyre and Steve Hamilton. There were a few players who
had been teammates on the Mantle-era Yankees, notably Roy White and
Bobby Murcer. But essentially, the rise of Thurman Munson in 1970 was the
first building block toward the three championships that awaited the team
later in the decade. Each year, one or two new additions would enhance the
roster, until the team was ready to return to an elite status.

Munson wasn't especially patient with that plan. A battler, a winner, a
guy who took every game as a challenge, he appreciated that the 1970 Yanks
were having a good year, but he wanted a pennant, not just a good year. He
took little pleasure in the team doing well so long as the Orioles were doing
better. He wanted to be those guys, and he'd pump his fist at the pitchers in key
situations and want more.

"Even as a rookie, he had a confidence and maturity back there," says
Stottlemyre. "We in turn had confidence in him. He was a kid, but he was very
mature as a major league player. We loved pitching to him."

The fans felt that spirit and liked to see a guy come along who didn't give
in to complacency and mediocrity. The fans were in love with Munson early
on, embracing him as New York fans can do—quickly.

A prime example of this came in August 1970, when he was on Reserve duty at Fort Dix and not expected back in time to play at all on Sunday in a doubleheader game against Baltimore. However, he drove impetuously and made it to Yankee Stadium—eighty-six miles—in a little over an hour, in time for the sixth inning of the second game. He listened to the game on WMCA radio as he rushed up the Jersey Turnpike. He went straight to the clubhouse and got into his uniform, emerging into the dugout, where Houk and his teammates greeted him warmly. "Grab a bat and pinch-hit," said Houk.

Out of the dugout popped Munson. In the press box, Bob Fishel tapped me on the arm with his pencil and pointed toward the on-deck circle. He was smiling. The fans did not expect to see him and his appearance on the field brought a tremendous roar from the crowd. To have been there at that moment was to see Thurman appreciated at a new level—our guy, and our hero.

He lined out to Brooks Robinson at third, but that wasn't the point. The response to his arrival signaled a bond between him and the fans that would never fade. If you could define the moment the fans fell in love with the future captain of this franchise, that was it.

Munson had arrived with a flourish, very much a part of the team, already emerging as a leader, and surely as "one of the guys."

"Thurm wanted so much to be included in the little 'side trips' that I would arrange on off days," recalls Fritz Peterson. "The routine was 'okay Tugs,' or 'okay, Beer Can' (nicknames I'd given him), 'you just wait out in the hallway [of the hotel] and we'll pick you up when we get up and you can come along,' when we would go to a lake or motorbiking, or whatever. He was great to have along.

"Once we went riding motorized trail bikes—Stottlemyre, Bahnsen, Munson, and me. All of a sudden he made a sharp curve and we all followed. He was going too fast. He missed the curve, went straight, and disappeared. He had driven right off the road into a deep ravine. The bike turned over twice, the headlights and tail lights were smashed, and Thurman was cut and bruised all over. He had so much pride in not getting hurt that when we reached him and saw he was alive, he just said, 'Let's go.'"

Munson kept lifting his average day by day until, on September 17, he went two for five against the Red Sox and reached the .300 mark. He never looked back and finished at .302 for the season, tops on the team. After the 1-for-30 start, he hit .322. After July 21, he hit .370. And he led all the league's catchers with 80 assists, half of them nailing would-be base stealers.

The line drives kept coming off his bat, and the team was playing very well. The Yankees had moved into second place on August 1—rarefied air for this team—and never relinquished it. The Orioles were so good that their ultimate margin was fourteen and a half games over New York, but the

Yanks won ninety-three games, certainly their best season since 1964, with Lindy McDaniel recording 29 saves and Peterson winning 20. Although it was embarrassing to those who remembered the Yankees winning pennants every year, the team celebrated the clinching of second place with a modest champagne celebration in the clubhouse.

"I know old Yankee purists must have been thinking that celebrating second place was really bush," said Munson, "but we enjoyed it."

The Baseball Writers' Association named him first on twenty-three of twenty-four ballots as he easily won the Rookie of the Year Award. The only strange thing about it was that *The Sporting News* Rookie of the Year Award, voted on by players, somehow went to Cleveland outfielder Ray Foster, who hit 23 homers to Munson's 6. (Foster would hit 45 in a three-season career.)

Players always like to think they are the best judges of other players, and while it is hard to dispute that intellectually, they have occasionally cast some really dumb votes when given the opportunity. Most notably, they awarded a Gold Glove for fielding prowess to Rafael Palmeiro in 1999 when he only played twenty-eight games at first base all season.

Thurman was the first catcher to win Rookie of the Year honors in the American League since the award was created in 1947, and the sixth Yankee to win the honor in that time. The only other catcher to win the award was Johnny Bench of the Reds, who had won it in the National League two years earlier. Here, then, you had the beginnings of a decade in which Munson and Bench would be the two premier catchers in their respective leagues, perennial all-stars, World Series rivals, and admirers of each other.

Bench would ultimately come to be thought of as perhaps the greatest catcher in the game's history. Prior to him, there had been no clear-cut winner. The debate would include Gabby Hartnett, Mickey Cochrane, Bill Dickey, Yogi Berra, and Roy Campanella, with a nod to Josh Gibson of the Negro Leagues. Although Bench's lifetime batting average would only be .267, he had a great highlight reel and revolutionized defensive play at the position. Thurman was honored to be compared to him.

Oh yes, but then there was Carlton Fisk.

Fisk was the anti-Munson. If Affirmed needed Alydar, if Ali needed Frazier, and if Evert needed Navratilova, Munson and Fisk needed each other.

Fisk first tasted the big leagues on September 18, 1969, about a month after Thurman did. It was enough to eventually make him a four-decade player.

He played a little bit in 1971, and then won the Rookie of the Year Award in 1972, making him the *second* A.L. catcher to nab the honor.

In many ways, he was everything Munson was not—tall, handsome, graceful, maybe even a little delicate in his movements and body language. The players would sometimes tease him about the latter as only players can. His famous "coaxing" of his walk-off homer in the 1975 World Series was an example of what opposing players saw as the delicate movements.

People think there was always a Yankee-Red Sox rivalry, going back to 1903, when the Highlanders (the original Yankees) were formed, and certainly heightened by the sale of Babe Ruth to the Yankees in 1920, and later by Joe DiMaggio and Ted Williams being opposing players.

In fact, there really wasn't much of a rivalry at all after the Sox fell into hard times after the Ruth sale. A rivalry can only be strong when both teams are strong. And for a long, long time, leading to the Munson-Fisk years, tickets to Fenway Park or Yankee Stadium for Yankee-Red Sox games were not that hard to get.

The Red Sox "Impossible Dream" pennant of 1967 turned a moribund team into a good one, something that, remarkably, is still going on. Not since Ruth helped the Yankees win the 1921 pennant—their first—has a single season so turned around the fortunes of a franchise.

But the Yankees didn't catch up right away. While the Red Sox remained strong after 1967, the Yankees were still down, save for the surprising 1970 finish. It wasn't until the mid-seventies that both teams peaked, and Munson and Fisk seemed to be the symbols of both.

Fisk was the New England lumberjack, Munson the Ohio blue-collar worker who led their teams to the top of the American League East.

Munson genuinely hated Fisk. And it was pretty mutual.

"I know they were aware of each other's presence," said Bill Lee, the Red Sox pitcher. "Munson was always checking Fisk's stats, and Carlton would go nuts any time a reporter mentioned Munson's name."

It was partly due to his competitive nature and of course it was fueled by the rising rivalry between the two glamour franchises, but Munson was also jealous and resentful of the attention Fisk was getting, and the All-Star elections he was winning.

"It's Curt Gowdy on the Game of the Week always playing him up," said Munson. "He used to be the Red Sox announcer, he loves them, and now he's on the national games and he's always talking about Fisk this and Fisk that. And you know what? Fisk is always getting hurt, and I'm always playing through injuries, and he's getting credit for things he might do if he was healthy. Gowdy has his thing for him."

True or not, it was what Munson believed. (Gowdy had earlier been a Yankees announcer.) Thurman thought you played hurt. "Whenever someone was complaining about anything, Thurman would look at him and say, 'So, retire!'" said Brian Doyle, later a teammate. "It was a wake-up call to remember how lucky we all were to be playing big-league baseball."

And the Fisk attention on NBC did tend to reflect itself in the annual All-Star Game fan voting, which had begun in 1969 by edict of Commissioner Bowie Kuhn.

Players always have an arm's-length regard for announcers anyway. They don't hear broadcasts unless they are in the clubhouse for a bathroom break or a change of jersey. Much of what they know about announcers is fueled by secondhand interpretations. One of my biggest problems when I was doing the Yankees' PR was trying to tame what the players' wives were telling their husbands that the announcers said about them. They often got it wrong, or misunderstood the context, and it invariably caused problems.

Munson's point about Fisk's injuries, though, was not off the mark. From 1972 through 1976, Fisk caught 516 games and was on the disabled list four times. In the same span, Thurman caught 728 games and was never on the disabled list. In fact, Munson would play his entire career without ever going on the DL.

Those were the years in which Munson formed his opinion about the brittle Fisk.

Of course, Fisk turned out to be one durable son of a gun. He would go on to be a four-decade player who would catch 2,226 games, including twenty-five games when he was forty-five years old. He played more games at the position than any man in history.

Munson would have come around and saluted his rival. He had a respect for durability because it was how he played the game, and he would have come around on Fisk, as he eventually came around on Reggie Jackson when they were teammates.

But for those early years of the rivalry, it was real and it was bitter. The two would take some shots at each other in the papers (when Thurman was choosing to talk to the press). And Munson told me that he'd speak to Fisk about things he didn't like seeing when Fisk came to bat. He'd call him by his last name.

"Listen, Fisk, I saw what you said in the paper this morning and it's bullshit," he might say as Carlton settled in at bat. Stuff like that.

Of course his Yankee teammates loved to tease him about Fisk. Gene Michael, who roomed with Thurman for five years, used to tear out good Fisk stories or handsome pictures from magazines about Carlton and put them in Thurman's locker just to get his reaction when he arrived in the clubhouse. Michael says he's sure that Thurman never knew who was putting them there.

Naming Names

From *Ball Four*

by Jim Bouton

In 1995, the New York Public Library named its "books of the century." Jim Bouton's Ball Four *was the only sports book on the list, appearing alongside classic works of literature like* The Great Gatsby *and* Catch 22. *Upon its publication, Commissioner Bowie Kuhn lambasted Bouton's book, labeling it "detrimental to baseball" and attempting to suppress it. Kuhn's actions backfired, garnering unprecedented exposure for the book and paving the way for other "tell-all" books by professional athletes.*

March 4

Mickey Mantle announced his retirement the other day and I got to thinking about the mixed feelings I've always had about him. On the one hand I really liked his sense of humor and his boyishness, the way he'd spend all that time in the clubhouse making up involved games of chance and the pools he got up on golf matches and the Derby and things like that.

I once invested a dollar when Mantle raffled off a ham. I won, only there was no ham. That was one of the hazards of entering a game of chance, Mickey explained.

I got back by entering a fishing tournament he organized and winning the weight division with a ten-pounder I'd purchased in a store the day before. Two years later Mantle was still wondering why I'd only caught the one big fish and why all the other fish that were caught were green and lively while mine was gray and just lay there, staring.

I also remember the time I won my first major-league game. It was a shutout against the Washington Senators in which I walked seven guys and gave up seven hits and had to pitch from a stretch position all game. They were hitting line drives all over the place and Hector (What a Pair of Hands)

Lopez bailed me out with about four leaping catches in left field. When the game was over I walked back into the clubhouse and there was a path of white towels from the door to my locker, and all the guys were standing there, and just as I opened the door Mickey was putting the last towel down in place. I'll never forget him for that.

And I won't forget the time—in 1962, I guess it was—in Kansas City. I was sitting alone in a restaurant, eating, when Mickey and Whitey Ford came in and Mickey invited me to eat with them and picked up the tab and it made me feel good all over and like a big shot besides.

On the other hand there were all the those times when he'd push little kids aside when they wanted his autograph, and the times when he was snotty to reporters, just about making them crawl and beg for a minute of his time. I've seen him close a bus window on kids trying to get his autograph. And I hated that look of his, when he'd get angry at somebody and cut him down with a glare. Bill Gilbert of *Sports Illustrated* once described that look as flickering across his face "like the nictitating membrane in the eye of a bird." And I don't like the Mantle that refused to sign baseballs in the clubhouse before the games. Everybody else had to sign, but Little Pete forged Mantle's signature. So there are thousands of baseballs around the country that have been signed not by Mickey Mantle but by Pete Previte.

Like everybody else on the club, I ached with Mantle when he had one of his numerous and extremely painful injuries. I often wondered, though, if he might have healed quicker if he'd been sleeping more and loosening up with the boys at the bar less. I guess we'll never know.

What we do know, though, is that the face he showed in the clubhouse, as opposed to the one he reserved for the outside world, was often one of great merriment.

I remember one time he'd been injured and didn't expect to play, and I guess he got himself smashed. The next day he looked hung over out of his mind and was sent up to pinch-hit. He could hardly see. So he staggered up to the plate and hit a tremendous drive to left field for a home run. When he came back into the dugout, everybody shook his hand and leaped all over him, and all the time he was getting a standing ovation from the crowd. He squinted out at the stands and said, "Those people don't know how tough that really was."

Another thing about Mantle. He was a pretty good practical joker. One time he and Ford told Pepitone and Linz that they'd finally arrived, they were ready to go out with the big boys. Mantle told them to get dressed up, tie and all—this was Detroit—and meet them in a place called The Flame. Mickey gave them the address and said to be sure to ask for Mickey Mantle's table.

Pepitone and Linz were like a couple of kids at Christmas. They couldn't stop talking about what a great time they were going to have with Mickey Mantle and Whitey Ford. They got all fancied up, hopped into a cab and told the driver to take them to The Flame. After about a half-hour the cab pulled up in front of a place that was in the heart of the slum section, a hole in the wall with a broken plate-glass window in front and a little broken-down sign over the door: THE FLAME. No Mantle. No Ford. No table.

◆ ◆ ◆

March 30, Holtville

Now about Roger Maris. Roger fought a lot with the people in the stands, especially in Detroit, where he used to give them the finger. He and the fans would get to calling each other names and then Maris would roll out his heavy artillery.

"Yeah? How much money are you making?"

Roger was making $70,000 a year.

After a while every time Maris got into an argument, the guys in the dugout would say, "C'mon Rodg, hit him with your wallet."

Thinking about the great Rodg reminded me of a brief encounter. One day there appeared a clipping on the bulletin board in the Yankee clubhouse. It was a quote from me after Mel Stottlemyre had hit an inside-the-park home run, which is very hard for a pitcher to do. One of the writers came to me after it and said, "What were you thinking when Stottlemyre was going around the bases?" It was a nice, silly question, so I gave him a nice, silly answer. I said I was hoping that Stottlemyre would fall down because if he hit an inside-the-park home run it would put pressure on all us other pitchers to hit inside-the-park home runs, and who needed that? And now it's on the bulletin board like I was serious.

I asked around to find out who put it up, but I couldn't, although I eventually decided it must have either been Clete Boyer, another one of my boosters, or Maris. So one day when they were standing together in the outfield, I went over and said, "I wish you guys would tell me who put that clipping up on the board, because I'd like to get my hands on the gutless son of a bitch who did it."

And although Maris had already denied to me that he put up the clipping, he said, "Don't call me gutless."

Somehow I managed not to get into a fight with him. But I felt I'd won the battle of wits. Which is probably why he didn't own up posting it the first time I asked him. He didn't want to contend with my rapier-like mind.

Maris' friend Clete Boyer was the kind of guy who would always tell me to be careful who I brought into the clubhouse. Yet he led the league in hosting the obnoxious offspring of clothing manufacturers. The way it worked, he'd get free sweaters and in return he'd have to bring the sons of the manufacturers into the clubhouse where they could run around, ask for autographs and make pests of themselves. He and Maris got the sweaters, and we got the kids.

And a final word about my favorite baseball writer, Jim Ogle, of the Newhouse papers. Ogle was a Yankee fan and he reacted to players purely on how much they were helping the Yankees to win. Charm, personality, intelligence—nothing counted. Only winning. Ogle didn't have even the pretense of objectivity. He was the only writer in the pressbox who would take the seventh-inning stretch in the Yankee half.

Once at a winter press conference, when the Yankees were announcing the signing of three or four guys, Stan Isaacs, who writes a really good column for *Newsday*, on Long Island, passed a note to Houk. It said: "Has Ogle signed his contract yet?"

Isaacs may not have known how ironic he was being. In fact Ogle's ambition was to work for the Yankees. But they would never give him a job.

Not that this prevented him from doing little jobs for them. Like when I was sent down he was on television with Yankee broadcasters and said that it wasn't so much that I was pitching poorly, but because of the kind of person I was. He said that none of the players liked me and there were some terrible things about me he couldn't even talk about. This left it up to the public imagination. What was I? Rapist, murderer, dope peddler? Jim Ogle wouldn't say.

◆ ◆ ◆

June 15

Today in the visiting dugout at Yankee Stadium, Joe Schultz said to nobody in particular: "Up and at 'em. Fuck 'em all. Let it all hang out."

I pitched against one hitter in the game, Jimmy Lyttle. Struck him out on five knuckleballs. Nothing to it.

I wonder how the Yankees feel now about picking up Johnson.

On the plane from New York to Milwaukee, where we play the White Sox in a game tomorrow, the stewardesses (we call them stews) were droning about fastening seatbelts. "Fasten your seatbelt," Fred Talbot said, "Fasten your seatbelt. All the time it's fasten your goddam seatbelt. But how come every time I read about one of those plane crashes, there's 180 people on board and all 180 die? Didn't any of them have their seatbelt fastened?"

People are always asking me if it's true about stewardesses. The answer is yes. You don't have to go out hunting for a stew. They stay in the same hotels we do. Open your door and you're liable to be invited to a party down the hall. They're on the road, same as we are, and probably just as lonely. Baseball players are young, reasonably attractive and have more money than most men their age. Not only that, baseball players often marry stews—and the stews know it.

Baseball players are not, by and large, the best dates. We prefer *wham, bam,* thank-you-ma'am affairs. In fact, if we're spotted taking a girl out to dinner, we're accused of "wining and dining," which is bad form. It's not bad form to wine and dine an attractive stew, however. A stew can come under the heading of class stuff, or table pussy, in comparison with some of the other creatures who are camp-followers or celebrity-fuckers, called Baseball Annies. It is permissible, in the scheme of things, to promise a Baseball Annie dinner and a show in return for certain quick services for a pair of roommates. And it is just as permissible, in the morality of the locker room, to refuse to pay off. The girls don't seem to mind very much when this happens. Indeed, they seem to expect it.

In Chicago there's Chicago Shirley who takes on every club as it gets to town. The first thing she does is call up the rookies for an orientation briefing. She asks them if there's anything she can do for them, and as the ballplayers say, "She can do it all." Chicago Shirley says that Chicago is a great place to live because teams in both leagues come through there. She doesn't like to miss anybody.

Seems Like Old Times

"Pinstripes Are Back in Style"
Sports Illustrated, July 2, 1973

by William Leggett

*It had been ten seasons since the Yankees' last championship, and
although it would be a few years yet before they fully returned to
glory, sportswriter William Leggett gave the baseball world fair
warning: The Bronx Bombers were on the rise. Led by Bobby Murcer,
Graig Nettles, Ron Blomberg, and an improving pitching staff,
the Yanks stood atop the league standings halfway through the
1973 campaign.*

AFTER YEARS OF DRAB MEDIOCRITY, THE ONCE LORDLY YANKEES ARE AGAIN
THE CLASS OF THEIR DIVISION—AND COLORFUL, TOO. WHO ELSE HAS NEW
OWNERS, NEW PITCHERS, AND BENCHES A .400 HITTER HALF THE TIME

The Yankees. Ah, the Yankees! The Babe, Iron Man Lou and Joe D., Whitey
and the Scooter and Mickey and Yogi. Monuments in center field in the great
Stadium. Pennants that came in waves. The lordly Yankees in their pinstripe
uniforms, always worn with the top button unbuttoned. Late summer trades
for insurance. Mel Allen. The cry was "Break 'em up." But as baseball goes, all
that was generations ago.

Last Saturday afternoon at Yankee Stadium after Bobby Murcer hit a
three-run homer to lead New York to its sixth victory in a row and 22nd in its
last 33 games, the organist could contain himself no longer; he boomed out "It
Seems Like Old Times." It was like old times. The Yankees were in first place,
seemingly out from beneath the large rock that had obscured them since 1964.
In the bars and supermarkets, on the trains and subways of the nation's largest
city, people were talking more about the Yankees than about the Mets. That

hadn't happened in—well, it had almost never happened. Pitching Coach Jim Turner, who has spent 51 consecutive years in a pro baseball uniform, more than any man in history, said, "It's so good to walk out there before a game and see so many people with notebooks, microphones and cameras interested in us again."

Not since they won their last pennant nine years ago had the Yankees been in first place this "late" in a season. One of their players, 24-year-old Ron Blomberg, was hitting .408 to lead the world in batting. Statisticians announced that not in a quarter of a century had anyone been hitting above .400 at this stage. The two who had last done it were named Ted Williams and Stan Musial. "Wow!" said Blomberg, learning of this, "those guys could *hit.*"

The team that Blomberg is playing with can hit, too. Especially when it must. Already this year the Yankees have won six games by coming from behind in the seventh inning or later. "Just about the entire difference between our team now and in the last couple of seasons," said Manager Ralph Houk, "is the hitting. It's fun to sit back and see our hitters do their job."

Houk was seated in his office last Wednesday evening after the Yankees had moved into first place by half a game, his stockinged feet crossed and a can of beer on his desk. He waggled an unlit cigar in his right hand. Two photographers came in and asked him if he'd mind lighting the cigar and leaning back in his swivel chair. "It's been so long since anyone asked me for my picture after a game," said Houk, "that I probably can't even remember how to pose." He remembered, all right.

The Yankees have a new pride in themselves this season, a sense of no longer being the No. 2 team in a city that in recent years endured them primarily by stifling yawns. For a long time during their dark ages the biggest news they made was when they fired an announcer, but not now. The Yankees of 1973 are interesting in themselves. Playing in poor or threatening weather over much of last week, they drew 148,084 people to a Stadium that has received reams of bad publicity—muggings, poor parking, etc.—and is about to be renovated.

Three weeks ago the Yanks went on a spending spree and bought two pitchers to help them win in this, their 50th year at their Stadium. Sudden Sam McDowell was extracted from the San Francisco Giants for $150,000 cash and Pat Dobson came from the Atlanta Braves for minor league players. All of a sudden, New York had a potentially strong pitching staff in a division notably short of quality arms. By adding McDowell (now 2-0 as a Yankee) and Dobson (2-1) to Mel Stottlemyre and Fritz Peterson, General Manager Lee MacPhail had stockpiled four men who had won 20 games at one time or another in the major leagues. Facing a schedule that forced them to play 24 games with no days off in the next three weeks, the Yankees could actually boast of six starting pitchers, George Medich and Steve Kline being the other two. "It's a situation you have to feel good about," said Houk. But feeling good costs money. By adding McDowell and Dobson the Yankees also hiked their player payroll to nearly $1.2 million.

Houk's six starters are pitching to one of the best catchers in baseball, Thurman Munson, who made it to the Yankees in 1969 with fewer than 100 games beneath his chest protector in the minors. In his rookie season Munson hit .302 and last year had more game-winning hits than any player on the club. This season he has scored more runs than anyone except Graig Nettles and Murcer and has driven in 33 runs, compared to 46 during all of last year.

No team has gotten as much run production from its designated hitters as New York. The DHs, most notably Jim Ray Hart, have driven home 44 runs, second only to Murcer's 47. Hart was purchased from the Giants in April in order to prevent a steady diet of lefthanders from minimizing the team's left-handed power: Murcer, Blomberg, Nettles and Matty Alou.

From the point of view of their gate, the new Yankees are a team with considerable personality and color, instead of the faceless mélanges of the recent past. The zaniest combination of this or many years—the one involving Peterson, Mike Kekich, their wives, children and dogs—was disbanded when Kekich was dealt off to Cleveland. But the Yankees still have a pair of Latin brothers in Matty and Felipe Alou; a Jewish wonder in Blomberg (who pronounces his name "Bloomberg"); an outstanding third baseman in Nettles, who came from Cleveland in the off-season and is reaching base nearly 50% of the time; and a proven batter in Murcer, who is not only hitting for distance and average but is scoring runs and driving them in. Then there is Sparky Lyle, who has already saved more games by himself (19) than any other entire bullpen in the league. Lindy McDaniel, still going strong at 37, again resembles the McDaniel of 1970 who saved 29 games with his fork ball. And there is Medich, a 24-year-old righthander who has pitched well despite only 16 major-league starts. Medich is a med student at the University of Pittsburgh and his presence on the team reminds Yankee fans of Dr. Bobby Brown, the third baseman/heart specialist who played so well for them in the '40s and '50s. Medich's nickname, of course, is Doc.

New York began the season as the favorite to win the East Division championship but got off to a horrendous start by losing its first four games by a combined score of 32-14. "It shocked us," says Blomberg, "but we knew we were better than that and we are proving it now." At 24 Blomberg has a delightful wit, a charming smile and an awful time hitting lefthanders. Counting spring training, he has managed only three hits in 53 bats against lefties, which is why Houk now stoutly declines to let him bat against them at all—whatever the game situation.

Naturally, the letters pile up on Houk's desk asking why he doesn't play Blomberg every day. "You would be amazed at how many of them there are, and how many stories are written about what a fool I am not to play Ronnie against lefties," says Houk. "But I'd be foolish to take a chance of losing a ball game by doing it. "Blomberg wants to hit against lefthanders but realizes the position he is in. "I'm young enough," he says, "and there is time for me to learn. When the season ended last year I went down to the Florida Instructional League to hit lefties and to learn more about playing first base. Well, there weren't that many left-handed pitchers down there, but I sure did get a chance to field a lot of ground balls."

Blomberg is known as a prodigious eater, capable of consuming a couple of ordinary meals at a sitting or one five-pound roast. He is also a first baseman of unusual capacities, most of them negative. Once this year all he had to do to complete a triple play was catch a ball at first base. He juggled the throw. "First time I ever had a chance to even see a triple play and I blew it," he said.

As a youngster in Atlanta, where he grew up a Yankee fan, Blomberg was dropped from one Little League team because his fielding was so bad. Next day, using a different name, he went to another tryout, made the team and finished the season with a .989 batting average. He learned to hit by picking berries off a bush in front of his house, tossing them up in the air and hitting them with a stick. "But there was nobody to hit berries to me so I didn't become a good fielder," he says.

When the Yankees won their last pennant in 1964, their image was so inflated by all the years of spectacular success, it was generally accepted that somebody's grandmother could manage them. Caught up in a fierce four-team pennant chase all during the season, the team, under Berra, took command in September by winning 11 straight. It was New York's 14th pennant in 16 years. That August it was announced that the Columbia Broadcasting System was buying the Yankees from co-owners Dan Topping and Del Webb for $13.2 million. The association was a near disaster from the outset. Shea Stadium had opened next door to the World's Fair in 1964 and the Mets were drawing more than 1,700,000 to the new ball park on their way to a 10th-place finish as well as a third consecutive season in which they would lose 100 games or more. Met attendance was nearly half a million higher with a last-place team than the Yankees with an exciting first-place team involved all summer in a pennant race.

Bobby Murcer was signed in June of 1964. Like Mantle, Murcer was from Oklahoma and, like Mantle, he was signed by scout Tom Greenwade. What swung him to the Yankees, he says, "was the idea that you would get a World Series check every year. You could just about bank on that. But when I came up in 1965 it was like I was some kind of an omen. The World Series supply for the Yankees had dried up."

Murcer joined the team as a shortstop and failed. Actually, his chances of living up to advance billing verged on the impossible. He was constantly being compared to his idol, Mantle. "It was tough going," he says now. By the end of 1966 he had a total of only 33 games in the majors. He lost 1967 and 1968 to the service, and when he came out for 1969 the Yankees were clearly a struggling club.

In 1969, of course, the Mets won the World Series while the Yankees finished fifth. The Mets by then were pulling more than two million a year and the Yankees barely a million.

"Some of us went through some rough times together," Murcer recalls, "but we learned about each other. In 1970 we finished second and last year we were in the race until very late. We just didn't have enough good players to win it."

Murcer is right about that, but there is an important difference between the 1970 and '72 performances. Houk had to keep his foot on the accelerator all of 1970 lest he lose sight of the Baltimore Orioles going around a curve in the distance. But last year the Yankees were in the race because Detroit and Boston played so-so and Baltimore just plain flopped. By the start of this year, the Yankees looked like a first-place team in a weak division.

Murcer tends to be critical of himself. "I'm hitting so bad," he said the other day, "that I've broken 12 bats in 15 games. I even went and got one that was made in 1965 and broke it the first time up." Notwithstanding, he had his batting average up to .285 and was a source of joy to the Yankees' new owners. In the off-season, George Steinbrenner and a group that came largely from Cleveland bought the Yankees from CBS. Steinbrenner watched his Pinstripes move last week and was pleased. So was Murcer. "I have a feeling about this team," he said, "a feeling that all the bad things are in the past, that we can win just like the Yankees are supposed to."

"That's for Trying to Fire Me"

From *Ladies and Gentlemen, the Bronx Is Burning*

by Jonathan Mahler

From disco to punk, political tension to urban blight, the Son of Sam to Mr. October, there was no place quite like New York in the late 1970s. Jonathan Mahler's Ladies and Gentlemen, the Bronx is Burning *captures the very essence of this unique time in the history of the Yankees and of the place they call home.*

Near the end of September, Yankee Stadium attendance passed the two million mark for the first time since 1949. Yankees' haters were no less committed to their cause than Yankees' rooters; the team drew nearly as well on the road.

For rhetorical purposes, the Yankees may have won their divisional flag during that dramatic mid-September series against the Red Sox, but it had been a long slog from there. Not until the penultimate day of the regular season in early October did they officially clinch, and they weren't even on the field when they did it. It was pouring in the Bronx, and the Yankees and Tigers were in the middle of a three-hour rain delay. During the extended pause the Orioles beat the Sox, officially eliminating Boston from contention.

The play-offs would be a rematch of '76: the Yankees versus the Royals. After finishing the season with the best record in baseball, Kansas City had both the oddsmakers and popular sentiment on their side. "All of baseball wants us to win," said the Royals' manager Whitey Herzog. "Not that they love us . . . they just hate the Yankees and their check writing."

The Yankees' clubhouse had been relatively calm for the last six weeks, but malice lurked not far below the surface. Near the end of the season *Newsday*'s Joe Donnelly, who'd been covering the Mets since mid-July, returned to the

Yankees' beat and was shocked to find Reggie and Munson kidding around with each other. "I went to Thurman and said, 'I'm not going to print this, but what are you doing hanging around with Reggie? Are you guys friends now?'" Donnelly recalls. "And Thurman said, 'How could I ever like that son of a bitch after what he pulled? But we need him to win. We need him to win.'"

The first squall of the postseason blew in on the eve of game one, when Billy Martin's fleeting moment of contentment at having again piloted his team into the play-offs curdled into a more familiar sentiment, underappreciation. Emerging from a preseries strategy session with George Steinbrenner and several Yankees' scouts, Martin declined to talk about his opponents for fear of saying something that might help them. But he was more than happy to talk about everything else, including what he called the turning point of the season, standing up to Reggie in the dugout at Fenway. And his boss. If the Yankees went on to win the World Series, Martin told the writers gathered in his office, and Steinbrenner *didn't* sweeten and extend his three-year, three-hundred-thousand-dollar contract, he was going to have to think seriously about asking for permission to talk to other clubs. With the first pitch scarcely more than twenty-four hours away, there was no way Steinbrenner could fire him. So Martin as much as challenged him to: "If he buys $50 million worth of players, I'll beat him with another club and he knows it . . . I'll make him cry."

The ritual resumed, it was now Steinbrenner's turn. "He's crazy if he tries to take credit for our success," the Yankees' owner told reporters, presenting them with evidence—the team's day-by-day won-loss record—that the season's real turning point had been August 10, when Martin finally started hitting Reggie at cleanup. "He is just trying to work up public support," Steinbrenner said dismissively.

Public support was one thing Martin didn't have to work up. When he was introduced before game one on October 4, which was played on a clear, mild afternoon in New York, the fans stood and cheered themselves hoarse. "This is in recognition of Billy telling off his boss," Dick Young wrote in the *Daily News*, "by 55,000 people who dream of telling off the boss."

Martin trotted out to the first base line and lifted his cap toward the sky. A wincing smile spread across his narrow face. Several Yankees joined the ovation. Martin looked younger than his forty-eight years, but he did not look good. There were dark circles under his eyes, and his shriveled frame had practically disappeared inside his increasingly baggy uniform. But for the moment anyway, he was happy.

Martin bathed in the clamor, unaware that his starting pitcher, Don Gullett, was having trouble getting loose. The lanky left-hander, who had torn his rotator cuff while fielding a bunt during the season, didn't tell anyone that the tightness in his shoulder was back. By the middle of the second inning, having surrendered four runs on four hits and two walks, he confessed to the team's trainer that he wasn't right. The trainer passed the word along to Martin, and Gullet was finished for the night.

So were the Yankees. Reggie went hitless, and the Yanks dropped the game, 7-2. The ailing Catfish Hunter, who hadn't set foot on a mound in three weeks, was already out for the series. Now Gullett appeared to be too.

The following morning the South Bronx got a surprise visitor. His presence was announced by a long line of motorcycle escorts and police cars. Sirens blaring, the caravan chugged up the Grand Concourse as helicopters buzzed overhead. In the back of the motorcade, peering through the windows of a cream-colored limousine at the grand facades of this once-opulent boulevard was President Jimmy Carter.

He was a couple of months late, but the president, in town to address the United Nations, had finally decided to pay a surprise visit to one of New York's worst ghettos, a neighborhood that had been ignored by most of the borough's blackout looters. By July 1977 there was virtually nothing there to steal.

Anticipating Carter's arrival a week earlier, the *Daily News* had taken the liberty of mapping out a more ambitious itinerary for him, beginning at St. Barbara's Church in Bushwick: "There the few working, middle-class families left in the dying neighborhood can give Carter the kind of first-hand knowledge of what's killing the nation's cities." But Carter had chosen to limit his slum tour to the South Bronx.

As the presidential caravan wended its way through this urban prairie on this mild, early fall morning, small clusters of people began appearing in front of burned-out and abandoned tenements, shouting, "We want money," and, "Give us jobs." The motorcade stopped abruptly along Charlotte Street, and the president disembarked to walk through the wasteland, a two-block stretch of rubble unbroken by so much as a single building.

It was a powerful image, a natural for front pages nationwide, and scores of politicians would soon follow in Carter's footsteps, all seeking to underscore their commitment to saving the neighborhood.

A closer look would have revealed that the neighborhood was already saving itself. By the time of Carter's visit, local community development groups with mottoes like "Don't move. Improve," had already begun to form. They beat back the city's wrecking crews, rebuilt battered buildings, and fought for the 1977 Community Reinvestment Act, a federal law requiring banks to provide loans in low-income neighborhoods. In time the city did its part too, earmarking some five hundred million dollars a year for affordable housing, much of which found its way to the South Bronx.

But these seeds of rebirth remained buried beneath the debris on October 5, 1977, the day the South Bronx became the most famous slum in America.

That night was a cool and windy one at the stadium. Guidry was serving smoke, but the Yankees still weren't hitting, even against Andy Hassler, the weakest of the Royals' starters.

It was 2-1 Yankees in the top of the sixth when Hal McRae came barreling into Willie Randolph, knocking the ball loose and sending the Yankees' second baseman tumbling head over heels toward the edge of the outfield grass. The Royals had tied the game, but they had also awakened the slumbering Yankees, who exploded for three runs in the home half of the inning. With Guidry going, that was more than enough to put the game away. They were now even at one, but with the series moving to the artificial turf in Kansas City for the last three games, the Royals still had the edge.

Whitey Herzog had been saving his best pitcher, Dennis Leonard, for game three in Kansas City and the young right-hander didn't disappoint. The Yankees managed just four hits, and Reggie was blanked. He was now one for eleven in the postseason, and his one hit had been an infield single.

For his part, Martin spent most of the night shrieking at the umpires. He knew there was more at stake here than a pennant. In case he didn't, Royals' fans held aloft a banner to remind him: BYE, BYE, BILLY. By the end of the night his voice had been reduced to a rasp. The next day would be an elimination game. Desperate for an edge, the Yankees' skipper set about tormenting the Royals' game four starter, Larry Gura, whom Martin had cut from his Texas Rangers team back in 1975. "If I had my way," Martin told every reporter he could, "I'd put a bodyguard around his house tonight and get him a chauffeur so he doesn't get into an accident on the way to the ballpark."

Gura made it safely to the ballpark but soon wished he hadn't. The Yanks touched him up for four runs on six hits in two innings. Just about everybody participated, with the exception of Reggie, who posted yet another oh-fer. When the Royals rallied to pull within one run in the fourth, Martin skipped right to his closer, Sparky Lyle, who pitched five-plus scoreless innings to force a winner-take-all game five.

At Royals Stadium the following afternoon, not long before the Yankees were scheduled to take the field for their pregame cuts, Billy Martin summoned his backup catcher, Fran Healy.

Poking his head into the manager's office, Healy, who'd been to the plate sixty-seven times all season, wasn't expecting to be told to be ready to play. He wasn't. Martin had an even more surprising request: "I'm sitting Reggie tonight, and I want you to tell him."

"I'm not telling him, *you* tell him," an incredulous Healy replied. "You're the manager."

"I don't want to tell him."

"Why don't you have one of the coaches tell him?" Healy asked.

"They don't want to tell him."

Healy pulled up a stool in front of Reggie's locker and told him.

Martin headed out to the dugout, took a seat on the top step, and informed the newsroom that Paul Blair, his late-innings defensive specialist, would be starting in right field. This time there were no winking references to Reggie's hyperextended elbow. The three-million-dollar slugger wasn't hitting for "spit" (as the papers wrote it), and he was butchering balls in the outfield. "If I played him and he dropped a ball that cost us the game, I wouldn't forgive myself for the rest of my life," Martin said. "I don't like to do this bastard thing, but if I don't do what's best for the club, I shouldn't be manager."

It was an act either of noble courage or of sadistic insecurity. An unconvincing argument could be made that starting Blair was the best thing for the club. Reggie was in the grip of a one-for-fourteen postseason swoon, and he looked about as surefooted as a beery weekend softballer on the artificial turf. What's more, he did have trouble with that night's pitcher, the left-handed junk baller Paul Splittorff. In fifteen at bats against Splittorff during the regular season, Reggie had picked up just two hits, a double and a home run.

But Martin never put much stock in stat sheets; number crunching, to his mind, was for managers who didn't trust their baseball instincts. More likely, the only calculus that Martin made was this one: If the Yankees won without Reggie, he would be vindicated. If the Yankees lost, well, he was going to be fired anyway.

Batting practice started, and Reggie, burning, remained in the locker room. Eventually he emerged and gave a disingenuously stoic interview to Howard Cosell, admitting that he was disappointed but adding—you could almost read the humiliation in his face now—that it had taken "guts" for Martin to sit him.

As the newspapermen stalked Reggie, hoping for a more honest comment, another bomb was ticking away. The Yankees' leadoff hitter, Mickey Rivers, was holed up in the trainer's room refusing to get dressed. He'd been having problems with his wife all year. Earlier in the season she'd reportedly chased him from their apartment in New Jersey up to the stadium and then repeatedly smashed into his car until a parking lot attendant intervened. Now she had racked up a huge shopping bill in their Kansas City hotel, and the front office was refusing to advance Rivers the money to cover it.

Rivers was eventually coaxed out, and the game got under way. By the end of the first the Royals' George Brett had slid into third spikes high, and the two benches had cleared.

The Royals took an early lead against a worn-out Guidry, who had pitched nine innings just three days before, and Martin quickly replaced him with Mike Torrez. The score was 3-1 Royals after three innings, and then the two teams started matching zeros. Every now and then NBC would advance the subplot, pointing a camera at the best-paid man in baseball history sitting on the bench in a warm-up jacket. No one believed it would end like this.

It didn't. In the eighth the Yankees mounted a rally, and Reggie got his chance. With one out and runners on first and third, Martin called on him to pinch-hit for the team's designated hitter, Cliff Johnson. The Royals' closer, Paul Bird, was on the mound. Reggie took ball one and then fouled off a pair of fastballs. Now Bird tried to sneak a slow curve by him. Reggie lunged, chipping the ball into center field for a run-scoring base hit, pulling the Yankees within one.

They won it in the ninth. The unlikely hero was Reggie's replacement, Paul Blair. Most baseball scouts believed that Blair had never really recovered from a cheek-shattering beaning a few years earlier and that he was at his most tentative when facing right-handed power pitchers, such as Dennis Leonard, who was brought in to finish the game for the Royals. Martin stuck with Blair anyway. After spoiling a good fastball and a couple of diving sliders, he caught a pitch on the bat handle and looped it toward shallow center for a base hit. Roy White followed with an eight-pitch walk. Mickey Rivers singled to drive home the tying run, moving White to third in the process. Willie Randolph finished it with a sacrifice fly.

Most of the nation's sports editors chose one of the two images to illustrate their game stories: a first-inning photograph of Royals' third baseman George Brett on all fours, with Yankees' third baseman Graig Nettles' foot embedded in his chest, or a postgame shot of the Royals' five-foot-four-inch shortstop, Fred Patek, sitting alone in the dugout, head in hands, his pants torn from a nasty spiking. Goliath had apparently defeated David. As one *Kansas City Times* columnist wrote, "Truth doesn't prevail. There is no justice."

In the locker room after the game, Billy Martin, for whom victory always tasted more like vindication, went looking for Steinbrenner with a full bottle of champagne. "That's for trying to fire me," Martin said, after sneaking up on his boss and soaking him from behind. Steinbrenner, a protective raincoat over his navy blazer, wheeled around. "What do you mean, *try*?" he said, half grinning. "If I want to fire you, I will."

Paul Blair hugged Munson and thanked him for working with him on protecting the outside part of the plate. "Yeah," Munson said, "the beachball can't stir the fuckin' drink, but he can teach you how to hit."

A few lockers away Reggie ended his short-lived experiment with stoicism. "Can I explain what it meant?" he blurted, reflecting on his bloop single to a few writers. "I can't explain it. I can't explain it because I don't understand the magnitude of Reggie Jackson." Not that he had forgiven Martin. On the team's charter plane a few hours later, Reggie sat alone in silence.

Martin was several rows up, listening to country music on a cassette recorder and wondering if any manager had ever gone into his second consecutive World Series still fighting for his job.

REG-GIE! REG-GIE!

From *Reggie Jackson: The Life and Thunderous Career of Baseball's Mr. October*

by Dayn Perry

Regardless of how he was received by his teammates or the media, in spite of his rocky relationship with manager Billy Martin, Reggie Jackson is most remembered for his on-field heroics, most notably in the 1977 World Series, when he blasted the Yankees back to glory. As Howard Cosell famously remarked during Game 6, "After all the furor, after all the hassling, it comes down to this!"

October 18, 1977, World Series, Game Six

The Yankees trailed 3-2. Thurman Munson led off the bottom of the fourth with a sharp single to left. Then Reggie stepped to the plate, leaned in, and cocked his bat. Burt Hooton's first pitch was a fastball low, but not inside where he aimed it. Reggie ripped at it. The ball climbed lazily across the outfield and just cleared the short fence in right. It was a home run—325 feet—without his usual shattering authority, but after Munson and Reggie touched the plate the Yankees led 4-3. In the dugout, Martin put a hand on Reggie's neck and embraced him for a moment.

Elias Sosa got up for the second time in the Dodger bull pen as Hooton worked uneasily to Chris Chambliss. With the count 2-1, Tommy Lasorda visited the mound to give Sosa more time. The camera cut to Reggie in the dugout. "Hi, Mom," he mouthed. "That's one of the few times I've seen him smile in the last seven days," said Tom Seaver in the broadcast booth.

Sosa trotted in while the grounds crew cleared trash from the outfield. Chambliss lifted a pitch from Sosa to shallow left. Bill Russell went back, Dusty Baker broke in, but the ball fell in between them. Chambliss wound up on second. Graig Nettles then grounded out to the right side, and Chambliss scurried to third. Lou Piniella pushed him across with a sac fly.

In the top of the fifth inning, Mike Torrez walked Bill Russell with one out to bring up the dangerous Reggie Smith. This time, Smith, who had powered a deep homer off Torrez in the third, swung over the top of a sinker and hit into an easy double play.

In the bottom half, Mickey Rivers led off with a single past Davey Lopes. Sosa, as in the prior inning, had little command. Lefty Doug Rau loosened in the Dodger bull pen. Willie Randolph dropped a bunt in front of home plate, but Steve Yeager pounced and threw to second just ahead of Rivers. Next was Munson, who lined out to Rick Monday in center for the second out.

Reggie asked coach Gene Michael what Sosa threw. Fastballs, Michael told him, all fastballs. Reggie stalked toward the plate. The scoreboard flashed: "REG-GIE!" Sosa threw to first to force Randolph back to the bag. Then he checked the runner again and brought the pitch. Michael was right: first-pitch fastball and on the outer third of the plate, exactly where it shouldn't have been. Reggie's swing was instinctive—almost involuntary. The ball was low and hard and fast off the bat.

In right field, Reggie Smith scarcely had time to turn around. As Reggie rounded first, he glanced into the Dodger dugout and tapped his chest with his right hand. The "Reg-gie!" chants started again. In the booth, Howard Cosell, no friend of Reggie, called his second home run of the night "something I'll always remember." Back in the dugout, Reggie waved at the camera and help up a pair of fingers. "Two," he mouthed. The Yankees led 7-3.

Lasorda, one batter too late, summoned Rau from the bull pen, and Chambliss grounded out to Steve Garvey at first. As Reggie took his spot in right field to start the sixth, the fans chanted his name, threw offerings at him, and brayed for his acknowledgement. He doffed his cap. "You might call it the aggrandizement of an athlete," said play-by-play man Keith Jackson.

Even as Sparky Lyle warmed up, Torrez cruised through the top of the inning. Rau did the same to Nettles, Piniella, and Bucky Dent in the bottom half. The seventh was no different. The Dodgers failed to threaten Torrez, and Charlie Hough, the new Dodgers pitcher, worked around a single by Rivers to pitch a scoreless frame. In the top of the eighth, Torrez allowed a leadoff single to Lopes and a hard hit lineout by Russell. Then Smith hit into an inning-ending double play.

In the bottom of the eighth, Reggie led off against the knuckleballer Hough. Any other night, Martin would've already replaced Reggie with Paul Blair, his defensive caddy. But not tonight. "Reggie Jackson has seen two pitches in the strike zone tonight," announced Keith Jackson. "And he's hit them both in the seats." The crowd's roar picked up as Reggie strutted to the plate.

The knuckleball was always an inviting pitch for a hitter like Reggie. Back in Puerto Rico in the winter of 1970, Frank Robinson had taught him to hit it, and Reggie hadn't forgotten. But Hough threw a tough one. The pitch fluttered to the outside corner, and Reggie cut the bat at it. Later, Dodgers manager Tommy Lasorda would call it "a perfect pitch."

At second base, umpire Ed Sudol doubted his own ears. Hough's tumbling pitch looked unhittable from hand to plate. But then Sudol heard the crack of the bat. He whipped around.

The ball sailed 475 feet to the blacked-out seats in distant center field. By the time Reggie reached second base, he realized the dimensions of what he'd done—three home runs on three swings, four on four swings going back to game five. Babe Ruth had twice hit three home runs in a World Series game, but nothing Ruth had ever done was so impossible, so hypnotic.

Reggie touched home plate to the loudest ovation he'd ever heard. In the dugout, he greeted them all—friends, enemies, and the once indifferent. But on this night Reggie allowed no indifference. Ray Negron pushed him out of the dugout and forced him to acknowledge the desperate cries of "Reg-gie! Reg-gie! Reg-gie!"

He emerged from the dugout, hands raised in triumph. "Thank you, thank you!" he shouted back at them. He thanked them, yet he chided them— chided them for taking so long to recognize his magnitude. "Fulfillment is written in his face," warbled Cosell. Reggie, with a smile that hid nothing, held up three fingers.

He took the field for the ninth heralded by desperate cheers. Keith Jackson announced that the decision was predictably unanimous: Reggie had won World Series MVP for the second time in his career. Again he raised three fingers for the fans in the right-field bleachers. Between outs and as Lyle warmed up yet again, the Dodgers pieced together three singles and scored a run, but history was already written. Monday drove a labored Torrez pitch to the wall in right, but Reggie steadied under it and caught the second out. Cops kneeled along the sidewalls, ready for what would happen next.

Martin considered a pitching change at the mound while fans perched themselves on the outfield walls. They threw firecrackers at Reggie. He jogged off the field. Then he stopped, retrieved a batting helmet, and returned to right field. Cosell called the fans' display "intolerable, unthinkable, disgraceful, and not worthy of this great city." With two outs, pinch hitter Lee Lacy popped up a bunt attempt to Torrez on the mound. Torrez clung to it.

Like sinners to a tent revival, fans—thousands of them—spilled onto the field. Reggie summoned his football skills, dodged most, ran over a few, and made it back to the dugout. The cops, overwhelmed at the perimeters, cracked heads with their nightsticks. Even the five police officers on horseback, even the helmeted members of the Tactical Patrol Force couldn't hold them back. Near third base, three cops gave a fifteen-year-old boy a concussion. "Jews for Jesus" leaflets swirled about the field. The fans tore up turf, bases, plastic seats—anything to help them remember what they didn't yet believe.

The celebration—the release—bled out into the neighborhoods. The police chased fans up 161st Street. Drivers around Yankee Stadium ran red lights and went the wrong way down one-way streets, all to avoid stopping, even for a moment, in the widening chaos. On 149th, the injured and already dead turned up at Lincoln Hospital. At the nearest precinct on 167th, the police began a long night of booking. At 125th and Seventh in Harlem, young black boys blocked traffic and held up newsprint photos and glossies of their new hero, Reggie Jackson. Over at the *New York Post*'s offices on South Street, they crafted an editorial on the miracles of the night. They wrote, "Who dares to call New York a lost cause?"

Reggie was burdened by a deep sense of occasion.

In the glow following moments when things went well for him—impossibly well on this night—he forgave too easily, was too heedless of the past. It was both a merit and a flaw.

In the Yankees clubhouse following a win that went beyond the extremities of the imagination, he was lost in the magnitude of it all. Eyes stinging from champagne, he took from around his neck the gold medallion of Jackie Robinson. He showed it to the press. "What do you think this man would think of me tonight?"

He rhapsodized to the writers at one turn and embraced his former—and future—enemies at another. "Anyone fights you, skip," he told Martin, his arm around the man who had terrorized him for months, "he's got to fight both of us."

Then someone told him his father, who had traveled from Philadelphia to see Reggie win the World Series for the fourth time, was asking for him at the door. "Bring my dad over," Reggie said. "Dad? Dad?"

Martinez, plumper and moving more slowly than he ever had, appeared. Reggie embraced him. "Get a picture of me and my dad for television, for the newspapers, and for the magazines," he said. "I must have a picture with my dad. I can't say too much for this man. He has been behind me all the way, even in my darkest moments."

After a moment, it was on to Steinbrenner. "Get my bat, Nick, please," Reggie said to a clubhouse attendant. He returned with Reggie's "dues collector," and the monologue began. "I started using this bat Saturday after

I broke one in Friday's game. Look at the wide grain. The older the tree, the wider the grain, the harder the wood," he said, pretending to be unaware of the scribbling writers in his audience. "I think I'll give this bat to George Steinbrenner."

On the other side of the clubhouse, others talked. "Reggie didn't do it," said Mickey Rivers to a nearby writer. "*We* did it."

"Stirs the drink, eh?" said Paul Blair. "Reggie doesn't do that. Rivers does that."

"Look," Munson said, "this was a team victory. It was the right fielder who hit the homers, not Reggie Jackson."

Baseball's Greatest Soap Opera

From *The Bronx Zoo*

by Sparky Lyle and Peter Golenbock

Forging down the path cleared by Jim Bouton's Ball Four, *Sparky Lyle recorded the mayhem of the entire 1978 Yankees season in his notebook, and* The Bronx Zoo *is what remains. A testament to the circus-like atmosphere created by George, Billy, and Reggie, Lyle's book is also a remarkable account of the resiliency of this particular Yankee team, which launched a remarkable comeback to reclaim the championship crown.*

Tuesday, April 18, New York

We go on the road tomorrow for a couple of days, so before today's game I went up to see Steinbrenner to tell him I'm quitting. I won the Cy Young Award last year: I'm the only left-hander in the bullpen, and I'll be damned if I'm going to play for what he's paying me. I went in and I said, "Why do I have to pitch to prove what I'm worth after what I've done already? You want more and more, but you won't compensate me for all I've done."

And he agreed with me. He said that I have a legitimate gripe. But George is in a corner because Gossage, who he paid two something million for, is 0 and 2, and if Steinbrenner renegotiates with me now, it'll look to the public like he's dealing from weakness.

He said, "If you wait and let everything quiet down, I'll take care of you, and you'll be happy. On the other hand," he said, "if you're going to quit, I'm going to have to let you do that." Then he said, "But you're not financially stable enough to do that, are you?"

What could I say? I told him I wasn't. So he said, "Wait till things die down. I'm not sure how long it will be. It may be a week, it may be a month. We'll have to see." He showed me the door, and as I was leaving, he said, "Don't call me again. I'll get in touch with you."

This contract thing has my head so messed up that I don't even want to go to the ball park. I told Steinbrenner, "Ordinarily I'm more relaxed at the ball park than anywhere, including my house." It's not that way anymore. Usually I go to the park at two o'clock for an eight o'clock game because I enjoy going there. Now I wait until the last minute.

The reporters have been asking me why I'm down because I've been really quiet, which is unusual. I can honestly say that until now I've never been depressed in the major leagues.

◆ ◆ ◆

Sunday, July 16, New York

We were losing 3 to 1 with the bases loaded. Lou Piniella got up against Larry Gura, and he hit a ball 430 feet—where it was caught by Amos Otis in the deepest part of Death Valley. Lou couldn't believe it! He thought he had a home run for sure, that he had won the ball game, and all he ended up with was a long out. After the game he was moaning and groaning about Yankee Stadium. Piniella was saying, "To hit a home run here you need help from Superman, Batman, Robin, Spiderman, Wonder Woman, Godzilla, King Kong," and he kept naming more and more comic book characters. We've lost eight out of ten. Boston is 13 games in front, and the way things are going, we'll be watching the play-offs this fall on Channel 4.

Gura, who's now 7 and 2 for Kansas City, played for the Yankees, but one morning last spring Billy saw him and Rich Coggins in their whites going to play tennis. Billy, who calls tennis a pussy game, went right up a tree.

You have to understand, Billy was seeing this guy who hadn't been pitching well going out to play tennis. Billy said to himself, "What the hell is he playing tennis for when he isn't pitching worth a crap? Swinging that racket can't be doing his pitching any good. No wonder he's horseshit." Gura, on the other hand, is thinking, "I'm keeping in shape playing tennis." They're looking at it from different standpoints. But the manager, of course, is going to win out. Billy said, "I'll get rid of them fuckers." And that's just what he did.

Reggie didn't play tonight. Gura's a lefty, and Billy benched Reggie in favor of right-handed Cliff Johnson, who is making the situation worse by going 0 for 4 every time he plays. These days when Reggie plays, it's only to DH, which I know he doesn't like. Even so, Reggie hasn't said very much. He told reporters, "I'm not talking anymore." Who knows what's lurking in the heart of Mr. October? I'm sure we'll find out soon.

On the surface it seems that Billy's sitting Reggie down against lefties is bad on Billy's part, and yet Billy isn't treating Reggie any different from the way he treats anyone else. A number of guys like Piniella, Thomasson, and Roy White were even hitting the ball and found themselves sitting. Spencer was one of the hottest hitters on the team for a little while, and all of a sudden he stopped playing. When you're struggling like we are, you have to try things, and Reggie hasn't been swinging the bat very well, and that's the reason Billy takes him out. Not for any other reason.

It's hard to tell what's running through Reggie's mind. Billy has finally been allowed to keep Reggie out of the outfield because he hurts us too much out there, but any time a manager does that to a ballplayer, especially a ballplayer with an ego as big as Reggie's, the ballplayer is going to go into a tizzy. No ballplayer likes to be told he sucks, even if he knows it's true, and what makes it worse is that because it's New York, the Yankees, the team of controversy, Reggie Jackson, Billy Martin, George Steinbrenner, it gets magnified way out of proportion, and everyone makes a big deal out of it. The writers are now going to run over to Reggie and ask him provocative questions like "Is Billy deliberately showing you up?" or "Do you think you're good enough to play right field?"; questions like that, and Reggie's going to say something bitchy, and then the writers will go back to Billy, and after the writers get finished with them, there's going to be some shit flying.

Billy didn't want Reggie on the Yankees. Billy wanted Joe Rudi, a right-handed batter who hits in the clutch and who's an excellent defensive outfielder. Rudi, however, isn't very colorful, and he isn't a draw. Reggie, with his big mouth and his big swing, puts people in the park. Plus he's a home run hitter and he makes a good play in the field every once in a while. George knew this and spent almost $3 million to sign him. What George didn't know was that this guy is a real piece of work.

After George signed him, when he told the papers, "I didn't come to New York to become a star. I brought my star with me," right then I knew. I said to myself, "This guy is going to be trouble." He's always telling everybody how great he is, and you never know whether he believes the stuff he says or not. This spring he told a TV reporter how important it was that people respect him. Then he said, "But to be respected, you have to be godly." Godly? Is he kidding? I respect plenty of people, but not one of them looks like the Pope, or Charlton Heston even.

Reggie's a mystery to me. He's a very intelligent guy. I've watched him on TV when he announces for ABC's Superstar competition during the offseason. He ad-libs, jokes around, uses the right words, and you can see that Reggie's a really smart person. If you listened to Reggie, you'd think he was the only intelligent guy on the whole Yankee team. That's what Reggie says—over and over. He told that to Carlos May once. May didn't give a damn what his IQ was and told him so. Reggie said, "You can't even spell IQ." Another time Reggie was giving Mickey Rivers the same jive. "My IQ is 160," he told Mickey. Mickey looked at Reggie and said, "Out of what, Buck, a thousand?" Cracked everybody up. Reggie's always trying to show Mickey how much smarter he is. One day he asked Mickey, "What am I doing arguing with someone who can't read or write?" Mickey replied, "You oughta stop reading and writing and start hitting."

Another thing I noticed about him. When Reggie was taking so much heat after his article in *Sport* magazine, he told a reporter, "The guys don't like me 'cause I'm black." The guys didn't like him 'cause he came to our team, and he wasn't here three months when he attacked Thurman in a magazine article and told everybody how great he was. Then we got pissed, and he said it was because he's black! Why did he have to say a thing like that?

Reggie isn't one personality. He's several. Some days he's real happy and friendly and nice, and other days he's nasty and surly and always growling at everybody. Then on other days he sits by himself and doesn't talk.

Reggie doesn't usually talk much with the other players anyway. Mostly it's with the press. We get to read the bull he says in the papers the next day. I don't pay attention to anything the guy says, never, and I'll tell you why. We were in Oakland for a game, and after it was over Reggie was being interviewed on the radio. Radios were on in the clubhouse, and we could hear what he was saying. Reggie's talking away, and he says, "You can't believe most of what the New York writers are saying about this team." Well, the New York writers are listening to him say this, and when he comes back to the clubhouse they are pissed. They ask him exactly what he meant by that. Reggie for a few seconds didn't know what to say, and then he said, "You guys heard that? If I knew you were listening, I wouldn't have said it."

When Reggie started playing with the Yankees last year, Billy discovered that Reggie wasn't nearly as good as Reggie thought or said he was. Billy started batting Reggie fifth, instead of fourth where he was used to batting, and George went crazy. George ordered Billy to bat him third or fourth. Billy told the press, "It's no big deal. Reggie's just not used to playing the way other people want him to." But it was a big deal because Reggie's George's boy, and for the two years Reggie's been here, Billy rarely can play Reggie the way he wants to, which is frustrating for Billy 'cause he feels a team should do everything it can to win, regardless of whose feelings get hurt.

Billy almost got fired last year over Reggie. We were getting our ass kicked by Boston, and George was on Billy's back because we weren't in first place, and in the middle of the game Jim Rice hits a pop fly to right field. The ball fell in, and Reggie trotted after it like it didn't matter at all, and he took forever to throw it back in. Billy walked out to the mound to take out the pitcher, Mike Torrez, and as I was walking in from the bullpen to relieve him, Billy also sent Paul Blair out to right to replace Reggie, who had without a doubt loafed after that ball. Billy was so angry he wanted to embarrass Reggie. If you lose, Billy always wants you to go down fighting, and Billy had been pissed off because even though Reggie had been winning some games for us, he was costing us a lot of ball games with his fielding.

Let's face it, Reggie's a bad outfielder. He has good speed to get to the ball, but the catching part is shaky. Before the game, Billy had wanted Reggie to shag fly balls during batting practice, but Reggie had refused. See, if Reggie had done that, I don't think Billy would have been as angry as he was. And Billy's taking Reggie out of the game embarrassed him in front of all the people in the park and all the people watching on national television, which really hurt Reggie a lot. Reggie hates to be embarrassed, especially in front of 50 million people. So when Reggie came in to the dugout, Reggie said, "What did I do? What did I do?" Billy said, "You know what you did." Reggie said, "You have to be crazy to show me up in front of all those people," and then Reggie made the mistake of calling Billy an old man.

When Reggie said that, something in Billy snapped. Billy hates to be embarrassed as much as Reggie does, and when he said that, Billy went for his throat. Ellie, Howser, and Yogi had to wrestle him to the bench to keep him from reaching Reggie. Reggie was yelling at Billy, "You better start liking me," as if to say, "If one of us is going to go, it isn't going to be me."

George had not been at the game. He was at a funeral someplace, and he had watched the game on TV and he saw the whole thing. A couple of days later he decided to fire Billy for losing his temper, but when Milt Richman of UPI leaked the story, the reaction of the fans was so hostile, George changed his mind.

When I heard that Billy was going to get fired, I went to him and told him, "I want you to know something. If you get fired because of this incident, I'm going home. I'm going to pack my bags and go back to New York for the rest of this road trip, and I'll show up when the team gets back." What I would have been saying was, if you fire Billy over an incident like that, where Reggie was loafing and Billy was punishing him for it, then you might as well have made Reggie the manager. "I can't see the manager taking the consequences when he's right," I told Billy. Not so much that it was Reggie and Billy. If it had been any manager and player, I would have felt the same way.

♦ ♦ ♦

Sunday, September 10, Boston

It's very hard to believe what's going on. For the fourth game in a row, we came out and started kicking ass and scored runs and hit the ball like I couldn't believe. Today we had 18 hits. We were ahead 5 to 0 in the second inning, and there was no way they were going to beat Figgie, and Goose, who pitched the last three innings. To sit there and watch it was really something. For five years I played with the Red Sox, and I've never seen a team come in and do that to the Sox. I think we even surprised ourselves. I mean, we came into Boston loaded for bear. We'd been hoping to win three out of four, and we got 67 hits and 42 runs, and they started making errors, and our pitching was solid, and after it was over, we were almost feeling sorry for them. Almost. Before we got here their momentum had never been taken away, and we completely destroyed them. In every game by the time we scored the third or fourth run, they'd be standing around in the field with their gloves off, their heads down, as if to say, "Oh, Goddamn, I hope we get a little luck and get out of this inning giving them only five runs."

I was talking with Piniella tonight, and he was saying how he's started to hit with his legs instead of with his hands and how much it's helped him. Evidently, it must be because he's hitting the hell out of the ball. They'll throw him a live fastball or a good pitch down and away, and boy, he'll hit the dogshit out of it, which is how he gets when he's hot. And he's been hitting like that for the last two weeks. In the four games against the Red Sox, he had ten hits, scored eight runs, had five RBIs, and had two doubles, a triple, and a home run.

Piniella doesn't get nearly the money he should be getting. Every year they tell him he's getting too old to play full time, and they tell him they're not going to raise his salary because he's only going to play against left-handers, but every year Lou starts hitting, and he'd be in there every day to where Lou would start saying, "Goddamn, they don't want to pay me for playing every day, but now they want me in there every day." But the way Lou is, he ends up saying to himself, "Screw it, what's another five thou? It ain't gonna make that much difference anyhow."

When Goose got the last out, it wasn't like winning the pennant. It was more like, "We've struggled all year, and here we're tied for first place where nobody thought we'd be, even us." I don't think any of us really thought we could overtake the Red Sox, but we never gave up. We always felt that if we got close to them, we'd have an outside shot at it. That was the best we were hoping for. But once we got within seven of them, we started thinking, "We just might have a chance at this. *If* we could keep on playing good ball. *If* this. *If* that. *If, if, if.* But all the ifs happened.

The past four days we weren't playing over our heads, even though it may have seemed that way scoring seven, eight runs in the first couple of innings every game. That was phenomenal. But this ball club is capable of doing that if everybody's healthy and has his act together, which is exactly what we have. Even the bench guys have gotten into winning this thing. They stopped talking about leaving. Winning solves a lot of problems.

For four days we had everything together to where you couldn't have planned it any better. If you had made a wish and said, "I wish such-and-such for these four games," you couldn't have had it any better.

No one is celebrating because we know we have our work cut out for us. We could very easily be three games back in three days, so everybody's keeping his mouth shut, and we're going to go out and play good baseball and not get too gung ho. Even though we just blew Boston away, it's not over. We can't be screwing around like we have a five-game lead.

Everyone's talking about how Boston's been so together all year, and now that we've kicked their ass and tied them for first, now all you hear about is the controversy on the Red Sox, that the players think George Scott is too fat and hasn't been trying, and stuff like that, that Zimmer is a lousy manager, and how Fred Lynn is jealous of Jim Rice and that Rice is angry because the Sox brought Lynn up before him. Crap like that. Ordinarily, you don't see dissension on a winning club.

Monday, October 2, Boston

It was strange, but for a game that was so important to both teams, there was very little tension. Last night a bunch of us went out and had a few drinks, and we were sitting at the hotel bar, and the general consensus was "We're gonna win tomorrow." We just knew we were going to win. And the Red Sox weren't tight because they had just had the Division championship taken away from them, and now they were getting a second chance. So they played as good a game as they could play because they felt they had absolutely nothing to lose.

It was a tremendous day, I'll tell you, it really was. It was like being in the seventh game of the World Series. Gid started and he didn't really have his good stuff 'cause he was going with only three days' rest again, but he was still good enough to hold them to two runs in six and a third, quite an accomplishment for a left-hander in Fenway. In the second Yaz got up, and he knew Gid was going to try to pump a fastball by him, and Gid got the ball up, and Yaz has such power in his hands, he just turned those wrists over and *boom* that ball was gone.

They scored again in the sixth when Rice singled Burleson home. Everything was real quiet in our bullpen, and I said to Tidrow, "We're just teasing them. In the ninth inning, we're gonna win this son of a bitch three to two and go home." Dirt said, "I think we're gonna win eight to two." We were both wrong—the score was actually 5-4—but we just knew, we had a feeling out there, that we were going to win. We had all those goose eggs up there on the scoreboard, but the way the game was going, Torrez had been lucky, and there was no way he was going to shut us out. And there wasn't.

In our half of the seventh Chambliss singled and Roy singled and Bucky Dent got up. Because Willie Randolphs's still out, Fred Stanley went in to play second when Len pinch-hit for Doyle, so they didn't pinch-hit for Bucky like they usually do. Torrez threw Bucky a slider, Bucky swung, and he hit the ball off his ankle. Bucky went down, and when he dragged himself back up, he hobbled over to third-base coach Dick Howser, and he said, "If that son of a bitch comes in there again with that pitch, I'm going to take him into the net." And Torrez threw it in there again, and *bang* there it went. Bucky hit it into the net for a three-run homer.

In the bullpen we were laughing because our shortstops have devastated Torrez. In June, Stanley hit that grand slam off him, and now Bucky hit this three-runner. Seven RBIs in two swings. Torrez just can't get our shortstops out! Then Rivers walked and stole second, and he scored when Thurman doubled off reliever Bob Stanley.

When Reggie got up in the eighth, Mr. October, as he likes to call himself, hit another home run to make it 5 to 2. Despite the fact that Reggie at times can be hard to take, there's no question that in the big games, he can get way up and hit the hell out of the ball. No one's ever denied him that. I can't figure out why he does it, but he does it. I think that in the big games a pitcher has a tendency to be finer around the plate, and that makes the hitter more selective. If Reggie could concentrate all year long like he does in the play-offs and the Series games, his records would be unbelievable. Reggie's so strong, and he has so much power that a pitcher can't fool with him. If he makes a mistake, and Reggie gets his bat on it, Reggie swings such a heavy bat that it's gone.

Goose relieved Gid in the seventh and got the last two outs, but in their half of the eighth, the Red Sox came back with two runs against him. Remy doubled, Yaz singled to drive him in, Fisk singled, and Lynn singled for their fourth run.

They got us out in the top of the ninth, so the score was still 5-4 ours when Boston batted in the bottom of the inning. Goose walked Burleson with one out. Remy then hit a line drive to Piniella in right. Lou lost it in the sun, which was beating right in his eyes, but he pretended he was going to catch it, pounding his glove, so Burleson had to hold up and could only go to second when the ball bounced in front of him. That won the game for us, 'cause Rice flied out, and had Burleson been on third, he would have tagged and scored and tied up the game. With Burleson on second, though, it was just a harmless fly ball.

Now there were two outs in the bottom of the ninth. The Red Sox were down to their last batter: Carl Yastrzemski. I had seen the way the game was going, and I was heating up pretty good in the bullpen cause I thought to myself, "Goddamn, the way this is going, I'm going to face Yaz if he comes up in the ninth." Even Tidrow had said, "They're gonna be using you. Stay ready." I guess he figured Yaz is left-handed and they'd bring me in to face the lefty.

If I could have gone in there and gotten him out and saved the game, that one out would have let me be part of something. Just one fucking out, which is all it would have been. I've always been able to get Yaz out, and if there was ever a time to bring me in, this was it.

I stood out in the bullpen waiting for Lemon to come out of the dugout and get Goose. Lemon, however, never left the bench. He left Goose in to pitch to Yaz. I said, "Screw it," and I stopped warming up.

I suppose I should have been annoyed, pissed off, angry, but I wasn't any of those things. You gotta look at it from Lem's way too. When you have a reliever like Goose—just like I was last year—you gotta go with the guy all the way. You can't be making too many moves.

Yaz stepped in. Goose fired the ball in there, and Yaz sent a high pop behind third. When Graig settled under the ball and caught it and the game was over, suddenly I felt a tremendous surge of happiness come over me. Even though I had hardly contributed at all, for the first time since the spring I really felt part of this team. I was proud of what we did, and all the records the team set. I was happy for Guidry, who won his twenty-fifth and I felt happy for Goose, who got his twenty-seventh save. I was thinking about how we came from 14 games back in July, and how no other team in the entire history of baseball had ever done that. The events were rushing through my mind. There were so many things that happened to this team this year, I'll probably remember this season more than any other season of my baseball career.

We were celebrating in the clubhouse, and I was feeling excited and happy, when I started thinking about what Steinbrenner had said to me during midseason: "I want you to know that just as much as you were responsible for getting us into the play-offs last year, you're just are responsible for our having to struggle so much this year. If you had pitched halfway the way you can, we would have run away with it."

Well, I'll be out of here by Christmas, I guarantee you that, and next year I'll come back and I'll get even with him. I'm going to miss the guys. I have no bitch with them. No team could have as great a bunch of guys as this team. But when I come back to Yankee Stadium, and I'm sitting in the opposite dugout, I'm going to break that man's heart, just like he broke mine. And that's a promise.

Bucky F---ing Dent

"Don Zimmer's Nightmare"
New York Times, May 14, 1979

by Eric Lincoln

Mention the name "Bucky Dent" to any Red Sox fan and you're likely to be met with exasperation, dejection, and perhaps some colorful language. Dent's home run in 1978's one-game playoff between the Yankees and Red Sox, which just barely cleared the towering left field wall at Fenway Park, was a shot through the heart of the Red Sox Nation. For Yankee fans, it was pure magic.

> The way the fans treat Zim is a sin, it's a sin.
> The way the fans treat him is a sin.
> —from "The Ballad of Don Zimmer"

BOSTON—Don Zimmer, the manager of the Boston Red Sox, has not yet forgotten it and says he believes he never will. He has replayed Bucky Dent's playoff home run over and over again in his mind, and he has had nightmares about it ever since that afternoon last October. In his nightmares Zimmer sees the ball rising in the wind toward the left-field corner of Fenway Park. This part of the dream is always the same. The variation is that sometimes the ball tails absolutely and unalterably foul, landing harmlessly on the roof. Most often, though, it stays fair.

Zimmer, standing in a corner of the Red Sox dugout last week, turned and pointed to the spot where Dent's home run had come to rest: slightly to the right of the yellow left-field foul pole, just over the ledge at the top of the 37-foot wall and on the net that hangs above Lansdowne Street. He had a large wad of chewing tobacco in his mouth, and he spit in the general direction of the wall. He thrust his hands forward, held them about two feet apart and told how close Boston had come to winning the American League's Eastern Division title.

"That much," he said. "Just that much."

Then Zimmer sat and stared vacantly at the wall. He lowered his head and said quietly:

"I've been in this game 30 years, and I've never been so disappointed. I thought I'd learned how to let go of things like that. But every time I come out of that tunnel leading to the dugout and look out at that wall, I see the ball going over it. It's been nightmares ever since."

He paused to spray some more tobacco.

"Nightmares, nightmares, nightmares."

It has been more than seven months since Oct. 2, when the New York Yankees defeated Boston, 5-4, in that one game playoff for the East crown, sending the Red Sox home from a season in which they once led the Yanks by 14 1/2 games. Still Don Zimmer can't forget.

The Boston players, by contrast, say they haven't had to cope with the nightmares, not for this length of time, anyway. Says Mike Torrez, the pitcher who gave up Dent's three-run homer: "Why hold on to it so long? It took me about two weeks to get over it. This is a new season, and I don't think anyone would want to carry the memory into next week." In a three-game series here starting Friday night, the Yankees and the Red Sox will be meeting for the first time since that October day. Tickets to the series were sold out within 24 hours after they had gone on sale one day last winter. But to Torrez it will be nothing more than just another duel between two of the four genuine contenders in the division: "Milwaukee, Baltimore, New York and us."

"Hyperbole," says Carlton Fisk. "I think the rivalry is nothing more than hyperbole at this point. It's the press and the fans who make something of it. They get hopped up, souped up and all excited. It's very strange."

Very strange, and Zimmer has taken the brunt. Upton Bell, the host of sports talk show on radio station WBZ here, says Boston fans speak of the October game in words that conjure the elements of "Greek tragedy." They talk of an ill wind that carried Dent's home run into the net. They curse the Fates and swear at the Yankees. And they swear at Don Zimmer, with invective from the stands, in letters to the newspapers and in telephone calls to radio talk shows. The criticism has been by and large unspecific.

"Overall the players have taken it well," said Bell, reflecting on the Red Sox's downfall of '78. "It's the fans who have reacted to this thing as though it was a matter of life and death. They've always been a little neurotic up here. They take the Red Sox very seriously. They call us on our show and ask why the Red Sox don't fire Don Zimmer. That's why we played 'The Ballad of Don Zimmer' on our show. The ballad says that Zimmer hasn't done too badly in winning 99 games last year. Still they go out to the ball park and boo him. It's something vicious in their New England heritage."

"I'm not concentrating on the Yankees this season," Zimmer said. "Last year it was supposed to be a two-team race. It's four teams; at least, this year, I know one thing for certain, though: When I do see those people come in here next Friday and I take a look at Dent, the nightmares will probably start all over again."

"You're either a hero or a bum to these fans," says Fred Lynn, the Boston center fielder.

And now Zimmer, who has played the bum, was sitting in the dugout and talking about the boss. He had heard them ever since he became the Red Sox manager in 1976, but they had become worse this spring—despite Boston's early-season position near first place, and despite Zimmer's winning percentage of almost .600 in his two and a half seasons here.

"My wife was sitting behind the dugout early in April when they started to boo me," he said. "She told me afterwards that she had cried. Now, that bothers me. These fans don't know what they're talking about. What have I done so wrong with this club, anyway? We got as close as anyone could get last season. And we're close now."

Haywood Sullivan, the executive president and general manager, sat down next to him. Sullivan, a former catcher for the Red Sox, and Buddy LeRoux, who was once their trainer, purchased the team from the estate of Thomas A. Yawkey for $15 million on Sept. 29, 1977. Since then Sullivan and LeRoux have been criticized for not buying enough free agents and for retaining Zimmer as manager.

"This afternoon we just had an executive meeting," Sullivan said. "Me, Don and Buddy. We talked about getting some players if we could. We need some extra pitching this year, and we need a backup catcher. We need to fill in some spots. We're trying to bring the people of Boston a pennant."

Sullivan stopped talking, looked at Zimmer and then turned away. He said softly: "You know, I hear the boos, and I guess it hurts me as much as it hurts Zim. Me and Zim go back a long way. You know what he just said to me? He said, 'One day, Haywood, you're going to have to fire me.' And I said, 'Yeah, Zim, but we'll still be friends, won't we?'"

Indeed they will. Under the terms of his four-year contract, which ends after next season, Zimmer would join the Boston front office if the manager's job were taken from him.

The Red Sox, now 21-11, have enjoyed a start reminiscent of last season's. "The only question mark," says Zimmer, "is pitching."

Last season Bob Stanley was the best pitcher in the bull pen, with a 15-2 record, a 2.60 earned-run average and 10 saves. Then Bill Lee was traded to Montreal, and Luis Tiant, another starting pitcher, signed with the Yankees as a free agent. Zimmer was confronted by a problem. "I had to look for some starters," he said, "I guess what I've done is what the Yankees did, only in reverse. I took Stanley out of the bull pen. They put Ron Guidry in it."

Stanley thus far is 3-2. Torrez is 4-1. Dennis Eckersley, who is relied on as the stopper, is 3-2, but his e.r.a. is 4.14. Chuck Rianey, a rookie started, yielded only two runs and three hits in beating Oakland yesterday, but he entered the game with an e.r.a. of 6.27. There are definitely questions, which are compounded by Bill Campbell's sore arm.

Nor do the questions necessarily end with the pitching, Zimmer's assessment notwithstanding.

Fisk, the Red Sox's No. 1 catcher the last seven years, played the last two months of the 1978 season with a ligament problem in his elbow. "I could hardly throw," he said.

Having rested over the winter, he arrived at spring training little improved. He has played in only one game this season, and whether he will return to the lineup as the regular catcher is uncertain.

"I gave it some thought," said Fisk. "In the past I was the type of guy who wanted to play 150 or 160 games. I felt the pressure from the front office, and I also felt the pressure within myself. I suppose you could say I'm a little bit older and wiser now. I'm not coming back to the lineup until my arm is perfect."

Fisk spent half an hour in the batting cage last Friday, then walked away shaking his arm and said, "It's stiff, and it still swells up on me."

His replacements have been Bob Montgomery, 35 years old, and Gary Allenson, 24. Zimmer is platooning them, hoping to blend experience with youth. But Montgomery has a career average of only .241, and Allenson is around .220 in his rookie season. "I'm hoping that Carlton will be back," Zimmer says. "I'm hoping and keeping my fingers crossed."

Lynn, meanwhile, is hitting at a marvelous pace. He leads the major leagues in home runs, with 13; he has already driven 33 runners across the plate, and his average has been around .300. He is batting third in the order now, just ahead of Jim Rice, last season's most valuable player. Last year Lynn batted either second in the order or as low as seventh. He lifted weights over the winter, though, and when he arrived at spring training he lowered the position of his bat. "My swing is quicker," he says. "I've always thought I could win the batting title. This year I think I have it."

If so, he will have to beat out Rice, who is near .340 and who got close to the triple crown last season. Carl Yastrzemski is hitting .308. Butch Hobson, the third baseman who underwent elbow surgery last winter, was kept on the bench for the first few weeks of the season because of the cold weather. He is just now starting to hit.

But Dwight Evans, the right fielder, has been hitting poorly. And George Scott, the hefty first baseman who was ordered by Zimmer to lose 20 pounds over the winter, is also struggling, around .235. Scott is rumored to be one of the players the Red Sox have discussed giving up for another starting pitcher, a pitcher they might not have needed had Tiant stayed. Says Zimmer:

"I take my cap off to George Steinbrenner." He tipped his cap and bowed. "The guy bought Tiant, and he can buy most any player he wants. People resent him for this. I don't. I think it's great. I'd like to have a team like that. I'd sure like to have that kind of money."

Ron Townsend and Sonny Billings have been working at Fenway Park for the last four seasons. They take turns, day by day, climbing a 37-foot ladder to scale the left-field wall, and then walking the two-foot-wide ledge to retrieve baseballs hit during batting practice and baseballs hit during games. Billings had the chore the day after the playoff game last October.

"I didn't even think about it," he said. "Nah, didn't cross my mind. It was the only ball up there, and I just picked it up and gave it to my boss. I guess the only person in the world who thought it meant something was Bucky Dent. Who knows? We could be using that ball for batting practice right now."

LeRoux laughed when he heard Billings's story. "Geez, if I'd been up on that ledge and picked that ball up, I would have flung it into the Charles River."

Said Don Zimmer: "I never want to see that ball again."

Captain Bad Body

From *How Life Imitates the World Series*

by Thomas Boswell

Thurman Munson died tragically in August 1979 while attempting to land his Cessna aircraft near his Akron, Ohio, home. Thomas Boswell eloquently described Munson as "Gruff in public, acerbic on the bench, maniacally intense on the field, [yet] . . . calm and unpretentiously puckish in private." For all these things, Munson is remembered and admired by many.

Chavez Ravine at sunset after a World Series game, with the crowds gone home and the San Gabriel Mountains aflame behind the outfield fence, is the most beautiful, transcendent setting in baseball. As Thurman Munson walked slowly around the upper deck of empty Dodger Stadium one such October evening, he shuffled along like an old man with sore feet, stretching the minutes before he reached the gate marked "Exit" and had to leave the place he loved best.

Because the game was over, the deadlines past and only an all-night flight from Los Angeles to New York was ahead of us, Munson was in no hurry—just talking softly about the sundown and the silence and about how the park was at its best when empty. This was how the New York Yankees usually saw their captain, their almost ideal leader and perfect teammate. Gruff in public, acerbic on the bench, maniacally intense on the field, Munson suddenly became calm and unpretentiously puckish in private. Munson's mouth played tricks under his walrus moustache as he walked, showing hidden glimpses of the mischievous, prankish nature buried deep under a layer of protective pride as bristly and thick as any animal hide.

"You've changed since you won the MVP award last year," Munson was teased. "You've gotta work to stay grumpy. Pretty soon you'll be a nice guy and a lousy ballplayer."

Munson liked that, since it flirted with bad taste, hinted at the truth, and dared him to make a denial. If humor holds a kernel of truth, then the adroit insult holds more—it was Munson's métier. "Now the guys can call me Captain Bad Body or anything they want," Munson said. "The Fat Kid's doing okay."

Thurman Munson, who died at thirty-two in a crash while piloting his private airplane, cultivated a misunderstanding with the world at large, just as he nurtured a powerful camaraderie with those he loved—his teammates and his family.

Small talk, which might only bore others, infuriated Munson. Good manners he disdained as weakness or fraud. Intransigence—take me or leave me—he had raised to a standard of personal integrity. Introduced to a stranger, he might begin, "Where'd you get that ugly shirt?" It was his method for finding his social bearings quickly. "The same place you got that ugly face" was always a proper answer.

A creature of the locker room, Munson was comfortable with conversation only when it was dangerous—balanced on the edge between humor and hostility. In the dugout world, where a fist-fight may be seen as only a minor incident that often clears the air, Munson's sharp-sighted straight-for-the-jugular salvos did not need to be muffled. In fact, they made him a sage among his peers. Being worthy of Munson's needle was a badge of honor. "It's unbelievable to other players that Munson is thought of as silent and surly," Baltimore captain Mark Belanger once said. "I'd say that he is the most talkative player in baseball, and maybe the funniest, too."

It may be Munson's unfortunate legacy that he is remembered as a caricature—almost the reverse—of himself, because he happened to disdain the sports media. Often the feeling was mutual.

"For the people who never knew him, didn't like him, I feel sorry for them," said Billy Martin.

"When I played against him, I hated him for years," Munson's Yankee friend, Graig Nettles, always said. "He was an absolute competitor. He wanted to be liked, but he was too proud to politic for it."

Many will be amused at perhaps the soundest of Munson's eulogies, that of Bowie Kuhn, who called him, "a wonderful, enormously likeable guy."

Since Munson's public manner did no public harm except to himself, it is only fair to judge him by his private face, which did much good, and by his style on the ball field, which ennobled his game.

"Nice guys are a dime a dozen," said the greatest Army football coach, Red Blaik, "but leaders are the rarest of breeds."

It was a nice irony that Munson found it incomprehensible that he was the first Yankee captain since Lou Gehrig. "If I'm supposed to be captain by example, I'll be terrible," said Munson, who was the heart of perhaps the most appealing of Bronx champions, those of '78.

"I seem to attract dirt," Munson once said with pride. "The game was only ten pitches old tonight and I was filthier than anybody else was all night." To those who appreciated him, Munson was a sweat hog, who, beneath the tools of ignorance, was the essence of pride and rude wit.

Great catchers bear a different dignity than other players, since what they do in their game is in every sense work and only in the highest sense play. He approved of that tradition which labeled a broken finger a sign of virtue. Although his statistics may one day squeeze his squatty body into the Hall of Fame, Munson's most indelible contribution to the game was his manner—a ring of roust-about power that seemed to encircle him and protect him in those moments of crisis that he relished.

At the plate, where he was a .300 hitter five times, batted .339 in three play-offs and .373 in three Series, Munson took his sweet time, digging in his back foot defiantly, adjusting his batting glove interminably, twisting the last kink out of his fidgety neck, then pawing, yanking, and nodding until he was absolutely ready. His message to the pitcher was evident to the entire stadium: "When I get all this finished, you're in trouble."

"You'd jam him with every pitch, the way you know you ought to," Jim Palmer said once, "but he'd actually move into the pitch and let it hit him."

On the bases, Munson revealed the all-sport athlete who was concealed under shin guards and chest protectors as he dashed first to third as though his britches were on fire, ending his digging, stumbling dashes with a variety of wildly improvisational slides that left him deliciously filthy. If Pete Rose epitomized conspicuous hustle in his era—flavored with a taste for self-promotion— then Munson was the greatest of hidden hustlers who disguised his injuries, never curried the crowd's favor, and was best appreciated by players who universally saw him as their model.

As a receiver, Munson had a jerry-rigged three-quarter-arm throw that made him seem comic, plus a scrambling style on low pitches that was weak. Yet on key plays, key steals, he usually seemed to win. And his secret strength was his studious knack for calling pitches and needling hitters. Munson spent countless hours gabbing around other teams' batting cages, pretending to chitchat but really studying stances. Everybody knew his motive, but was helpless.

"Munson always said, 'How's it going, kid?' to rookies, and 'How's the family?' to veterans when we come to the plate," Belanger said. "One day, I got furious and said, 'Thurman, we all know what you're doing. You're trying to distract me and I'm hitting .190. Just leave me the hell alone. Just shut up when I'm up here or I'll hit you with the bat.'

"He got this terrible hurt expression and said, 'Jeez. Blade, I didn't know you felt that strongly. I swear I'll never say another word to you.' "

On his next at-bat, Belanger was all ready to swing when the high-pitched penetrating voice behind him said, "How's the family, Blade?"

If Munson had an instinct for victory on the field with his indestructible will, he had a penchant for feeling bitterly slighted at other times. For years, he felt he played in the shadow of glamorous Carlton Fisk of Boston. He almost had apoplexy when Cincinnati Manager Sparky Anderson said of Munson, "Don't embarrass him by comparing him to Johnny Bench." When the Yankees paid Reggie Jackson, a slugger of a few all-around baseball skills, more than Munson, the catcher was permanently galled. The list of indignities, real and imagined, was long.

Yet Munson, contrary to his image, often laughed about his annoyances, saying, "I'm just happy to be here," or "The Fat Kid was not consulted." Those who thought Munson obnoxiously serious in all his grumbling about money were unaware of Munson's guileful and lusty ability to acquire capital—and real estate. The dugout scuttlebutt on Munson was that he would eventually own Ohio as Ty Cobb wished to acquire Georgia. Munson flew airplanes for two reasons central to his misunderstood personality: 1) because he disliked big-city bluster and loved his family in Canton, Ohio, and 2) because he planned on owning not just one airplane but eventually an entire commuter airline.

Ballplayers do not leave epitaphs, only memories and friends. Munson, the man who may have been baseball's ideal teammate, was rich in both.

Though some may wonder why, the mourning for Munson will be just as genuine and deeply felt within baseball as it was for the last Yankee captain who died too young. The Fat Kid left memories of a style of play as indelible as those of any man of his time.

PART VI

Tough Times for Donnie Baseball

1982–1995

Don Mattingly holds a spot in Yankee Stadium's Monument Park alongside the likes of Ruth, Gehrig, DiMaggio, Mantle, Berra, Jackson, and other heroes who made this franchise the winningest organization in the history of professional team sports. Among the 18 players, 3 field managers, and 3 front-office men honored with plaques or monuments at the Stadium, "Donnie Baseball" is the only one who never played on, managed, or ran a World Series team. His 14-year career (1982–1995) exactly coincided with the Yankees' longest pennant drought since the team's first 18 seasons in New York. But Mattingly's accomplishments—including one batting title, one RBI crown, and three straight 200-hit seasons—are nonetheless worthy of celebration; two pieces by eminent *Sports Illustrated* writers describe the pinnacle seasons of his career.

As the Yankees of the 1980s struggled to regain championship form, George Steinbrenner brought in a parade of high-priced free agents and continued his revolving-door approach to hiring managers. Billy Martin took the helm on three different occasions during the decade, and esteemed *New York Post* columnist Phil Pepe attempts to make sense of the madness.

Hall of Famer Dave Winfield and four-time all-star Tommy John provide an outsider's view to joining the Yankee fray, while longtime Bombers Graig Nettles and Lou Piniella reflect on the ever-evolving zoo in the Bronx. And although all-stars and big-name free agents define the Yankee mystique, the views of a humble bat boy and the remarkable achievement of a pitcher facing incredible odds bring a human side to the Yankee story.

Don Mattingly, circa 1985. *Focus on Sport/Getty Images*

"I Can Wear My Hat Any Way I Want"

From *Balls*

by Graig Nettles and Peter Golenbock

In his third stint as Yankees manager, Billy Martin got right back to being Billy Martin. After declaring war on umpires at the start of the 1983 season, the Yankees ended up on the wrong end of some pretty tough calls. In this piece, third baseman Graig Nettles recalls a particularly tough day at the ballpark for Billy.

Billy was having trouble with the umpires all night one game against Texas, and a couple times he was right. I was involved. There were two outs and I was batting against Rick Honeycutt. I had two strikes, and Smalley tried to steal home.

I'm up there guarding the plate, trying to get the run in, and on the next pitch, I hear someone running down the line yelling, "Don't swing, Puff, don't swing," and I look up, and it's Smalley.

You never—I mean never—steal home with two strikes on the batter. You can get killed that way. The pitcher throws it over, you have to swing, otherwise it's strike three, and the inning is over. When I'm out in the field, and the runner is bluffing to steal home with two strikes, I yell, "Take it if you want it." What good's it going to do you if the pitcher throws a strike? I didn't want to hit Smalley, so I just stood there scratching my head. I didn't know what the heck was going on.

Smalley comes sliding across the plate, and he's safe, and the umpire, who was blocked by the catcher, calls him out. Billy came out and argued that—to no avail.

I later found out the reason he went with two strikes. An earlier pitch had been way inside and almost hit me—it was right under my chin—and everyone assumed it was a ball, but the ump had called it a strike, making the count one and two. The next pitch was called a ball, and so Zimmer, the third-base coach, thought the count was three and one when it was really two and two.

A couple innings later, I was on first base, and I was running, and there was a grounder to second, and I came sliding in just as the shortstop was about the make the relay, and I threw a shoulder into him. He was right on the base, and I had the right to do that, and the umpire called an automatic double play. Billy came out and argued that.

And then later in the game, a Texas player hit a ball that we thought bounced over the fence, which should have been a double, but the umpire said it hadn't bounced. The ump may have been right on that, but Billy argued that one too.

And then the next inning Billy stood in the dugout with his cap turned sideways, and before I knew it, the umpire called time and looked into the dugout and pointed at Billy. Billy came out of the dugout, and the ump screamed, "If you don't turn your hat around, I'm throwing you out of here." Billy screamed, "I can wear my hat any way I want." The ump said, "That's it. You're out of here. You're gone." And then Billy started kicking dirt on him.

As he was leaving the dugout, Billy ordered all our starting pitchers who weren't going to play that day to wear their hats sideways. And they sat that way the rest of the game. I really didn't know you could be thrown out of a game for wearing a hat sideways. Earl Weaver used to wear it backwards but not sideways.

The fact is that a lot of the players think that the umps are getting on Billy because of the Yankee ad campaign that features pictures of Billy kicking dirt on an umpire. Everyone knows George rehired Billy because he draws fans, and before the season started, he made these posters, and the yearbook shows the same picture, and it's only going to make it tough on us.

The second game of the season, Billy told the press, "I'm declaring war on the umpires." Hell, that doesn't do the players any good. It just makes it tougher to do our jobs when the umps are against us. But that's the way Billy likes to do things. Plus the fact that any time a play is called against us, George gets tapes and sends them to the league office to prove how the umpires are wrong. So the umps are going to have a hard-on for us all the time, which makes it that much tougher. We can't say anything to anyone. Billy isn't going to change. He's been successful doing it his way. I don't think the umps would consciously screw us, because they have a lot of integrity, but if it's a close call, all this is not going to influence them in our favor either.

My second big league at bat I was standing at home plate. Ed Runge was the home plate ump. I walked up to hit. While the catcher was out on the mound talking to the pitcher, Runge said to me, "You're from San Diego, aren't you?" I said, "Yeah." He said, "San Diego High?" I said, "Yeah." His son had been there a couple years ahead of me. He said, "Good luck to you. I'm pulling for you guys from San Diego, especially San Diego High, to make it." I said, "Thanks a lot, Ed. I appreciate it." Joel Horlen was the pitcher, and the first pitch he threw me was a curve outside, which the catcher caught on a bounce almost. Runge went, "Strike one." I didn't say anything, because I had heard you don't say anything to Ed Runge, because he likes to test rookies. I just stood there. The next pitch I figured Horlen was going to throw outside, so I was leaning way out, and he threw it inside and it must have had six inches of the plate, and Runge says, "Ball one." From then on, when Runge was behind the plate, I had a very small strike zone, and he was an umpire pitchers ordinarily loved. Six inches from the plate either way was a strike, usually. But he gave me pitches like no other umpire. Because I didn't complain to him when he tested me.

It taught me a lesson right there—not to give umpires a lot of grief. And I never have. I tell the young players coming up, "Don't give the umpires crap. Don't say anything. Accept the calls, because in the long run you'll get the breaks."

Sweet Lou, the Someday-Manager

From *Sweet Lou*

by Lou Piniella and Maury Allen

Ten seasons after making his (brief) big-league debut with the Orioles, Lou Piniella came to New York in 1974 as an outfielder and part-time DH. Approaching retirement in 1984, "Sweet Lou" didn't take long to entertain thoughts of entering the managerial realm. The Yankees initially brought Piniella on as a hitting coach, and he finally got the call to manage in 1986.

I have admired a lot of hitters in my time: George Brett, Carl Yastrzemski, Tony Oliva, Rod Carew, and, for power, Reggie Jackson. Another hitter I admire, not so much for style or mechanics or stance as for sheer durability and hitting success, is Pete Rose. I had 1,705 hits in my career and thought I was a pretty good hitter. Here is a guy who will finish up with nearly 2,500 more hits than me and who has played the game with intensity all these years. I can't comprehend a guy getting 4,200 hits. It could be 10,000 hits. It all seems astronomical. He has 700 more hits than Carl Yastrzemski, who was the best hitter in our league for all those years. I'm just amazed that a guy could eat, sleep, and live baseball for so long. It was his job, but he always kept it a game. I was a high school senior when he broke in with the Tampa Tarpons in 1961, and I always rooted for him. It's incredible to me that he was a professional player before I was, and he was still playing long after I was finished. He did it all with hard work.

As the 1984 season wound down, more and more people—newspaper reporters, Yankee officials, fans—began discussing my future. Would I ever manage the Yankees? Would I ever manage any other big league club? Did I want to?

A baseball career takes funny turns. There is no way to predict the future. Yes, I wanted to manage the Yankees someday. I also thought I'd be damn good at it. I knew I wouldn't have any trouble handling the offense and generating runs. Whether I could handle the pitchers and the personalities of twenty-five players were more legitimate questions.

Nobody handled pitching better than Yogi Berra did in 1984. He taught me one thing of paramount importance about managing: Pitchers have only so many throws in their arms. You have to treat them with kid gloves—they're different from the rest of the club. You can't abuse their arms. The first lesson Yogi taught me was to get the pitcher out of there at the right time, no matter whether you're way ahead or way behind. You want the pitcher to last eight or ten years, not three or four. George Steinbrenner taught me how much money it takes to develop a younger pitcher. You cannot destroy all you have invested in a kid just to win this game or that one. You must understand the long-range goals of the organization. When I broke in, pitchers used to be concerned about coming out of games. They thought more innings meant more money. Now everybody makes enough money. If you have a good young pitcher, protect him. Stretch his career out.

Yogi did a magnificent job in making Dave Righetti a fine relief pitcher. Yogi protected Righetti, brought him along slowly, and was cautious as to how he used him. When he had pitched two or three times, Yogi would sit him down for a while.

"We may lose today," Yogi once told me on the bench when he refused to warm Righetti up in a close game, "but it will win us five or six down the road." By the end of the season, Righetti was comfortable and confident as a relief pitcher.

A manager has to look at the entire season. If you jump out fast, you have a chance to win wire to wire. If not, the idea is to keep yourself in position through the middle of the summer, so you can win it in September.

One other important aspect of successful managing is using all your personnel, not only the on-field but also the off-field people. You have to learn to depend on your specialty personnel, your pitching and hitting and fielding coaches, your front office, your scouts, all the people in the organization. Nobody is so smart that he can run a ballclub all by himself. You have to hire good people and give them authority. When I manage, my coaches will be ambitious. I don't intend to surround myself with old buddies who just want to add pension time. I want guys who want to manage, who want to better their position. They will be on top of their game. It would be a thrill to have my coaches picked as big league managers.

Just as I don't want yes men as coaches, managers shouldn't be yes men for the front office people. I will work with them, understand what they have to do, and appreciate their efforts—as a coach I've learned to understand the business aspects of the front office. It's important to work well with the front office. But I will make my own decisions.

Remember, you heard it here first!

In 1984, we salvaged some pride by finishing third. Yogi had the club playing good ball in the second half, and could be especially proud of the second half record of 51-30. The most thrilling part of the year was the batting race between Don Mattingly and Dave Winfield, with Mattingly giving me too much credit for helping him win. That kid can flat-out hit, and will be a threat to win batting titles for years to come. In the final weeks of the season, George asked me several times what I thought of Yogi's handing of the club. I had no idea which way George was leaning—toward bringing him back or toward letting him go—but I tried to give him my honest opinion. I told him I thought Yogi had rebuilt the pitching staff. I thought he was more aggressive, in better control of the team, and had turned the place around. I didn't tell George what to do or what not to do about Yogi. Whichever way George went, I would not be surprised.

Mattingly vs. Winfield—The 1984 Batting Race

"And May The Best Man Win"
Sports Illustrated, September 10, 1984

by Steve Wulf

*Though it wasn't exactly Ruth vs. Gehrig or Mantle vs. Maris, the
1984 batting race was something special in the Bronx. In the end, it
was Don Mattingly edging out Dave Winfield with his .343 average.
Winfield finished at .340, the highest mark of his Hall-of-Fame career.*

TEAMMATES DAVE WINFIELD AND DON MATTINGLY ARE IN A TIGHT
BATTLE FOR THE BATTING CROWN

David is Goliath. The big guy stands 6'6", bats righthanded, pulls the ball, makes
about $1.5 million a year, strides as if he owned the place and spits out half of
Kansas's sunflower seed crop. In the other corner is The Kid. He's 5'11", only 23,
lefty, a spray hitter earning $130,000 this year, one of the boys and up to snuff.

Dave Winfield and Don Mattingly are the unlikely opponents in the
American League batting race, as well as teammates on the New York Yankees.
"They're 1 and 1A," says the Yankee batting coach, Lou Piniella. "It doesn't
matter which stablemate wins, so long as they flash that number on the tote
board after it's over."

What a race they're in! In seven games last week, Sunday to Sunday,
the lead changed hands 11 times, sometimes during games. At week's end
Winfield was hitting .351812 and Mattingly .350806. Their nearest pursuer,
Eddie Murray of Baltimore, was batting a mundane .322. The feats of 1 and

1A require the special perspective of their manager, Yogi Berra. "Three-fifty," mused Berra one day last week. "That's a lot of hits."

Those are hard .350s, too. Mattingly has 20 home runs and 89 RBIs, and following games last weekend against California, in which he singled, doubled and homered twice, he led the league in slugging percentage at .548. Winfield, sixth in slugging, has 16 homers and 81 RBIs. Together, they've helped turn the Yankee season around, pulling the team up from last on May 20 to fourth in the AL East.

With 27 games left, Mattingly, who has 174 hits, and Winfield, who has 165, could become the first Yankees since Bobby Richardson in 1962 to have 200 hits, and either one could become only the sixth Yankee ever to win a batting title. To the accompaniment of harps, the five previous winners are Babe Ruth . . . Lou Gehrig . . . Joe DiMaggio . . . Mickey Mantle and—who let him in?—Snuffy Stirnweiss.

Neither Winfield nor Mattingly was a preseason candidate to win a batting title. Winfield had a career average of .284 for his 11 seasons, never batting higher than .308. Mattingly, who hit .283 as a rookie in '83, wasn't even assured of a regular job.

Winfield got off to a slow start, spending 15 days on the disabled list with a hamstring injury and sinking as low as .242 on May 7. "When I came off the DL," says Winfield, "[Dave] Kingman had like 11 homers and 27 RBIs, and I was sitting at 2 and 5. I had nothing left to shoot for but the batting title. When I started to get serious I was around .269, and I said, 'Let me get out of here.' Then it was .270, .280, .290. I skipped right over the .300s, spent a few days in the teens, missed the 20s. . . ." On July 5, after a month-long 58-for-121 (.429) tear, Winfield reached a high of .377.

Winfield says he became a better hitter because of an almost mystical weight/exercise program known as Sagekinetics, developed by a former minor league pitcher named Steve Sagedahl. The Sage-kinetic machines simulate the batting and throwing motions of baseball, building both strength and speed.

Winfield thinks it's amazing he's done so well, considering his ongoing feud with a certain owner who shall remain nameless. "He tried to trade me [to Texas] and assassinate my character," Winfield says. "I have had to fight adversity and animus, and I've answered: one, by the way I play, two, by speaking up when nobody else would, and three, by taking him to court and winning the money he owes the [David M.] Winfield Foundation. But none of this has been a motivating factor."

Winfield's real motivation is that he feels he has never gotten his due. For someone who puts up some great numbers, plays very hard, gives a lot of time to the public and stands up to an obnoxious owner, he has remained remarkably unpopular. "I know people are rooting for The Kid," says Reggie Jackson, who likes to keep an eye on his old team. "I hear people knocking Dave because he's sacrificed his home-run power for his average. But the man has over 80 RBIs. The only thing you can knock him for is that he's never won."

The Kid carries no such burdens. In fact, he's almost carefree about the batting race. "I think it's kind of neat," says Mattingly, "the two of us fighting for the title. Just think, we don't have to check the papers to see which one is ahead, not as if it was Dave and, say, Kent Hrbek. I like it this way."

Mattingly simply loves to hit. He went to Puerto Rico over the winter because he was a little disappointed that he tailed off at the end of '83, and he won the winter league's batting championship with a .368 average. He and Piniella practice together frequently, and Friday night they could be seen in the runway behind the dugout, working on mechanics.

"I just wasn't feeling right," says Mattingly, who was batting .350 at the time. "Lou got me to put a little more weight on my back foot and stay down." The next night, Mattingly touched the Angels' Geoff Zahn for an opposite-field single, an opposite-field double and an impressive home run into the Anaheim Stadium terrace in rightfield, all on first pitches.

Mattingly's power has been a revelation, even to him. "I never hit more than 10 homers in a season, in any league," he says. "I think it's amazing enough that I'm going for a batting title. But for me to be up there in slugging percentage is even more incredible." Actually, Mattingly is proudest that he has liberated the Yankee farm system: The team is no longer afraid to bring up its good young prospects. One of them, in fact, outfielder Vic Mata, is challenging Winfield and Mattingly at .339, although he has only 62 at bats.

Winfield regained the batting lead in the first inning Sunday, singling after Mattingly flied out. Their race was briefly interrupted by a beanball war and a fifth-inning fight, and if either player was worried about protecting himself, he didn't show it. Winfield took responsibility for the strongest Angel, Brian Downing, and Mattingly ended up on the bottom of a pile. In the sixth, Mattingly dusted himself off, then hit a Ron Romanick pitch over the rightfield fence, which started the winning rally in the Yankees' 5-3 victory and also gave him the batting lead. That lasted only a few moments, though, because Winfield followed with a hustling double to left.

Both Winfield and Mattingly want the title, but while Winfield wants it badly, Battingly—as he is coming to be known—wants it goodly. "If I don't win it," he says, "I won't be disappointed, because I didn't expect it and I'll know I had a very good year. I'll be very happy for Dave. Just so long as one of us wins it."

Winfield is trying to steer clear of the entire subject. "I don't like to get into it," he said Sunday. "With the pressures of the New York media, I don't think it's going to be a nice situation at the end."

Winfield has experience on his side, and if he gets hot again, well, nobody gets hotter, even if he does have a sore left wrist. Mattingly will have the benefit of seeing more righthanders the last month, and he's the better contact hitter. Nobody on the Yankees will say it, but there is a slight pull for Mattingly. One observer says, "Mattingly might have a great game, but if the team lost, he won't do anything but throw his glove in the locker. Winfield, if he does well in a loss, will sometimes shrug his shoulders as if to say, 'Hey, it wasn't my fault.'"

Says outfielder Steve Kemp, who's very close to Mattingly, "I hope it ends in a tie, I really do. I know most people are rooting for Don, but that's because he's sort of the underdog. Who knows? Someday he might be the veteran fighting it out with The Kid for the batting title, and people will be pulling against him."

One of them is an expensive thoroughbred and the other a quarter horse, but they're 1 and 1A.

Mr. May

From *Winfield: A Player's Life*

by Dave Winfield with Tom Parker

*After signing Dave Winfield to the most lucrative contract ever in
1981, George Steinbrenner grew impatient with his big investment.
After a key loss to the Toronto Blue Jays late in the 1985 season,
Steinbrenner lamented, "Where is Reggie Jackson? We need a Mr.
October or a Mr. September. . . . Dave Winfield is Mr. May." There
was plenty of love lost between the owner and his star player.*

By the close of spring training, the 1985 Yankees were the closest knit team I'd
ever been on. There wasn't a bad apple in the bunch. It was also a team capable
of scoring a lot of runs, creating havoc for the opposition. There were Mattingly,
Randolph, Baylor, and George's newest acquisition, Rickey Henderson. Plus,
the strongest pitching staff since I'd joined the team—Guidry, Phil Niekro,
Righetti. You could just sense the excitement. Let's go! Let's go!!!

You could also feel the pressure. Steinbrenner had fielded an *expensive*
team, he said, and we'd have to earn our keep right out of the starting gate
or the crap would really hit the fan. It did. After the first few games, Yogi,
who always did his damndest to protect himself and the team from outside
pressures, could sense things coming down around him. Sixteen games into
the season Steinbrenner fired him and brought back Billy Martin for his fourth
stint at the helm. Many players were pissed, not just that Billy was coming in,
but that Yogi was on his way out. Most of them felt that the team would have
righted itself, but our opinions didn't count. Steinbrenner responded in the
press by saying that if we liked Yogi so much, we should have won for him.

Billy was cool about it, though. The players' reaction, the press, public
opinion, he shrugged it all off. He knew how we felt. "Yogi understands," he
told us the first day he was back on the job. "He's a great guy but it happens
to all of us. He stepped in for me once. Now I'm stepping in for him. If we

lose it, I'll be the one to take the blame. If we win it, everyone gets the credit, including Yogi."

Class. But that wasn't the feeling in the clubhouse. Everyone knew that things were going to be different. First, because it was Billy, there'd be even more reporters hanging around, looking for dirt. Next, a lot of the guys feared they'd be in Billy's doghouse. After all, he had his reputation as a disciplinarian to uphold. Billy's arrival didn't matter to me, though. While their styles were markedly different, I'd play the same for either Yogi or Billy; which is to say, after my experiences in 1984, I'd run, hit, and throw as well as I could, and help the team win, but I wasn't going to kill myself emotionally. Also, I knew that Billy respected my play and would back me up. That's all I really wanted from a manager.

Like any season with Billy in charge, 1985 sees a lot of hustle, a lot of wins. But there's also the psychological toll Billy's presence takes on the players and some coaches, coming from the tacit pressure from the top. Will Billy make it through the year? What happens if we drop a key series? How much slack before the noose tightens?

In 1985 the noose tightens in August. We're having a terrific month, are really on a tear, with the best record for August in professional baseball. We're only two games behind the division-leading Blue Jays, who are coming to Yankee Stadium for a series. But we're ready. We're hot, we're confident, we're cruising.

Then Steinbrenner shows up in the locker room: "This is the most important series of the year. We've got to sweep. This is a test of Yankee heart and Yankee pride. We can't let Toronto shame us in our own ballpark. This is the whole season right here."

That sure relaxes everyone on the team. Especially Billy who—known for his laid-back style—goes on a spree issuing contradictory commands and cussin' people out right and left. Willie Horton, one of our coaches, takes the worst of it. It's Willie do this, Willie do that. Billy resented Willie to begin with because rumor was that Steinbrenner had hired him to be Billy's chaperon. But the plan misfired because Willie didn't drink, leaving Billy to his own devices during off-hours.

Anyway, we take the first game—a Friday nighter—a sloppy win, but a win. Saturday we lose a close one. The locker room is pretty subdued afterward, the sentiment being: We're not ashamed, we played hard; they're a good team, the Yankees don't own all the talent; we'll win tomorrow.

Then Steinbrenner blasts into the locker room again, a single reporter in tow. George looks around and says, "The pitching's okay, but the hitting sucks!" Soon he's on a roll. We've got no Yankee pride. We should be ashamed to pick up our paychecks. We'd better not count on getting those paychecks indefinitely. Nobody looks at anybody else, everybody stares into his own locker.

Sunday morning we read in the paper that Steinbrenner says the Yankees are being "outplayed, outhustled, outmanaged, and outowned." Steinbrenner also names a few players, all black, who've really let him down. I'm number one on the list, "Mr. May." He wants "Mr. October" back.

Okay, my average is a little low, but I'm still driving in runs at a rate of 100+ a year for the fourth year in a row. The only guy to match me in the eighties was Eddie Murray.

Come the third game the team is disorganized and demoralized. Toronto knows it and kicks our butts all over the field. Steinbrenner's strategy was, I suppose, let me just whip my guys and they'll perform. That kind of rah-rah Vince Lombardi tactic might work in football, but not in baseball. We're whipped in the papers and Toronto comes in for the kill. After that, we get into a losing groove, although we eventually come back to make it close. But as far as I'm concerned, *that* was the season, right there.

The mindset of a team, I feel, is absolutely critical to how the players will perform. Professionals or not, there has to be some joy in it, if only to relieve the pressure that builds over a 162-game season. A team doing well can have a lot of fun, talk some outrageous trash in the locker room, on the bus, on the plane. There's fun to be had on the field, too. Hitting back-to-back home runs. Stealing bases, sliding, scoring. Throwing the other guy out at the plate. You can have a *great* time. With Steinbrenner, though, it's win or lose, live or die. The man shows up and the fun's gone, the pressure's on.

George wants controversy in New York; he creates it because he thinks it brings fans into the stadium. Billy is used to seeing his name in boldface so everyone will know who's really responsible for those wins when they come. The New York reporters are always sniffing around hoping for the apocalypse. Most guys in the league think a year in New York is worth three anywhere else. The attention can make a career take off, the pressure can shorten it. In Detroit if you play well for three weeks they let you slide for a month. In New York, performance isn't even judged day to day; it's play to play. And George Steinbrenner's got the shortest memory in town.

You're Hired. . . .
You're Fired!

From *The Ballad of Billy & George: The Tempestuous Baseball Marriage of Billy Martin and George Steinbrenner*

by Phil Pepe

Baseball is a cut-throat business, and managers know their jobs are rarely safe—especially if your boss was George Steinbrenner. Manager Billy Martin was hired, fired, and re-hired so many times it's tough to keep straight. All told, Martin had five separate tenures as Yankees manager from 1975 to 1988, each one as tumultuous as the next.

In the beginning, Billy Martin and George Steinbrenner got along swimmingly.

"Their common denominator," said Martin's lawyer, Judge Eddie Sapir of New Orleans, "was that every day they won a ball-game, the Lord added some life back into each of them. That was their common denominator: their burning desire to win."

The Yankees won five of their first six games in 1976 and 15 of their first 20. On May 8, they were in first place by three games. By mid-July, their lead was double digits, and the Yankees were off and running to their first American League pennant in 12 years.

For the most part, the season would pass without incident . . . well, almost without incident. In retrospect, there were some small, subtle signs of discontent between Martin and Steinbrenner that, in the years ahead, would bubble over into what would become an ongoing soap opera.

As July drew to a close, the Yankees went into a mild slide. They lost 11 of 15 games, their lead melting from 14 1/2 games to a still commanding 8 1/2, sending Steinbrenner into what would become a familiar panic mode. He told

Martin he wanted to go into the clubhouse and talk to the pitchers. Billy was against it, but he agreed to let Steinbrenner have his say.

"He gave the pitchers a rah-rah talk like they were high school kids, not professionals," said Martin, who often accused Steinbrenner of having a football mentality, of not understanding the pitfalls of a 162-game schedule.

"In football, they play once a week," Martin said. "Baseball is played every day, day in, day out. You have to grind it. You're going to hit your bumps in the long season, but you just have to ride them out, and you can't ride them out with pep talks."

"I went in and I got tough," Steinbrenner said. "I told them we're going for something here. You're going to get along, and if you can't get along with your teammate, then just ignore him."

Steinbrenner made his Knute Rockne speech, and Martin stood by silently, shifting embarrassingly from one foot to the other. When it was over, and the owner had left the clubhouse, the pitchers began to mock Steinbrenner and his sophomoric speech.

"They had hardly paid attention to anything he said," said Martin.

Said Graig Nettles: "We had a lot of veteran guys, and George would come in and yell at us, or he'd rip us in the newspapers. We knew how to turn him off and put that out of our minds and go out and play the game. And we played well after he'd rip us, and he thought he actually spurred us on to victory. He didn't, but in his mind he thought he did."

Not long after Steinbrenner's clubhouse caper, Martin took another subtle hit. As he walked to home plate to present the lineups to the umpires before a game, he noticed that sitting in the owner's private box was Dick Williams, the man Steinbrenner tried to hire as his manager before settling on Bill Virdon.

Steinbrenner explained to inquiring members of the media that Williams's presence was meaningless and innocent.

"Dick was in town," the owner said. "We're friends and he called me, so I invited him to come to the game. There's nothing to it."

Martin, perhaps somewhat paranoid, read something else into Williams's presence—a form of intimidation by Steinbrenner, an implied threat that Billy had better get the Yankees straightened out because another manager was waiting in the wings, and available.

A five-game winning streak and eight victories in nine games in August reversed the trend and restored the Bombers' lead to 10 1/2 games. They would go on to coast to a wire-to-wire victory in the American League East, finishing 10 1/2 games ahead of Baltimore.

"Billy was a real tactician," said Chris Chambliss, who would have a powerful impact on New York's first pennant in 12 years. "He knew how to get the best out of his players. As far as his off-the-field stuff, you knew that, but we had all kinds of other stuff going on with our club anyway. When it came to between the lines, I thought he was an excellent manager."

The Yankees would beat the Kansas City Royals in the five-game American League Championship Series, clinching the pennant in dramatic fashion on Chambliss's home run in the bottom of the ninth.

As soon as Chambliss's blast disappeared into the right field stands, Yankee Stadium exploded as long-suffering Yankee fans celebrated their team's return to glory. Billy Martin had done it. He had made good on his boast to George Steinbrenner. But his job was not complete.

No sooner had the Yankees clinched their 30th American League pennant—the first in Steinbrenner's regime—the owner let Martin know that he would not be content unless the Yankees won the World Series against the Cincinnati Reds, the vaunted "Big Red Machine" of Johnny Bench, Pete Rose, Joe Morgan and Tony Perez.

When the Reds blew the Yankees away in four games, Steinbrenner went into a rage. The Yankees had won their first pennant in 12 years and had gone over two million in home attendance for the first time in 26 years, but Steinbrenner was not satisfied.

He stormed into the Yankees clubhouse looking for Martin. He found him in the trainers' room, sobbing hysterically in defeat.

"We won a pennant, but I want a ring," Steinbrenner raged and put his manager on notice that getting swept in the World Series rendered the American League pennant meaningless and was therefore unacceptable. He would settle for nothing less than a World Series championship.

To make matters worse, Martin never received the tugboat he said Steinbrenner had promised him. Steinbrenner's defense was that he had mentioned giving Billy a tugboat as a joke, and that Martin understood it to be in jest. It would not be the first time that Martin and Steinbrenner would draw different conclusions on an issue.

On thing, however, was becoming abundantly clear: The honeymoon between Steinbrenner and Billy Martin was nearing an end.

◆ ◆ ◆

If hiring Billy Martin as his manager for the fifth time was George Steinbrenner's way of looking for a quick fix for his Yankees, that's exactly what he got. Billy V started spectacularly, the Yankees winning their first 5 games and 9 of their first 10.

This was Billy Martin at his best, back where he believed he belonged, managing a baseball team: not just *any* baseball team, but the team he loved.

It was typical Billy, doing what he had done so often, coming in and taking over, putting his imprint on a team, improving them immediately. It was inevitable. Also inevitable was Billy being Billy, looking for trouble, finding it, and self-destructing.

On May 2, the Yankees began a seven-game trip. They swept a two-game series in Chicago, then swept a two-game series in Kansas City. The Yankees had a record of 20-8 and a two-and-a-half game lead in the American League East, and Martin was eagerly looking forward to the next stop, a three-game series against the Texas Rangers in Arlington. There he would meet up with his old pal Mickey Mantle and with his son, Billy Joe.

The Yankees lost the first game of the series, 7-6, but Martin made note of how his team battled, fighting back from a 7-1 deficit to score five runs in the top of the ninth. The rally fell short, but Martin took pride in the fact that his team refused to quit.

When the game was over, Martin, as usual, headed straight for the bar at the Arlington Hilton, where he met up with Mantle, Mantle's son, Danny, and Yankees coach Mike Ferraro. After a few drinks, the group decided to move the party to Lace, a nearby topless nightclub.

What transpired next is unclear. What is known is that the Mantles and Ferraro decided to call it a night and left Martin alone at the club. At some point, Martin went into the men's room, where he proceeded to get involved in a skirmish with another patron. Soon a club bouncer and another customer arrived to act as peacemakers, grabbed Martin, and led him out of the men's room.

When Martin loudly objected to their interference, he was led to a rear door and tossed out of the club. In so doing, Martin hit his head on a stucco wall and suffered cuts on his ear and the side of his head. (Martin's version was that the bouncer sucker punched him, but police records made no mention of a punch.)

A bloody mess, Martin climbed into a taxi and headed back to the hotel. There is no record of how many times Martin avoided detection of his late-night dalliances by hopping a cab and returning to his hotel. This time, however, he was not so fortunate, the victim of bad timing.

When he arrived at the Arlington Hilton in the wee hours, there were dozens of witnesses waiting on the front lawn of the hotel. The hotel's fire alarm had gone off, causing the guests, Steinbrenner included, to be evacuated.

Seeing the condition of his manager, Steinbrenner was horrified. Ordinarily, he might have fired Martin on the spot for this latest episode. But the Yankees had a record of 20-9 and were in first place, so Steinbrenner issued a statement defending his beleaguered manager. Privately, he put Martin on a short leash.

"I felt responsible for the Lace incident because I wasn't there," said Billy Martin Jr., who, at the time, was a student at Texas Tech University in Lubbock, some 250 miles from Arlington. He was supposed to meet up with his father that night, but he had just finished his final exams and, rather than make the five-hour drive to Arlington, decided to get a night's sleep and set out fresh the next morning.

"If I had been there," said Billy Joe, "it never would have happened. I would have gotten him out of the club and back to the hotel before any of that. Dad never got into trouble when I was around."

The Yankees lost all three games in Texas, but won 5 of their next 6 and 11 of 14, including 5 in a row, which left them in first place. Martin seemed to have dodged another bullet . . . but only temporarily.

On May 30, the Yankees lost a 3-2 14-inning heartbreaker to the Athletics in Oakland. Martin had been ejected in the third inning when umpire Dale Scott ruled a line drive to shortstop Bobby Meacham was trapped. Martin argued that Meacham had made a clean catch of the ball and went off on an expletive-filled tirade at Scott, kicking dirt on the umpire. As a result, Martin was fined $1,000 and suspended for three games.

Without Martin, the Yankees won two out of three in Baltimore and returned home to lose two out of three to the Red Sox.

In Cleveland on June 19, they were routed by the Indians, 11-3, when Martin, obviously intending to prove a point, let pitcher Tim Stoddard absorb a beating that enabled the Indians to build on a 4-3 lead and put the game out of reach. For weeks, Martin had been begging the Yankees to release Stoddard, and his decision to leave Stoddard in to take his lumps was no doubt done to force the issue.

A witness to this was Clyde King, who had been sent by Steinbrenner to observe Martin and report back to the owner. What King reported was that Martin was out of control and the team's pitching was in disarray.

"My advice to you is that we make a change," King told Steinbrenner.

From Cleveland, the Yankees went to Detroit for a three-game series. The Tigers won the first game, 2-1, when reliever Cecilio Guante gave up a home run to Tom Brookens in the 10th inning.

The next night, the Yankees took a 6-1 lead into the bottom of the ninth. The Tigers rallied, and Martin again called on Guante to pitch to Alan

Trammell with the bases loaded. Trammell belted a grand slam to climax a six-run rally and gave the Tigers a 7-6 victory.

The Tigers won again the next night, scoring a run in the bottom of the 10th for a 3-2 victory in the final game of the series, and the final game of Martin's managerial career.

Steinbrenner had seen enough. He decided to make a change. Martin was fired on June 23 and replaced by Lou Piniella, who just a year before vowed he would never work for Steinbrenner again.

Twenty-two days later, the Yankees released Tim Stoddard. It was vindication, but small consolation, for Billy Martin.

Donnie Baseball Sets the Big Leagues on Fire

"The Banger in the Bronx"
Sports Illustrated, April 14, 1986

by E. M. Swift

Don Mattingly's 1984 batting title was only the beginning for this budding star. He racked up over 200 hits, 100 RBI, and 30 home runs in each of the next two seasons, leading the league in doubles both seasons as well. "Donnie Baseball" barely lost out to Boston's Wade Boggs for the 1986 batting crown and then finished second to Red Sox pitcher Roger Clemens in the MVP race.

IN ONLY HIS THIRD SEASON, DON MATTINGLY INVITES COMPARISON WITH
GEHRIG, DIMAGGIO, AND OTHER YANKEE STARS OF YORE

Don Mattingly is prowling the kitchen like a caged cat, looking for something, *anything*, that remotely resembles a baseball bat. A jammed thumb has forced the American League's MVP to miss batting practice the past four days, and there is a bridled restlessness about him, like that of a heavy smoker in his third day of trying to kick the nic. Mattingly wants to play. He wants to play so badly that, jammed thumb or no, he was diving for ground balls on this, the seventh day of spring training, saying to himself, "Seventh game of the World Series . . . two out . . . two on . . . " like some 9-year-old with a new glove.

The handle of a vacuum cleaner finds its way into Mattingly's hands, and he checks his stance. It is not exactly textbook stuff, hunched over as he is with his bat an inch off his shoulder and his right leg open and his left foot pointing backward "almost like a duck's," as he describes it. But textbook or no, this stance is one of the keys to Mattingly's success.

"I never thought I'd drive in 145 runs," says the 24-year-old Mattingly, taking a practice cut in the direction of his 1-year-old son, Taylor, who looks up from his animal crackers and giggles. Taylor was last publicly seen on the pages of the *New York Post* wearing Jim McMahon-style sunglasses and a headband bearing the name STEINBRENNER. This was a gentle dig at the Yankee owner, who, after signing Mattingly to a $1.375 million, one-year contract the day before arbitration proceedings were to begin in February, is considerably more popular in the Mattingly household now than he was a year ago. "I thought I might hit 35 homers," Mattingly adds, "but I didn't think it'd be last year."

He sure didn't after reaching the midpoint of the 1985 campaign with only nine round-trippers in 337 at bats. Then it was instant Popeye. Unexpectedly, Mattingly, who before making the big leagues had never had more than 10 home runs in a season, slammed 26 homers in the second half of the year, batting .340 over the same span to finish the season at .324. He also scored 107 runs to go with his 145 ribbies and 35 homers. All this from a 19th-round draft choice, for heaven's sake, who was thought to be too slow ever to make it as a singles hitter and too punchless ever to make it at first base. Mattingly's 217 runs produced (runs scored plus runs batted in, less homers) were the most by a Yankee since—no, not Reg-gie, not even Mantle or Maris, but—Joe DiMaggio, who drove in 155 runs, scored 110 and hit 39 homers in 1948.

"He had as good a year as anyone I've ever played with—or against," says rookie Yankee manager Lou Piniella, who has been Mattingly's batting instructor the past three years. "You knew the numbers were going to be good, but he put them up so easily that until you took a step back at the end of the year, you didn't realize *how* good."

Numbers are just, well, numbers. But consider these comparisons with Mattingly's 1985 totals. He had 48 doubles, second on the all-time Yankee list to the 52 by Lou Gehrig in 1927. Mattingly also became the first American League player to lead the majors in doubles two years in a row since Tris Speaker did so from 1920 to '23. He rapped 211 hits, the most by a Yankee since Red Rolfe had 213 in 1939. His back-to-back 200-plus-hit seasons were the first by a Yank since DiMaggio did it in 1936 and '37.

Yankee co-captain Ron Guidry thinks it's no mere coincidence that Mattingly's stats invoke such hallowed names. "By the time his career is over," says Guidry, "he could be one of the best who ever played this game. He may not turn out to be quite what Lou Gehrig was, but he'll be closer than anybody else."

Here are some more Mattingly figures: He had 370 total bases, four more than Roger Maris had when he walloped 61 in '61. And with only 41 strikeouts in 652 at bats, Mattingly became the first major league player since Ted Williams (1957) to homer 30 times or more while fanning 50 times or less. "I used to think of Donnie as a line-drive hitter with home run power," says Piniella. "Now I'm starting to think of him as a home run hitter who *can* hit .300."

Can hit .300? In 1984, his first full season in the majors, Mattingly won the AL batting title at .343—the first Yank to win that crown since Mantle (1956). That .343 was the highest average by a Yankee lefty in almost 50 years, since Gehrig's .351 in 1937. In four years of minor league ball Mattingly's average was .332, and before that, at Reitz Memorial High in his hometown of Evansville, Ind., he hit .500 and .575 his last two years. "If he hit less than .300, I'd be ashamed, and he'd be sleeping in the living room," says his wife of six years, the former Kim Sexton. She's a lady who understands motivation because she's the daughter of Mattingly's high school football coach. "But those homers seem kind of weird to me," she admits. "I'm afraid they'll go away."

No one expected them. Not Piniella, not Mattingly, certainly not the Yankees, who were trying just about anyone at first base who could swing a bat and chew gum back in 1983, when Mattingly was first given a shot at the job over the likes of Bobby Murcer, John Mayberry, Butch Hobson, Roy Smalley, Ken Griffey and Steve Balboni. It was, like so many others in the Yankees organization, a temporary appointment. "I started the first game at home and had three tough plays at first that didn't go my way," Mattingly, a Gold Glover last year, recalls. None of the plays was scored an error, but Mattingly, who had gone 1 for 3, was promptly benched by manager Billy Martin. The day he and Kim moved into their 18th-floor apartment in Hackensack, N.J., he was returned to the minors. "It was kind of sad," Kim recalls.

"It wasn't that sad," says Mattingly. "Every minor leaguer has stories like that. It's good that it didn't all come so easy. One thing I can say about the Yankees: They've never *given* me a thing."

Kim digests this for a moment and shrugs. "Well *I* was sad," she says.

It's not so much that nothing bothers Mattingly. Things bother him all right: losing, Yankee politics and, to a degree, celebrity—to name three. It's more that nothing distracts him from the business at hand, which for the past couple of years has been learning to hit the bejesus out of a baseball. At the time Mattingly was returned to Columbus, Ohio, he was primarily a leftfield hitter with an inside-out swing. "I never used to pull the ball," Mattingly says. "I imitated [Rod] Carew a lot. Mickey Vernon, who was my minor league hitting coach, used to tell me, 'You don't have to change to hit in the big leagues. Just put the barrel of the bat on the ball.'"

Late in '82 and early '83, Piniella began talking to Mattingly about some of the theories of Charlie Lau. He experimented with Piniella's ideas throughout the rest of '83, and then while playing winter ball in Puerto Rico, where he led the league with a .368 average. When Mattingly showed up for spring training in 1984, Yankee manager Yogi Berra told him that he would be his swing man, alternating among first base, leftfield and rightfield to give Yankee regulars a rest. No problem, said Mattingly. Then he added, "But once you get me into the lineup, you're going to have trouble getting me out."

Cocky? Well, of course. When every baseball looks to you not like an aspirin tablet but like a cantaloupe, who wouldn't be cocky? *"When I'm seeing the ball good,* I'm seeing it early," Mattingly says. When I'm seeing the ball good. It's a phrase Mattingly uses a lot, an effort to demystify what, to him, seems the most natural, least explicable of tasks. "I see it right out of the pitcher's hands, seams and all. I'm not looking for any particular pitch, just hard stuff. Then it's pure reaction." Mattingly makes it sound as if every pitch—slider, curve, fastball, forkball, change—looks so big floating down the pipe that the suspense lies not in whether he will hammer the baseball but in whether he will hammer it *where they ain't.*

Whether there's a game, a pennant race, a batting title or his financial security on the line, Mattingly has positively raked the opposition. He went 4 for 5 on the last day of the 1984 season to edge teammate Dave Winfield for the AL batting crown. In 10 straight games last year between Sept. 20 and Sept. 30, Mattingly drove in at least one run as the Yanks battled to gain ground on the Toronto Blue Jays. For the season he led the league with 21 game-winning RBIs, and over the past two years Mattingly has batted an astounding .393 with runners in scoring position. Increasingly, it is Mattingly—not Winfield—to whom the Yankees have turned for leadership, both on and off the field.

"If he made one dollar a year or two million a year, he'd have the same intensity," says former teammate Don Baylor. "I love to watch him practice," says Angel manager Gene Mauch. "He's very serious during infield, never wastes a swing in the batting cage. From there on I don't want to look at him."

"He's the best in the league," sums up the White Sox' Carlton Fisk. "He hits for average, he hits for power, he plays defense. The best."

Such compliments run off Mattingly's back like Ohio River water off an Evansville duck. Evansville is the Hoosier city where he and Kim still live in the off-season, and it was there that he learned early on to keep his athletic achievements in perspective. A three-sport star at Memorial High, Mattingly was the youngest of four athletic brothers. The eldest, Jerry, died at 23 in a construction accident. Don was eight at the time. Another brother, Randy, kicked around the Canadian Football League for five years as a quarterback and punter. Being a high school hotshot didn't seem terribly significant in the Mattingly family. "I didn't expect any special treatment at school for being an athlete," Mattingly says. "I never wore my letter sweater or anything like that. I'm not shy—just not a ham. My personality doesn't need that sort of adulation. I'm not flashy. I still don't think of myself as a great player. I think of myself as an everyday player. A worker type. Consistent. On time. You have to see my game over a long time to appreciate it."

"At first," says the Royals' George Brett, with whom Mattingly is often compared, "he was one of those guys who seemed to hit a lot of lazy fly balls against lefthanders. But then late in the '84 season he was hanging in better, and last year it didn't seem to matter who was pitching, left- or righthanded. He was going to hurt them."

Indeed, 18 of Mattingly's 35 homers in 1985 came against southpaws. *When I'm seeing the ball good . . .* no one sees it better.

One thing about playing on the Yankees, you also get a pretty good look at the cowhide of life—seams and all. When something does get under his skin—as was the case last June when, in the midst of a home stand against the Blue Jays and the Tigers, Steinbrenner suggested that the Yanks hold yet another in a succession of off-day workouts—Mattingly speaks out once and that's the end of it. Tied for the league lead in RBIs at the time, Mattingly remarked to a couple of reporters, "Guys need a day off sometimes. We don't get any. Having a break, getting a chance to get your head together, could be more helpful than a workout."

When that hit the newsstands, it unleashed this Steinbrenner tirade: "If he's tired of working out, that's too damned bad. He ought to get a real job, be a taxi driver or steelworker and find out what life and hard work are all about. I'm getting fed up with his attitude. Last year I thought he was the all-American boy, but now I'm not so sure."

One can only wonder what Steinbrenner's perception of the all-American boy may be. "When I spoke out about practices, it was something that had to be said," Mattingly says now. "George wants to win. But I want to win as much as he does, and I was always taught that we're all in this together, that the team was more important than any one player. There's not a franchise player in baseball. So when he goes off and says stuff about Dave Winfield being Mr. May, like he did last September when we were playing Toronto, or starts firing back at me about steelworkers and farmers just because I'm from Indiana, I don't agree with it. So I'll say something to get it off my chest. Then in two or three days it all passes over. I don't mind George. Sometimes I kind of like his little mind games."

That's spring-training talk. Steinbrenner has twice refused to sign Mattingly to a long-term contract, and don't be stunned if Mattingly flees to saner pastures when he becomes eligible for free agency in 1989. After Mattingly won the batting title in 1984 on a $130,000 salary, the Yankees broke off negotiations for the '85 season and simply renewed his contract for $325,000, take it or leave it; Mattingly wound up also receiving $130,000 in incentive bonuses. "It wasn't the money that upset me," Mattingly said later. "It was the way things were handled. I said I wouldn't forget it, and I won't. Baseball is all business to the owners. At least our owner. That's the lesson. I'm a piece of property, a tool. I'm not a family member or anything like that. But to me, baseball's still a game. I don't want it to be work. I want it to be play.

"I'll tell you, the athlete I admire as much as anyone is Julius Erving. That's who I want to be like. I remember a few years ago watching a playoff game between Philadelphia and Portland, and there was a fight or something between Maurice Lucas and Darryl Dawkins and things were getting crazy on the court. Everybody's pushing and jumping around. Then the camera pans over and shows a picture of Dr. J. He was watching from the bench, totally composed and within himself. That picture goes through my mind whenever I feel myself losing control."

Composure. That's what Mattingly has. It is what any young player needs in order to thrive on Steinbrenner's Yankees, or to win a batting title or to drive in runs during a pennant race. In Mattingly's rookie year, in man-on-base situations, he used to think, "I'm going to show them I can drive in runs." And he would tighten up. Now, he just looks out at the pitcher and relaxes. Maybe he conjures up a picture of Erving. "The pitcher's the guy in trouble, not me," Mattingly thinks.

Then the pitcher starts his windup. *When I'm seeing the ball good. . . .* Yes, the pitcher is in trouble.

T. J.'s Remarkable Comeback

From *T. J.: My 26 Years in Baseball*

by Tommy John with Dan Valenti

Before his first (and only) season as the manager of the Yankees, Dallas Green made it very clear to Tommy John that he had no chance at pitching for the team at age 45. T. J. had Green singing a different tune by the end of spring training, and he was named the opening day starter in his 26th and final major league season.

My final appearance of spring training came on March 30, 1989, a start against the Orioles at Miami. It was the bookend to my very first appearance against the Birds on March 3. My final tune-up went seven innings, good for two runs, six hits, three walks and four strikeouts.

There were media types swarming all over me, wanting the story about how I had turned from Sayonara to Cy Young. Even while I was warming up, people were requesting interviews. It was chaotic, but I had fun with it.

"Look what you've created," I kidded Dallas, "I can't even work."

Generally, the media weren't a distraction, because at Yankee camp they couldn't follow you everywhere, like they could at Dodgertown. The press could only be in the Fort Lauderdale clubhouse at specified times. Also, the New York beat writers, guys like Moss Klein, Bill Madden, Mike Martinez, and Murray Chass were friends, and almost did as much as I did to get me on the ball club. In their stories they created a Robin Hood underdog figure out of me.

New Yorkers love underdogs, and the fans were captivated by this old pitcher who just wouldn't give up. The fans who followed me through spring training felt special when I made the club; it was almost as if *they* had made it.

The New York fans and I have a very special feeling for each other, stemming from their tremendous support in seeing us through Travis's ordeal in 1981. That special relationship with the fans of New York shall remain intact for the rest of my life.

The theme of the fans was "Tommy showed Dallas, didn't he?" But I didn't feel that way at all. As camp started to wind down, my feeling was one of joy over having made the team, not one of satisfaction for having "shown" Dallas. I just wanted to pitch. I felt light as a rookie. I was enjoying myself. Baseball was fun again.

And then Dallas made his bold decision: forty-five-year-old Tommy John would start on opening day when the New York Yankees faced the Minnesota Twins at the Hubert H. Humphrey Metrodome in Minneapolis on April 4 against Frank Viola, the previous year's Cy Young winner.

Logically speaking, the move was understandable. The other four starters were Andy Hawkins, Al Leiter, Dave La Point, and John Candelaria. All but Hawkins were left-handers, so Dallas wanted to use Hawkins in the middle, with two lefties on either side. La Point and I were similar pitchers. It was clear Dallas wouldn't start us one-two, and with Dave's injury problems, he would not be the opener. That left either Candelaria, Leiter, or me. Leiter was twenty-three and too young. If they had named him to start on opening day, he wouldn't have slept for a week. That's how high-strung he was. He was a rookie bouncing off the walls. But there was no choice between Candelaria or me, either, since Candy was recovering from a knee injury, and Dallas wanted to give him extra rest.

But logic or not, it was still incredible to find myself in position as the opener. What were the odds?

I had come into camp with "no chance" of making the team; I would be given no help from the manager or his coaches. Yet here I was, accorded the honor reserved for a team's best pitcher. Upon hearing the news, I didn't feel surprise as much as validation. I never stopped believing in myself, never stopped hoping and working for the best. Those feelings were proven out. Now, even the doubters had faith.

Dallas's postmortem to my final spring outing against the Orioles: "He can pitch, can't he?"

The Bronx Bombers Fall on Hard Times

"The Empire Strikes Out"
Sports Illustrated, May 27, 1991

by Franz Lidz

*It's at once sadistic and enlightening to compare the legendary 1961
Yankees to the team that donned the pinstripes 30 years later in 1991.
It's also surreal to see George Steinbrenner referred to in the past tense
(his "lifetime ban" would be lifted in March of 1993), but
Frank Lidz puts the Yankee struggles of the previous decade in
fascinating context.*

ON THE 30TH ANNIVERSARY OF PERHAPS THE GREATEST SEASON OF THEIR
LONG REIGN, THE NEW YORK YANKEES' ONCE-PROUD DYNASTY HAS
BECOME A TRAVESTY

My uncle Danny lived to be 77 years old, and he had an opinion for every
minute of those 77 years. And though he spent half his life in the Bronx, his
opinion of the New York Yankees remained unchanged: He didn't care for
them. Particularly the 1961 team. "They're Roman Yankee imperialists," Uncle
Danny complained. "They only have three honorable men." He refused to
reveal their names, possibly to protect them from the dishonorable ones.

But to my nine-year-old eyes, the Roman Yanks of '61 seemed to have
descended from the gods. And I worshiped them accordingly: Mars Maris,
Mercury Mantle, Bacchus Berra, Somnus Skowron, Apollo Arroyo. I'd listen
raptly to victory after glorious victory issuing from my radio, like news
from some ancient oracle. I composed a paean called Mick and Maris, to be

sung to the tune of Love and Marriage. I wore my hair in a Roger Maris-like butch, bandaged my knees in tribute to Mickey Mantle and erected an altar to them on my desk next to my Clete Boyer autographed baseball. Along about September I offered up a mason jar filled with lightning bugs, adding a new firefly every time an M&M boy hit one out. By Oct. 1, when Maris took Boston's Tracy Stallard deep for No. 61 (to go with Mantle's 54), that jar glowed and shimmered.

Those Roman Yankees were triumphal, imperial in a way no team may ever be again. Eight were All-Stars. Six hit more than 20 homers. So murderous was this Murderers Row that first baseman Moose Skowron (28 dingers) batted seventh. Whitey Ford went 25-4; Ralph Terry, 16-3; Luis Arroyo, 15-5 with 29 saves. New York amassed 240 home runs and 109 victories and sacked the Cincinnati Reds in the World Series. "Some say the Yanks of 30 years ago were the greatest team ever," says Ralph Houk, who was their manager.

This Yankee juggernaut had not one but two Babe Ruths, and the drama of the home run derby staged by Maris and Mantle held the entire nation in sway. Stadiums were jammed wherever they played. Film crews tracked them. Newspapers trumpeted their feats. Magazines heralded their heroics. The Game of the Week, NBC's Saturday showcase, became, in effect, the Yankee Game of the Week. The Yanks' domain extended beyond the Empire State to the far corners of the Empire. Factory workers in Japan made book on them. Israeli newscasters ran nightly updates. Yet, through it all, Uncle Danny remained unswayed. "Remember the Roman Empire," he intoned darkly. "Remember its decline and fall."

Uncle Danny was right, of course. Within a few years the Yankee Empire had collapsed. The Yanks limped on like defeated centurions through Mesopotamia. Their collection of fading stars and failed journeymen (see Tresh, T. and Womack, D.) sank dismally into last place in 1966. Two years later they batted a collective .214 (see Clarke, H. and Kosco, A.). Management, grown fat and arrogant from winning so long, fiddled while every team that came into the Bronx burned them. It was only after a Visigoth from Cleveland seized control (see Steinbrenner, G.) and started enlisting legionnaires from the outer provinces that the Yanks rose anew.

George Steinbrenner's hire-and-fire tactics afforded him early victories. But eventually Yankee Stadium became the House That Ruthlessness Tore Down, and Steinbrenner was driven into exile last year, retaining his ownership but being excluded from baseball operations. His 1990 Yanks were the worst team in the American League, and this season New York is battling the Baltimore Orioles and the Cleveland Indians for last place in the AL East. Last week the Yankees went 32 innings without a run, their worst string of futility in 22 years.

Even confirmed Yankee haters sympathize. "The current team is not even worthy of my contempt," laments Jeff Wernick, a Los Angeles businessman who has detested the Yankees since he was born, in Brooklyn, when there was still an Ebbets Field. "With Steinbrenner gone, there's nothing left to despise."

Whom can we compare Emperor Steinbrenner to? Maybe Nero. Or maybe Caligula, whose reign began peacefully enough but became increasingly despotic, grotesque in its excesses. Caligula, too, spent money extravagantly, banished many of his subjects, became convinced he was a god and demanded to be worshiped that way. And just as Steinbrenner once claimed to have punched out a fan in an elevator, Caligula insisted he had defeated Neptune one-on-one.

But Steinbrenner may be closer to Diocletian, the fourth-century general who briefly restored the empire to preeminence. Diocletian proclaimed himself Jupiter on earth and took the title Jovius, which is Latin for "the Boss." His reign was one of intense persecution: He expected total obedience under penalty of death. When he finally abdicated, Rome was in even worse shape than before.

"George's legacy is not the World Series winners of '77 and '78 or having the best record of any team in the '80s, " says Tony Kubek, the noble shortstop of that 1961 team and a linchpin of that Yankee era, who speaks his mind even though he's now a broadcaster for the team. "His legacy is these past five seasons—teams with worse and worse records culminating in last year's last-place finish."

In the lost golden age of Yankees past—from 1926 to '64—New York never had a losing record and won 26 American League pennants and 19 world championships. "Winning breeds tradition," says another Yankee announcer, Phil Rizzuto, who played in nine World Series during his 13 years in pinstripes. Under Steinbrenner, the only tradition has been turmoil and turnover. "George talked a lot about tradition, but it was all phony," says Kubek. "It was just him trying to be part of the tradition. You can't manufacture tradition in a plastic way. You have to have a certain class to go with it."

Tradition alone used to be good for 10 wins a year. The crowd and the stadium, the ghosts and the legends inspired uncertainty in the opposition and game-winning hits from the Yankees. "When we crossed the white line, we didn't think anyone could beat us," says Bill Stafford, who won 14 games for New York in 1961.

Though the Yankees still drew more than two million at home last year, New Yorkers have come to view the team the way they view their city—with a sort of morbid fascination with its decomposition. "As far as Yankee pride goes, I haven't felt a whole lot of it," says rightfielder Jesse Barfield, a Yank since 1989. "I think you're only going to feel that when you win."

Steinbrenner's successor as managing general partner of these damned Yankees comes, appropriately enough, from the Broadway stage: Robert Nederlander is a theater impresario. The casting almost guarantees a flop. The Yankee lineup is short on lefthanded power in a ballpark where the rightfield porch has immortalized those who hit lefty and long. New York's pitching consists mostly of memories, the most recent being that of Dave Righetti, who saved 36 games last season and then escaped to San Francisco. The Yanks' best third baseman may still be Graig Nettles, their 46-year-old first base coach. The four guys who have hung out at third this year had totaled, through Sunday, one home run, four RBIs and a .152 batting average.

Hampered by a chronically bad back, Don Mattingly, who used to hit about .340 every year, now hovers around .280. He used to poke 30 homers; if he keeps up his present pace, he'll hit 10 this season. Mattingly at least still plays a creditable first base, Roberto Kelly flashes brilliant in center, and Kevin Maas is an acceptable designated hitter. Maas averages better than a walk a game. If he continues his pace, he'll break Babe Ruth's single-season major league record of 170. That passes for big excitement in the Bronx these days, considering that last year's Yankee record-breaker was Barfield, who set the club strikeout mark of 150.

In an off-season move, second baseman Steve Sax—the Yankees' best trade bait—was signed to a four-year, $12.4 million contract extension despite the fact that New York's top young prospect, Pat Kelly, plays the same position. Kelly was called up from the minors on Sunday; now Sax will take a fling at playing third.

Back in 1961, the defense was nearly as good as the offense. The '91 infield is anchored by Alvaro Espinoza, a ukulele-hitting shortstop with quicksilver hands and lead feet. "What other shortstop in the majors gets pinch-run for in the seventh inning?" asks Kubek, who never was.

Does Espinoza compare favorably to Joe DeMaestri, Kubek's 1961 backup?

"Not really," says Kubek. "DeMaestri was a better fielder."

Kubek, in fact, contends that not a single 1991 Yankee would have cracked the '61 starting lineup, with the possible exception of the Mattingly of a few years ago. In his current condition, though, Mattingly "would have been a late-inning defensive replacement" for Skowron, Kubek says.

"Do you see a Mantle on this team?" Kubek asks. "Or a Maris? Or an Elston Howard? I don't see a Boyer. I don't see a Bobby Richardson, although the catcher, Matt Nokes, reminds me a little of Johnny Blanchard." Blanchard, you'll recall, was the 1961 Yanks' second-string catcher.

Maas and leftfielder Hensley Meulens, who some have tried to tag as the contemporary M&M boys, are a thin candy shell of the originals. "We don't have any true Yankee sluggers anymore who people will come out to see," says Rizzuto. "Reggie Jackson played in New York for five years, but even he wasn't a true Yankee. They'll retire his number in Oakland, not in New York."

"Mantle was the last true Yankee slugger," insists New Jersey bartender Bob Pezzuti, a true Yankee fan. "When he retired in 1968, Yankee tradition became frozen in time."

Time literally stopped at Yankee Stadium during the fourth inning on May 15. The scoreboard clock stuck at 8:53 with New York trailing the California Angels 6-2. During the time warp, two innings passed, and four more Angel runners crossed the plate. In that game, Yankee starter Chuck Cary was relieved—if that's the word—by Eric Plunk, who finished the week with a 9.90 ERA. Plunk's most notable pitch last Thursday was a fastball that went behind a batter. Poor Plunk may be the only '91 Yankee with a '61 counterpart: He pitches like Ryne Duren without glasses.

And whatever happened to good old Yankee spirit? "The team I played for knew how to root," says 1961 alumnus Hector Lopez. "Every inning we'd be up on the dugout steps, hollering, shouting, slapping each other on the backs. Very seldom do you see today's Yankees pulling for their teammates. They just sit on the bench watching the game as if it was on TV."

Complacency had no place in Yankeedom in 1961. "I never felt secure," says Skowron. "I remember checking out the minor league statistics to see who was after my job." Says Kubek, "I get the feeling now that some guys [free agents] join the Yankees because it's easy to play for them. You're not expected to win anymore. They think, 'Hey, the Yanks lost 95 games last year. What the hell, I'll take the money and put up with everything.' So much for Yankee tradition."

In recent years, pinstripe tradition came to be worth exactly zero to a free agent confronted by the specter of Steinbrenner and offered $17 million by someone else. "Most quality free agents haven't wanted to sign with the Yankees," says agent Arn Tellem, whose most prominent client, pitcher Mark Langston, spurned Steinbrenner in 1989. "They were scared off by the pressure of having to perform for George. They feared his capriciousness. After leaving the Yankees, players are so mentally drained that they have to go through a kind of detoxification. But that's not the main reason the better free agents have stayed away. It's that the Yankees just aren't competitive anymore."

Could New York's free-agent fortunes improve? Among the premier players who will enter the free-agent pool at the end of this season are three who grew up within a short train ride of Yankee Stadium: the New York Mets' Frank Viola, the Pittsburgh Pirates' Bobby Bonilla and the Chicago Cubs' Shawon Dunston. "The Yankees need every one of them," says Tellem. "I'd bet they'll all be offered mammoth contracts. It wouldn't surprise me if all three wound up Yankees."

Still, the Yankee future is not in the pool, but on the farm. The Diocletian Yanks traditionally sacrificed their young (see McGee, W.; Drabek, D.; Rijo, J.) for seasoned gladiators. They tried to dump Roberto Kelly on Atlanta two years ago, but the Braves—not noted for talent judgment themselves—turned down the offer. Now the Yankee bushes are flowering again: Besides Pat Kelly, watch for outfielders Bernie Williams and Gerald Williams and pitchers Wade Taylor and Jeff Johnson. "The Yankees' bright spot is on the horizon," Rizzuto says. "They just can't trade any of the kids."

Yankee fans react to this with mild diffidence. "If Roberto Kelly continues to develop, if Mattingly gets his power back, if Maas hits homers, if Pat Kelly stays up, if Steinbrenner stays away—if all that happens, the Yanks might have a bit of a nucleus," says Manhattan lawyer Joe Villella, a Yankee diehard. "It's not much, but you've got to start somewhere."

Even Rome wasn't rebuilt in a day.

A Left-handed
Bat Stretcher

*From Batboy: My True Life Adventures Coming of Age
with the New York Yankees*

by Matthew McGough

*What young baseball fan hasn't seen the kids with "BB" on the backs
of their jerseys and longingly wished they could land such a gig?
According to Matthew McGough, all it took was a simple letter and a
bit of perseverance—and, once on the job, a good sense of humor.*

I walked into Yankee Stadium the morning of Opening Day again dressed for a holiday dinner and with my book bag over my shoulder.

The security guard in the Yankees lobby checked my name off a list and pointed me through a door just inside the Stadium press gate.

"Down the stairs and follow the blue strip on the floor," he said.

I recognized the tunnel from my interview in October and soon found myself standing before the heavy clubhouse door. I took a deep breath, pulled the door open, and walked inside.

The last time I'd seen the clubhouse it had been empty, save for the trunks and boxes of clothes that Nick had strewn across the clubhouse floor. Now, the sight and sound of at least a hundred people hit me head-on.

A leading sign that spring has arrived in New York. Opening Day at Yankee Stadium has always been among the most newsworthy of the City's annual sports events. That year was no exception, and the fact that the Yankees were opening the season against the Boston Red Sox only heightened the already significant fan and media interest in the game.

Dozens of reporters rushed around the room, camera crews in tow. Carpenters, electricians, and painters hurriedly put the final touches on different parts of the clubhouse. An entourage from Mayor Dinkins's office milled around, mixing with uniformed cops and security men in dark suits. And weaving through the mob, in various states of dress, were the ballplayers, most of whom I recognized from TV, but none of whom I'd ever seen except across rows and rows of Stadium seats. One with a barrel chest and huge biceps strutted past me across the room. Another sat at his locker doing a crossword puzzle. Two younger guys in pinstriped uniform pants and blank Yankees T-shirts—rookies, I guessed—stood to the side and spoke quietly while they too eyed the crowd. Veterans joked loudly and looked very much at home. And on the far right, in the corner locker twice the size of any other, sat Don Mattingly, Yankees captain. Donnie Baseball. The guy in midswing on the poster in my room at home. I swung my book bag off my shoulder, inadvertently bumping a camera and drawing a midinterview scowl from the cameraman. I thought I'd better go find Nick.

I approached him at his picnic table, where he stood with a black marker, purposefully printing players' names in big block letters on the collars of baseball undershirts.

"What do you want me to do, Nick?" I asked.

"Stay the fuck out of the way," he answered. Two players walked over a second later and impatiently began listing their grievances: "Nick, I can't find the bag I packed in spring training; Old man, I need Nike batting gloves, I can't wear Adidas; Nicky, you have four AA batteries?

I must have looked as lost as I felt. I backed away and stumbled toward a distant corner, next to the trainers' room, that seemed slightly less chaotic than the rest of the clubhouse. I found myself in front of one locker, unlike all the others, that bore not a nameplate but a number: 15. Save for a catcher's mask and pair of shin guards that hung from a hook on the side of the cubby, it was forlornly empty.

I realized suddenly whose locker it had been, whose locker it still was. "Thurman Munson," I said to myself in wonder. "Wow."

Munson, a catcher, was a beloved Yankee, the captain of their championship teams in the late seventies. His career had ended near its peak when he was killed in a midseason airplane crash. The Yankees had evidently preserved his locker as a monument and memorial. I reached out to run my fingers across the gashes in Munson's battered shin guards when I felt a tap on my shoulder.

I turned away and was suddenly face-to-face with the team's current captain, Mattingly, the man himself. He extended his right hand to me.

"Hey, I'm Don Mattingly," he said. "You're going to be working with us this year?"

It took me a moment to process my hero's simple question. I realized that Mattingly could have introduced himself with any number of other less generous but still thrilling questions: Are you the new bat boy? Who are you? What's your name? Are you going to be working *for* us this year? But he hadn't. Of all that I had imagined in the days before the season opener, I'd never thought about my new job in these terms: working *with* the Yankees, in common pursuit of a common goal.

"Uh, I know who you are, Mr. Mattingly," I managed to stammer. "I'm Matt, the new bat boy."

"Nice to meet you," Mattingly said with a firm handshake.

"Thanks," I replied instinctively. "I mean, nice to meet you, too."

"Listen, Matt," he said, as if I could have done anything else. "I've got an important job for you. I just unpacked all my bats from spring training. I don't know if it was the humidity in Florida or the altitude of the flight or what, but they're all coming up short. The game starts in a couple of hours. I need you to get me a bat stretcher."

After Mattingly returned to his locker, I ran a lap around the clubhouse looking for Nick. I found him a minute later, digging through a trunk of underwear over by the coaches' room.

"Nick," I said. "I need a bat stretcher for Don Mattingly."

I'd barely gotten the words out of my mouth when Nick hit my virgin ears with a stream of expletives terrifying in their intensity and earnestness. Spittle hit my cheek as he screamed at me. I'd never heard such a tirade before, not even in the movies, let alone one directed at me. I scurried away, leaving Nick over my shoulder cursing loudly into his pile of underwear. Nick's assistant, Rob Cucuzza, sat at a picnic table, and I blurted out the mission with which I'd been entrusted.

"Don Mattingly asked me to get him a bat stretcher, and Nick, uh, Nick told me not to bother him."

Rob put his hand on my shoulder and smiled.

"Try Tartabull, Matty," he told me kindly. "I think I saw him using one earlier this morning."

Danny Tartabull, the Yankees' new high-priced, power-hitting right fielder, was getting dressed at his locker all the way on the other side of the clubhouse. He had just pulled his jersey over his head when I summoned up the courage to approach and ask if I could borrow his bat stretcher.

"Uh, Mr. Tartabull," I offered. "I'm Matt, the new bat boy. Don Mattingly just unpacked his bats from spring training, and they're all too short. I heard you were using the bat stretcher earlier this morning."

Tartabull kicked at some boxes and baseball spikes at the foot of his locker before turning to face me.

"It's Matt?" he asked. "I was using it earlier, Matt, but I must have left it in the manager's office. Try in there."

I thanked him, checking my watch as I took off in the direction of the office. Time was short, and I felt a heavy burden of responsibility. First pitch wasn't more than a couple of hours away, and more than fifty-six thousand fans were coming from all over New York City, on Opening Day, to see Don Mattingly lead the Yankees against the hated Red Sox. I didn't need anyone to explain to me that Mattingly wouldn't be able to do much against Roger Clemens, then Boston's hard-throwing ace, with a shrunken piece of wood in his hands. He had asked me to help him, and I couldn't fathom what it might mean—for him, for the team, and for my job prospects—to let him down.

Yankees manager Buck Showalter sat behind his desk surrounded by half a dozen reporters, holding what appeared to be an impromptu press conference. I entered and waited patiently, a few feet inside the door, until the conversation fell silent. All eyes turned to the nervous kid in the blue blazer and the baseball themed tie standing in the middle of the Yankees manager's office, in the heart of the Yankees clubhouse, on the morning of Opening Day.

"I'm, uh, really sorry to interrupt, Mr. Showalter," I began. "I'm Matt, the new bat boy. Don Mattingly needs a bat stretcher because his bats shrunk on the way up from Fort Lauderdale, and Danny Tartabull had it before but, uh, he says he left it in there with you this morning." Everyone was listening intently. Showalter scanned the floor at the feet of the beat writers and peered for a second around his desk.

"He left it in here?" he mused aloud. "It's possible, I guess. But do you need a right-handed one or a left-handed one?"

I knew that Mattingly was one of the best left-handed hitters in baseball.

"I need a left-handed bat stretcher," I answered confidently.

"Well, Tartabull's isn't going to do Mattingly any good at all then, is it, Matt? You better try down at the Red Sox clubhouse." I grinned weakly at the writers and excused myself from the room.

The Boston clubhouse was a lot less crowded than the Yankees', and thankfully I was able to find the Red Sox equipment manager right away. I recounted for him what I'd been through that morning—from Mattingly, to

Nick Priore, to Tartabull, and now Showalter, who I thought maybe had a right-handed bat stretcher but not the lefty one that Mattingly needed immediately. He patiently heard me out, and given the traditional enmity between the two teams, I was relieved that he seemed willing to help. He checked his watch.

"You don't have much time," he said. "We didn't bring any bat stretchers at all with us, but we could use one, too." He dug into his pocket and produced a twenty-dollar bill. "Go to the sporting goods store on 161st Street and buy two, a left-handed one for Mattingly and a right-handed one for us."

By the time I got up to street level, fans had begun to descend on the Stadium en masse, and it took me a good ten minutes walking against the human tide to make it to the corner of 161st and River Avenue. I was about to cross the street when the thought crossed my mind that, for someone about to pick two up at the store, I didn't even know what a bat stretcher looked like. I crossed under the elevated tracks, then stopped dumb at the door of Stan's Sporting Goods. I'd played and followed baseball my whole life, but before that morning, I was pretty sure, I had never even heard of a bat stretcher.

The possibility that this might be a joke scared me even more than the thought of failing in my first assignment as Yankees bat boy. If there were bat stretchers for sale in the sporting good stores around Yankee Stadium, there could be only one outcome worse than failing to produce one for Don Mattingly in his time of need.

What if I rolled back into the clubhouse and told Mattingly I was too smart to fall for his BS about stretching shrunken bats—and was wrong? I'd be ostracized at school. I'd be back in the bleachers, permanently. I mulled over my prospects during three full laps around Yankee Stadium, convincing myself that it had to be a prank, before I worked up enough courage to walk back into the clubhouse and confront the ballplayers.

The room erupted into laughter. Mattingly smirked at me from his corner locker. I tried to smirk back, trying hard to let him know: Yeah, you got me. But that's cool. I can take it.

Jim Abbott:
Against All Odds

"Not a Hit, Not a Run, Not a Doubt"
New York Times, September 5, 1993

by Jennifer Frey

*There have been 269 no-hitters pitched in the history of major league
baseball, 11 of them by Yankees. And 268 of them were thrown by
pitchers with two hands. As was the case for much of his life,
Jim Abbott was the remarkable exception.*

Jim Abbott has spent his entire career—his entire life—exceeding expectations,
and that was no different yesterday afternoon. The Yankees handed the baseball
to Abbott, their struggling left-hander, and asked that he simply keep the team
competitive in this pennant-race game against the Cleveland Indians.

Abbott gave them much more.

On a cloudy day at Yankee Stadium, Abbott, 25, threw the eighth no-
hitter in the 90-year history of the Yankees' franchise, blanking the Cleveland
Indians, 4-0. The last Yankee to throw an official no-hitter was Dave Righetti,
who beat the Boston Red Sox at Yankee Stadium on July 4, 1983.

"Nobody in this clubhouse is more deserving of this than Jim is," said
shortstop Randy Velarde, who fielded a Carlos Baerga grounder for the final
out. "We all have so much respect for him."

The no-hitter is only the latest in a long list of remarkable achievements
for Abbott. A star at the University of Michigan and a member of the 1988
gold medal-winning United States Olympic baseball team, Abbott takes the
greatest pride in his ability to make others forget that he was born without a
right hand.

"So many things have been nice in my career, and this is certainly at the
top of them," Abbott said.

In Control in the Ninth

With the crowd of 27,225 on its feet and screaming in the ninth inning, Abbott retired first Kenny Lofton, then Felix Fermin, then forced Baerga, the Indians' best hitter, to ground softly to short. Afterward, he did not quite know how to react as his teammates mobbed him near the pitcher's mound. Should he be cocky? Calm? Grateful? Exuberant?

"I did not know how to act out there," said Abbott, who walked five batters but never allowed a base runner past first base. "I didn't know whether to be supremely confident or supremely thankful. I guess it's a little bit of both."

The glory of this Yankees' season—New York moved one and a half games behind the division-leading Blue Jays, who played a late game against California last night—has not included a stellar year by Abbott, who came to the Yankees in an off-season trade and has admittedly found the transition difficult. For Abbott, it has been a season filled with sleepless nights and self-described "irrational" ramblings to his wife, Dana, who trembled when she congratulated her husband yesterday afternoon.

"I'm thrilled to come out of that last start and pitch a game like this," said Abbott, who had struggled to a 9-11 record heading into yesterday's game. "It makes it doubly nice being in September and being in a pennant race."

The last time he pitched, in Cleveland six days ago, Abbott gave up a dreadful 10 hits and 7 runs in three and two-thirds innings, then left the field, the clubhouse and the stadium, his uniform exchanged for a pair of shorts and some running shoes. The outing sent his earned run average up to 4.31 and his frustration level right off the chart. Heading into yesterday's game, Abbott had lost three of his last six starts—and that's not counting the outing against the Indians in Cleveland, which miraculously turned into a no-decision for Abbott after a Yankee offensive outburst.

Confidence Was Down

This was a key start for Abbott, then, key for both him and the Yankees, who had lost three of four on this homestand. Abbott admitted this week that he had let the Indians dictate his pitches last week in Cleveland, that his confidence level was down after watching Jimmy Key and Melido Perez get battered around in the previous two games. This time, Abbott insisted, he would throw his own game and let things happen as they would.

"I think no-hitters take a little bit of luck," said Abbott, who went seven and one-third hitless innings against the Chicago White Sox on May 29 before Bo Jackson singled. "To be honest, I can hardly tell you the difference—other than a little bit more command on my breaking ball—between this start and the last one."

In the opening minutes of the game, Abbott did little to relieve the nervousness on the Yankee bench. Abbott got behind his first batter, Lofton, then walked him on five pitches. His first pitch to his next batter, Fermin, was a ball as well. Then came a double-play ball and a flyout, and Abbott chugged off the mound looking somewhat relieved, if not relaxed.

Staked to a 3-0 lead after the third inning and consistently backed by solid defense, Abbott settled down and got the Indians on infield grounder after infield grounder, with the occasional walk and a couple of fly balls. The closest thing to a hit came with one out in the seventh, when third baseman Wade Boggs dived to his left to stab an Albert Belle grounder and beat Belle with the throw.

Abbott turned and waved his glove in Boggs's direction afterward, clearly grateful for his effort. Boggs easily fielded a grounder from the next batter, Randy Milligan, to send the no-hitter into the eighth.

Unfazed by Bunt Attempt

"I felt a little tired in the seventh inning," Abbott said, smiling, "but in the eight and ninth, with the crowd, I didn't feel it at all."

The crowd stood for every pitch in the last two innings and was whipped into an angry frenzy when Lofton led off the ninth with an attempt to bunt. Abbott, though, was unfazed. Lofton—to the crowd's great pleasure—grounded weakly to second, then Bernie Williams chased Fermin's fly ball to the warning track in center for the second out. That brought Baerga to the plate.

"You never want to get no-hit," said Baerga, who went 0 for 4 on the afternoon. "That was really on my mind in my last at-bat. I just wanted to get a hit in any way possible. But this was Jim Abbott's day."

The Future of the Franchise

From *The Record* (Bergen County, New Jersey)

by Bob Hertzel

In 20-year-old minor leaguer Derek Jeter, sportswriter Bob Hertzel saw a nascent superstar with the potential to lead the Yankees back to greatness, comparing his arrival to that of Babe Ruth. Though Ruth and Jeter are vastly different types of players—and people—each has left an indelible mark on the franchise and the game of baseball.

August 21, 1994: Rapid Rise

NORFOLK, VA.—Nearly 80 years ago it was a franchise on the verge of a championship, one special player away.

That player was the Babe.

Today things are not much different for the Yankees, who again find themselves looking at a championship so near yet so far.

To win it they may turn again to a babe, lowercased.

His name is Derek Jeter, chronological age 20, baseball age closer to 30.

Jeter is two years out of high school and maybe less than a year from the major leagues.

"It's gone by kind of quick," he said. "It seems like just the other day I was in high school but that's two years now."

Jeter was talking as he dressed. His team, the Columbus Clippers, the Yankees' Class AAA affiliate, was about to play the Norfolk Tides in a game that would be televised to the New York City area, which has been starved for baseball during the players' strike. It would be the area's first good look at the Yankees' latest phenom.

Someone wondered what Jeter's high school buddies would be doing while he was playing.

"They're probably going out," he said. "They're doing what they want to do. I'm doing what I always wanted to do."

A gifted athlete, Jeter's rise through the Yankees' farm system has been meteoric, especially considering how the club takes its time with prospects. Don Mattingly, for example, was in his fifth professional season before he reached the Yankees to stay.

One reason could be the Yankees' perception of a need at shortstop, which might become urgent next season. Mike Gallego and Randy Velarde will be free agents next year. To sign either would take a lot of money.

Having lost faith in Dave Silvestri's ability to play shortstop in the major leagues, the Yankees might be willing to gamble on Jeter, who would work cheap.

Other teams took such gambles this year and lost. Toronto tried to go with 20-year-old Alex Gonzalez at short but he couldn't cut it. Seattle tried Alex Rodriguez, 18, as a midseason replacement but had to send him down.

Can Jeter do it? No one knows yet. He's getting his first taste of top minor league competition and is showing no signs it is too much for him.

It is a lot different from his first minor league season, which came after the Yankees made Jeter—who was born in Pequannock and lived in West Milford until moving to Michigan when he was 4—their No. 1 draft pick, sixth overall, in 1992.

That turned into a disaster. Jeter was homesick, distressed, depressed.

"I called home all the time," he said. "I'd never been away before. It's just something you have to get used to."

His parents are level-headed, professional people. His father, Charles, is the head of the Gateway Clinic for Alcohol and Drug Abuse in Michigan. He has a doctorate from Fisk University in Nashville, Tenn. His mother, Dorothy, is an accountant and has done graduate work.

Their advice?

"Stick with it," he recalled.

So he stuck with it, but it was difficult.

He'd just come out of a high school season at Kalamazoo Central where he had hit .508, down from the .557 he'd hit as a junior. He was all-universe . . . and then they started throwing curveballs in the minor leagues.

If you were to give his first professional season a name it would be "Homesick and Hitless." He hit .202 at Tampa, not a whole lot better in the 11 games he played at Greensboro.

"I was trying to figure it out and I couldn't," he said. "I began thinking, maybe I should have gone to school."

The University of Michigan would have been glad to have had him in its baseball program, just as it was glad to get Jalen Rose and Chris Webber into its basketball program. After all, they played an important role in Jeter's life.

"They're why I'm playing baseball," he said.

He thought he might be a basketball player, right up until he ran head on into each of their teams.

"They killed us. Right then I decided baseball was my game," he said.

Jeter attended Michigan in the off-season, then returned to Greensboro, where everything came together for him in a .295 season.

Asked to explain it, he simply said, "Confidence."

The confidence began in the spring when he was invited to the major league spring training camp.

"I saw how the big league players carried themselves. I saw how they went about their work."

He also saw that the talent gap wasn't all that great.

"The difference was mostly consistency. Don't get me wrong, they're better. But the big thing was the consistency," he said.

Coming off the solid season at Greensboro, Jeter geared himself up this year to begin at Class AA Albany. What he didn't take into account was the Yankees' penchant for aging draft choices like fine wine rather than hurrying them along.

They sent him to Tampa.

"I was upset when they first told me," he said. "I'm not in a hurry to get to the big leagues but you ask anyone and they'll tell you they'd like to get there as soon as possible. But I got over it. It's something I can't control, so why worry about it?"

He went to Tampa and proved himself to be advanced far past a Class A classification, leaving his mark on the Florida State League by being named in a recent poll of managers as the league's most exciting player, best hitting prospect, and best infield arm.

He was promoted to Albany, where he overwhelmed the Eastern League. The Yankees could not ignore his progress and did something they almost never do with someone as young and inexperienced as Jeter.

They moved him to Class AAA Columbus.

He was neither awed nor overwhelmed.

"The kid has come in and looked like he belonged from the day he got here," said Columbus manager Stump Merrill.

"He's definitely not in over his head," said Tom Spencer, the third base coach.

It was a difficult position for Jeter to be in. He was being summoned to play shortstop on a team that had two shortstops who had played in the major leagues this year—Silvestri and Robert Eenhoorn.

"Didn't phase him a bit," said Merrill.

Merrill called him into his office the first day, not sure what he was getting.

"I was expecting a kid who was a bundle of nerves but he wasn't. I told him this was a different level but the plate was still 17 inches wide and the bases were still 90 feet apart. They don't throw the ball any harder, just locate it better, so when they find a weakness, he'll have to adjust but that he shouldn't do anything special, just go have fun," Merrill recalled.

And that is what he has done. Oh, there are still some defensive shortcomings and those must be overcome. Yankees manager Buck Showalter says that the No. 1 thing he will need in a shortstop next season is the ability to catch and throw consistently.

"He's come a long way defensively," Merrill said, recalling 56 errors in Jeter's season at Greensboro. "He works hard. I think back to the 1970s. The Red Sox had this kid in Bristol who could hit but who wasn't real good on defense. Now I see what Wade Boggs has become and it shows what you can do when you dedicate yourself to working on a phase of the game that is giving you trouble."

May 30, 1995: Yanks' Star Prospect Jeter Gets Call to Bail Out Infield

SEATTLE—There were no private jets, no limos. Hardly the way you'd expect the future of the Yankees to arrive.

"A long trip," Derek Jeter assured those who were listening. "Norfolk to Dallas, three hours; then here, four more hours."

And so began the major league career of one of the most highly touted Yankees prospects to arrive in the big leagues since Thurman Munson and, at 20, the youngest since Jose Rijo. He joined a team riddled by injury and stepped right into the starting lineup Monday night, albeit in the No. 9 spot in the order.

In a way, Jeter's arrival signaled a New York changing of the guard, so to speak, for to make room on the roster the Yankees designated shortstop Kevin Elster for assignment, probably bringing to the end a career that began with the World Series champion '86 Mets.

The Yankees have 10 days to trade Elster, who's hitting just .118, or for him to accept an assignment to Columbus.

Jeter's career is being born out of the rubble of a Yankees roster that has been decimated by injuries to shortstops Tony Fernandez and Dave Silvestri, pitchers Jimmy Key and Scott Kamieniecki (all four on the disabled list), outfielder Paul O'Neill (just off DL), and second baseman Pat Kelly (unable to play).

The question was whether Jeter's promotion was a short-term, stopgap move or the start of a career with limitless potential, which could move Fernandez out of the picture.

Manager Buck Showalter would not speculate on whether Jeter would become his everyday shortstop.

"We'll address that when the time comes," said Showalter. "It will depend on how he performs and on Tony's health."

Fernandez is recovering from a rib-cage injury and was hitting just .206 when put on the DL.

As for Jeter, he just says: "All I can do is play hard and do the best I can. They're just not going to give someone the shortstop job."

One thing Showalter did vow: "If he's here, he will play."

That indicated Jeter could, with a fast start, win the job from Fernandez. There are some other scenarios that could keep him around, one being the possible placement of Kelly on the DL, which would keep a roster spot open.

The other, which the Yankees must be considering, is putting first baseman Don Mattingly, whose vision continues to be a problem, on the DL even though he has been playing against right-handers.

If Mattingly's vision continues to plague him, Showalter may put him on the DL, move Wade Boggs to first, shift Fernandez to third, and play Jeter at short.

As for Jeter, he's unaware of any of this or the hype that surrounds his promotion.

"You try not to pay too much attention to things like that," he said. "You can go crazy trying to think about what might happen."

The only advice he got from Showalter was "to keep doing what I've been doing. It's the same game here. It's still baseball."

If it is the same game, then Jeter figures to be a star for he comes with the proper credentials, including 17- and 10-game hitting streaks at Columbus this year, leading to a .354 average. He was first in the International League in hits, doubles, and triples, and was third in runs and batting average.

PART VII

The Core Four and a Dynasty Reborn

1996–2010

The arrival of Derek Jeter—whose rise through the minor leagues closes out the preceding section of this book—as the Yankees' starting shortstop in 1996 was not the single act that led to the revival of a dynasty in the Bronx. Nor was the development of an untouchable pitch—the cutter—by reliever Mariano Rivera, or Jorge Posada's longevity and reliability behind the plate, or Andy Pettitte's clutch October pitching. But taken together, these four acts, these four men formed the foundation on which a winning tradition was rebuilt at Yankee Stadium.

The four World Series titles won by the Yankees from 1996 to 2000 (and a fifth in 2009) not only restored pride and a sense of tradition to the franchise, but they inspired the era's top sportwriters to explore the Yankee legacy once again. Roger Angell reflects on the remarkable series of events of 1996 that brought about the first Yankee championship in nearly two decades, and Tom Verducci enjoys the rare privilege of sitting down with the "Core Four" to discuss the achievements, challenges, and relationships that have kept the team near the pinnacle of baseball for more than a decade.

As with previous Yankee juggernauts, it took a seasoned manager and leader of men to keep this talented group of players on task. Throughout his "Yankee years," Joe Torre directed many of the game's top pitchers and lineups. And the man who, for better or worse, defined Yankee baseball for nearly four decades, George Steinbrenner, receives a thoughtful tribute from newly inducted Hall of Fame journalist Bill Madden.

Derek Jeter, 2004. *Brad Mangin/MLB Photos/Getty Images*

The Bombers Are Back

From *Game Time: A Baseball Companion*

by Roger Angell

The 1996 season put the Yankees back on the track to greatness, and Roger Angell's postseason recap is as classic as the games themselves. From the incredible Tony Tarasco fan interference non-call in the ALDS to the unlikely comeback in Game 5 of the World Series, 1996 will go down as one of the most memorable seasons in franchise history.

An umpire died on the field on opening day in Cincinnati; Roger Clemens struck out twenty batters in a September game against the Tigers, just ten years after he first performed the feat (he walked no batters in either game); Tom Lasorda at last stepped down as Dodger manager; and the Mariners displayed their new, six-foot-three shortstop Alex Rodriguez, who batted .358, with thirty-six home runs, in the first flowering of what looks like a remarkable career. Nothing further will be offered here in summation of the 1996 season and its divisional-level playoffs—there it goes: bye-bye!—except a numerical footnote to mark the 4,962 home runs smacked this year (five hundred and four more than the old record), and the seventeen hitters who attained the once sacrosanct forty-homer level. I was there, in any case, for the most famous round-tripper of the year, which was hit by Derek Jeter and caught (in slipshod fashion) by Jeffrey Maier, a foot or two above the up-stretched glove of Oriole outfielder Tony Tarasco at the foot of the right-field porch at the Stadium. My seat for the notorious event was deep in the auxiliary press rows behind third base, and for a time I had no more idea about what happened (our pressbox TV monitors were down) than Rich Garcia, the right-field-line ump, who amazingly only saw the ball disappear into the stands. Then I realized that Tarasco, pointing upward and shooting out his other arm like a cash-register drawer, was reenacting the caper a la Marcel Marceau. (He was lighthearted about it in the clubhouse later on, repeatedly describing the kid's swipe as a magic trick. "Merlin must be in the house," he said.) The homer stood, after an epochal beef, the Yanks won, and Jeff Maier got to come back to the Stadium the next day and sit in the *News* box behind the Yankee dugout. His fame, it is certain, will last a bit more than fifteen minutes. Whatever his fate or future, every year or couple of years or five years for the rest of his life he can expect a telephone call on the date—perhaps to the site of his archeological dig in far Uzbekistan, or his dental clinic in the Paramus Mall—and the voice of some scrounging far-away feature writer, saying, "Hello, Dr. Maier? Jeffrey? Aren't you the Jeff Maier who—Jeff, say hello to Ralph Branca."

The Orioles didn't play very well in the League Championships, which the Yankees walked away with after three stifling wins at Oriole Park, thus sustaining their deep-voodoo 9-0 winning spell over the O's at home. The critical truth that came over me (and the Orioles' home rooters, too, I imagine) as play unfolded was the insufficiency or unreliability of air power— the home run, that is—as a reliable strategic force. From my seat in the second row of the left-field upper deck, the cramped Camden Yards playing field, with its tight foul lines and short, quirkily angled outfield fences, felt like a subdivided suburban plot. You could go out and play here, but watch out! I could easily see how the O's had whacked their record two hundred and fifty-seven homers here this year, but even as the variously arcing or streaking or ricocheting dingers now began to fly about the place—some suddenly disappearing below my feet—they seemed to become less interesting as the games progressed, if only because the Orioles offered so little else in their own behalf. Thirteen of their nineteen runs in the series were scored on homers, but they never stole a base, rarely moved a runner, and left ten men to die on second or third base in the late innings. The celebrated center of their defense showed startling flaws—a weakness in Cal Ripken's throwing, and even some uncertainty by Robbie Alomar, an infield star of the first magnitude, whose between-the-wickets error in the final game opened the floodgates for a six-run Yankee inning. Nothing is gained by replaying here the infamous earlier moment when Alomar, in a late-September game, spat in the face of umpire John Hirshbeck after a disputed call at home plate. It might be noted, though, that the ultimate victim of the league's insufficient response to this offense (a five-day suspension, to be served when play resumes next April) wasn't the fans or the umpires but Alomar himself. Unshriven by the more obvious and appropriate penalty of immediate dismissal from all further games this year, he will now always be remembered, I believe, not just for his incomparable skills but for a guttersnipe moment that he cannot retract or repay.

"How come baseball makes everybody feel so happy?" a New Jersey woman (a daughter of mine, if truth be told) asked me over the phone the morning after David Cone's critical and steely 5-2 win over the Braves in the third game of the World Series. I can't remember what I said, but part of the answer could have been that the game, often at the very last instant, allows half the fans to feel the excruciating relief of not being on the other side. As parable, let's cut to the fourth Series game, down in Atlanta, where the Braves, the defending World Champions and familiar October-baseball habitués, had matters well in hand after five innings, leading by 6-0 and heading smoothly toward a 3-1 lead in this Series, which they'd begun by simply trampling the Yankees in the Bronx, winning by 12-1 and 4-0—and thus sustaining a post-season outburst of unmatched offensive ferocity in which they'd outscored their opponents by forty-eight runs to two. (Perhaps understandably, a dangerous smugness had begun to infect the Atlanta sports philosophes, with one local columnist suggesting that it was scarcely worth the bother of playing out such a one-sided Series, and another murmuring of the Braves, "Theirs is a higher standard.")

Now, to be sure, the visitors scored three comeback runs in the sixth inning, on some singles, a walk, and a little Braves error out in right field, but the home-side reliever, Mike Bielecki, quickly struck out three Yanks in a row, ending the threat. Not to worry. Hanging around for the seventh-inning stretch, the happy Atlantans root-root-rooted for the home team, essayed a bit of farewell woo-wooing and forearm chopping, here and there flaunting those foam-rubber tomahawks, and then, in considerable numbers, began to file down the aisles, headed for home. You couldn't blame them: it was after eleven, and tomorrow was a school day. This Series was a lock, and they'd catch the rest of the Braves' win on the car radio. In one respect, at least, Yankee fans now suddenly had the better of it, for the vast majority of them were already at home, eight hundred and fifty miles to the north, where they were following the gloomy proceedings via Fox TV. Well, maybe one more batter, most were thinking—you couldn't blame them, either; it was another one of those late, overstuffed games—and they waited while Charlie Hayes's little lead-off number in the eighth rolled gently up the third-base line like a windup toy and died there, still two inches fair: an eighty-five-foot single. Laughing and shaking their heads—isn't baseball weird—they hung on a bit longer, waiting for the next thing.

All sports are eventful, but baseball, unlike the others, sometimes becomes situational as well, suddenly presenting its participants—the players and the fans together—with as many interconnections and possibilities and opportunities for interesting disaster as a Cheever Thanksgiving dinner. More and more relatives turn up and crowd in around the table, some of whom you didn't expect to see here at all, somebody is pouring another round of drinks, and suddenly there doesn't appear to be enough silverware or stuffing to go around. Nerves and certainties are fraying, cousins are eyeing each other apprehensively, voices are raised in the kitchen. Something awful is about to happen. How hot it is in here. How fraught.

Three batters along, with Mariano Duncan on first and Hayes now on third, Jim Leyritz, a late replacement, stood in to face the Braves' fireballing relief stopper, Mark Wohlers—a right-hander-vs.-right-handed-batter setup, and thus comforting for the Braves. Wohlers threw a fastball—a ninety-eight-mile-an-hour streak that Leyritz swung at smoothly and fouled back. Leyritz, a backup catcher, has a quirky style at the plate. After each pitch, he spins his bat forward in his right hand like a baton twirler, and when he steps back in, ready to swing, he stiffens his left leg and delicately points the foot forward in an almost feminine balletic gesture. On this at-bat, he also wore on his left elbow a thick, clunky-looking brace that looked like Japanese armor: protection for a painful bruise he'd sustained when struck on the biceps by a pitch in a playoff game against the Orioles.

Leyritz took a ball, then another, and, still putting a good swing on the ball, fouled off two more pitches. The home crowd had gone quiet, and up in the pressbox behind the plate you could hear the Yankee players, on the top step of their dugout, barking encouragement to Leyritz. Another pitch arrived—a slider this time, a slider that didn't slide—and Leyritz hit the ball over the left-field fence, tying the game and changing this World Series for good.

Although altered, the game situation persisted, thickening in detail and possibilities as the pitchers and batters came and went for both sides. We were in Atlanta, which meant National League rules: no designated hitter. Under these classic conditions, a tie game in late innings becomes a crisis in slow motion, with each manager glancing at his bullpen and his dwindling list of pinch-hitters, which he must match up, of course, against the right-handed or left-handed remaining pitchers on the other side, while also focusing on the possibilities from the point of view of his opposing skipper. Fans, happily surveying the field and studying their filling-up scorecards, in fancy begin to enter the minds of the rival managers:

Joe Torre (top of the ninth; two on and two out): Look at Cecil out there, leading off second again. I sure don't want to lose his bat if this goes another inning, but he's no Road Runner, and how will I feel if we get a safe knock here and he gets thrown out at the plate? Damn . . . To run for him or not to run, that is the question. Well, O.K.—get Andy Fox out there. Sorry, Cec. Now we'll get a hit and go ahead in this thing, for sure.

It didn't happen.

Bobby Cox (top of the tenth, two out, with Yankee base runners Tim Raines on second base and Jeter on first): Well, here comes Bernie Williams up, wouldn't you know it? This guy killed the Rangers and killed the Orioles, and I'm not going to let him kill us here. I'll never hear the end of it if I put him on and the front guy scores, but it's sure as hell the right thing to do this time. (He signals for the intentional base on balls to Williams.) Who will they bat here—it's gonna be Boggs, bet your butt on it.

Joe Torre: Yes. Now. Finally it's Boggs time. All we need is ball four, Wade baby!

Torre had already wheeled in five pinch-hitters or runners, and six pitchers (forty-one players got into this game before it was done, including thirteen pitchers and five different third basemen), and for him to have Wade Boggs, a five-time American League batting champion with a deadly eye for the strike zone, still available to pinch-hit in this extremity was a miracle of conservation. Steve Avery, the incumbent Braves pitcher, worked manfully at the task, throwing a one-and-two strike or near-strike that Boggs let go by and that ump Steve Rippley called a ball instead. Wincing, Avery delivered another ball and then ball four, forcing in the go-ahead run.

The thunderstruck Bobby Cox (we will skip a further visit to his noggin here, out of respect), beckoning in a fresh pitcher named Brad Clontz, also took care of the suddenly imperative need to play his last offensive card by simultaneously inserting his left-handed slugger, Ryan Klesko, in the game, routinely switching the two names on his lineup card so that Klesko would lead off the Braves' half of the inning. Nothing, however, can be routine about a tenth-inning contretemps in the World Series. Idly regarding the Troy-like panorama below, the baseball gods noticed that Klesko, an indifferent fielder who had to take the field somewhere on this no-d.h. diamond, was playing first base, and arranged for the next Yankee batter, Charlie Hayes, to send up a soft little pop fly that Klesko somehow lost in the lights as the Yankees' insurance run came barreling home. Later on—after Joe Torre and Don Zimmer had finished pounding and yelling at each other ("Wow! Wasn't that—!" "Shut up—who's pitching next?") and Klesko had struck out and Wetteland had come on to finish up and the reporters had cranked out their comparisons between this epic and the Mookie Wilson-Bill Buckner sixth game in the 1986 series—Torre said, "That was the best game I've been involved with, ever. Nothing else comes close."

Baseball anxiety, which is to say baseball happiness, came in a different flavor the next night, when Andy Pettitte, matched against the Braves' John Smoltz in a face-off of this year's potential Cy Young Award winners, fired an edgy, hold-your-breath shutout that the Yanks won, 1-0, thanks to a fly ball that Marquis Grissom dropped in center field for a two-base error, and a Fielder double. Pettitte, who numbed the Atlanta batters with his tailing fastball, also contributed a pair of breathtaking defensive plays in the sixth, nervily barehanding a bunt and firing to third base for a force, and then, on the very next pitch, pouncing on a comebacker to begin the game's backbreaking double play. Sudden events like this can make careers, and for Pettitte—David Cone said it—this game was a defining moment. The win, nailed down where O'Neill caught up with Luis Polonia's drive to deep right center, wrapped up the Yanks' unlikely sweep down in Atlanta. They had won all eight of their post-season road games this year, which is unheard of, and that 8-6 comeback, the longest post-season game ever played, was the second-biggest turnabout in World Series history.

We know the rest. The Yankees, back before their home hordes, scored all three of their runs in a third-inning flareup against the near-invincible Greg Maddux, with Joe Girardi contributing that rarest and most thrilling sight in baseball's catalogue, a triple over the center fielder's head. Jimmy Key, the Yankee starter, had inordinate trouble throwing strikes but never gave in, refusing to deliver the inviting, problem-solving, game-risking pitch up over the plate. Wetteland wrapped up, after practically inducing mass heart failure when he gave up three singles and the Braves' second run in the ninth, and the Yanks went into their pigpile. They had conquered a proud and powerful and (I heard this everywhere) unlikable team, after beating their unmatched trio of starters: Tom Glavine, Smoltz, and Maddux. They beat them in the toughest, most grudging competition imaginable, because the three did not exactly fold up: their combined earned-run average in these games, as they probably won't forget, was 1.23. Maddux, a four-time winner of the Cy Young Award, went out in style, saying, "Obviously, it hurts losing, but the atmosphere here is matched nowhere. It's exciting to be out there on the mound in front of people going freaky. It's wild. Even though we lost, in a while we're going to appreciate being in this place."

As always happens, I wanted the baseball back, even at the moment of its ending. Watching Wade Boggs up on that police horse, with his hat off and his fist in the air, and the field full of cops and debris, I kept turning back in my mind to the pleasures of Yankee baseball as it had been at this game's beginning, with the crowd, a mass somehow more tightly packed into a single body than at any other park, weaving and writhing together, rocking and boogying along between innings, to the enormous music from the videotron and sound system blasting out "Cotton Eye Joe" and "Rock and Roll (Part II)." It was better, of course, during the action, when everyone was jumping up for the play or the third strike, with their arms raised, and with that motion turning into a front-to-back moving wave, as its leaders—rows of friends together in their gear and their high spirits, all hand-slapping and high-fiving—began making those everybody-up gestures that drove me bananas even while they made me smile and got me up, too. There was the crowd sound, too—that many-thousands roar around you and above and below you, a curving, enveloping noise so deep and thick that you felt it inside your head and your stomach and lower inside you as well; sometimes the noise was so loud that the Stadium became a part of the instrument, trembling and thrumming with it, the way it has always done and was meant to do. The fans' joyfulness was there as well, along with their apprehension, with the crowd feeding on its own noise and its brash energy and laughing at the power of its familiar deafening yells: "Oooh-oh! Oooh-oh! Oooh-oh!" and "Let's go, Yank-ees! Let's go, Yank-ees!" or, a quicker, "Le'sgoYank-ees! Le'sgoYank-ees!" or the ancient, brisk clap-clap clapclapclap staccato—a one, two, threefourfive beat that zinged around the stands and lifted us with a quicker insistence.

This Yankee crowd is quick and dead sure of itself, and proud of its harsh, vulgar, big-city reputation as the most demanding and judgmental body in sports: the La Scala of the pastime. It knows baseball, it misses nothing, and it makes up its mind in an instant: that sudden deep "Booo!" or the irredeemable "Aaaah-sole! Aaaah-sssole!" Plus it's funny. When the estimable Bobby Cox, his world in pieces around him, headed back to his dugout after protesting a terrible ump's call out at second base, and then got himself thrown out of the game by third-base umpire Tim Welke—they'd been wrangling all week—the bleachers and back-rows chorus did a triumphant parody of that gruesome Atlanta tomahawk chant, with its own fresh lyrics: "Fuck the Braaaves!" Fuck thuh Braa-aves!" and then had to stop; it had broken itself up. Yes, we had the nice victory parade and the ticker tape, with the Mayor and the Governor in their Yankee caps, and our guys, the smiling players, up on the trucks, but never mind all that now. This other stuff is what we'll want to hold on to, with winter coming along. Never mind the monuments.

Championships Begin with Starting Pitching

From *The Yankee Years*

by Joe Torre and Tom Verducci

David Cone's perfect game was just a sliver of the story of New York's pitching rotation in 1999. Roger Clemens (who had an underwhelming first season as a Yankee) and Andy Pettitte (whom George Steinbrenner was hell-bent on trading) both came up big in the postseason, and Joe Torre's Yankees of 1998–1999 became the first team to sweep consecutive Series since the Bombers of 1938–1939.

The 1999 Yankees were not quite the machine that was the 1998 Yankees, but they were a reasonable facsimile—except for Clemens falling short of replacing Wells' excellence. They held first place for 131 days, including all of them after June 9. On July 18, two months into Torre being back on the job, and 14 months since Wells threw his perfect game, all about the Yankees was perfect again. It was a Sunday afternoon in which the Yankees honored Yogi Berra before an interleague game against the Montreal Expos. Don Larsen, the author of the only perfect game in World Series history, was there to throw the ceremonial first pitch to Berra, a nod to their collaboration in the 1956 perfecto. Larsen and Berra watched the game from Steinbrenner's suite-level box. They saw history repeat itself.

Cone, the Yankees' starting pitcher, dominated the heavily righthanded Expos, none of whom had faced him before, with fast-balls and sliders that disappeared from their swing plane. After only five innings, the thought occurred to Cone that he might have a shot at throwing a perfect game. The Expos kept going down with amazing ease; Cone would throw only 20 balls to 27 batters. After almost every inning on the 98-degree day, Cone would return to the clubhouse to change one of the cutoff undershirts he wore beneath his jersey. By the time he retreated to the clubhouse in the eighth inning, the perfect game still intact, he noticed there was nobody in there. Nobody wanted to break the tradition of not talking to a pitcher when he has a no-hitter or perfect game in progress.

"It was a ghost town," Cone said. "Even the clubhouse attendants were gone."

Cone kept the perfect game going through the eighth, though to do so it took a backhand grab of a grounder and surprisingly true throw from the unpredictable Knoblauch at second base. Now Cone was only three outs away from baseball immortality. He walked back to the clubhouse. Again, the place was deserted. He changed undershirts again, then walked into the bathroom, stopping at one of the sinks in front of the large mirror. Alone, he looked at himself in the mirror and spoke aloud.

"What do we have to do to get this done?" he said. "This is the last chance you're ever going to have to do something like this."

He bent down, ran cold water from the faucet into his cupped hands and splashed the water over his face. He stared at himself in the mirror again.

"Holy shit," he said. "How am I going to do this?"

For a moment he was caught in a very awkward place between doubt and desire, trying to beat back one while encouraging the other in a battle inside his head.

Don't blow it, he thought to himself.

And then he shook his head.

No, don't think that way! That's negative.

But doubt crawled back.

Don't blow it.

No. No negative thoughts. Get it done!

But don't blow it.

Finally, he stopped the internal doubt for good. Still staring into the mirror, he thought to himself, *Screw the psychobabble! Go out and there and get it done!*

Cone was 36 years old, a survivor of a scary aneurysm three years earlier, and well aware of his pitching mortality. He could not know it at the time, but this would be the last complete game he would ever throw, the last shutout, too. In fact, Cone would make 131 starts in his six seasons with the Yankees, and this would be his only shutout.

"I went out there for the ninth and—boom, boom, boom—struck out the first guy on three pitches," Cone said. "Then I got a humpback liner to left, which Ricky Ledee kind of lost in the seats or sun or whatever."

Ledee, though, caught the ball, however ungracefully. Cone needed one more out. The batter was Orlando Cabrera, a 24-year-old shortstop. Cabrera swung and missed at the first pitch and took the second one for a ball. On the next pitch, a slider, the 88th pitch of the game for Cone, Cabrera lifted a pop-up into foul ground near third base. Cone looked up and couldn't find the ball.

"I remember the sun was setting on that side of Yankee Stadium," Cone said. "As I looked up I got blinded by the sun, so I pointed, thinking Brosius was already camped under it at that point. I never saw the ball."

Brosius squeezed the pop-up in his glove. Cone was perfect. He dropped to his knees and reached for his head, in a sweet combination of disbelief and relief.

Torre always believed championships began with starting pitching and 1999 was no different, even with Clemens underperforming. Torre's rotation was remarkably durable and reliable once again. Cone, Clemens, El Duque, Pettitte and Irabu made 152 of the teams' 162 starts, posting a 68-36 record. Steinbrenner, though, considered Pettitte a drag on the staff and wanted him gone, especially after Pettitte could not get out of the fourth inning of a game against the White Sox on July 28, 10 days after Cone's perfect game and three days before the trade deadline. Pettitte was 7-8 with a 5.65 ERA at that point. Steinbrenner had a deal in place to ship Pettitte to the Phillies.

While the Yankees were in Boston just hours away from the deadline, Steinbrenner conducted a conference call with Cashman, Torre and Stottlemyre. Steinbrenner said he was ready to trade Pettitte.

"I can't believe you would even consider doing it!" Stottlemyre said.

Torre and Cashman also spoke out against trading Pettitte. Finally, Steinbrenner gave in. He called off the deal.

"You better be right," he said to the three of them, "or you know what's going to happen."

Over the next 4 1/2 years, or until Steinbrenner let Pettitte walk as a free agent, Pettitte went 75-35 for Steinbrenner's Yankees, a .682 winning percentage. Over the rest of that 1999 season, Pettitte was 7-3 with a 3.46 ERA before tacking on a 2-0 postseason. Pettitte never truly engendered confidence from Steinbrenner, possibly because he carried himself with a sensitivity that belied his competitiveness.

Torre remembers one of the big first games Pettitte pitched for him, on September 18, 1996, against Baltimore. It was the first game of a huge three-game series at Yankee Stadium against the second-place Orioles, whom the Yankees led by three games with 13 games to play. Pettitte, 24, was pitching against veteran Baltimore righthander Scott Erickson. Torre walked into the trainer's room before the game and happened to find Pettitte there.

"He looked scared to death," Torre said. "He was just sitting there, staring."

Torre learned to interpret such a look from Pettitte as intense focus. Pettitte pitched magnificently against Baltimore, allowing the league's top home-run-hitting team just two runs over 8 1/3 innings. Pettitte did leave trailing, 2-1, but the Yankees rallied to tie the game in the ninth and win it in the 10th, 3-2.

"One thing I learned about Andy," Torre said, "is he thought you weren't allowed to be nervous. Jeter, as far as handling the pressure, is the best I've ever seen. But Andy, in spite of getting excited, managed to handle it the right way. The game never sped up for him.

"He's so honest, which is so refreshing, because not too many people own up to their shortcomings. He does. Whether it's a particular at-bat or pitch, he'll tell you. Andy is very honest.

"In fact, I remember when I talked to him about the possibility of coming back to the Yankees after he pitched those years in Houston. He said, 'I thought I had everything where I wanted it: coming home, being with family. . . . I just didn't have fun playing. There was no fire. Just the thought of going back to New York has gotten me excited.' Probably the worst word in sports is being 'comfortable.' There's something about comfort that doesn't seem to fit with what you need to do. Andy missed New York. Andy was great. I think he taught Roger how to pitch in New York. And Roger taught Andy how to be stronger. Back then Andy was a little soft physically, but not mentally, that's for sure."

The trade for Clemens, meanwhile, did not turn out the way the Yankees expected. Clemens missed three weeks early in the season with a leg problem, and when he did pitch he looked nothing like the best pitcher in baseball as he had been in Toronto. He was 8-4 with an unseemly 4.98 ERA through the middle of July. He struck out 10 batters in a game only once. He looked far too ordinary.

"Roger struggled early on," Cone said. "He was getting booed at Yankee Stadium. Roger was always kind of aloof. He was kind of shy and insecure. People don't realize that about him. A lot of superstars are like that, surprisingly so. Roger was like that. He struggled to fit in. He struggled with New York. He was not pitching too well and in fact had trouble just hanging out. He would be disappearing before games. He was always hiding in the weight room or on the couch in the traveling secretary's office. Just kind of hiding out a lot. During the game he wasn't on the bench very much. He got better as he started to pitch better and got used to the guys."

One day in August, while the Yankees were in Seattle, Clemens asked Torre if he could use his office to call his mother. Torre said of course. A while later Torre stepped into the office to retrieve something and heard Clemens tell his mom, "I'm still just trying to fit in and be one of the guys."

When Clemens was done with the call, Torre told him he wanted to speak to him.

"'Fit in' my ass," Torre told him. "You be who you are. Be Roger Clemens."

"I know," Clemens said. "That's what my mom is always telling me."

"Listen," Torre said, "you're allowed to be selfish. We traded for you because we wanted the guy who was pitching in Toronto, not somebody different. Not somebody who is just trying to fit in. You're just trying to sort of blend in here and that's not what we want. That's not what we traded for. You're too tentative."

Clemens agreed with Torre's assessment and vowed to become more assertive, though the Yankees still didn't see the dominating version of Clemens. He pitched only marginally better over his final 11 starts, going 5-6 with a 4.34 ERA.

"The thing with Roger that I found was you loved him," Torre said. "There are all the bells and whistles that you get with Roger but his heart was always in the right place. He was a good team-mate, and that sort of surprised me, because before he got to us he had this reputation about being able to go home and not be around the team. And I told him. 'You can't do that,' and it was never a problem.

"He was a cheerleader in between starts. And he reminded me of Bob Gibson when he did start. We wouldn't be scoring for Gibby and he'd go, 'You guys . . . you've got to be shittin' me.' And he'd go inside the clubhouse. Roger would do that. He was very outgoing, and yet it wasn't an act. If it was, he had himself convinced of that.

"He also had tremendous belief in himself and his pitching. If you don't believe that pitch is going to go exactly where you want it, then it's not going to go there. Roger believed every pitch was going where he wanted it to go."

Clemens did not come close to replacing Wells' production with the 1999 Yankees. He finished 14-10 with a 4.60 ERA, the worst ERA of his 24-year career. The Yankees still won that AL East with 98 wins, four more than second-place Boston. On the final weekend of the season, Torre sat down with Stottlemyre to map out their pitching plans for the playoffs when Torre decided to include Clemens in the discussion. Clemens, by reputation, was a protypical Game 1 starter, but in reality he had not been that kind of pitcher for the Yankees all year. Orlando "El Duque" Hernandez had led the staff that season with 17 wins. Torre decided he wanted Clemens to recognize that reality himself.

"Roger, who do you think should start Game 1?" Torre asked him.

"Duque," Clemens said.

Torre was a bit relieved to know he would not have to convince Clemens otherwise.

"What I like to do is see if people evaluate the same way I do," Torre said. "I figured, 'As much as he thinks of himself, let's see what he said.'"

If Clemens had said he deserved the ball for Game 1, Torre said, "We would have talked him out of it. We would have explained why that's not true. I always liked to believe that you could always try to make sense to people. I always try to make these guys understand there is another perspective other than theirs."

Clemens was Torre's number three starter, behind Hernandez and Andy Pettitte. The Yankees blew through the Texas Rangers in the Division Series again, allowing only one run in the three-game sweep. Torre used the same order of pitchers in the American League Championship Series against Boston, an arrangement that left Clemens returning to Fenway Park to pitch against Pedro Martinez in Game 3. The game was promoted in the manner of a heavyweight fight, a bout between Clemens, the expatriate Red Sox star, and Martinez, his replacement in Boston as the best pitcher in baseball and the soul of the franchise. The crowd arrived with the meanness and edginess of a mob. Indeed, before the day was done packs of fans would climb over themselves trying to claw down a canvas mural hung in one of the concourses in the celebration of Clemens's two 20-strikeout games with Boston.

Clemens, a shell of himself all season, failed miserably amid the hostility. Torre removed him after only one batter into the third inning with a score of 4-0. Clemens walked off the mound and down the dugout steps gingerly, having something of a ready-made excuse because of some back stiffness. Clemens was charged with five runs in what became a 13-1 Boston victory, its only one of the ALCS. In the middle innings, with Clemens long gone and Martinez cutting apart the Yankees lineup, the crowd mocked Clemens by chanting, "Where is Roger?"

Part of what made Clemens great as a pitcher was his inflated sense of self, the same trait that prompted Torre to check with Clemens before aligning his postseason rotation. There is almost no concession in the man. He enjoyed not being just Roger Clemens, but also playing the role of Roger Clemens.

"He is needy, and he's got his own world he lives in. As far as competing, they're different people. Roger's always going to go out there and have that positive attitude. That's the way he has to think."

Said Brian McNamee, Clemens's former personal trainer, and the one who told baseball special investigator George Mitchell in 2007 that he injected Clemens with steroids, "The worst day was the day after Roger lost a game. Because he would blame everybody on the field. It was the umpire, it was the fielders, it was Jeter can't go to his left, it was the outfielders playing back too deep . . . it was always something. The ball. The ball's too slick. Oh, Posada? All the time. It was just a nightmare."

Torre never knew Clemens to look for excuses. He understood that Clemens's knack for ignoring reality at cost of preserving his grand sense of self would not play well in the wake of his debacle in ALCS Game 3 in front of the Boston mob. Blaming his third-inning knockout on a stiff back, for instance, would invite his critics to diminish him further. Torre was concerned about what Clemens might say to reporters after the game.

As Torre took Clemens out of the game, he told him on the mound, "Just do yourself a favor. When they come in and talk to you, just tell them you were horseshit. Because I know you're hurting. You know you're hurting. But that won't play well."

After the game, first the reporters asked Torre if Clemens, by evidence of the pained look he gave leaving the mound, was diminished by an injury.

Said Torre, "I think the score was making him grimace."

Then the reporters approached Clemens. Would he blame the results on his back? Was the ball too slick? This time, thanks to Torre's intervention, he actually revealed some concession.

"I think the thing for me tonight was location," Clemens said. "I didn't have good command. I fell behind and they made me pay for it."

Rebirth of the Subway Series

"October Best"
The Sporting News, November 6, 2000

by Michael Knisley

*When the Dodgers and Giants left for sunny California, they took the
Subway Series tradition with them. The Mets, born in 1962,
were relative newcomers, and their success had never coincided with
their cross-town rivals'—until 2000, when New York's first Subway
Series since 1956 was played.*

THE YANKEES GO THROUGH A WORLD SERIES LIKE A MERCEDES ON THE
AUTOBAHN. TV VIEWERS MAY PREFER AN ECONOMY CAR, BUT THE TEAM
FROM THE BRONX HANDLES WELL ON ROUGH ROADS AND IS QUICK TO
REPLACE ANY WORN-OUT PARTS.

"You've just got to tip your hat to them. They get out there, and they get after
it. They get it done. They play good, sound, fundamental baseball. They do all
the little things, and that's what it takes to win championships. Not that we
didn't, but there are some places along the road where we stumbled a little bit.
They do what it takes. They did what it takes."

—Mets pitcher Turk Wendell

Something about the Yankees rings the same bell year after year. Wendell
may not realize it, but he's tapping into a baseball tradition that's become as
predictable as the seventh-inning stretch, the ceremonial first pitch and World
Series games ending so long after midnight that even the vampires are tucked
back into bed before the last out is made.

The Yankees are world champions now for three years running and for four out of the last five. That's a truly remarkable feat in this era of free agents and tiered playoffs. Because players have the freedom to change teams now and because a World Series winner needs to beat three clubs in October now to finish on top of the heap, the Yankees' string of titles looks more formidable than the Oakland A's three straight from 1972 to '74, the last time a team was this dominant.

In fact, Yankees manager Joe Torre makes a case, a strong case, for the 1996–2000 Yankees' being baseball's best team ever, and any counter to that argument isn't going to be entirely persuasive.

So the team wins consistently. But it's the consistency of the way it wins that really distinguishes the Yankees. You score one; they score two. You throw a play away; they make you pay. You get picked off first; they snuff your rally. It happens over and over and over, and it happens year after year after year.

It happened to the Mets last week almost exactly as it happened to the Braves in 1996, to the Padres in 1998 and to the Braves again last season.

The Mets put up a bold front in their five-game loss. They lost four games by a total of five runs. Every game was in doubt until the very end. A break here, a break there and maybe the overall outcome would have been different. Todd Zeile, for instance, came within a total of perhaps two inches of hitting two home runs, but instead wound up with a double and a long out in Games 1 and 2. The Mets lost both games by a single run.

Yankees shortstop and Series MVP Derek Jeter simply may be practicing Subway Series diplomacy, but he sent kudos in the direction of Shea Stadium when he said, "We made it look easy in three out of the last four years, but this one was a little bit of a struggle for us. It's been up and down. It seems like it's been one continuous game. I haven't slept in a week."

The Mets did manage to end two notable Yankee streaks. When they took Game 3 (by a 4-2 score), they stopped both the Yankees' unprecedented 14-game World Series victory string and pitcher Orlando "El Duque" Hernandez's personal postseason unbeaten record. (He was 8-0 in nine starts.)

Hey, it's something.

And yet, as the Mets' Wendell stood in front of his locker late last Thursday night and delivered his postmortem, his comments were practically indistinguishable from the analyses of other National League representatives who had fallen to the Yankees in previous years.

A season ago in a hushed visiting clubhouse at Yankee Stadium, Braves infielder Keith Lockhart said, "It's hard to take anything away from that team. You can start to turn the tide just a little bit, and it's like they just smell blood over there. They just keep battling and battling. You can't just shut down one or two guys in their lineup and beat them. They're all tough outs."

In 1998 the appraiser was Padres right fielder Tony Gwynn and the scene was Jack Murphy Stadium, but the meaning of the words were the same. "Just as soon as you get the lead, they turn it around," Gwynn said. "They get two and then three, and you're in the hole again. So, yeah, it's frustrating as hell."

Even in 1996, when the Yankees dropped the first two games to Atlanta, they came back and won four straight and captured the Series, employing the embryonic stages of the modus operandi they've used over the last three seasons.

"Sooner or later," said Braves general manager John Schuerholz back then, "somebody has to say to that team over there, 'Well done, guys. You're the champions, and your play and your fight and grit demonstrate that.' I'm not ashamed to say it. I'm surprised and disappointed we didn't win. But I'm also cognizant of the fact that those guys in the other uniforms over there battled their hearts out."

It doesn't seem to matter much whom the Yankees play in the World Series. All comers walk away shaking their heads. They all walk away in awe. They all walk away losers.

The Yankees have been doing this for so long that it's almost as if they win by rote. Even their jubilation scene near second base after this year's Series-clinching, 4-2 victory seemed more pure reflex action than true joy. They came running together in a teamwide huddle with the requisite jumping up and down, but none of them even hit the turf.

Several Yankees did hoist a visibly emotional Torre to their shoulders to carry him toward the dugout, but the onfield celebration was over almost as soon as it began.

Could be that they were too exhausted for more. Each game, as Jeter suggested, was close and tense, including Game 5, in which the Yankees didn't score the winning runs until the top of the ninth inning. The pressure on both teams to win the first Subway Series in 44 years was draining. Lose to the crosstown Mets, and much of what the Yankees built over the last few years would be undone.

Could be, though, that this is just old hat to them, as it apparently is to much of the nation outside New York City. Fox's ratings for the World Series were astronomical in New York but dreadful elsewhere, partly because of the length of the games, partly because of the provincial flavor and, probably, partly because baseball fans didn't see much new from the Yankees this time around.

In some ways, the games played like a series of reruns, a too-familiar show already in syndication and playing in a late-night time slot. As close as each game was, the ratings were by far the worst in the 40 years the World Series has been televised. This in a year in which Major League Baseball set a new single-season total attendance record.

In any event, these Yankees aren't exactly an openly emotional bunch. They don't readily provide the golden video moments, save maybe for Torre's post-Series tears and Roger Clemens' irresistible impulse to hurl a broken bat in the direction of Mike Piazza.

"This team is very low-profile," said first-base coach Lee Mazzilli. "These are mild, low-key people. You get on a bus or a plane with us and you would not know if we won, 10-1, or lost, 10-1. We don't get too high, and we don't get too low. That comes from the Godfather in there (Torre), and it funnels down. They don't wear their emotions on their sleeves.

"That's just the experience we have. I think if the experience factor wasn't there, if these guys hadn't been here before, they may not have been able to make the adjustment from the regular season to the postseason. But when we enter the postseason, I can honestly say that we expect to win. It's a confidence thing. This team believes. I mean, this is not a cocky team. They don't pop off. They don't talk much. They just believe."

Winning is a learned behavior, and the Yankees seem able to call on the lessons they've learned whenever they come up against a postseason opponent who isn't as familiar with the process—which, of course, by now is every postseason opponent.

As much as anything, that was the difference between the Yankees and the Mets.

The Mets, for instance, played charitably in Game 1, when they made four baserunning blunders that kept a 3-2 late-inning lead from being any bigger. Two of those mental errors were committed by young outfielders Timo Perez and Jay Payton, neither of whom had been in a major league playoff game until this year. When the Yankees tied that game in the ninth, somehow you knew they were going to win it. In the 12th, they did.

The Mets, who hadn't been in a World Series in 14 years, essentially gave that one away. There was no give-back from the other dugout in any of the other meetings. After that first game and in the context of the Yankees' past performances, the Series carried a sense of inevitability with it through closer Mariano Rivera's two saves (he now holds the World Series career record with seven) and the Yankees' two-run rally in the ninth inning that won the deciding fifth game.

It isn't fair to say they play on autopilot because baseball is a very difficult, very cerebral game that demands concentration as well as physical tools. Nobody just goes through the motions and wins a World Series, and that includes the Yankees. Torre, a former National League manager, still knows the National League game and kept as much pressure on the Mets as possible with that style—hit-and-run plays, moving runners, manufacturing runs. It's a good, exciting brand of ball.

But the Yankees are so efficient in October after October that at times it seems they're sitting back in their seats with the cruise-control button pushed.

"I would say this club is one that knows how to win," says Reggie Jackson, Mr. October himself and now a Yankees front-office employee. "They feel like, 'If I get beat, I get beat. But I'm not going to lose.' They don't strike out at the wrong time. They don't throw the ball away. They keep themselves close, and they bite and scratch and claw. The wrinkles go out of the uniform when you do that. This club understands that."

The Yankees have done this so often in October that even the unpredictability of their offensive heroes is becoming predictable. It was Jim Leyritz in 1996, light-hitting third baseman Scott Brosius in 1998, reserve outfielder Chad Curtis in 1999.

In 2000 the incomparable Jeter was the World Series Most Valuable Player for his .409 batting average, his two key home runs and his sparkling play in the field. But Jose Vizcaino, obtained only for bench depth at midseason, collected four hits and drove in the winning run in the 12th inning of Game 1. And utility infielder Luis Sojo, cut by the Yankees last offseason and dropped even by the Pirates this year, accounted for the winning runs in both the fourth and fifth games.

All that said, we've probably seen the last of some of the core group of players that won those four world titles in the last half-decade. Even though at the end of the postseason the Yankees appear almost as invincible this year as they did in years past, they won only 87 regular-season games. Eight other teams won more than that.

Torre himself points out their good fortune to have played in the American League East. In either of the other A.L. divisions, an 87-74 record wouldn't have even made them the wild-card play-off team. Nor would it have been good enough to qualify from the National League.

"If we were in a different division," Torre says, "we'd have a pipe sent down to see daylight."

And at that, they won a handful of regular-season games with little more than a wing, a prayer and Yankees mystique. They won on a phantom double play in Texas, on boneheaded baserunning by the Indians in Cleveland, on a bases-loaded walk in the 10th inning against Tampa Bay. In September they were abysmal. They lost 15 of their last 18 regular-season games and were taken to the limit in the first round of the playoffs by the A's.

Joe Sparks, a scout for the Cardinals, watched the Yankees in the first two rounds of the postseason and was completely baffled by their September.

"All of a sudden they're good," Sparks said at the end of the ALCS. "Two weeks ago, they were worried to death about everything. I've watched them play two series now, and I can't imagine those guys struggling at all. I can't imagine them losing all those games. I think the big story is how quickly they went from being real bad to real good. There was no middle ground in there. I mean, you just don't go from one extreme to the other like that, from playing awful to playing like I'm seeing them play now.

"I'm glad I didn't write my report two weeks ago. If I did, I'd have to change it. I'd have said they were pushovers."

The Yankees are what in the corporate world is known as a mature business. In other words, they aren't going to get any better than they've already been unless they make significant changes. The front office knows that and knew it even before the 2000 season began. For the first time in recent years, the club purposely avoided negotiations with its potential free agents during the season, presumably to keep options open for major changes this winter.

Now, management is unencumbered by unattractive contracts to players such as Paul O'Neill (who is 37), David Cone (also 37), Dwight Gooden (36 on November 16), Jose Canseco (36), Glenallen Hill (35) and World Series Game 4 starter Denny Neagle, whose hold on a spot in the rotation is tenuous at best.

At the expense of some of those veterans, principal owner Steinbrenner and general manager Brian Cashman will work to free up the cash to sign some of the high-priced free agents on the market, primarily outfielder Manny Ramirez and either Mike Mussina or Mike Hampton, both pitchers. They'll have to sign Jeter, who can be a free agent after next season, to a new contract, too, and after his performance in 2000, that contract likely will be worth considerably more than the $118 million, seven-year deal that didn't get finished last spring.

The Yankees already are by far the highest-salaried team in the game, which likely is another factor contributing to World Series disinterest from the country at large. That isn't going to change. The payroll will move in 2001, and the movement won't be in a southerly direction.

Brosius may not be back at third, Chuck Knoblauch may not be back at second, and Tino Martinez may not be back at first. The Yankees have at least three prospects who probably are major-league-ready in infielders Alfonso Soriano and D'Angelo Jimenez and first baseman Nick Johnson, who missed the 2000 season with an injured wrist but has begun hitting against live pitching again in Florida this fall.

And they'll regain the services of two of their younger stars-in-waiting, left fielder Shane Spencer and starter/long reliever Ramiro Mendoza, both injured this season.

The Yankees may be back in the World Series again next October. But if they are, it will be with a decidedly different look than they took into the 2000 postseason. Ramirez replacing O'Neill in right field? Mussina replacing Neagle in the rotation? In the afterglow of their championship celebration last Thursday night, someone broached the likelihood of another championship with Steinbrenner.

"Isn't this the end?" Steinbrenner was asked.

"Don't bet the house on it," he said.

"Well, then, how long can it go on?"

"I don't know. I hope forever."

That is not, it's probably safe to say, the hope of the National League. Or Fox Sports.

So Many Dereks

"The Death of Derek Jeter"
Esquire, November 2006

by Michael Martone

In this fictional vignette, writer Michael Martone takes a surreal
trip into the mind of "Mr. November" as he ponders the significance
of his own signature. You can be sure that opposing pitchers have
equally convoluted thoughts running through their heads when
Derek Jeter steps to the plate.

Derek Jeter Derek Jeter Derek Jeter

Every year I change my signature. I'll print. Or I'll slant it more, make more loops. I'll switch-hit, writing left-handed in a cramped, crabby left-leaning scrawl. I have no notion of the effect on the aftermarket for the autographs. Is it even authentic, each rewiring of my hand? I imagine the hubbub in a card shop, the gaggle of collectors squinting, loupes screwed into their eyes, bent over the memorabilia, trying to make sense of the snowflake variations, no two alike.

This summer I tried calligraphy, bamboo brush and that block of ink I have to wet and mix myself. Matsui Sensei took time to study my technique, sidelined as he was with his broken wrist. He had me draw a perfect circle. It was hard. "Yes," he said. "Now we should consider your breathing." We sat in center field. I held my brush poised ready to become one with the paper. I closed my eyes and felt myself breathe out the me-ness of me. Or so I thought. It wasn't working. I peeked out of one eye. The grounds crew was working quietly around us, raking the infield into lazy wavelike furrows, arranging the bases to look like floating islands. This is all an illusion, I remember thinking. But it didn't take. I sighed and signed his cast with my 2001 signature, the *e*'s like *o*'s. We bowed to each other, and Hideki said that I should repeat this koan:

Walk when you walk. Talk when you talk. Die when you die.

And I do. I do. After I'm dead, all these scratches I have made will be what's left of me, and then, they say, we'll see what I was really worth. I think about it. I sign this thing or that. A contract. A warrant. A credit-card slip. A scorecard. A pennant. My will. Someone's belly. So many Dereks, still in circulation.

The Dominance of the Sandman

"Mariano Rivera's a true Yankee,
almost mythical in his dominance"
Sports Illustrated/SI.COM, July 2, 2009

by Joe Posnanski

There's no better word than "dominant" to describe Mariano Rivera's career. With the heart of a winner and nerves of steel, Rivera ruthlessly slams the door on his opponents, working primarily with an infuriatingly effective cut fastball. Through 16 seasons, Rivera's 2.23 career ERA is lowest among all active pitchers, and he has allowed only 11 earned runs in nearly 140 postseason innings. Dominant.

"They say his father was a fisherman. Maybe he was as poor as we are and would understand."

—Ernest Hemingway, *The Old Man and the Sea*

There is a Yankee mythology that sustains New York fans and drives everybody else crazy, and it goes something like this: To play for the New York Yankees, you need to have a certain quality—quiet dignity, maybe, that's part of it, or valor or a sense of the moment. All of that. More. To be a Yankee, the mythos goes, you should suffer your pain in private like Mantle, and keep hitting home runs even when your hair falls out like Maris, and find your true self in October like Reggie. You can be larger than life, like the Babe, and call yourself lucky when dying like Gehrig, and see the world through your own eyes like Yogi. You can even punch out marshmallow salesmen like Billy Martin. As long as you win almost every time out, like Whitey, and make perfectly timed moves, like Casey, and are willing to dive headfirst after victory like Jeter.

No team has so many legends . . . and no team celebrates their legends to New York Yankee excess. This is what makes the Yankees so beloved and despised, depending on which side of the pinstripes you stand. And the man who probably represents the Yankee mythology better than anyone is the man who, according to the Yankee legend, never threw to the wrong base. "I thank the good Lord for making me a Yankee," Joe DiMaggio famously said, and he hit in 56 straight games and made plays with grace. People wrote songs about him. Hemingway wrote literature about him.

"I must have the confidence," Hemingway's old man says to the sea, "and I must be worthy of the great DiMaggio, who does all things perfectly even with the pain of the bone spur in his heel."

The funny part is there is actually a Yankees player who, perhaps even more than DiMaggio, lives up to the Yankee mythology. He too is the son of a fisherman, and he grew up poor enough to understand. His career almost ended before it began, and he was almost traded (twice) before the Yankee pinstripes looked right on him. On the field, he has triumphed under the most intense glare in American sports. Off the field, he has been quiet to the sound of invisible. And all the while, he has looked calm, stunningly calm, the sort of superhuman calm that Hollywood gives its heroes.

Yes, if there is an expression that conveys the Yankee myth, it would be the countenance of Mariano Rivera in the ninth inning.

"Have faith in the Yankees, my son," Hemingway's old man says to the boy. "Think of the great DiMaggio."

If Ernest Hemingway was alive and writing today, those words would be: "Think of the great Rivera."

One pitch. Think about that. Mariano Rivera has saved 502 baseball games by essentially throwing one pitch, that same cut fastball. And, of course, he has done much more than save 502 baseball games with the cut fastball . . . you can choose a thousand numbers to show his eminence. Consider ERA+, a statistic that measures a players ERA against the pitchers of his own era. In ERA+, 100 is exactly league average.

Here are the greatest ERA+ in baseball history (more than 1,000 innings pitched):

1. Mariano Rivera, 198
2. Pedro Martinez, 154
3. Lefty Grove, 148
4. Walter Johnson, 147
5. Five pitchers tied at 146

Look at that—Rivera's ERA+ is more than FORTY POINTS higher than anyone else in baseball history. How about WHIP—walks-plus-hits per inning pitched?

1. Addie Joss, 0.968
2. Ed Walsh, 1.000
3. Mariano Rivera, 1.02
4. John Ward, 1.044*
* You will note the other three on the list are all pitchers from the
  Deadball Era.

How about number of seasons with an ERA under 2.00? Walter Johnson did it 11 times—all in the Deadball Era. Mariano Rivera did it eight times during the biggest explosion of offense since the 1930s. Of course, you can't compare Rivera to Walter Johnson or any other starter; Rivera has not even thrown 85 innings in a season since he became a closer in 1997.

Then again, you cannot compare Walter Johnson or any other starter to Rivera either because, of the 1,055 innings the man has pitched, about 900 of them were eighth inning, ninth inning or later, with the game on the line, with the crowd freaking out, with the metropolis tabloid editors holding the back pages (How's this for the headline: "Cry Me A Rivera?" Or "Oh no Mariano!"), with the opposing team, as it says in Casey at the Bat, clinging to the hope which springs eternal in the human breast.

And with Rivera on the mound, Mighty Casey did strike out time and time and time again. Rivera struck them out and busted their bats on that same pitch over and over and over, one pitch, a low-to-mid-90s cut fastball. One pitch. It seems impossible.

But what a pitch. Jim Thome calls it the greatest pitch in baseball history, and who could argue? There's Sandy Koufax's curveball, Satchel Paige's fastball, Steve Carlton's slider, Carl Hubbell's screwball, Bruce Sutter's splitter, Gaylord Perry's spitter, Pedro Martinez's change-up, but all of them threw other pitches, set-up pitches. Rivera has no opening act. He comes at hitters with the same pitch, one pitch, again and again, hard fastball, sharp break to the left at the last possible instant, that pitch has undoubtedly broken more bats per inning than any other, it has left more batters frozen per inning than any other, it has broken more hearts than Brian's Song.

Rivera says he learned the pitch while fooling around one day in 1997, playing catch with his friend and Panama countryman Ramiro Mendoza. By then, Rivera was already the Yankees closer. And he was already terrific—he was coming off a superhuman 1996 season. That year, as a setup man to John Wetteland, he had pitched 107 innings, struck out 130, and allowed the league to hit only .189. But he had done that with pure power—a high-90s fastball and impeccable control. And such things don't last.

Rivera remembers playing catch with Mendoza, coming up with a new grip, and coming out of it with this monster—"A gift from God," he always says—a cut fastball that bore in on lefties and made righties give up.

And suddenly, he was even better. That year, 1997, he finished with his first sub-2.00 ERA. And from that point on, Mariano Rivera threw that one pitch in ballparks across America, to the best hitters of his generation. The best hitters of his generation could not catch up. They have not caught up still.

"You know what's coming," a five-time All-Star Mike Sweeney once said. "But you know what's coming in horror movies, too. It still gets you."

Mariano Rivera grew up in Puerto Camito, Panama, and he happily will admit that he did not grow up with big dreams. He never expected to leave. He worked as a fisherman as a young boy—cleaned fish, pulled up nets, like the boy in Hemingway's vision. He wanted to play ball. The Yankees signed him for $3,000, Rivera promised his mother he would always come home, and when he was 22 years old he had Tommy John surgery. Nobody was predicting great things.

His first game in the big leagues in 1995—Rivera was 25 already—he started against the California Angels and lasted just 3 1/3 innings. After four starts, his ERA was 10.20, and he didn't pitch again for more than three weeks. Then, on the Fourth of July, he threw eight innings, allowed two hits and struck out 11 against the White Sox. The Yankees were not entirely sure what they had.

They would not really know what they had until (fittingly) the playoffs—the Yankees' first playoff appearance in 14 years. Rivera pitched 5 1/3 scoreless innings in relief against the Seattle Mariners. He dominated those innings too, something seemed to light up inside him when the pressure was its heaviest. The next year, with Joe Torre as the new Yankees manager, Rivera was moved to the 'pen, and he was immediately so awesome that in late April, Twins manager Tom Kelly made this statement: "He needs to pitch in a higher league, if there is one. Ban him from baseball. He should be illegal."

Of course, quite a few closers have been virtually unhittable for one year, two years, three years. But sooner or later, something happens. Hitters figure something out. The constant duress wears the pitcher down. The closer's money pitch loses one mph of speed or one millimeter of break. And then, like an NFL cornerback who loses a half step, the closer is lost.

But Rivera's one pitch has never lost its power. He just keeps going, year after year. Here's a challenge for you: pick out Mariano Rivera's best year. Do you want 1998, when he saved 36 games for the almost unbeatable Yankees and posted a 1.91 ERA? Or do you prefer the next year, when he led the league with 45 saves and opposing batters hit .176 against him? Do you like 2004 when he saved 53—32 by the All-Star Break—or 2005 when he had a 1.38 ERA and had an absurd 38 1-2-3 innings?

Then again, you could always choose last year, when Rivera had a 77-to-6 strikeout-to-walk ratio and punched up a .665 WHIP—only Dennis Eckersley in his heyday had ever put so few batters on base.

He has always looked so comfortable in the moment. It isn't that Mariano Rivera has never failed —he actually has three of the most famous defeats in recent memory. In 1997, he gave up an eighth-inning home run to Sandy Alomar with the Yankees just four outs away from clinching a spot in the ALCS. In 2001, he gave up two broken bat singles—Rivera breaks bats the way Chuck Norris breaks bones—and committed an error and allowed two runs in the ninth in Game 7 of the World Series. In 2004, he blew two saves against Boston, a performance so shocking that the next year Red Sox fans wildly cheered him when his name was announced.*

*Rivera just smiled, of course. "I felt honored," he said. "What was I going to do? Get upset and start throwing baseballs at people?"

No, it isn't that Rivera never failed, it's that he never let that failure define him or knock him off course. Even with those three defeats, he's the greatest postseason closer in baseball history, maybe the greatest postseason pitcher ever. He is 8-1 in the postseason with 34 saves (nobody else has even half of that) and a ludicrous 0.77 ERA. Sixty-six times in his postseason career, Mariano Rivera has appeared in the late innings of a playoff or World Series game and not given up a run—nobody else is even close.

Rivera does not talk much about it, at least not publicly, but he will say that to pitch well in those heart-pounding moments you have to enjoy the heart-pounding moments, you must have balance in your life (the moment is important but not THAT important; losing is difficult but it won't kill you), and you have to forget the failures and successes of the past. Rivera does not seem the type to write a book, but if he ever did it should be something about peace—Zen and the Art of Closing Out A Baseball Game—because that seems to be his greatest gift of all. Mariano Rivera always seems at peace.

It's probably worth noting here that Mariano Rivera has not written a book. Other Yankees have—Derek Jeter has written two, Paul O'Neill wrote one about his father, Jorge Posada has written a children's book and so on. Rivera doesn't claim to have anything to say. He seems happiest in the stillness of the background, a hard place to find in New York City.

But he has found that quiet place in New York. And this, perhaps, is the most remarkable thing about Mariano Rivera. He's the ultimate Yankee, the embodiment of the Yankee myth, and yet for 15 seasons now he has not sparked a controversy, not been caught in the bright lights, not inspired the boos anywhere in America.

Oh, every so often, for a couple of weeks or a month, he will give up a few runs and look to be human, and there will be some who will start to prepare the eulogy, most recently a few weeks ago after a rough patch, but then he will emerge again, throwing that one matchless pitch. He's 39 years old now. He has saved 48 games in his last 50 chances. This isn't to say that Mariano Rivera is underrated—everyone knows. Yankees fans love him. Opposing fans respect him. It's just that as good as people think he is, he might even be better.

He comes into a game—Metallica's *Enter Sandman* blaring over Yankee Stadium—and he begins to warm up, and the crowd's going wild, and the opposing players are psyching themselves up, and he has that look on his face, that placid look, that look that says that everything will be all right.

"They have other men on the team," the boy said to Hemingway's old man.

"Naturally," the old man said. "But he makes the difference."

Back in the Canyon of Heroes

"'09 Yankees Reminder of Big, Bad Bombers"
New York Post, November 6, 2009

by Mike Vaccaro

*In his second season as Yankee skipper, Joe Girardi took the team
back to the place that fans most love to see them—in the "Canyon
of Heroes," parading down lower Broadway toward City Hall Park,
with thousands celebrating and showering the champions with
confetti. The 2009 title was the team's first since 2000, an eternity
by Yankee standards.*

It took a while for the city and the Yankees to get together with this parade
business, if you want to know the truth. Babe Ruth never got to see the
Canyon of Heroes. Neither did Lou Gehrig, or Joe DiMaggio, or Lefty Gomez.
Phil Rizzuto had to wait until he'd taken up residence in a broadcast booth to
go. Casey Stengel had to wait until he was the manager of the expansion Mets
to go.

Bobby Jones got two ticker-tape parades and Ben Hogan got one before
anyone ever thought to invite the Yankees to the Canyon of Heroes. The
first baseball man of any kind to be showered in confetti wasn't even a New
York baseball man, but Connie Mack, honored on Aug. 19, 1949, on his 50th
anniversary as manager of the Philadelphia A's, feted in the afternoon and
bombed in the evening by the Yankees.

The city threw a parade for the New York Giants' baseball team after it
clinched the 1954 pennant but before it won the World Series. In fact, it wasn't
until April 10, 1961, that the Yankees finally made their way downtown . . . and
that was to honor them for a World Series they'd lost the previous October.

Since then, of course, the Yankees have all but adopted Lower Manhattan as their second home, sort of a satellite office for the big room up in the Bronx, and when they climb onto their floats this morning at Broadway and Battery Place, and make their way to Chambers Street, it'll mark the ninth time the Yankees have taken the trip, more than any other team, group or individual ever.

"It's the greatest ride you can take," said Derek Jeter, who will be taking his fifth such trip, which is as many as Admiral Byrd (three) and General Eisenhower (two) combined. "It's you and your teammates sharing in a great victory. And it's all of you and the fans, sharing one last moment together. I'm happy for all these guys who've never done this before. It'll be the time of their lives."

It will be. Someone asked Alex Rodriguez about the parade just as Wednesday night turned into Thursday morning, just as the reality of being a world champion had begun to sink in, begun to register, and Rodriguez could barely keep himself coherent he turned so instantly giddy.

"It's going to be the best party of our lives," A-Rod said.

It will be a hell of a party, that much is certain, and it will commemorate a different kind of Yankees championship team, one that, you can argue, we really haven't seen in a couple of generations. It was unlike the Dynasty Boys of 1996–2000 because those teams were as beloved for their large home-grown core and for others—Tino Martinez, Paul O'Neill, Scott Brosius, Chuck Knoblauch, even David Wells—acquired the old-fashioned way, through smart trading and savvy dealing.

It may resemble the 1977–78 Bronx Zoo battlers because there are so many fat contracts assembled in one relatively small room, but that is where even that resemblance ends, because these guys got along far better than those guys ever did. You were never going to catch Mark Teixeira saying that he was the straw that stirs the drink, hinting that CC Sabathia could only stir it bad. Not this bunch.

Really, in many ways, the era this team most resembles is the Old-Time Dynasty Yankees, the ones that inspired such devotion among their fans and such resentment everywhere else, teams built to batter you and to better you, teams that inspired so many fans in American League outposts like Detroit and Cleveland and Chicago to wail, "Break up the Yankees!" You hear that a lot now, and those shouts are sure to get louder, and you know something? That's OK. Let them all roar. Today, in the Canyon of Heroes, nobody will be able to hear anything other than a city and a baseball team thanking each other, loudly, for the ride of their lives. It's a rite of autumn the Yankees know better than any who ever lived.

Baseball Loses Its Last Lion

"George Steinbrenner, owner of New York Yankees, has died in
Tampa at age of 80 after heart attack"
New York Daily News, July 13, 2010

by Bill Madden

*The multifarious characterizations of the life of George Steinbrenner
can all be thrown out the window. In baseball, all that counts at
the end of the season is who stands atop the great heap, and there
was nothing the Boss would not do if he thought it would improve
the team's chances of being the last team standing. For that, he is
a true Yankee champion.*

George Steinbrenner, a towering and intimidating figure who dominated the
New York sports scene for 35 years, winning 11 American League pennants
and seven world championships as owner of the Yankees, in and around
two suspensions from baseball and multiple feuds and firings, died Tuesday
morning in Tampa after suffering a massive heart attack. He was 80.

"The Boss"—as he was so aptly named by *Daily News* columnist Mike
Lupica, his longtime antagonist—died at around 6:30 a.m. He had been
suffering from failing health, the result of a series of strokes, for the past
few years.

His family released a statement Tuesday morning. "It is with profound
sadness that the family of George M. Steinbrenner III announces his passing,"
the statement said. "He was an incredible and charitable man. First and
foremost he was devoted to his entire family—his beloved wife, Joan; his
sisters, Susan Norpell and Judy Kamm, his children, Hank, Jennifer, Jessica
and Hal; and all his grandchildren. He was a visionary and a giant in the

world of sports. He took a great but struggling franchise and turned it into a champion again."

In Steinbrenner's blustering and bombastic reign as the longest-termed owner in their history, the Yankees recovered from the rubble of their darkest era under CBS' ownership (1964–72) to win world championships in 1977 and 1978, only to fall and then rise again with another dynastic string of four championships under manager Joe Torre from 1996–2000 and then winning a seventh world championship for him under Joe Girardi this past season.

At the same time, the franchise that Steinbrenner and a group of 15 limited partners purchased on Jan. 3, 1973, for $8.8 million from CBS (or $4.4 million less than the network had paid for it), skyrocketed in value to over a billion dollars, according to analysts, after Steinbrenner brokered unprecedented worldwide marketing deals for the Yankees and formed his own cable television network (YES) to broadcast the team's games. Steinbrenner's personal initial investment in the team was $168,000.

"George was a giant of the game, and his devotion to baseball was surpassed only by his devotion to his family and his beloved New York Yankees," said Major League Baseball commissioner Bud Selig. "He was and always will be as much of a New York Yankee as Babe Ruth, Lou Gehrig, Joe DiMaggio, Mickey Mantle, Yogi Berra, Whitey Ford and all of the other Yankee legends."

As news of Steinbrenner's death spread Tuesday morning, words of praise and admiration poured in from across the sports world and beyond.

"He was truly the most influential and innovative owner in all of sports," said former New York Mayor Rudy Giuliani. "He made the Yankees a source of great pride in being a New Yorker. George Steinbrenner's Yankees represent the will to overcome all odds, which is precisely the will New Yorkers display when meeting every challenge they face."

Until his mostly glorious sunset years, during which his management team of chief adviser Gene Michael, GM Brian Cashman and Torre remained intact and the team payroll escalated to the $200 million plateau, Steinbrenner's operation of the Yankees was one of constant upheaval, turmoil and instability. This was no better evidenced than by his hiring and firing of 12 managers (including Billy Martin five times) between Ralph Houk (whom he inherited in 1973) and Torre. And prior to Cashman's ascension at age 30 to the Yankee GM role in 1998, no less than 14 people (including Michael twice) held that position before ultimately finding the working conditions intolerable and, in many cases, hazardous to their health.

Hard as he was on his managers and general managers, Steinbrenner feuded with his players as well, the most notable being Dave Winfield, whom he signed to a 10-year, $23 million free-agent contract in 1980, then a record. The ink was barely dry on the deal when Steinbrenner discovered his lawyers had neglected to inform him of cost-of-living clauses in it that greatly enhanced its value. This, in turn, led to a bitter feud between Steinbrenner and his new superstar left fielder that culminated with the Yankee owner's second suspension from baseball, July 30, 1990, after it was revealed he'd paid $40,000 to a self-described gambler, Howie Spira, to provide dirt to him on Winfield.

Through the years, Steinbrenner had acrimonious fallings out with many of his star players such as Reggie Jackson, Lou Piniella, Goose Gossage, Graig Nettles and Sparky Lyle, only to later patch things up and welcome them back into the Yankee fold. With Yankee icon Yogi Berra, however, the feud was a lasting one. Berra, who Steinbrenner fired as manager just 16 games into the 1985 season, vowed never to return to Yankee Stadium "as long as [Steinbrenner's] there," and was estranged from the organization until January 1999, when a peace pact was finally brokered between the two, with Steinbrenner issuing a public apology to him.

"He was a very generous, caring, passionate man," Berra said Tuesday. "George and I had our differences, but who didn't? We became great friends over the last decade and I will miss him very much."

When Steinbrenner wasn't publicly sparring with his own Yankee underlings, he was seemingly in constant war with commissioners, league presidents, umpires and other team owners and officials. From 1983 until 1995, it was calculated that he'd accrued $645,000 in fines stemming from those feuds. In 1983 alone, Steinbrenner was levied fines totaling $305,000 for various offenses against baseball mankind, as well as being suspended for a week by American League president Lee MacPhail for making derogatory remarks about umpires Darryl Cousins and John Shulock.

If nothing else, Steinbrenner's public jabs at his many targets of derision and contempt were colorful. He once called White Sox owners Jerry Reinsdorf and Eddie Einhorn "those two pumpkins" and "the Katzenjammer twins" (for which he was fined $5,000). Responding to a 1981 off-the-cuff remark by Mets GM Frank Cashen about Yankee Stadium being "Fort Apache," Steinbrenner referred to him as "that pus-sy face little man"—a term he used a variation of some 25 years later when he called his Japanese pitching prodigy Hideki Irabu "a fat pus-sy toad." And during the height of the Yankee-Red Sox hostilities in 2003, he referred to Boston CEO Larry Lucchino as a "chameleon" after Lucchino labeled the Yankees "the evil empire."

The low point of the Steinbrenner-created turmoil in 1983 came when The Boss was fined $250,000 by baseball commissioner Bowie Kuhn for his actions and statements surrounding the infamous "Pine Tar Game" in which MacPhail overturned an umpires' ruling disallowing a game-winning home run by the Kansas City Royals' George Brett because of excessive pine tar on his bat. MacPhail ordered the game to be picked up from the point of Brett's home run when the Royals returned to New York 3 1/2 weeks later.

In the meantime, Steinbrenner, with notorious rogue attorney Roy Cohn as his point man, filed lawsuits against baseball in the courts of Manhattan and the Bronx in an attempt to prevent the game from being restarted. The final straw for Kuhn was when Steinbrenner, in an obvious attempt to incite the New York fans against the AL president, suggested publicly that "MacPhail ought to go house-hunting in Kansas City."

It was Kuhn who handed down Steinbrenner's first suspension, barely 23 months after he'd purchased controlling interest in the Yankees. Having pled guilty to one count of conspiracy for making illegal contributions to Richard Nixon's 1972 presidential campaign, Steinbrenner was suspended in November 1974 for two years by Kuhn for actions detrimental to baseball. The suspension was lifted by Kuhn after 15 months for "good behavior" but by then Steinbrenner had already been working undercover to buy and build the Yankees into a superpower again.

In December 1974, Oakland A's ace right-hander Catfish Hunter was declared a free agent by baseball arbitrator Peter Seitz on the grounds that his contract had been breached. A wild bidding war ensued, and on New Year's Eve, the Yankees announced they had signed Hunter to what was later revealed to be a five-year, $3.35 million deal.

Although Steinbrenner was on suspension at the time of the Hunter signing, there was no question he had engineered it, and from there the Yankees became the biggest players in the advent of free agency. Hunter was the cornerstone to their renaissance, followed by the high-profile signings of Jackson and pitcher Don Gullett in 1976 and the fearsome closer, Gossage, in 1977. More than any other owner at the time, Steinbrenner understood how, through free agency, a team could go from the bottom to the top in a hurry, and he, of course, had the resources to do it.

But after the back-to-back world championships in 1977 and 1978 and winning 103 games in 1980 (after which he still fired manager Dick Howser because the Yankees got swept in the ALCS by the Royals), Steinbrenner began to get carried away with signing free agents, to the detriment of the Yankee farm system. For all his free agent successes of the '70s, there were just as many expensive flops in the '80s—singles-hitting outfielder Davey Collins (three years, $2.4 million), pitchers Ed Whitson (five years, $4.5 million), Pascual Perez (three years, $5.1 million), outfielder Steve Kemp (five years, $4.5 million), reliever Rawley Eastwick, (five years, $1.1 million), all of which were considered at the time to be market-busting deals.

Steinbrenner's nadir as a meddling, destructive owner came in the 1981 World Series, when he ordered the benching of Jackson and got involved in a fistfight on the elevator of the hotel in Los Angeles where the Yankees were staying. He claimed at the time he was defending the honor of his players against two unidentified ruffians who had been making taunting remarks about the Yankees. The two never materialized and after the Yankees lost the Series in six games to the Dodgers, Steinbrenner ordered his public relations director, Irv Kaze, to read a public apology to the Yankee Stadium fans, further infuriating his players.

As a result of Steinbrenner's failed excesses, the Yankees, beginning in 1982, endured the longest pennant drought (15 years) in their history, and as their decline deepened, even their money couldn't lure the better free agents to New York. It was not until Steinbrenner was serving his second suspension, this one levied by commissioner Fay Vincent, that the Yankees, under Michael's stewardship, began planting the seeds to a new era of prosperity and refreshing stability.

A primary factor in the '90s Yankee renaissance was the farm system, which for years Steinbrenner had ravaged with impulsive "win now" deals in which he sacrificed top prospects like outfielders Jay Buhner and Willie McGee and first baseman Fred McGriff. With Steinbrenner again on suspension, the farm system was allowed to flourish, and homegrown talents Bernie Williams, Derek Jeter, Andy Pettitte, Jorge Posada and Mariano Rivera—any and all of whom would have likely been traded under Steinbrenner's operating policy of the '80s—instead made it to the Bronx to form the nucleus of the Torre-managed championship seasons.

The October 1995 hiring of Torre—whose managerial term far exceeded any of Steinbrenner's previous 13 pilots—was the end result of another tempest. After leading the Yankees to the playoffs for the first time since 1981, Buck Showalter balked at the two-year, $1,050,000 contract extension offered him, prompting Steinbrenner to take the offer off the table and sever ties with him. Steinbrenner then issued a statement in which he wished "nothing but the best for Buck and his little family."

But, as with Howser (whom he called from a roadside pay phone in Tampa, to say he'd reconsidered his decision to fire him), Steinbrenner had second thoughts about letting Showalter go and actually drove to his home in Pensacola, Fla., a few days later, asking him to come back. Like Howser in 1980, however, Showalter said "no thanks," pointing out that Steinbrenner, on the advice of Michael, had already hired the Brooklyn-born Torre as his new manager.

Although they had their inevitable clashes, Steinbrenner admitted that he never had a better relationship with a manager than he had with Torre, although that, too, ended badly when Torre turned down an incentive-laden contract after another quick playoff exit in 2007. It was at that fateful meeting in Tampa that Torre looked Steinbrenner in the eye and called the offer "insulting." In turning down the offer, Torre told Steinbrenner that The Boss would never have become a billionaire without Torre and his winning teams. Torre was replaced by Girardi, his former catcher, and went on to manage the Los Angeles Dodgers.

"I will always remember George Steinbrenner as a passionate man, a tough boss, a true visionary, a great humanitarian and a dear friend," Torre said Tuesday. "I will be forever grateful that he trusted me with his Yankees for 12 years. My heart goes out to his entire family. He will be deeply missed in New York, Tampa and throughout the world of baseball. It's only fitting that he went out as a world champ."

Born July 4, 1930, in Cleveland, Steinbrenner spoke often about his demanding father, Henry, as having been the most influential person in his life. Henry Steinbrenner had graduated from MIT, where he was an NCAA hurdles champion. Young George tried to emulate his father (whose dictum was "Always work harder than anybody else") but, by his own admission, he was never able to please the old man.

After attending Culver Military Academy in Indiana, Steinbrenner didn't have the grades to follow his father to MIT. But he did get admitted to Williams College, where he, too, excelled in running the hurdles. It was at Williams where Steinbrenner developed a passion for the classics, as well as Gen. George Patton. Throughout his years running the Yankees, he would readily recite his favorite quotes of various philosophers, poets and military leaders, many of which are also inscribed on the clubhouse walls of both Yankee Stadium and the team's spring training complex in Tampa.

Upon graduation from Williams, Steinbrenner went into the military service for three years and, at Lockbourne Air Force base near Columbus, Ohio, set up a coffee cart franchise that served 16,000 soldiers and office workers. After his discharge, he stayed in Columbus to coach football and basketball at St. Thomas Aquinas High School. It was also there that he met a local student at Ohio State, Joan Zieg, whom he married.

In 1955, Steinbrenner was hired as an assistant football coach at Northwestern under Lou Saban, who remained a lifelong friend and even served a brief term as Yankee president. In 1956 and 1957, he served as Jack Mollenkopf's backfield coach at Purdue. Then, in 1957 he elected to enter his father's shipbuilding business, Kinsman Transit, which had been a fixture on the Great Lakes since 1882.

By this time, the elder Steinbrenner had grown weary of trying to compete against the larger shipbuilding corporations, which was fine with his hard-driving son, who relished the challenge of butting heads with big business. Steinbrenner later became part of a group that purchased American Shipbuilding Co., and by 1972 the company's gross sales were more than $100 million annually.

In the early 1980s, however, the government had eliminated shipbuilding subsidies and American Ship began a long decline—ironically paralleling that of Steinbrenner's Yankees. In 1983, Steinbrenner shuttered the company's Lorain, Ohio, offices and moved all his operations to Tampa. Mounting losses, however, prompted the company to file for Chapter 11 bankruptcy in 1993.

Throughout his tenure of running the shipbuilding business, Steinbrenner maintained a connection to his real passion, sports. In the '50s, he owned the Cleveland Pipers of the ill-fated American Basketball League, and he was a longtime member of the U.S. Olympic Committee. After moving to Tampa, Steinbrenner became actively involved in horse racing. He briefly owned Tampa Bay Down and bred horses on his farm in Ocala, Fla. He was also presented with the prestigious Gold Medal award from the National (college) Football Foundation in 2002.

But his sports legacy, of course, is the Yankees. "I've just bought the Mona Lisa of sports teams," he said upon closing the deal with CBS for the team in 1973—to which his father said to him: "You finally did something right."

But of all the quotes uttered by and about him, the one that probably best summed up the essence of Steinbrenner was that of John McMullen, one of his early limited partners with the Yankees. When asked why he was selling his share of the Yankees, McMullen replied: "Because I came to realize that there is nothing quite so limited in life than being a limited partner of George Steinbrenner." Beside his wife, Joan, Steinbrenner is survived by two sons, Harold and Hank, and two daughters, Jennifer and Jessica, all of whom reside in Tampa.

Funeral arrangements will be private. There will be an additional public service with details to be announced.

The Core Four

"So Far, So Good"
Sports Illustrated, May 3, 2010

by Tom Verducci

In the era of big money free-agent acquisitions and blockbuster trades, it's becoming almost common for a team to assemble a group of star players with the short-term of goal of wining a championship. It's much less common to keep those stars together for an extended run, which is exactly what the Yankees have achieved with Jeter, Posada, Pettitte, and Rivera.

THEY'VE WON WORLD SERIES, CONQUERED NEW YORK AND HANDLED THE BOSS. BUT IN 16 YEARS THE YANKEES' CORE FOUR HAD NEVER SAT DOWN FOR LUNCH TOGETHER—UNTIL AN *SI* ROUNDTABLE LAST WEEK

Beginning in February 1990, the Yankees signed Mariano Rivera, Jorge Posada, Andy Pettitte and Derek Jeter within 28 months of one another. All four made their big league debuts in 1995, and except for the three seasons when Pettitte played for his hometown Astros (2004–06), they have been together ever since, sharing championships and life's milestones, big and small, like brothers.

The Core Four—Rivera is 40; Posada, 38; Pettitte, 37; and Jeter, 35—have combined for 27 All-Star selections, 11 division titles, seven American League pennants, five world championships and $562 million in career earnings. In accomplishment and longevity, the sports world has seen nothing quite like this quartet. This year Rivera, Posada and Jeter became the first trio of teammates in any North American sport to stay together for 16 consecutive seasons. And there is no indication that any of the four, fresh off winning World Series ring number five in 2009, is close to being finished. Rivera (six saves, 0.00 ERA through Sunday), Posada (.315 batting average), Jeter (.316) and Pettitte (3-0, 1.29) helped the Yankees win their first five series of the season—the first Yankees team to do so since 1926.

Mo, Sado, Andy and Jeet, as they call one another, have spent more of their adulthood with one another than their own families. (Since they first met, all but Jeter have become husbands and fathers; Jeter was the best man at Posada's wedding.) One finishes another's sentences, they can communicate with just a look, and they operate a kind of elders' tribunal in the New York clubhouse. They also have built virtually spotless reputations, save for when Pettitte admitted in 2007 to twice using human growth hormone. When he faced questions from reporters about his transgression, Rivera, Posada and Jeter were, of course, near his side.

In all those years, however, Rivera, Posada, Pettitte and Jeter had never shared a meal except as part of larger groups—until *SI* gathered the Core Four for lunch last week at the St. Regis Hotel in San Francisco, for a discussion moderated by senior writer Tom Verducci. Rivera, the closer, was the first one to show—two minutes early. Asked to predict who'd be the last to arrive, Rivera said, "Sado. Jeter, then Sado will be last."

Pettitte, the starting pitcher, arrived next, and then, just as Rivera was lecturing on punctuality and half-jokingly threatening to leave, Jeter, the captain and shortstop, walked in. "What time is it?" Rivera asked him.

"Seven after," Jeter said.

"You were supposed to be here seven minutes ago," Rivera said.

Posada, the catcher, was indeed the last to arrive. "Look at this," Rivera said, bowing his head at the table and rubbing the top of his balding pate. "See this? This is from Sado. He did this."

The Core Four were just getting warmed up. What follows is a transcript, edited for length and clarity, of their rare conversation: a celebration of their careers, their successes, their memories, their fears, but mostly their friendship.

SI: I want to go back to 1992, when Andy was throwing to Jorge, a converted second baseman, in Class A in Greensboro, N.C.

Posada: Go back to 1991. I was catching a bullpen from him [at short-season Class A] Oneonta, and he's throwing me knuckleballs. The ball hit me right in the knee. I said, "No more knuckleballs."

Pettitte: I had a knuckleball when I signed.

Jeter: Yeah, you're still throwing knuckleballs.

Pettitte: I'd get two strikes on somebody and throw it as hard as I could. Struck everybody out. And then they told me after the first year, "You've got to can it." They said, "After you've pitched for 10 years in the big leagues, if you want to break it back out, you can."

SI: So now you can throw it again.

Pettitte: It's no good now. I lost it.

SI: How about when Jeter showed up in Greensboro? He joined you guys on August 20, 1992.

Posada: [Laughs.] Good-looking fellow.

Rivera: Where was I?

SI: Fort Lauderdale, High A.

Posada: You were older. Let's make sure everybody knows that. He's the oldest.

Rivera: I saw Jeet. . . . Oh, my God. I was with my cousin [former major league outfielder Ruben Rivera] in Tampa. We were playing, if I'm not mistaken, the Cardinals in St. Pete. I looked at Jeet [who was in the Gulf Coast League before Greensboro]. . . . *I* was skinny? This boy was *dying*. I was like, Who is that?

Posada: He comes in the clubhouse, and he's got high tops, with an ankle brace. And remember that Louisville Slugger bag that you stick your bats in? He had that. I was like, Wow, this is our first-rounder?

Rivera: And throwing the ball away. . . . But I saw the hitting. He hit the ball hard, and far. I said, "Wow."

Posada: They changed the Peter Pan Section [in Greensboro]. It used to be behind first base. They had to move it to third base.

SI: That was where the kids sat?

Posada: Yeah, it was too dangerous [because of Jeter's throws].

Jeter: The stories get better and better every year.

SI: Mariano, I remember you once said you cried a lot in the minor leagues, right?

Rivera: Not that I cried a lot. I did cry, like two, three times. That was my second year, in Greensboro, 1991. Because I couldn't communicate. But imagine, I came from Panama. My first year, in Tampa, most of the people I played with spoke Spanish. So I was fine. My second year I went to Greensboro. And no Spanish at all. It was hard. I think that was one of the toughest times that I had.

SI: I think people would be surprised how tough it can be starting out for young players. You guys probably all had moments of doubt or thoughts of, Wow, I don't know if I can make it.

Jeter: I cried all the time—1992, when I first signed, similar to Mo. I had no roommate, because I signed late. Third baseman spoke no English. Second baseman spoke no English. I struggled for the first time. [Jeter hit .210 in his first season as a pro.] I cried almost every day. That was tough.

Posada: I went to junior college [in Decatur, Ala]. So I cried there. When I got to the pros it was, "This is what I want." It was exciting for me. But junior college was tough. I didn't know any English. I mean, I got to know it a lot better during junior college.

Pettitte: I didn't cry at all. But the toughest part for me was . . . I got called up to Oneonta [in 1991, during his first season in the minors], and it's where all the older guys and the prospects were. Those were the guys from the four-year colleges, mostly. I'll never forget, they moved me up and I had nowhere to stay. They told me to get in touch with [former Yankees farmhand] Lyle Mouton and a couple of other guys living together in a house. It was like a two-bedroom home. They put a cot in the pantry of the kitchen for me, and I bought a little thing to hang my clothes on, like a hanging rack. That's where I stayed for the last month and a half that I was there. So that was a real tough time. I felt real uncomfortable because those guys were older than me.

SI: What about when you got to the big leagues? You all got there in 1995. Derek and Jorge, did you room together?

Posada: Well, they put us in the same hotel in New Jersey. We shared a car, to go back and forth to the ballpark. A Dodge Neon. It said NEON on the steering wheel, and if you [barely] touched it, touched the O just like this, it would honk the horn. *Eh-eh.* Just touch it. So Derek and I would be back and forth in the Neon. But in '95 we were watching most of the games. We didn't have a chance to play.

Jeter: That was in September. Mo and I came up earlier in '95, and they sent us down the same day [in June].

Rivera: I gave up a home run against Edgar Martinez. They got mad at me and Jeet and sent us both down.

Jeter: He gave up a home run and they sent me down! We were miserable.

SI: What about 1996? You won the championship, but is there something else about that year that's particularly memorable?

Posada: I got sent down like 10 times. I was in the big leagues for 60-something days. [He actually made four round trips between the minors and majors.] Up and down. I was in that elevator the whole year.

SI: Did you guys all have that moment of, I belong here. I can do this.

Jeter: Probably Opening Day in '96.

Pettitte: Didn't you hit a home run on Opening Day?

Jeter: Yeah.

Rivera: We were in Cleveland. We were snowed out, and then rescheduled.

Pettitte: For me that's when it all started. I mean, when Derek came along there was so much talk about him. I can't remember a whole lot of stuff. Like '95, I can't really remember . . . I remember Mo coming up and making some starts and being in the rotation and stuff like that. But everything's kind of like a blank for me in '95. But then in '96 when Derek came up, there was so much anticipation about him being our shortstop and Opening Day and that home run. I can remember that like it was yesterday.

SI: So how does your friendship come about? Do you start hanging out together off the field?

Jeter: Just around each other [at the ballpark]. You see them more than you see your family.

Pettitte: These guys [Jeter and Posada] are together 24/7, it seems like. But the four of us . . . I don't think we hang out. . . . I don't think we've ever been to lunch, us four, one time.

Posada: I don't think so.

Pettitte: But we spend so much time at the ballpark together, just talking.

Posada: We get on each other, we make fun of each other, we laugh. . . .

Pettitte: If something's going on in the room, we can look at each other . . .

Posada: . . . and know what's going on—without even saying anything. I can just look at Derek, and he knows exactly what I'm thinking about. Mo same thing, Andy same thing.

Rivera: We have been together so long, but the four of us together, just us, like having breakfast, being all together at the same time? No, I don't think ever.

Posada: Maybe dinner, but part of a big group.

SI: If I wanted to get, say, restaurant advice, which one of you guys should I go to?

Jeter: Where are we?

SI: It depends where we are?

Rivera: [Points to Jeter.]

Posada: See, Mo goes to Benihana every day. So he would tell you to go to Benihana wherever we are.

Rivera: Listen, I like to simplify things.

SI: O.K., what if I was a young kid on the team and I wanted financial advice. Which one of you guys should I talk to?

Posada: Mo.

Rivera: You know what my son says? That I still keep the first dollar I made. I understand that we do this in a period of time. We cannot do this forever. So whatever you make, you have to make sure that you take care of it. At least that's what I do. I know I'm going to play this game for . . . a period of time.

Posada: Yeah, how long are you going to play, Mo?

Rivera: I have this year. After this year I don't have a contract. I don't have a job. I'm going to do whatever it takes to save the money that I have made, because I know that I'm not going to be working after that, or making the kind of money that we are making now. So you have to watch what you do, where you invest, and always make sure you do the right thing, and ask God definitely for directions.

SI: That was a good question, Jorge.

Pettitte: What was the question?

SI: How long are you going to do this? I'm assuming you guys all are in the same boat as far as that goes. Does anybody plan out, "I want to play X number of years?"

Rivera: I don't think so. I mean, how many times have I retired?

Jeter: He retires every other year.

Rivera: Every contract I think, Well, this is it for me.

Jeter: [Points at Pettitte.] Him, too. "This is my last year. One more year."

Pettitte: What are you talking about? I was [retired]. I was.

Rivera: I was retired every year after my contract was up. [But] I'm still going.

SI: This game keeps pulling you back.

Rivera: I love this game. This is what I know how to do. For me, it's kind of hard to just leave and be competitive. I'm competitive.

Jeter: It's tough to leave when you're having fun.

SI: You guys look like you still have fun after all these years, all these games, all these road trips. Am I right?

Jeter: You have to have fun. If I wasn't having fun, I couldn't play.

Pettitte: Especially after all the success we've had, right?

Rivera: I think it's easier for [Jeter] because he doesn't have a family. He can do this until . . . he'll be 40 and have no kids still. But to me, and I can talk about Andy and also Sado, you miss your kids. You miss your family. This year it has hit me hard, especially in spring training. My kids were in New York. I was in Tampa. And I was missing them a lot. So that line, where's your family and where's your game . . . how do you draw that line? How long are you going to do this? How long are they going to support you? And then flying, and those things that petrify you. I'm petrified by flights. I suffer on those flights.

SI: You guys must have fun with him about that.

Rivera: Are you kidding me? *Everybody.*

Posada: Every time the plane goes up and down we go, "Mo! Are you O.K.?"

Rivera: I loved it when we had [relief pitcher] Tom Gordon on the team. Because he would literally grab my hand. We'd be holding hands. He would say, "Mo, grab my hand!" He was maybe [more scared] than me. . . . You go through all those lines, but there is a line [where you can't play anymore]. And that's why I say [Jeter] is in a better position than us, to continue playing the game. I don't know how long I'm going to do this.

Pettitte: Because the older [your children] get, it gets harder. [Rivera's] oldest [16] is a year older than my oldest. More complications. It's pretty easy when they're small.

Posada: You've got kids who are driving now, right?

Pettitte: Not yet. Mo does. [His son] got his permit, so I guess he is driving.

Posada: So he's got the Challenger driving around? [Rivera owns a custom-built 2009 Dodge Challenger SRT8.]

Rivera: He wishes. But it's amazing. I remember my kid being this small, and now all of a sudden. . . . That's why I say it's hard. That's why I say there's a line and you have to know when to stop, even knowing that you love the game. To me my family is more important than the game.

SI: So tell me one thing about you guys that might be surprising. Like Derek, I know, is a practical joker.

Jeter: Me?

SI: He once tried to pull that trick on me about getting me to try to swallow a spoonful of cinnamon.

Posada: Well, he does that cinnamon thing, but that will be it for the whole year. He tries to see how many people he can get. And he will talk to every security guard, every new reporter. Derek's quiet, you know. He gets quiet.

Rivera: He's an instigator! Instigator!

Posada: The biggest instigator is over there—that lefty guy.

Pettitte: Actually, *they* all are!

Rivera: Whoa, time out. Time out. These three? Me? I'm in my corner. They all say, "Mo, this guy is talking about you!" Who do I instigate? Nobody. I'm on my own. This guy [Jeter]? The worst.

Pettitte: I'd say, to be fair, me, Jorgie and Jeter, we stir it up pretty good.

Jeter: Yeah, we keep the clubhouse loose.

Posada: Mo, he's in charge of the relievers.

Pettitte: Mo's kind of the quiet assassin type. It goes on all the time. [Other players say] "Get Jeter off me." "Get Mo off me." I can't tell you how many times somebody has walked up to me and said, "What are you saying about me?"

Rivera: The beauty about this group of guys is it's family. As a family we all pull for one another. It's beautiful. I don't think you will have this, or see this, again—in any other sport. Period.

Posada: I have never been mad at any of these guys. I swear to God. Mad like we don't talk to each other? Never. If we have a problem, we talk about it and that's it. I don't think there's ever been any problem. I think we understand each other so well that we've never had a problem.

Jeter: What it comes down to is that I never have to worry about these guys being ready to play.

Pettitte: It's all about trust.

Jeter: I mean, it never crosses my mind. I don't have to worry about them. I know they know how to win. I know that's the only thing they care about. They don't care about their personal stats.

Rivera: No egos. No jealousy.

SI: It seems like you've always been that way.

Jeter: We learned that coming up. The Boss [George Steinbrenner], all he cared about was winning.

Rivera: Whatever they did, I think they brainwashed us! They did a good job, put it that way.

Posada: They taught us well. The coaches, the front office, the director of player development . . . they taught us well.

Rivera: You won't see this again. In any sport. Take a picture. And keep it.

SI: It seems like you guys always know you can count on one another.

Pettitte: Nothing against anybody else, but there are things I'll talk to these guys about that I may feel it's not appropriate to talk to somebody else about. There are certain things that may not need to be out there in the clubhouse. There's some stuff you feel like needs to be said between the four of us, and we'll say, "Hey, keep an eye on it."

Posada: Little things. We'll talk to each other and say, "What do you think about this?" And then we . . .

Jeter: . . . we've got to talk about it and make sure it doesn't happen again, things like that.

Posada: I bet you if we put our families together, they're very similar. I think my mom and dad are very similar to their moms and dads. Very, very similar.

Pettitte: No doubt. Very close.

Rivera: Strong families.

Posada: So I think *that's* why we're sitting here today.

SI: Thanks for your time, guys.

Jeter: Mo's going to Benihana's now.

Permissions and Credits

Every effort has been made to identify and properly acknowledge the copyright holders of material published in this book. We invite copyright holders to inform us of any oversights or improper acknowledgments, and any errors and omissions will be corrected in future editions.

"Home Nine Incorporated" first published in the *New York Times,* March 15, 1903.

"New York Team Plays in Washington and Loses to the Local Nine—Score, 3 to 1" first published in the *New York Times*, April 22, 1903.

"Pitcher Chesbro Tells for the First Time of His Famous 'Spit Ball,' and Shows How It Is Thrown," by Jack Chesbro and Frederic P. O'Connell, first published in the *Boston Post,* January 22, 1905.

Excerpt from *The Black Prince of Baseball: Hal Chase and the Mythology of Baseball,* by Donald Dewey and Nicholas Acocella, is reprinted by permission of the authors.

"From Griffith to Stallings to Chase—or Owner Frank Farrell in search of someone who will give him a ride for his money," by Ring Lardner, first published in the *Chicago Daily Tribune,* September 23, 1910.

"Yankees Lose with Victory in Sight" first published in the *New York Times,* April 12, 1912.

"Giants to Share Polo Grounds with Yankees" first published in the *New York Daily Tribune,* January 23, 1913.

"The Yankees' Chief Slugger: Walter Pipp, Who Robbed Frank Baker of His 'Home Run' Title," by J. J. Ward, first published in *Baseball Magazine,* January 1917.

"The Sport Light," by Grantland Rice, first published in the *New York Daily Tribune,* April 19, 1917.

"Carl Mays Twirls Yanks to Victory" first published in the *New York Times,* August 8, 1919.

"Rapid Rise," by Bob Hertzel, first published in *The Record* (Bergen County, New Jersey), August 24, 1981.

"Yanks' Star Prospect Jeter Gets Call to Bail Out Infield," by Bob Hertzel, first published in *The Record* (Bergen County, New Jersey), May 30, 1995.

Excerpt from *Game Time: A Baseball Companion*, by Roger Angell, © 2003 by Roger Angell, reprinted by permission of Houghton Mifflin Harcourt Publishing Company.

Excerpt from *The Yankee Years*, by Joe Torre and Tom Verducci, © 2009, 2010 by Anjoli, Inc. and Tom Verducci. Used by permission of Doubleday, a division of Random House, Inc.

"October Best," by Michael Knisley, first published in *The Sporting News*, November 6, 2000.

"The Death of Derek Jeter," by Michael Martone, first published in *Esquire*, November 2006. Used by kind permission of the author.

"Mariano Rivera's a true Yankee, almost mythical in his dominance," by Joe Posnanski, first published in *Sports Illustrated*/SI.COM, July 2, 2009. Reprinted courtesy of Sports Illustrated, © 2009 by Time Inc. All rights reserved.

"'09 Yankees reminder of big, bad Bombers," by Mike Vaccaro, first published in the *New York Post*, November 6, 2009.

"George Steinbrenner, owner of New York Yankees, has died in Tampa at age of 80 after heart attack," by Bill Madden, first published in the *New York Daily News*, July 13, 2010.

"So Far, So Good," by Tom Verducci, first published in *Sports Illustrated*, May 3, 2010. Reprinted courtesy of Sports Illustrated, © 2010 by Time Inc. All rights reserved.

Index